WASHINGTON'S
IMMORTALS

Also by Patrick K. O'Donnell

*First SEALs: The Untold Story of the Forging of
America's Most Elite Unit*

*Dog Company: The Boys of Pointe du Hoc—The Rangers
Who Accomplished D-Day's Toughest Mission
and Led the Way across Europe*

*Give Me Tomorrow: The Korean War's Greatest Untold Story—
The Epic Stand of the Marines of George Company*

*They Dared Return: The True Story of Jewish Spies
Behind the Lines in Nazi Germany*

*The Brenner Assignment: The Untold Story of
the Most Daring Spy Mission of World War II*

*We Were One: Shoulder to Shoulder with
the Marines Who Took Fallujah*

*Operatives, Spies, and Saboteurs: The Unknown Story
of the Men and Women of World War II's OSS*

*Into the Rising Sun: In Their Own Words, World War II's
Pacific Veterans Reveal the Heart of Combat*

*Beyond Valor: World War II's Ranger and Airborne Veterans
Reveal the Heart of Combat*

WASHINGTON'S IMMORTALS

THE UNTOLD STORY OF AN ELITE REGIMENT WHO CHANGED THE COURSE OF THE REVOLUTION

PATRICK K. O'DONNELL

Atlantic Monthly Press
New York

Published simultaneously in Canada
Printed in the United States of America

FIRST EDITION

ISBN 978-0-8021-2459-3
eISBN 978-0-8021-9071-0

Atlantic Monthly Press
an imprint of Grove Atlantic
154 West 14th Street
New York, NY 10011

Distributed by Publishers Group West

groveatlantic.com

16 17 18 19 20   10 9 8 7 6 5 4 3 2 1

To the men and women of the Revolution who sacrificed everything for an idea—the United States. You are the greatest generation.

CONTENTS

PREFACE

The sign is rusted and scarred. Its aqua-blue surface bears the fading words "MARYLAND HEROES." Suspended from a piece of corroded iron, it marks a mass grave:

> Here lie buried 256 Maryland soldiers
> Who fell in the Battle of Brooklyn
> August 27, 1776

I encountered that neglected piece of history in September 2010 during a walking tour of the neighborhood where the Battle of Brooklyn, also known as the Battle of Long Island, took place. Today it is a depressed area filled with auto repair shops and warehouses. The bright spot is a well-worn, decades-old American Legion post. Several blocks northeast are the elegant brownstones of Park Slope. Somewhere beneath the surface, perhaps under a garage or below a paved street, are the Marylanders' undiscovered bodies. Their remains lie intermingled in what should be hallowed ground.

In the revolutionary summer of 1776 these courageous patriots, known as "gentlemen of honour, family, and fortune," gave their lives in a desperate series of bayonet charges against British troops, who were bunkered in a stone house that was still standing just a few blocks away from where I stood. Their assault on that house arguably remains one of the most important elite small-unit engagements in American history. It bought precious time for the Patriot cause, allowing hundreds of colonial troops to retreat through a gap in British lines.

The lonely weathered placard nestled among the auto-body shops of present-day Brooklyn bears silent witness to the drama that once unfolded in this place and the extraordinary men who changed history.

* * *

"Close up! Close up!"

Over the crackle of musket fire and boom of cannon, the indomitable Major Mordecai Gist and many of the founding officers of the Baltimore Independent Cadets ordered their men forward.

Shots tore through the ranks of more than two hundred Marylanders. Undaunted, the men continued to surge toward an old stone house occupied by British General Lord Cornwallis (Charles, Earl Cornwallis) and his Redcoats.

A century earlier, the home's massive walls had been built to fend off potential Indian attacks. Now, these same barriers that had shielded Americans were called upon to repel them. Cornwallis's men trained a light cannon and musket fire on the advancing Marylanders, who launched a preemptive strike aimed at protecting their brothers-in-arms.

The British "[continued] pouring the canister and grape upon the Americans like a shower of hail." In the melee "the flower of some of the finest families of the South [were] cut to atoms."

Defying the carnage unfolding around them, Gist's men "closed their ranks over the bodies of their dead comrades, and still turned their faces to the foe."

The boldness of the Marylanders' charge initially unhinged Cornwallis's defenses as his gunners nearly abandoned their artillery, but intense fire from the house and fresh reinforcements compelled the Marylanders to retreat and then mount yet another charge.

From a distant hill, General George Washington watched the gallant display through his spyglass. As the Marylanders began to fall, he cried out, "Good God! What brave fellows I must this day lose!"[1]

Yet not all was lost. Scores of Marylanders, led by Major Gist, held off the British long enough to help save a corps of Washington's troops and arguably the bulk of the nascent American army from destruction. The Marylanders' forlorn assaults delayed a British attack on American

1. Their bravery and sacrifice gave rise to the Maryland nickname, the Old Line State.

fortifications at Brooklyn Heights and allowed hundreds of Americans to escape to the temporary safety of their entrenchments. The soldiers who participated in that unorthodox assault would become known as the Immortals or the Maryland 400. With their blood, these men bought, in the words of one American, "an hour, more precious to American liberty than any other in its history." Gist and several men in his group escaped to fight future battles that changed the fate of a nation.

Reading the solemn words etched on that metal sign made me curious. I wanted to know what really happened to these men, who they were, and why citizen-soldiers—amateurs—fought and sacrificed their lives and fortunes to fight the most formidable army in the world. Over the years, I unearthed a hidden war buried in letters and diaries. Forgotten pension files bore testament to heroism and sacrifice, and even to betrayal by fellow Americans. It wasn't the Revolution of famous men trapped in the amber of fading oil portraits, but an alive, boots-on-the-ground, brutally long conflict that pitted brother against brother in a war that America wasn't preordained to win. These sacrifices by a small group of men—in the right place, at the right time—who were willing to march thousands of miles and endure years of unimaginable hardship, made the difference between victory and defeat.

Their nine-year saga has remained untold for over 239 years and nearly forgotten, much like the mass grave in which their comrades now lie. Gist and hundreds of Marylanders from all walks of life became an elite corps that formed the nucleus of the greatest fighting regiments of the war. They helped to keep the Continental Army intact through the darkest days of the Revolution. It is also a story about close friends whose fellowship in battle kept them together in the most impossible circumstances, enabled their survival, and helped them emerge as some of the most decorated and successful battle captains of the war. This book is the first *Band of Brothers*-style history of the Revolution; rather than providing a regimental history, it focuses on the actions of these men. Facing tremendous adversity, these Americans were often called upon by Washington to play a pivotal role in the war's decisive battles just as they did that day in Brooklyn.

A pockmarked sign memorializes the beginning of an epic journey that started on a winter day in 1774.

But a metal sign isn't enough to commemorate a mystery, the unknown resting place of so many Americans who willingly gave their lives for a nation yet to be born.

1774–75

CHAPTER 1

"GENTLEMEN OF HONOUR, FAMILY, AND FORTUNE"

Snow gently fell outside a Baltimore tavern on December 3, 1774, as thirty-two-year-old Mordecai Gist addressed the city's social elite. On his own initiative, Gist had gathered together a group of freemen, merchants, shipbuilders, and businessmen who were interested in forming the first independent military company in Maryland to protect their rights and potentially to break away from Britain.

At the time, Baltimore, one of the primary trading centers in the colonies, was a boomtown with a seedy, rough-and-tumble quality about it. One member of the Continental Congress described it as "infinitely, the dirtiest place I was ever in." Another piled on the accolades and called it "the Damndest Hole in the World."

A second-generation Baltimore native, Gist was the son of a prominent surveyor who had helped lay out the city's streets. His uncle, Christopher Gist, had served with George Washington in the French and Indian War, and on two separate occasions he had saved the future general's life. The younger Gist had already established himself as a sea captain and merchant, dealing primarily in textiles and firearms, which had earned him a sizable fortune. He was also a widower. Four years earlier, his first wife had died during the birth of their daughter, who then perished in infancy. At six feet tall, he was a man of impressive stature for his day. Others described him as having a "frank and genial manner." A natural leader known for his forceful opinions, Gist was among the colony's first agitators for independence and later emerged as one of America's most powerful Freemasons.

In October he had participated in the burning of the *Peggy Stewart*. In an incident reminiscent of the Boston Tea Party, a captain had brought a ship loaded with tea into Annapolis harbor despite a colonial boycott. Outraged Marylanders gave the *Peggy Stewart*'s captain a choice: either burn his ship and all its cargo or be hanged at his front door. The captain chose to run his ship aground and torch it.

The *Peggy Stewart* incident occurred ten months after the Boston Tea Party, in which American demonstrators, some disguised as American Indians, had dumped an entire shipment of tea from the East India Company into Boston harbor to protest taxes levied by the British on the tea. It echoed the American cry "No taxation without representation." Many Americans demanded the right to elect the representatives who imposed taxes and passed regulations. The Crown had responded to the Tea Party swiftly with draconian measures that became known as the Coercive Acts or Intolerable Acts. Among other provisions, they allowed British officials to be tried in Britain for crimes committed in the colonies. Another of these acts required colonists to house and feed British soldiers in their homes.

British troops led by General Thomas Gage disbanded the elected colonial government in Massachusetts and shut down the port of Boston, throwing thousands of men out of work. The crisis in Boston escalated and fomented discord throughout the thirteen colonies, resonating strongly in Baltimore, where trade was the lifeblood of the community.

On that December night in the tavern, like-minded Patriots had gathered to hear Gist, whom they elected as captain of their company, read aloud the articles of incorporation for the Baltimore Independent Cadets. The charter called for sixty men—"a company composed of gentlemen of honour, family, and fortune, and tho' of different countries animated by a zeal and reverence for rights of humanity"—to voluntarily join and tie themselves together "by all the Sacred ties of Honour and the Love and Justice due to ourselves and Country."

Gist's gravitas and presence reverberated through the room as he read the articles:

We, the Baltimore Independent Cadets, Impress'd with a sense of the unhappy [state] of our Suffering Brethren in Boston, the Alarming conduct of General Gage, and the oppressive Unconstitutional acts of Parliament to deprive us of Liberty and enforce Slavery on His Majesties Loyal Liege Subjects of America in General,

For the better security of our lives, liberties, and Properties under such Alarming Circumstances, we think it highly advisable and necessary, that we form ourselves into a Body, or Company in order to [learn] the military discipline; to act in defence of our Country agreeable to the Resolves of the Continental Congress.

The cadets promised to march within forty-eight hours to the aid of any sister colonies that needed their help, to obey their elected commander, to purchase their own uniforms and equipment, and to submit to a court-martial for any default "contrary to the true Intent and Meaning of this Engagement." However, as true gentlemen, they would not submit themselves to corporal punishment.

The young merchant and the other newly inducted members of the company made history that day. Gist's independent company was the first of its kind in Maryland, but similar companies soon sprang up across the colonies. Unbeknownst to them at the time, the men in that tavern would become one of only a few core units crucial to the continued existence of the entire Continental Army throughout the Revolutionary War. At key points, their participation made a difference that allowed the army to survive—often at an enormous price. Sickness and privation of the most severe kind (including marching barefoot for thousands of miles over many years), British bullets, and the hazards of imprisonment would take their toll. Very few of the men who gathered that night at the tavern or those who joined them later would survive eight years of war, multiple campaigns, and dozens of battles unscathed.

The cadets, later quietly renamed the Baltimore Independent Company, formed a cadre that was incorporated into multiple companies and regiments that played a key role in many battles of importance during the American Revolution and fought in both the North and the South. Built on personal relationships with deep family ties that spanned decades, the Baltimore Independent Company was a tight-knit group of close friends who forged one of the most legendary units of the American Revolution.

One of those men crucial to the company was twenty-three-year-old Samuel Smith. A born leader, Smith was first elected sergeant within the company and quickly rose through the ranks as an officer. Like many of the cadets, he had been trained in the classics, studying Latin and Greek at school. As a young man, he had worked in his father's countinghouse and traveled to Europe on one of his father's merchant ships. He proved to be charismatic and a natural battle commander. Eventually, he would assume command of the Baltimore Independent Company and many other units. In time, he became one of the finest regimental commanders of the war.

Like Gist and Smith, many of the company's members were prosperous merchants. For them, the decision to join the company meant sacrificing their livelihood—the ability to trade with Great Britain. For years they had been on the sharp end of onerous taxes and restrictions that required the colonies to trade exclusively with Britain. Responding to the spiraling crisis in Boston, delegates from the American colonies met in the First Continental Congress. Formed at the urging of Benjamin Franklin and first organized in 1774 in Philadelphia, Congress comprised representatives from twelve of the thirteen colonies (initially Georgia didn't participate, since it felt that it needed British protection from hostile Indians). The Congress remained undecided on the issue of declaring independence from Great Britain, but its members firmly believed that King George III owed the people of the colonies better treatment. The representatives wanted their voices heard in London. On September 5, 1774, Congress adopted the Articles of Association, which declared that if the Intolerable Acts were not repealed by December 1, 1774, the colonies would boycott British goods. A provision in the articles also called for an embargo of British goods by September 1775 if the acts weren't abolished. It was a bold move: Americans struck at the heart of British trade, which heavily relied on the North American economy. The Continental Congress's actions were a serious challenge to imperial rule, essentially amounting to a declaration of economic war against the Crown.

The independent spirit that gave rise to this decision to rebel against Britain had been fomenting in Maryland since its founding. In 1632 the king granted the ownership of the colony to George Calvert, Lord Baltimore, a Catholic, who was designated the "proprietary." Unlike most of the colonies, which answered to the king or to locally elected governments, Maryland answered to the proprietary, who set up the government as he saw fit. The arrangement essentially created "an empire within an empire" and made it easy for the people who lived in Maryland to see themselves as independent of the Crown. This unusual form of government persisted until 1691, when Britain appointed a royal governor for the colony.

In the middle of the eighteenth century, the French and Indian War planted seeds of discontent in America and had an impact on many of the Maryland officers. Also known as the Seven Years' War, the war was a worldwide conflict between Britain and France that began in 1754. Both countries had extensive holdings in the New World, and disagreements arose over disputed territory and trading rights in the Ohio Valley. The governor of Virginia sent twenty-one-year-old Major George Washington and a small group of men to evict the French from the area, but the French refused to leave, pushing the two countries on the path toward war. On May 28, 1754, Washington led the British troops to victory in the Battle of Jumonville Glen, which is generally regarded as the first battle in the French and Indian War.

In the early days of the conflict, both sides developed irregular warfare techniques, such as the use of proxies and the use of ranging forces. The proxies included Rogers' Rangers, Americans who fought for Britain. The British and the French also developed light infantry, which were lightly armed forces known for their quickness, speed, and flexibility. More importantly, the colonists learned to train, organize, and move large numbers of men through untamed wilderness. Americans fighting for the British—including George Washington, William Smallwood, and Daniel Morgan, along with future Americans and British officers Edward Hand, Horatio Gates, and Charles Lee—gained invaluable battle experience in the conflict. They also learned Indian tactics. Many Native American tribes fought on the side of the French during the conflict. Unlike the Europeans, the tribes often struck in surprise attacks with small raiding parties that hit the enemy hard and then retreated before casualties could mount, and they fired from behind trees and other natural obstructions rather than out in the open. The seeds of an American way of waging war were planted.

By 1760 most of the fighting in North America had come to end, although battles continued to rage in the West Indies and Europe for some time. The North American portion of the war officially came to a close on February 10, 1763, when the two sides signed the Treaty of Paris. Five days later, they ended the European war with the Treaty of Hubertusburg. Under the terms of surrender, France gave up all rights to the mainland of North America but held on to its island colonies in the Caribbean and the Gulf of Saint Lawrence. Spain, which had entered the war on France's side, agreed to cede Florida to Britain in exchange for regaining control of Cuba and gaining control of Louisiana. Britain was left as the primary power in control of Canada and the thirteen colonies that would become the United States.

While the British were victorious, the cost was exorbitant. The war had nearly doubled the empire's debt. To offset this enormous financial burden, the Crown began raising taxes on its colonies so that they would pay for their own administration and defense, allowing the government in London to put more money toward its war debts. When Parliament passed the Stamp Act in 1765, the colonists were primed to revolt. Extremely unpopular in the American colonies, the onerous act required that all printed materials, including legal documents and newspapers, use specially stamped paper produced in Britain. The colonists objected to this regulation on the grounds that they shouldn't be taxed without their consent. Although Parliament eventually repealed the Stamp Act, it passed a series of other laws and taxes that the Americans found objectionable, including a law that forbade the colonies from issuing currency and a fateful tax on tea.

Outraged by the new and oppressive laws, Massachusetts appealed to its sister colonies for support. In a show of solidarity, the Continental Congress agreed to ban the import of British goods. It went one step further, by placing an export ban on American commodities that were valued by the Crown, such as tobacco, rice, and a long list of naval products. The men in Maryland who joined the cadets certainly objected to the taxes, but for them the Revolution wasn't only about money. They were motivated by ideals of freedom and liberty, and they didn't want their daily lives and business decisions at the mercy of the bureaucracy in London.

While war seemed inevitable in hindsight, it was not a foregone conclusion, even as the various independent companies throughout the colonies began to organize. In fact, many of the colonies hoped for a diplomatic solution to the crisis that would keep them as part of the British Empire. The act of rebellion—if it came to that—would be a last resort.

With the clouds of war gathering on an uncertain horizon, the Baltimore cadets began to arm and outfit themselves with the best weapons and uniforms money could buy. This company of wealthy Baltimoreans went into battle carrying a "good gun" with a bayonet plus a brace of pistols and a sword. However, most of the other American units could not afford such expensive guns and supplies; many of their brothers-in-arms would fight with old hunting rifles or makeshift weapons. And while many Americans marched in the leather or homespun clothing they wore every day, Marylanders of this company wore "a Uniform Suit of Cloathes turn'd up with Buff, and trim'd with Yellow Metal, or Gold Buttons, White Stockings and Black Cloth half Boote." Emboldened by their example, numerous independent companies formed across Maryland for the defense of the state.

Shortly after the signing of the company's articles of incorporation, training began. Drilling occupied the bulk of each day. Cadets learned how to march and create battle formations. They also practiced loading and firing their muskets as a group and possibly engaged in target practice. Gist's men had their own drillmaster, a cadet named Richard Cary. Cary had previously served as a member of the Ancient and Honourable Artillery Company of Boston, which was commanded by John Hancock.[2] Cary's high-quality training and the company's expensive equipment set Maryland's troops apart from those of other colonies as war unfolded and turned them into, arguably, the first elite infantry unit in the Continental Army.

Voluntary enlistment in these independent companies violated British imperial law. Doing so represented open defiance of Crown rule and constituted an act of treason potentially punishable by death. The sixty Patriots who first signed the articles of incorporation for the Baltimore Independent Cadets were effectively signing their own death warrants. That threat was quite real. When the British had put down an insurrection in Ireland around the same time, a judge decreed to the captured revolutionaries, "You are to be drawn on hurdles to the place of execution, where you are to be hanged by the neck, but not until you are dead, for while you are still living your bodies are to be taken down, your bowels torn out and burned before your faces, your heads then cut off, and your bodies divided each into four quarters."

Elite warriors throughout history have believed that willpower and determination can overcome all odds. This thoughtful, independent company of men ardently embraced their ideals, making a purposeful decision to sacrifice their fortunes, their livelihood, and possibly their lives for the promise of an idea with the risk of an unknown future. Gist, like many Patriots, believed that his men's fervor would help them overcome the much larger, better-equipped, and highly trained British army.

Gist was not alone in his belief. Among Gist's papers is a letter addressed to the Baltimore Independent Company. Full of classical

---

2. Formed in 1637, the artillery company was one of the first citizen militias in the colonies. It still exists today, serving primarily as an honor guard for the governor of Massachusetts, and is the one of the oldest chartered military organizations in North America.

allusions, the letter was signed by an admirer of the company who called himself Agamemnon,[3] the name of the Greek king who united his countrymen to fight against the Trojans. After asking that his letter be read aloud to the group, he refers to Xerxes's army of Immortals and compares the Marylanders to the Spartans who stood against a much larger force at the Battle of Thermopylae. The letter explains, "About three hundred men who's hearts were warmed with patriotism, [held off] an Army of Twenty thousand." The letter writer believed that Gist's men, like the Spartans and other elite units throughout history, could play a crucial role in shaping the future of the new nation.

The comparison would prove eerily accurate. In a little over a year, Washington would call upon the Marylanders to make an epic stand of their own against overwhelming odds.

3. The original letter used the Latin spelling of Agamemnon.

CHAPTER 2

SMALLWOOD'S BATTALION AND THE BIRTH OF AN ARMY

On May 5, 1775, swept up in revolutionary fervor, the Baltimore Independent Company traveled to the outskirts of Baltimore, where delegates to the Continental Congress were due to pass through the city on their way to Philadelphia. The honor guard waited in eager anticipation. Their patience was rewarded when George Washington and several other delegates—soon to be heroes of the Revolution—rode into town.

The Marylanders eagerly accompanied these dignitaries to the lavish Fountain Inn, located near present-day Light Street and Redwood Street, which boasted excellent wine cellars, twenty-four bedrooms, and six mahogany-finished grand parlors. On the inn's grounds, the cadets lined up in formation and discharged their muskets into the air three times in salute of the cavalcade. The pomp and ceremony continued through the next day when Washington, then a colonel, reviewed the troops on the town common. He expressed "satisfaction in the appearance and behavior of the officers and men." Mordecai Gist's Independent Company then led the way to the courthouse, where the city fathers entertained the dignitaries in style. During the proceedings, the delegates offered a toast: "May the town of Baltimore flourish and the noble spirits of the inhabitants continue till ministerial tyranny be at an end." The defenders of Maryland were about to take their first steps as defenders of a larger cause.

After their brief stay in Baltimore, the southern delegates arrived in Philadelphia, where the Second Continental Congress convened on

May 10, 1775. On the 19th of the previous month, the Patriots had fired the "shot heard round the world" at the Battles of Lexington and Concord. It was the start of open conflict between the colonists and their mother country.

The siege of Boston followed these initial clashes. Massachusetts militia and other American troops, furnishing their own clothing, equipment, and arms, blockaded all land routes out of Boston, trapping the British garrison there despite the fact that no American army existed and none of the colonies had declared independence. Instead, in Washington's own words, there was "a mixed multitude of people . . . under very little order or government. . . . Confusion and disorder reigned in every department."

In June, the Second Continental Congress made a momentous decision. In spite of the fear that an army could someday be used against its own people, Congress established a military force and commissioned Washington as the "General and Commander in Chief of the Army of the United Colonies." Eventually, resolutions from Congress called it the "Continental Army" or "American Army."

A second-generation Virginian born to moderately prosperous planters, Washington had been educated in the colonies and had become a surveyor before serving with distinction during the French and Indian War. Rising to the rank of colonel and regimental commander in Virginia's provincial forces, he gained the military and political skills he later needed as the leader of a fledgling American army. Six-foot-two and handsome with a commanding presence and countenance, Washington was one of the best riders in the colonies and possessed enormous physical strength. His inheritance of the plantation at Mount Vernon, along with real estate holdings of his wife, Martha Custis, made him a wealthy man. That status thrust him into the upper echelons of colonial society. With his contacts, temperament, and martial record, Washington seemed to be an excellent choice for the role of commander in chief. But he was far from the only option.

Washington's chief rivals for the position included two veterans of the French and Indian War: Horatio Gates and Charles Lee. Lee had considerable experience fighting overseas in various European wars, and Gates had distinguished himself fighting in North America. But perhaps Washington's most serious rival was the president of the Continental Congress, John Hancock, who had never been in battle and whose only military experience was commanding parade ground maneuvers for the Ancient and Honorable Artillery Company of Boston, the same unit to which Richard Cary belonged.

John Adams noted that Washington had two invaluable leadership skills: "He possessed the gift of silence and had great command." As the most crucial officer of the Revolution, Washington had to transform citizens from all walks of American life and all thirteen colonies, including the Marylanders, from undisciplined neophytes into soldiers. Eventually, the commander in chief formed a special relationship with the elite fighting soldiers of Maryland, one of the few units to fight in both the North and the South, men who would hold the army together in the darkest hours of the Revolution.

After establishing that Washington would lead the colonial army, the penniless Continental Congress set about raising that army. In a series of resolutions, the Congress recommended that each of the thirteen colonies establish a battalion[4] "at the expense of the Continent." Maryland answered this call in a unique way: a battalion with a core cadre of officers and NCOs from the independent cadets at its heart. Smallwood's Battalion was born.

In December 1775 the Maryland Convention, Maryland's Patriot government during the early part of the Revolution, resolved to raise an army of 1,444 troops "in the pay and for the defense" of Maryland. The following month, the government finalized its plan, determining that the force would consist "of a battalion of 9 companies, 7 independent

---

4. Even though a battalion is typically about a third the size of a regiment, the size and strength varied by unit, and "battalion" could also mean any subdivision of a regiment. The military of the time often used the terms "battalion" and "regiment" interchangeably.

companies, [and] 2 companies of artillery." Each company consisted of at least sixty-eight privates, and some included as many as one hundred. All the men were to be volunteers, described as "young hearty robust men, who are tied by birth or family connection or property to this country; and are well practiced in the use of firearms."

Answering the call of the Second Continental Congress to enlist regulars for a Continental Army, Maryland created a force unique in the thirteen colonies because it was neither militia nor Continental; instead, it was a state-funded (from taxes levied from Marylanders and later the seizure of Loyalist property) defense force created to protect Maryland from the British and from the internal threat of Americans loyal to the Crown.

These volunteer regulars enlisted for a year and earned wages paid by Maryland for their service. Privates initially received five and a third dollars; sergeants eight dollars; and the highest-paid member of the unit, the colonel, fifty dollars. These wages, even when they were paid, were barely enough for any member of the force to scrape by. Many of them never received their full wages, which were docked to pay for uniforms. Some soldiers in good standing later received a land bounty.

Smallwood's Battalion also had a tiny contingent of musicians, specifically drummers and fifers. In the eighteenth century men could hardly hear shouted commands over the roar of cannon and muskets, so they learned to follow orders given by the beat of a drum. Each army had scores of drum signals, and men who drilled to them instantly followed these commands. Fifers and drummers also played marching music, popular tunes that the men sang along to. Slowly, these drills and martial music welded men together as they formed a sense of unity.

The men needed shoes, buckles, stockings, shirts, overalls, a hat, a comb, a blanket, a knife, tents, a camp kettle, and other related items in addition to weapons. In the beginning, they supplied many of these needs themselves. Housing and tents were also in short supply. One officer noted that his company was so poorly equipped that the men had to "encamp out among the pines without Blankets or Tents." He complained, "We stand here exposed and remain in a most Defenceless state." Over time, they needed replacements for their clothing and equipment. Sometimes Congress or the states provided these for the troops, but more often, the men went without.

The new troops also needed food. Officers exchanged many letters on the subject of acquiring meat and bread to fill the battalion's stomachs. Congress fixed rations at a pound of beef, three-quarters of a pound of pork, or a pound of fish per day. Provisions also included peas, beans, vegetables, "cyder," and molasses. But like the uniforms and equipment, the rations were more hope than reality. As the war progressed, many Marylanders starved, wore rags, and went barefoot.

Informally, the Marylanders referred to these companies collectively as Smallwood's Battalion, as the colony placed the bulk of the existing independent companies, including Gist's, under the leadership of Colonel William Smallwood. Born in Charles County, Maryland, and educated at Eton College in England, Smallwood came from a family of politicians. After serving in the French and Indian War, he was elected as a representative in the Maryland provincial assembly, the local government for the colony. At the time of his appointment, he was a portly forty-three-year-old planter who was highly respected in Maryland but who also possessed a pettiness that didn't endear him to many of his men.

Being placed under Smallwood's command did not sit well with Gist, who sent a letter to the Maryland government demanding that he be allowed to continue as commander of his company. It stated that Gist, on his own time and at his own risk, recruited the company that had twice elected him as commander. Gist imbued a winning tradition in the troops, teaching them that "Success alone is merit." Finally, he concluded, "If appointed to an office (not beneath what my former rank entitled me to) I shall endeavor to acquit myself with honour to those who are pleased to appoint me." He signed the missive, rather ironically, as "Your most obedient, humble servant, Mordecai Gist."

The convention not only acceded to Gist's request, but promoted him, making him a second major of the entire regiment under Smallwood. Gist's former company retained something of its independence although it was now under Smallwood's command. In addition, many of the men from his company were given high positions in the newly established battalion. Former members of the Baltimore Independent Company made up a quarter of the commissioned and noncommissioned officers in Smallwood's Battalion.

Many of the officers in Smallwood's companies possessed strong leadership qualities. Those characteristics allowed many to attain prominent positions in politics after the war. Several became congressmen or state senators, and Smallwood himself eventually became governor. The original slate of officers in the battalion included Nathaniel Ramsay, a lawyer from Cecil County, who was a captain in the unit. Educated at the College of New Jersey (today Princeton University), Ramsay was thirty-four when the Maryland Battalion formed, and so was one of the older men in the regiment. Ramsay's family included several notable figures. His brother David Ramsay became a prominent early historian of the American Revolution, and his brother-in-law was the famous artist Charles Willson Peale, who served with the Pennsylvania militia. Peale painted several portraits of America's founders, including nearly sixty portraits of George Washington.

Charles Willson Peale's younger brother James was also a renowned artist, although not as highly regarded as Charles Willson. The two lived and worked together for a time, with James focusing on miniatures. In January 1776 James accepted a commission as an ensign in Smallwood's Battalion at the age of twenty-six. The ensigns, junior officers, had a special place in a company or regiment, as they took turns carrying the colors. After about two years of service, Peale was promoted to captain.

Finding enough officers with natural leadership qualities proved challenging, as was the case for any fledging military unit formed from scratch. One Baltimorean wrote to the Maryland authorities, "There are a good many more vacancies in the 8th Battalion as soon as they can be collected together a list will be laid before you in order that they may be filled up." He added, "The men are undisciplined they therefore more especially require to be full officer'd. But as we may want time to do that. I am determined to march with what we have."

Another of those new officers was Edward Veazey, a fourth-generation American from Cecil County who was named captain of the 7th Independent Company under Smallwood. Like many of the young officers, Veazey was from one of Maryland's leading families. His relatives were wealthy, slaveholding plantation owners, and many of them held public office in Maryland during and after the Revolution. Also from a prominent family was Bryan Philpot Jr., a twenty-year-old who obtained a commission as an ensign. Philpot's father was very influential in Baltimore as a successful merchant and landowner. Later, the city named a street, bridge, point, and hill after the family.

Many of the Maryland officers were quite young when they assumed their ranks. William Sterrett was only eighteen years old when he became a first lieutenant in the Maryland Battalion in January 1776. Descended from Irish immigrants, the Sterrett family ran a very successful store in Baltimore, John Sterrett & Company, which sold imported goods like cloth and salt; the Sterretts also owned shipping interests and land in the area. The family ardently supported the Revolution, and William's brother John served as a captain in the Baltimore County Militia. His sister Mary, known as Polly, later married Mordecai Gist. A large number of the men in the battalion were bound together by friendship or family ties.

These young officers were often promoted through the ranks quickly. James Fernandis originally entered Smallwood's Battalion as an enlisted soldier on January 30, 1776. Of Spanish ancestry, the Fernandis family had immigrated to Maryland more than 120 years before the Revolution broke out. Within six months of enlistment, Fernandis had received a commission as a lieutenant. Six months later, he was a second lieutenant, and by April 1777 he had become a first lieutenant. Another, John Bantham, a twenty-year-old from Kent County, enlisted as a private but became a sergeant within just a few days, likely because of his innate ability to lead men.

*   *   *

As the acid test of leadership, the officers were required to recruit their own men, who commonly included people from their hometowns. Each company quickly filled up. The Marylanders spanned the spectrum of socioeconomic classes but were largely farmers (and their sons) and some artisans, like ship's carpenters, brewers, bakers, and blacksmiths. One officer stated when writing to Smallwood that he hoped to "have a very Respectable Company of farmers sons as I am determined I will take very few, if any, out of this Town."

The muster rolls from 1775 to 1776 are fragmentary. Based on information about one company, the average age of the recruits, who hailed from all of Maryland's counties, was just under twenty-five years, and the average height was around five-foot-seven. A variety of factors motivated the men to join: For many, it was patriotism; for others it may have been a chance to improve their standard of living. Still others, green and unaccustomed to the horrors of war, may have been seduced by dreams of glory and honor.

In all wars, the privates do most of the fighting; Smallwood's Battalion was no different. The enlisted ranks were filled with men who signed up for one year of service, such as John Hughes, a twenty-six-year-old Marylander from Frederick County. Some, like John Boudy, a young teenager who lived with his parents at Bald Friar's Ferry on the Susquehanna River in northern Maryland, served through the entire war. Many sets of brothers also joined Smallwood's Battalion, including the Scottish-born McMillan brothers, who were likely poor tenant farmers raising tobacco in the eastern portion of Harford County in the Chesapeake region. Both men started out in the militia, enlisted in the battalion in the spring, and were quickly promoted to sergeant in a few months.

Free African Americans also joined the ranks of Smallwood's Battalion. While the exact number who served the unit through the course of the war is impossible to determine, estimates say around five thousand African Americans served in the entire Continental Army and twice as many fought for the British. This was not only America's first army, but America's first integrated army, the likes of which wouldn't be seen again until after World War II. In a cruel irony, thousands of black men fought for the values of liberty and freedom while tens of thousands of their brothers remained enslaved.

Indentured servants were not eligible for service unless they had permission from their master or mistress. Indentured service and slavery were both fairly common in Maryland at the time: a 1752 census of Baltimore County listed 11,345 free whites; 1,501 white indentured servants and convicts; 4,143 black and mulatto slaves; and 204 free blacks and mulattoes. Sometimes servants signed up illegally. One such case was Daniel Brophy, who joined Smallwood's Battalion in the spring of 1776. Brophy was later returned to his master after the man demanded restitution.

The company's noncommissioned officers helped with recruitment. Sergeants were specifically assigned this task. Twenty-three-year-old Gassaway Watkins began his career as one of those NCOs. Born and raised in Anne Arundel County, Maryland, he attained the rank of ensign the year he enlisted and later became a captain. A "man of magnificent physique, six-feet-two inches in height, well-proportioned and developed," Watkins had statuesque height that made "him conspicuous in battle."

As the companies filled up with men, the next task was to provide training, equipment, and arms.

CHAPTER 3

GIRDING FOR WAR

Arming Smallwood's Battalion was a nightmare. Most of the firearms were personally owned by the soldiers who carried them, and this situation led to a hodgepodge of makes, models, and calibers. In the beginning, many of the newly minted soldiers didn't have any weapons at all during their drill. As supplies came in, they received muskets, sometimes called firelocks.

Operating this kind of weapon was a time-consuming chore. Troops like the Marylanders carried cartridge pouches that held twelve to thirty-six prepared cartridges. The cartridges were tubes of paper with the same diameter as the musket bore. Each contained a ball and a premeasured amount of black powder, and they were crimped on the end. To fire, the soldier would pull out a cartridge, rip off the top of the paper with his teeth, pour a small amount of powder into the priming pan, pour the rest of the powder into the musket barrel, and then insert the ball and paper into the barrel and ram them down. Only then was the musket ready to fire. Under the best possible conditions, a well-trained and well-supplied soldier could load and shoot four or five times per minute. In the heat of battle, distracted by the smoke and sounds of conflict and with adrenaline surging through his veins, a soldier often forgot or skipped essential steps in the intricate process, which could lead to misfires that had deadly consequences.

Technology drove tactics. Because muskets were so inaccurate, troops practiced laying down concentrated fire in large numbers. Soldiers of the time lined up in rows, sometimes eight or ten ranks deep, and fired en masse, meaning that everyone in the front ranks who had a clear line of sight to the opposing side pulled his trigger at the same time. This massed fire improved the odds of hitting the enemy.

As formidable as they sound, most of these volleys weren't very successful. "It was just possible for a good marksman to hit a man at 100 yards; a volley could be fired with some chance of obtaining hits on a mass of troops at 200 yards; but at 300 yards fire was completely ineffective." One trial in France showed just how inaccurately muskets performed: 60 percent hit the target at 82 yards, 40 percent hit at 164 yards, and a mere 23 percent at 300 yards. An observer wrote, "Powder is not as terrible as believed. Few men in these affairs are killed from in front while fighting. I have seen whole salvoes fail to kill four men." The reality is that parade ground trials did not translate into battlefield actuality: men had adrenaline surging, smoke obscured lines of sight, misfires occurred with regularity (sometimes as high as 25 percent), and often the enemy was barreling down with fixed bayonets. In the chaos, men sometimes broke from fear, and even a well-trained soldier couldn't get off as many well-aimed shots in combat as in a trial setting.

All firearms of this era were made by hand—like everything else a soldier wore and carried—and some gunsmiths were better than others. The officers set about testing every gun provided to the regiment by Baltimore manufacturers. Evidently, some of the gun makers were cognizant that their wares weren't up to the challenge; as one Marylander reported in February 1776, "Mr. Keener [a local gunsmith] after seeing the rest try'd refus'd to have his proved but upon my threatning him a good deal he comply'd." In fact, more than half of the guns Keener supplied failed the test. A higher percentage of the guns from other makers passed, and the tester "stamp'd all that prov'd good." In another message, one officer reported that only eight of twenty-nine muskets in his company were working. The rest were "vile trash" that couldn't be made to function.

Smallwood's Battalion also requisitioned some "of the guns which were in the hands of the minute Company" that had formerly been defending the colony. Minute companies were made up of militia sometimes called minutemen, local civilians in the area who could answer the call to arms in an emergency. This wasn't a good solution, however, as the minute company's guns were "very indifferent, indeed so bad that twould be cruel to set me to work with them," noted one officer. That insufficiency left the militia without the weapons it needed. "The militia are thro' this county in a most defenceless state, and my Company if possible in a much worse one," the officer added.

Inequities in the supply of various units impacted the troops' morale on several occasions. Captain Edward Veazey, stationed on the Eastern Shore, said the lack of arms and uniforms made him "very uneasy." It became a problem because the officers "understood the troops on the W. Shore are generally well armed & provided with Cloaths."

In an effort to address the problem, William Smallwood sent Jack Steward to search for arms and gunpowder. Known for his sizable ego, Jack was the son of Stephen Steward, who owned a forty-three-acre shipyard south of Annapolis. Six feet tall, Jack Steward was a handsome man and well built. A former Quaker, he was courageous and lived by his personal motto, "You only live once." Commissioned a first lieutenant on January 14, 1776, he quickly rose through the ranks and became a captain in charge of a company that same year.

Likely accompanying Steward was his lifelong friend Benjamin Ford. The two men were neighbors, and Ford's grandfather built Steward's house. Like Steward, Ford was a strong and charismatic leader. Both proved practically fearless in battle.

Steward's quest for gunpowder was indicative of America's need for military supplies. When the war began, the colonials had only about half a pound of gunpowder for each of their soldiers. Throughout the conflict, this was an Achilles' heel of sorts for the Revolution. Powder enabled or curtailed success on the battlefield. As Americans manufactured only about 10 percent of what they used, 90 percent of it had to be imported.

British military planners recognized the importance of gunpowder. In October 1774 the Crown advised its colonial governors to "take the most effectual measures to arresting, detaining and securing any Gunpowder, or any sort of Arms or Ammunitions which may be attempted to be imported into the province." British troops soon began seizing or destroying stores of ammunition and gunpowder whenever they found any. The colonists scoured the earth for powder and saltpeter (potassium nitrate, one of the key ingredients in explosives) to replenish their stores. They sent agents to Canada and the Caribbean and brought in imports from France and the Netherlands. They also attempted to produce their own gunpowder from locally mined materials. These efforts were so ineffective that Benjamin Franklin thought they might as well revert to bows and arrows.

The Marylanders received bayonets, which were unusual for colonial troops. A typical bayonet at the time was a triangle socket bayonet that was fitted on the end of the musket. These deadly blades were stabbing weapons that could impale a man's guts, leaving mortal wounds. Proper training allowed the men not only to withstand a bayonet charge from an enemy force but also to make an attack of their own.

Once the companies were formed and equipped, they were positioned in the spring of 1776 to defend Maryland's most important economic centers. Six companies, the majority of Smallwood's Battalion, were stationed in Annapolis, while the remaining three, commanded by Mordecai Gist, went to Baltimore. The independent companies were sprinkled throughout Maryland.

Also sprinkled throughout Maryland were many families who remained loyal to the Crown. Exact figures on the number of American Loyalists are impossible to determine, but by the end of the war, more than eightly thousand Loyalist Americans would be banished from America. One of those men found his name in the *Maryland Journal and Baltimore Advertiser* because Gist placed the following advertisement there:

Deserted. From the Baltimore Independent Company on the night of the 24th instant, a certain Thomas Freshwater. He is an Englishmen, about 5 ft. 7 in. high, swarthy complexion, long black hair, much given to drink, and when drunk very impertinent; had on a sute of drummers clothes. It is suspected that some

of the Tories in this place have been affiliated with his escape
and forwarded him to Annapolis, where he has been since seen.
Whoever apprehends said deserter and shall deliver him to me,
shall receive a reward of forty shillings.

A civil war raged throughout the colonies and separated many of the
citizens of Maryland.

CHAPTER 4

AMERICA'S FIRST CIVIL WAR

A low murmur ran through the crowd of Marylanders gathered for a meeting of two militia companies in Frederick County, Maryland, northwest of Baltimore on February 6, 1776. Robert Gassaway rose to his feet and began speaking. Although all present had volunteered to defend their homes from British forces if the need should arise, many retained some feelings of loyalty to the Crown. More than a few were also uneasy about the new colonial organizations that were taking on the role of government. Gassaway gave voice to their secret fears, saying that "it was better for the Poor People to lay down their Arms, and pay the Duties and Taxes laid upon them by the King and Parliament, than to be brought into Slavery and to be commanded and ordered about as they were" by rippling effects of the crisis in Boston and by the Patriot government in Maryland. He intimated that Marylanders, including his sons, were compelled to sign up for the militia because they feared what the local Committee of Observation, the group charged with suppressing Loyalists, would do if they refused to join. "My brave boys fight away," he added with his hands clasped around his neck, "for fear their necks should be stretched."

Angrily, the more patriotic among the group told Gassaway to keep his opinions to himself.

But the outspoken Marylander wouldn't be silenced. Gassaway claimed he "was satisfied he was right," and he called on the militia to lay down its arms.

Gassaway's dissent provides an example of the stark divisions between Loyalists and Patriots that tore many colonies—and many families—apart during the war, which wasn't only a revolution but a civil war as well.

As for Gassaway, the threat of imprisonment later convinced him to sign a poorly written confession, which said, "I confess that I am sory to think that I should have said enni thing that should have given enny purson reson to think that it was my deiser to disunite the peopel and, And acknowledge my error in so doing, and do promis for tim to cum to behave myself carfully."

This civil war was particularly evident in Maryland, where Chesapeake Bay divided the colony in half, effectively creating two factions. Those who lived on the Eastern Shore tended to be Loyalists, or Tories, while other areas were home to more Patriots.

From Maryland's founding in 1632, its geography had separated it into two sections. On the western shore of the Chesapeake, the towns of Annapolis, Saint Mary's City, and Baltimore served as way stations for travelers and merchants journeying to and from other colonies. Trade flourished and residents were in regular communication with the other colonies. The Eastern Shore, by contrast, was much more isolated. The farmers, plantation owners, and fishermen of the area tended to keep to themselves, with religion often playing a major role in the colonists' lives. Although the colony had been founded as a haven for Catholics, by the end of the seventeenth century, Protestants were asserting more control in the colony, just as they were in Britain. On the Eastern Shore, the Church of England dominated the religious landscape. The local church leaders encouraged their congregations to remain loyal to Great Britain and, in many cases, the people followed the recommendations of the clergy. However, supporters of both sides could be found throughout the state and the rest of the colonies, often living close together. In the crucible of insurgency, ethnic, religious, and secular divisions resulted in bitter rivalries, pitting neighbor against neighbor and brother against brother.

Dealing with the numerous Loyalists in Maryland fell to the colony's Council of Safety. This euphemistically named body provided a mechanism for military planning and hoarding of supplies and weapons, as well as administering the government and clamping down on dissidents.

At the urging of the recently convened Second Continental Congress, each of the colonies formed a similar council. Marylanders who refused to sign an oath of association were labeled "Non-Associators," and the state required them to pay fines and forfeit their firearms; in some cases it also seized their property.

At the local level, towns like Baltimore established Committees of Observation, which provided extralegal courts to administer regulations. There were approximately nine hundred such committees across Maryland. They served to intimidate Loyalists, confiscate their property, and enforce laws. Mordecai Gist and other prominent members of the Baltimore Independent Company were heavily involved with both the Council of Safety and the Committee of Observation, taking orders from both groups.

The new government organizations effectively kept many Loyalists and those with mixed allegiance in check. The committees also had a financial component; they suspended British debt laws and collection activities from Britain. In the Chesapeake region, debt owed to British factors and agents was a major issue, as many Patriot planters were overextended. After examining British Treasury records, one historian claimed that more than fifty-five members of Virginia's House of Burgesses were in hock to the Crown. George Washington and Thomas Jefferson each owed between one thousand and five thousand pounds—a fortune at the time—and many prominent Marylanders joined their ranks. In addition, the state owed £289,000, largely from a trade deficit in which imports outstripped exports.

Loyalty to the Crown and loyalty to the Patriot cause divided several of the families of Smallwood's Battalion. Eastern Shore native John Gunby was a fierce Patriot, but his father "was an ardent supporter of the Crown; in other words, a Tory." Called "one of the most gallant officers of the Maryland Line under Gen. Smallwood," John Gunby was born in Somerset County. At the age of thirty, he volunteered as a minuteman, despite the objections of his father, who warned that he could be hanged for treason. The younger Gunby replied, "I am determined to join American forces; I would sooner sink into a patriot's grave than wear the crown of England." Like Gist, he raised an independent company that became part of Smallwood's Battalion.

Despite their disagreement, Gunby continued to respect and admire his father. He wrote that "Tory" was

> a name to which a great deal of undeserved odium has been always attached in America. Yet Toryism in principle was nothing but a conservative attachment to the government and institutions of the Mother country. . . . This admirable sentiment of loyalty to the king was so strong that it required almost the bitterness of death to break it. All the more, we must admire the heroic manhood of the colonies, which threw off these attachments in the cause of freedom and endured all kinds of pain and suffering rather than endure oppression.

These competing desires—loyalty to the Crown and the desire to be free from oppression—warred within the hearts of many colonists, causing some of them to change their allegiance during the course of the Revolution.

One Tory who didn't have divided loyalties was Eastern Shore mogul and pamphleteer James Chalmers, owner of an island on the Chesapeake. With his fortune of more than ten thousand pounds, he had purchased several sprawling tobacco plantations on the Eastern Shore and owned scores of slaves. He had an inner circle of many influential and wealthy Loyalists. An Englishman described the recent Scottish immigrant by saying, "The worthy proprietor lives in a manner independent of mankind, the *monarch* of his little fertile territory." Zealously opposed to revolution, Chalmers published scathing rebuttals to Patriot literature, including Thomas Paine's *Common Sense*. He wrote that Paine, "shamefully misrepresents facts, is ignorant of the true state of Great Britain and her Colonies, utterly unqualified for the arduous task, he has presumptuously assumed; and ardently intent on seducing us to that precipice on which himself stands trembling." He concluded, "Volumes were insufficient to describe the horror, misery and desolation, awaiting the people at large in the Syren [Siren] form of American independence. In short, I affirm that it would be most excellent policy in those who wish for TRUE LIBERTY to submit by an advantageous reconciliation to the authority of Great Britain; 'to accomplish in the long run, what they cannot do by hypocrisy, fraud and force in the short one.' INDEPENDENCE AND SLAVERY ARE SYNONYMOUS TERMS."

After refusing to sign an oath of fidelity to the Maryland Council of Safety and being beaten nearly to death by a mob in Chestertown, Chalmers prepared to "repel force by force." Within a year he was talking to the British commander in North America. In time he became a mirror image of Gist, raising his own regiment of Loyalists, just as the Baltimore merchant had assembled his Patriots.

In the cauldron of competing ideals and with less-than-ideal training and preparation, the Marylanders went to war against people who had been their countrymen. To quash this nascent insurrection, the Crown planned to intimidate the rebellious colonies with a show of force.

1776

CHAPTER 5

THE *OTTER*

Water splashed against the side of the *Defence* as the vessel navigated the Chesapeake on March 9, 1776. Captain Samuel Smith looked around at his men who had enthusiastically volunteered for the mission to confront the British warship *Otter*, which lay at anchor up ahead and threatened the cities of Baltimore and Annapolis. So many of Smith's men had wanted to take part in the action that the *Defence* couldn't hold them all. Some had clambered into small boats that were now accompanying the converted merchant ship, which carried twenty guns.

Like so many of the men who made up the core of the new battalion, Smith was one of the original sixty cadets in the Baltimore Independent Company. Smith was close to Mordecai Gist and Nathaniel Ramsay and particularly close to Jack Steward. Smith and Steward actually once fought a duel, "becoming, subsequently, on the most friendly terms."

Over a year had passed since Smith and the other cadets had formed Maryland's first independent military company, and many dramatic events had shaped the first twelve months of the Revolution. The siege of Boston had been lifted after Patriots seized the heavy artillery at Fort Ticonderoga and hauled it hundreds of miles across the New York and Massachusetts countryside before positioning it over Dorchester Heights in south Boston. With the artillery on fortified high ground overlooking Boston harbor, the British commander saw that his position in Boston had become indefensible and withdrew his troops to Halifax, Nova Scotia. The Americans won a string of victories in 1775 and suffered one epic defeat while assaulting Quebec in the midst of a snowstorm on the last day of the year.

In the South a Patriot militia numbering nearly one thousand men crushed a Loyalist militia of equal force outside Wilmington, North Carolina, dampening the Crown's influence in the state for years. In Virginia the colony's firebrand governor, John Murray, also known as Lord Dunmore, attempted to disrupt Whig units outside Norfolk. In the Battle of Great Bridge, Patriot forces annihilated Dunmore's troops, slaying or wounding nearly one hundred British regulars, while the only American casualty was a single man with a slightly wounded thumb. Trounced, Dunmore, with a small contingent of British regulars, Loyalists, and several hundred former slaves he dubbed the Ethiopian Regiment, boarded royal ships, including the man-of-war *Otter.* Next, Dunmore's force bombarded and torched Norfolk, and what it didn't destroy Whig militia finished off, burning and looting many Loyalist homes. Most Americans didn't know the full truth of the episode and assumed it was a British atrocity. The supposed atrocity, combined with an earlier incident at Falmouth, Massachusetts, where the British torched hundreds of houses, galvanized calls for independence. With Norfolk in ashes, Dunmore's flotilla sailed across the Chesapeake to Portsmouth, Virginia, before turning north and raiding the coastline.

In a show of force, Dunmore sent a group of warships including the *Otter* up the Chesapeake toward Baltimore and Annapolis in March 1776. Their arrival caused great consternation in the colony, and people who lived near the shore quickly evacuated out of fear that they would meet the same fate as Norfolk. The Council of Safety immediately sent a note to the battalion, saying, "We hear that the 44 Gun Man of War and two Sloops are on their Way up the Bay: the City [Baltimore] is now weak and we judge it necessary to have all the Men drawn to Town we can for its Defence; we should be glad you will give Directions to all the Companies and Men in your Battalion that can be got ready to repair as soon as possible to Town. We shall be glad to see you as early in the morning as you can."

Preliminary intelligence proved to be somewhat exaggerated, as later reports counted only eighteen guns on the *Otter*. Nevertheless, the battalion "moved with astonishing dispatch, and as soon as the Vessels hove in Sight [the Maryland] Coast was lined with Men." As a show of strength, the battalion mustered ranks near the shoreline. To make it appear that it had more men than it did, the same soldiers lined up over and over in different locations as the British ship moved up the coast.

Adding to the tension, the *Otter* had set fire to a small boat carrying a load of oats. The *Otter's* captain claimed it "was done without order and done by an inconsiderate midshipman," but the move fanned the flames of hostility in Annapolis and Baltimore. Making things worse, the captain next demanded that the governor of Maryland turn over to him the vessel *Defence*, which was currently being fitted out for war and which the British called a presumably hostile privateer. In addition, he wanted provisions, which he would take by force if the Marylanders refused to sell them to him.

While the negotiations were still in progress, the captain of the *Defence* called for volunteers to challenge the *Otter* and recapture other vessels that were in convoy. Samuel Smith's company enthusiastically volunteered. The American ship, accompanied by a few others, approached the British flotilla. Surprised by such resistance, the *Otter* turned tail and ran to Virginia, pillaging Maryland's Saint George's Island on the way to get the supplies denied it at Baltimore. During this withdrawal, the *Otter* attempted to capture an American schooner in a nearby creek, but the local militia drove the British ship away. Meanwhile, the triumphant Marylanders returned to Baltimore with the vessels that they had retaken.

Although the encounter with the *Otter* had been a minor incident, the Marylanders had received their first taste of victory. The Maryland Council of Safety heralded their bravery, writing, "We cannot sufficiently commend those brave Sons of Liberty who this Day stood forth so gallantly in Defence of their Country. Be assured that we shall afford them every assistance in our power."

The second task entrusted to the regiment was more distasteful. Virginian Patriots had intercepted some correspondence between Maryland's British-installed governor, Sir Robert Eden, and a renowned Loyalist and close associate of firebrand James Chalmers. One Patriot general forwarded the letters to the Council of Safety, which then asked Smith's company to arrest the governor. The Council wrote, "It evidently appears that Mr. Eden has been carrying on a dangerous Correspondence with the Ministry of Great Britain, who seem desperately bent on the Destruction of America. The Congress therefore have come to a Resolution that the Person and Papers of Governor Eden be immediately seized, from which there is Reason to believe, we may not only learn but probably defeat, the Designs of our Enemies."

However, the governor enjoyed great popularity among the people. A consummate politician, he attempted to walk both sides of the fence; he understood their grievances yet opposed taking up arms.

Despite the fact that Eden was Britain's representative, when Smith and his men arrived in Annapolis to carry out their duty, the Council of Safety suddenly changed its mind and ordered them back home. Eventually, an investigation found that Eden had no malicious intent, but the Council of Safety requested that the governor leave the colony, which he did. As Eden was leaving, the largest invasion of North America was about to begin.

CHAPTER 6

THE ARMADA

On the cool summer morning of June 29, 1776, Marylander Private Daniel McCurtin seated himself in an outbuilding that afforded a panoramic view of the blue-green, wide-open waters cradling the lower harbor of New York City. As McCurtin turned his gaze to take in the picturesque vista, he instead witnessed a jarring sight. The bay seemed to resemble "a wood of pine trees trimmed," as hundreds of ships sporting naked masts approached shore and dropped sail to anchor. Astonished by this strange development, he continued, "I declare, at my noticing this, that I could not believe my eyes, but Keeping my eyes fixed at the very spot, judge you of my surprise when in ten minutes, the whole bay was full of shipping as ever it could be. I declare that I thought all London was afloat."

McCurtin, part of a small advance group of Marylanders in New York, saw the harbinger of a vast flotilla carrying more than twenty-three thousand British regulars and an initial complement of ten thousand Hessian allies to American shores. Over the next six weeks, more than five hundred transports and seventy British warships sailed into New York's harbors. The show of strength comprised half of the British navy and a large portion of the British army. Some of the first ships to arrive dropped anchor off Sandy Hook, New Jersey, while others landed troops to invade Staten Island. The island contained a rebel flagstaff fort to signal the arrival of British troops. It also provided an ideal staging area for the invasion of Long Island and Manhattan. The British ships bided their time until the rest of the transports bearing the Hessians and other reinforcements arrived.[5]

In response to the British invasion, John Hancock, then president of the Continental Congress, put out a call to the colonies for troops. In a letter to the Maryland Convention, he wrote, "The Congress have this day received intelligence which renders it absolutely necessary that the greatest exertion should be made to save our country from being desolated by the hands of tyranny." Congress asked the colonies to send reinforcements to New York. Hancock's closing words demonstrated the gravity of the situation. He wrote:

> I do therefore most ardently beseech you and require, in the name and by the authority of Congress, as you regard your own freedom, and as you stand engaged by the most solemn ties of honour, to support the common cause:—to strain every nerve to send forward your militia. This is a step of such infinite moment that in all probability your speedy compliance will prove the salvation of your country. We should reflect, too, that the loss of the campaign must inevitably protract the war; and that, in order to gain it, we have only to exert ourselves, and to make use of the means by which God and nature have given us to defend ourselves.

After the letter was received in Maryland, nine companies of Smallwood's Battalion set out for Philadelphia. Congress ordered the Marylanders to join troops in Phildelphia and then report to General George Washington in New York. Two of the independent companies stayed in Maryland a while longer in the event the British attacked. They soon joined their brethren.

---

5. Howe also put his men to work constructing landing barges, precursors of World War II's landing craft infantry (LCI). The barges had high gunwales and a crude ramp that dropped in the front, allowing the men to exit quickly on a landing beach.

Smallwood's Battalion, already an elite unit by virtue of training, equipment, and motivation, was about to become amalgamated into the Continental Army. This force had some success on the battlefield in 1775, but most of the world at the time believed it ludicrous to suppose that the ragtag assortment of amateurs with their unique set of principles could stand up to—let alone defeat—one of the finest armies in existence.

The top flag officers the king sent to America were considered exceptional in the British military. Leading the British forces in New York were the Howe brothers: General William Howe, a thirty-year army veteran; and Admiral Richard Howe, who commanded the British navy in North America. Sons of a viscount and of royal blood, they had enjoyed an aristocratic upbringing. The two mirrored each other in many ways: both were tall and dark-complexioned, both were quiet and brave, and both entered the military at an early age. Both also held seats in Parliament and had excellent military records. Richard Howe had fired the first shot in the Seven Years' War and became a very influential admiral, revising the navy's signals and advancing its amphibious warfare capabilities. William Howe had served in the French and Indian War, which gave him a good understanding of conditions in North America and the tactics likely to succeed there.

However, the Howe brothers had very different personalities. Richard, the more taciturn one, earned the nickname Black Dick both for his dark complexion and for his morose personality. One contemporary described the admiral as "silent as a rock."

William, on the other hand, had a reputation for gambling and whoring, and he frequently brought his married mistress, Elizabeth Loring, known as the Sultana, to public events. She was the wife of Loyalist Joshua Loring, who held the position of commissary for prisoners. Public accounts mocked the cuckolded Loring, saying that he "had no objection. He fingered the cash, the general enjoyed madam."

Despite their differences in temperament, the brothers both expressed sympathy for the colonists. As a member of Parliament,

William even voted against the Coercive Acts. They served in America as a matter of duty, not out of any dislike for the Americans. Understanding that a political solution was the best way to end the Revolution, they also sought and received the authority to act as peace commissioners who could grant concessions to the colonists in order to halt hostilities. However, their authority to negotiate and bind the Crown to a peace settlement was extremely limited; they could grant pardons but not much more. Their dedication to seeking peace greatly affected the strategy they pursued throughout the war.

General Howe's top lieutenant, General Sir Henry Clinton, had a very different view; he believed the aim of the war should be to destroy the American army. Clinton wasn't particularly likable and even described himself as "a shy bitch." He frequently clashed with William Howe. Clinton's father, George Clinton, was an admiral and also served for a decade as governor of New York—an assignment that brought Henry Clinton to the state as a twelve-year-old. He later fought in the French and Indian War, during which he developed friendships with Charles Lee and William Alexander (otherwise known as Lord Stirling), whom he later faced as enemies on the battlefield. Descended from a noble family, Clinton, like the Howe brothers, held a seat in Parliament in addition to serving in the military. Although fairly unimpressive looking, Clinton was brilliant, and this brought him to the attention of his superiors even before the start of the Revolution. He often suggested plans that, if they had been followed, could have allowed the British army to flank and destroy the Americans. At Bunker Hill, he offered an alternative attack plan that might have resulted in enveloping American forces and reducing British losses. A superb strategist, Clinton believed that the key to winning the war was annihilating the Patriot forces, not just conquering territory.

The British army that landed on Staten Island in 1776 was one of the most proficient armed forces in the world. Its ranks were filled with volunteers who viewed the military as a career and had a great deal of experience, much like today's U.S. military. For example, the fifteen generals serving at the time averaged thirty years of service, and even the privates averaged nine years in the military. A substantial portion of the army consisted of seasoned combat veterans tested in the wilds of North America during the French and Indian War or in the killing fields of Europe during the Seven Years' War. Its members took pride in Britain's long history of imperial supremacy, leading one American to label it "the most arrogant army in the world."

By contrast, the American army was a mongrel group made up of amateurs. Ambrose Serle, private secretary to Admiral Richard Howe, sneered, "Their army is the strangest that was ever collected: old men of 60, boys of 14, and blacks of all ages, and ragged for the most part, compose the motley crew." The typical American soldier had less than six months of combat experience—or more likely, none at all. Unlike the long-serving British troops, the American generals averaged just two years of experience, while most of the rank and file had been serving on active duty for mere months.

The British army included a number of specialized departments covering everything from hospitals to engineers and quartermasters, making it one of the first global bureaucracies. British officers leading these departments and units differed greatly from their American counterparts, who were typically elected and were often responsible for raising their own troops. British leaders purchased their commissions, which weren't cheap. In a typical regiment, it could cost five hundred pounds sterling to become a lieutenant, fifteen hundred for a captaincy, twenty-six hundred to be a major, and thirty-five hundred to be named lieutenant colonel. As a result, most came from the upper ranks of British society. Becoming a British officer could also prove to be a pathway to wealth. Officers got to keep the pay for any of their men killed in battle, and some who served during the Revolutionary War made as much as eight hundred pounds, the equivalent of a senior officer's salary, in this manner.

But the heart of the British army was its regiments: each with its own identity. Made up of about four hundred to six hundred[6] troops, a regiment recruited its own members. While a few were pressed into service from prisons and given the choice of imprisonment or the army, most were common men—tradesmen, farmers, and laborers. Some sought adventure, and others enlisted to escape poverty and starvation. Several of the regiments had existed for more than a century and had impressive, proud battle histories. They possessed cherished traditions that they passed on to each member of the regiment. Many thought, and were encouraged to believe, that their unit was the best in the army. They also felt a deep loyalty to their king that set them in firm opposition to the Americans they were battling. As one historian has noted, "For men on both sides who actually did the fighting, the war was not primarily a conflict of power or interest. It was a clash of principles in which they deeply believed." This army, highly motivated and imbued with its own principles and traditions, invaded the shores of Staten Island in the summer of 1776.

The grenadiers led the assault on Staten Island. Chosen for their immense size and strength, the grenadiers accentuated their impressive height with caps that made them look a foot taller. As the name suggests, men in the grenadiers originally carried grenades. However, at the time of the American Revolution, the grenades had fallen out of use, and the men carried muskets and bayonets like other British soldiers. Every infantry regiment had its grenadiers, who tackled the toughest jobs in battle—they led daring assaults and stormed the beaches during amphibious landings.

Disembarking alongside the grenadiers was another type of elite unit—the light infantry. Known as the Light Bobs, these soldiers were chosen not for their size, but for their endurance, intelligence, and mastery of firearms. Rather than the regimented drills of the regular army,

6. British regiments were normally divided into ten companies. They had a peacetime strength of thirty-five officers, twenty sergeants, thirty corporals, ten drummers (one per company), two fifers, and 380 privates. Understanding the challenge of fighting in America, Parliament typically increased a regiment's authorized strength by 200 men.

these men practiced "leaping, running, climbing precipices, swimming, skirmishing through woods, loading and firing in different attitudes, and marching with remarkable rapidity." This was a relatively new concept of a military unit, first deployed during the French and Indian War, when British officers attempted to adopt some of the nimble fighting techniques of the American Indians. Based on that experience, General William Howe himself convinced the king to authorize the formation of light infantry companies within each regiment. These were some of the most battle-hardened and bloodied troops in the British army, having lost many men in the battles at Lexington, Concord, and Bunker Hill. The American army (including the Marylanders) later adopted light infantry.

The British also had light cavalry, known as the Light Dragoons. These were often gentleman warriors, highly educated and drawn from the upper crust of society. Originally formed to handle reconnaissance and scouting duties, they were later renowned for their charges. Typically, each carried a small arsenal: "two pistols, a short-barreled carbine, and a long cavalry sword." Their sabers, used for hacking and slashing, were among the most feared weapons of the war in the hands of an experienced rider. Well-armed and mounted on fast horses, these recently created units, which often fought dismounted, were a force to be reckoned with throughout the Revolutionary War.

The British forces on Staten Island also included several companies of the Royal Regiment of Artillery, equipped with seventy-two guns. Its members wore dark blue uniforms instead of red, and it promoted officers based on merit rather than allowing men to purchase commissions. Because getting a cannonball to reach its target was cutting-edge science at the time, they were among the most highly trained specialists in the British military. They studied mathematics, engineering, and chemistry at Woolwich Military Academy, affectionately known as the Shop. These artillerists brought with them a variety of field pieces: three-, six-, eight-, and twelve-pounders (so named for the weight of the cannonball), among many other sizes. A crew of several men manned each gun. For added mobility and to deal with the rough terrain of America, the artillerists also towed lighter, three-pound brass cannons known as grasshoppers that they utilized during the war.

The artillery fired a variety of projectiles. Solid shot was just that, iron spheres or cannonballs. Howitzers and mortars, artillery which lobbed high altitude shots at the enemy rather than firing directly, sometimes shot balls that had been hollowed out and filled with explosives. These shells had fuses that were ignited by the blast when fired. The artillerists carefully prepared the fuses to ignite the ball approximately when it hit the ground or for air bursts. In addition to single iron balls, cannons could also fire a "canister," a tin can filled with lead or iron balls which let out a terrible squeaking sound and acted like shotguns at close range. They used "grape," a canvas bag filled with lead or iron balls, resembling a bunch of grapes, for longer-range shots. Each type of ordnance had a devastating effect.

The invading forces included two armies within the army: the Scottish Highlanders and the Hessians. The Highlanders initially fought against the English during the failed Jacobite Rebellions between 1688 and 1746, but the British skillfully turned their former enemies into allies and integrated them into their army. Often extremely poor—though fiercely proud—these Gaelic-speaking clansmen were frequently recruited by and served with members of their own families. For this reason, the men were intensely loyal to their units. A typical Highlander viewed "any disgrace which he might bring on his clan or district as the most cruel misfortune." Most served for life, including one record-setting private who spent seventy-five years in the service. Dressed in kilts and heavily armed with muskets, bayonets, pistols, broadswords, and various knives, they cut an impressive figure and often struck fear into the hearts of their enemies.

Ten thousand Hessians arrived in New York in mid-August, the first of many who fought beside the British. Professional soldiers primarily from the Hesse region of Germany, the Hessians were "the largest suppliers of troops in the world, [and] also the most expensive." All together more than thirty thousand of them took part in the American Revolutionary War. The king compensated them well for their service, and officers and enlisted men alike expected to make their fortune fighting in America. One Hessian captain noted, "Never in this world was an army as well paid as this one during the civil war in America. One could call them rich." Looting was an expected benefit of service for some European soldiers, and in spite of repeated orders against it and strict punishments, opportunistic soldiers availed themselves of whatever booty they could acquire. This rampant looting undermined the Howe brothers' intended strategy of protecting the Loyalist population, who they incorrectly believed vastly outnumbered the insurgents.

Hessian boys registered with the military at age seven and came before the recruiters as teenagers to see if they would be needed in the army or would be considered "indispensable personnel" who were more valuable to the country as farmers, merchants, or skilled craftsmen. Many of the rank and file began life as peasants but enlisted because the pay was better than that of a farmworker or servant. Others were "expendable people"—bankrupt or unemployed men, some kidnapped and forced into service against their will. Discipline was brutal, as the officers often beat or hanged soldiers for various offenses. In some cases, they also inflicted punishments on soldiers' families at home. The result of this harshness was an army that obeyed orders immediately and unquestioningly. They were professional warriors who looked down on the American rebels.

With the arrival of the British fleet, George Washington faced a nearly impossible strategic situation. Surrounded entirely by water, New York was vulnerable to invasion by the British navy at every point, making it virtually indefensible. At the time, New York was home to around twenty thousand residents and had a sizable Loyalist population. The main thoroughfare was Broadway, a wide, tree-lined street with many houses and churches, while City Hall dominated Wall Street. A sound move would have been to evacuate the city, but that was politically untenable. Local leaders and the Continental Congress urged Washington to defend New York. Washington attempted to turn the city into a fortress, constructing forts and defensive works throughout Manhattan and on Long Island.

Washington also worked to build up the morale of his men, proclaiming in his general orders, "The time is near at hand which must probably determine whether or not Americans are to be free men or slaves. . . . The fate of unborn millions now depend, under God, on the courage . . . of this Army." His stirring words had the intended effect. One of his men wrote in a letter to his wife, "The whole army is in better spirits than I have known it at any time." He added, "Indeed, the city is now so strong, that in the present temper of our men, the enemy would lose half their army in attempting to take it."

At 6:00 p.m. on July 9, 1776, their spirits got another boost. The few Marylanders and the rest of Washington's army in New York assembled by unit at various parade grounds and common areas. They listened intently as the head of each brigade read aloud the Declaration of Independence. The men greeted the words with various cheers and "Huzzahs!" Shortly after the reading, a mob formed and marched down Broadway, where they tore down the lead- and gold-leaf-adorned equestrian statue of King George III. The Declaration effectively made traitors of all Americans who bore arms against the Crown.

Despite the rhetoric, the Howe brothers attempted to set up a peace summit to end the rebellion through negotiation. The meetings went nowhere because the Americans understood that the Howes had no power to negotiate an overarching treaty. Ambrose Serle succinctly summed up the only official meeting between the two governments till the end of the war: "They met, they talked, they parted."

The Battle of New York moved closer.

Chapter 7

Maryland Goes to War

Nearly seven hundred men strong, Smallwood's Battalion marched proudly into its nascent country's capital—Philadelphia, Pennsylvania. It was the middle of July 1776 and the Marylanders had traveled by barge up the Chesapeake, and marched on foot the rest of the way to the city to parade in front of the Continental Congress. An officer in the city at the time made note of the Marylanders' arrival, writing in his diary, "Never did a finer, more dignified, and braver body of men face an enemy. They were composed of the flower of Maryland, being young gentlemen, the sons of opulent planters, farmers and mechanics. From the colonel to the private, all were attired in hunting-shirts." Another of the city's residents agreed, noting, "Colonel Smallwood's battalion was one of the finest in the army, in dress, equipment, and discipline." They were distinguished by "the most macaroni cocked hat, and hottest blood in the Union." After a brief stay in the City of Brotherly Love, the Marylanders continued the long journey to join the forces already assembled in New York and arrived on July 30.

Smallwood's Battalion included not only men: wives, mothers, daughters, mistresses, and other assorted women marched along with the men, looking for safety and work. These camp followers, as they later became known, had a complicated relationship with the military hierarchy. Many of the officers despised having these women and their children along, believing that they distracted the soldiers, slowed their movements, and consumed food that could have fed the men. Others were more pragmatic, noting that the men might not continue to fight if they couldn't bring along their wives. Washington wrote that he "was obliged to give Provisions to the extra Women in these regiments, or lose by Desertion, perhaps to the enemy, some of the oldest and best Soldiers in the Service."

In addition, the camp followers provided valuable services for the Continental Army. Many worked as laundresses, earning rations and small fees for their labor. Others cooked for their husbands or paying customers, often the blacksmiths, wheelwrights, and other workmen who performed necessary tasks for the army. The army also employed many of the women as nurses in the field hospitals. Because this was one of the dirtiest and most dangerous occupations for women, the officers often had to bribe or coerce reluctant women to care for wounded and dying men. However, a few brave women volunteered for an even more perilous job: while working as cooks or laundresses in the British camps, they spied on the Redcoats' movements and brought back word of their plans to the Americans.

One woman who was soon traveling with Smallwood's Battalion as a camp follower was the beautiful Margaret Jane Peale Ramsay, known as Jenny, who was the wife of Nathaniel Ramsay and the sister of painter and ensign James Peale. "Having fondness for reading . . . she was refined in her intellect and she was beautiful in her person. . . . She had many admirers, some of them, afterwards became great note in the revolution." Mrs. Ramsay traveled in a small carriage with a servant and endured many of the hardships of army life in order to be with her husband. Her brother Charles Willson Peale noted, "She said she would rather be with the army whatever might be her suffering, than be at a distance and so much tormented, for if she was near the army in case of misfortunes she possibly might be aiding to help those most dear to her." Unlike many of the women accompanying Smallwood's Battalion, Jenny didn't perform manual labor. Instead, she acted as a hostess, and her tent or quarters became the center of social life for the officers: Samuel Smith, Jack Steward, Mordecai Gist, Benjamin Ford, and the other officers gathered where she set up camp. She wielded a considerable amount of influence; one fellow camp follower said to Mrs. Ramsay, "You can aid me in my many difficulties, for everybody seems to pay more regard to what you say than I have ever seen before."

After arriving in Manhattan, the battalion bivouacked on a hill about a mile outside the heart of the city (today's lower Manhattan), waiting for further orders, but the downtime soon began to wear on the men. Washington's hastily assembled army in New York began to diminish in number owing to desertion and sickness. Maryland Sergeant William Sands wrote in a letter to his parents, "We are advised to hold our Selves in Readyness we Expect an Attack hourly we have Lost a great many of our Troops They have deserted from us at Philadelphia and Elisabeth Town and a Great Many Sick in the Ospitals."[7] The enlisted men, like John Hughes and the McMillan brothers, William and Samuel, quickly adapted to the abysmal conditions of camp life in Manhattan.

Thousands of people bivouacked in such close proximity to one another, combined with a lack of discipline, produced sanitation problems with horrific results. In August, about 25 percent of the American army was listed as sick and unable to serve. Typhoid fever, dysentery, malaria, and other maladies spread rampantly throughout the filthy camps. The Maryland troops were no exception, and sickness greatly reduced their numbers. In an attempt to check the spread of disease, American officers, including General Nathanael Greene, tried to enforce sanitation rules, but to no avail. Greene, a thirty-four-year-old Rhode Islander and former Quaker, had been a successful businessman prior to the war. He stood about five-foot-ten and was broad-shouldered, although a childhood accident had left him with a stiff right leg and a pronounced limp. He also suffered from asthma. His piercing blue eyes radiated confidence, but beneath the veneer, Greene was very sensitive to criticism. A born leader, he was also a student of military history, which served him well. Joining the Rhode Island militia as a private, he quickly rose to the rank of general thanks to his keen mind and natural battlefield acumen. Over the course of the war, he became Washington's

7. Sands was killed in battle before his message could be delivered to his family.

favorite general. On this occasion Greene's blossoming military genius
was diverted to the practical basics of running an army. Greene noted
the men "typically easing themselves in the ditches of the fortifications."

Venereal disease ran rampant. With so many soldiers encamped in
New York and Long Island, the bordello district in Manhattan, known
as the Holy Ground, mushroomed, pandering to the carnal needs of
the men—even the most chaste. "The whores (by information) continue
their employ, which is become very, very lucrative," recalled one observer.
"Their unparalleled conduct is sufficient antidote against any desires that
a person can have that has one spark of modesty or virtue left in him to
blast atum [*sic*] must certainly be lost before he can associate with those
bitchfoxy jades, jills, hags, strums, prostitutes, and these multiplied into
one another." A New York City survey shortly after the war estimated
that 20 percent of women of childbearing age were prostitutes. Tarts
who entered the Maryland camp in an unauthorized manner could be
seized. Then their heads were shaved, and they were drummed out of
camp at a slow cadence known as the whore's march.

Smallwood's Battalion wasn't the only group of Marylanders that
marched toward New York; the colony also sent 3,405 militiamen to
serve as part of a "Flying Camp."[8] Established directly by the Continental Congress, the Flying Camp carried no heavy equipment so that it
could move quickly to wherever it was needed—in this case, New York.
Officials in Maryland agreed to provide the troops based on a couple of
strict conditions: Flying Camp members from Maryland fought only in

8. Joining the Flying Camp and Smallwood's Battalion, a number of independent Maryland companies also made their way toward New York. Several arrived and distinguished
themselves; others never completed the journey. The latter category included Captain
John Watkins, who left Maryland later than Smallwood and lingered in the City of
Brotherly Love. One writer noted, "Capt. Watkins and his men we are sorry to inform
you are on very ill terms, the Capt. has beat some of them, he says he had great cause,
they say he had none, some of them have said nothing shall induce them to continue in
the company under Capt. Watkins." He added that the captain "is addicted to Drink and
his appearance at several Times we have seen him bespeaks it." The Maryland Council
of Safety soon removed the inebriate officer.

the area from their colony to New York (not New England), and their service expired on December 1, 1776. Eventually, many of the enlisted men and officers of the Flying Camp amalgamated into Smallwood's Battalion. On August 16, Maryland informed Congress, "We shall have near four thousand men with you in a short time [including independent companies and Smallwood's Battalion]. . . . We are sending all we have that can be armed and equipped, and the people of New York, for whome we have a great affection, can have no more than our all."

The militiamen of the Flying Camp are largely a footnote in history and weren't as well trained or equipped as Smallwood's Battalion, but they produced several outstanding officers including Marylander John Eager Howard. Humble yet a charismatic leader, Howard was appointed captain of the Flying Camp's 2nd Battalion. The son of a prosperous farmer, the tall, handsome Howard had no military background, yet the Baltimore scion emerged as one of the great natural battlefield commanders of the Revolution. In his private life, he was known for his graciousness, "the amenity of his manners, his hospitality, and his extensive and useful knowledge." His memory for facts was quite remarkable, leading one person to call him "perhaps the most accurate repository of the history of his own time, in this or any other country." He was a very disciplined man, and "his habits of life were contemplative, cautious, scrupulously just, and regulated by the stricted method." He had many close friends, and one biographer noted, "Few men have enjoyed a more enviable lot: his youth distinguished in the field, his age in the council, and every period solaced by the attachment of friends." He "deserves a statue of gold no less than Roman and Grecian heroes," one newspaper later wrote. He officially joined the military when he put on his uniform in July 1776 at the age of twenty-four. Like the other officers in the Flying Camp, Howard was responsible for recruiting his own men. Although he was an exceptionally modest man, Howard was extremely popular in Baltimore and needed just one day to find all thirty men for his company.

Captain William Beatty from Frederick County, Maryland, who kept a diary throughout the war, "was apptd. an Ensign in ye flying Camp raised in the state of Md the 3d July." His father, also named William, served as a colonel in the American forces. The younger Beatty was just eighteen when he received his first commission as an officer, and he rose in rank steadily as the Revolution progressed.

Marching with Beatty and Howard was twenty-two-year-old Lawrence Everhart. Born of German parents near Frederick, Maryland, Everhart was "tall and brawny with powerful limbs" and "a noble countenance." He was also described as "having an eye beaming with the luster of genuine courage."

The Flying Camp reached New York City shortly after Smallwood's Battalion arrived. Congress named Brigadier General Rezin Beall as overall commander of the Maryland Flying Camp but designated no overall commander of Maryland forces. The two commanders began arguing between themselves almost immediately, disagreeing about who had the higher rank. The dispute continued to fester as the real battle was about to begin.

CHAPTER 8

THE STORM BEGINS

"In a few minutes the entire heavens became black as ink, and from horizon to horizon, the whole empyrean was ablaze with lightning," recalled one observer who experienced the spectacular natural pyrotechnics on the night of August 21. "The lightning fell in massive sheets of fire to earth and seemed to strike incessantly and on every side." Legend holds that a single lightning bolt killed three American officers and "the tips of their swords and the coins in their pockets had been melted, their bodies as black as if roasted." The portentous storm seemed to serve as a prelude to the thunder of cannon and chatter of small arms that soon sounded throughout New York.

The next day after that violent storm, the British invasion of Long Island commenced, led by two frigates that tested American defenses as they sailed up the East River, largely unscathed. Admiral Richard Howe's secretary, Ambrose Serle, described the intimidating, yet breathtaking scene he encountered on the picturesque day, detailing the armada of "ships and vessels with their sails spread open to dry, the sun shining clear upon them, the green hills and meadows after the rain."

The first waves of roughly twenty-two thousand British troops began disembarking at Gravesend Bay on Long Island. Misinformed about the strength of the actual invasion, George Washington erroneously believed that only half that number had landed, that the amphibious landing on Long Island was a feint, and that the main blow would fall on Manhattan.

As the British and Hessian troops disgorged from their landing boats onto the island, they discovered a land of abundance. "The peach and apple trees are especially numerous [and] the furnishings in the [houses] are excellent. Comfort beauty and cleanliness are readily apparent," one soldier wrote. Serle watched with amusement as the troops "regaled themselves with fine apples, which hung everywhere in great abundance. . . . It was really diverting to see sailors and apples tumbling from the trees together." Most of America's colonists were of middling class and enjoyed a higher standard of living than the rest of the world. For many of the British, the perceived wealth and plentitude seemed to be proof that the colonists got rich off the Crown.

Howe's men made camp as additional reinforcements streamed in. Some fighting broke out, as Major Mordecai Gist noted: "The Enemy being now landed on Long Island and little Skirmishes happened [by the] lines." Washington rushed additional reinforcements, including Smallwood's Marylanders, across the East River toward the American defenses in Brooklyn, bringing American strength to about six thousand men.

Days earlier, before the British landings on Long Island, Nathanael Greene, who was helping oversee the preparations of the defenses, had fallen gravely ill. Washington replaced him with General John Sullivan, whose ability and leadership paled in comparison to Greene's. Worse, Sullivan didn't know the American defenses or Brooklyn's terrain. The vain New England lawyer was marked by an "over desire of being popular." Prior to the war, the forty-four-year-old Sullivan had handled foreclosures and had served with Washington in the Continental Congress. The abrupt change of command at the top was symptomatic of the chaos that reigned throughout the American camp. Unlike their well-ordered British counterparts, the Americans had "carts and horses driving every way among the army," wrote one observer. "Men marching out and coming in. . . . Small arms and field pieces continually firing. All in tumult."

General Washington inspected the defenses on Long Island. Concerned about Sullivan's ability to lead, Washington placed Israel Putnam, nicknamed Old Put, in charge of Sullivan on August 24, just days after calling in Sullivan to replace Greene. A veteran who served in Rogers' Rangers, a French and Indian War reconnaissance and early special-operations force whose tactics inspired many generations of warriors, Putnam was fifty-eight years old; his age led many of the troops to refer to him as "Granny." In the Battle of Bunker Hill on the outskirts of Boston on June 17, 1775, General Putnam had led the forces in the field and became famous for saying, "Don't fire, boys, until you can see the whites of their eyes." While the British captured the hill and expanded the territory under their control, the cost was high: 226 killed and 828 wounded. The Americans, by contrast, had around 140 killed and 310 wounded and were able to retreat and regroup after the battle, leaving themselves in a much better position. Clinton wrote, "A few more such victories would have shortly put an end to British dominion in America." Putnam's exploits throughout the war became the source of many legends. His appearance in Long Island was highly popular with the men but did nothing to curb the chaos in camp. Washington instructed Putnam to stop the "irregularities" and informed him, "The distinction between a well regulated army and a mob is the good order and discipline of the first, and the licentious and disorderly behavior of the latter."

As a forward defense, Washington instructed Old Put to position three thousand troops, including elements of Smallwood's Battalion, atop a wooded ridge of hills that cut through Brooklyn, known then as the Heights of Gowanus. Eighty feet high at points, the forested spur offered a natural defensive position to the Americans. One nineteenth-century historian wrote that they were "a continuous barrier, a huge natural abatis, impassible to artillery, where with proportionate numbers a successful defense could be sustained." On Washington's orders, Putnam sent his best men—led by General Sullivan and General Stirling (William Alexander)—forward on the wooded ridge; there they could meet the enemy in the trees, where they hoped to use the ground to their advantage. Another six thousand men remained in the fortifications at Brooklyn Heights. The Americans designed a collapsible defense: the Marylanders and other forward troops were to hold the British off as long as possible, inflict maximum casualties, and then fall back toward the forts on Brooklyn Heights. The American generals irrationally expected

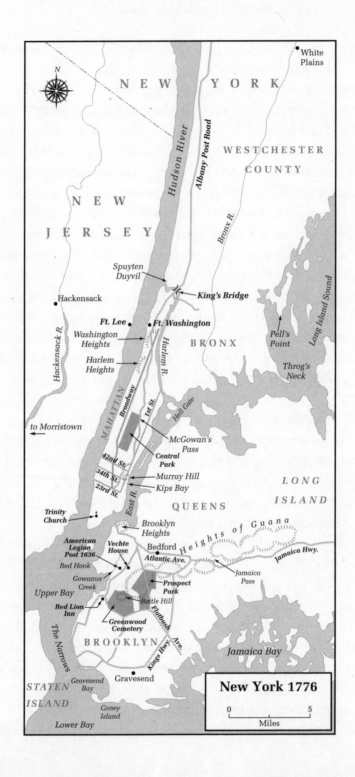

White
Plains

N E W   Y O R K

WESTCHESTER
COUNTY

Hudson River

Albany Post Road

Bronx R.

N E W

J E R S E Y

Hackensack R.

Long Island Sound

Spuyten
Duyvil

King's Bridge

Hackensack

Ft. Lee   Ft. Washington

Washington
Heights

BRONX

Pell's
Point

Harlem
Heights

Harlem R.

Throg's
Neck

to Morristown

MANHATTAN

Broadway

1st St.

Hell Gate

McGowan's
Pass

Central
Park

42nd St.

34th St.   Murray Hill

23rd St.   Kips Bay

East R.

L O N G

I S L A N D

QUEENS

Trinity
Church

Brooklyn
Heights

Heights of Guana

American
Legion
Post 1636

Vechte
House

Bedford

Atlantic Ave.

Jamaica Hwy.

Red Hook

Gowanus
Creek

Prospect
Park

Jamaica
Pass

Upper Bay

Red Lion
Inn

Battle Hill

Greenwood
Cemetery

Flatbush Ave.

B R O O K L Y N

Kings Hwy.

Jamaica Bay

The Narrows

Gravesend
Bay

Gravesend

STATEN
ISLAND

Coney
Island

Lower Bay

New York 1776

0 ————————— 5
Miles

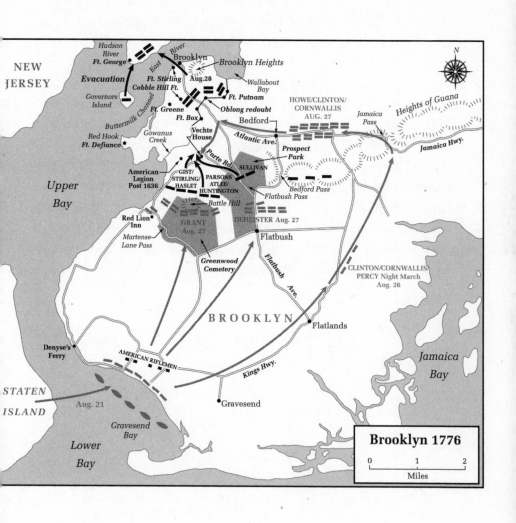

NEW
JERSEY

Upper
Bay

STATEN
ISLAND

Lower
Bay

Hudson
River
Ft. George
Evacuation
Governors
Island

Buttermilk Channel
Red Hook
Ft. Defiance

Gowanus
Creek

American
Legion
Post 1636

Red Lion
Inn
Martense
Lane Pass

East River
Brooklyn
Aug.28
Ft. Stirling
Cobble Hill Ft.
Ft. Greene
Ft. Box

Vechte
House

Porte Rd

GIST/
STIRLING/
HASLET

Brooklyn Heights
Wallabout
Bay
Ft. Putnam
Oblong redoubt
Bedford

HOWE/CLINTON/
CORNWALLIS
AUG. 27

Atlantic Ave.

Prospect
Park

SULLIVAN

PARSONS
ATLEE/
HUNTINGTON

Battle Hill

GRANT
Aug. 27

DEHEISTER Aug. 27

Greenwood
Cemetery

Flatbush

Heights of Guana

Jamaica
Pass

Jamaica Hwy.

Bedford Pass

Flatbush Pass

Flatbush Ave.

CLINTON/CORNWALLIS/
PERCY Night March
Aug. 26

BROOKLYN

Flatlands

Jamaica
Bay

Denyse's
Ferry

AMERICAN RIFLEMEN

Aug. 21

Gravesend
Bay

Kings Hwy.

Gravesend

N

Brooklyn 1776

0   1   2
Miles

the green troops to somehow hold the six-mile forested ridgeline for an extended period of time and "at all hazards prevent the enemy's passing the wood." But the heavy foliage also limited the line of sight to a hundred feet and hampered communication among Patriot units. Putnam assigned the bulk of the Marylanders along the Gowanus Road, a key artery that hugged the shoreline of Brooklyn's Gravesend Bay. Sullivan had command of about one thousand troops and controlled the center of the Gowanus Heights near Flatbush. Eight hundred Pennsylvanians held the Bedford Road on the Americans' far left flank. The roads cut through three passes that the Patriots felt were defensible. A fourth pass, known as the Jamaica Pass, lay three miles north of the American left flank on the Bedford Road. It remained unguarded until the last minute, when five young militiamen on horseback were ordered to patrol Jamaica Pass. It was the blind spot in the American defenses. It was also exactly where General William Howe's main force was headed.

CHAPTER 9

THE BATTLE OF BROOKLYN

Early on the morning of August 27, 1776, two British scouts drew closer to the Red Lion Inn in Brooklyn, near the present-day intersection of Fourth Avenue and Thirty-Fifth Street. Something off to the side of the road caught their eye. Despite the darkness of the night, they could discern twisting vines and the unmistakable bulbous green bulges of ripe watermelons. The fruit was uncommon in Britain and highly prized. A savvy innkeeper had planted the melon patch to woo the many tourists who came to see the area's attraction—a striking, otherworldly-looking indentation in a nearby rock that many claimed was the devil's hoof-print. The sharp-eyed observers were quick to attack the field in hopes of enjoying the harvest.

However, the Redcoat scouts weren't the only ones awake at eleven that night near the inn. Former British officer and Pennsylvanian physician Colonel Edward Hand had riflemen stationed as lookouts nearby. They fired a few rounds at the would-be thieves. With those shots, fired in the middle of a watermelon patch, the largest battle of the Revolution began.

The two Brits quickly retreated into the night unharmed, making their way back down the Gowanus Road until they linked up with the main British force commanded by General James Grant, a rotund, pompous, opinionated Scot who was a veteran of the French and Indian War. Grant was leading five thousand Redcoats toward the Marylanders and other American troops dug in on the Heights of Gowanus. He intended to pin down a large portion of the American army as part of General Henry Clinton's grand plan, essentially a large-scale hammer-and-anvil maneuver. The part of the anvil would be played by Grant's forces, which would attack the right side of the American line that included Mary-lander units deployed along the shore or Gowanus Road. A column of Hessians, under the command of General Leopold von Heister, would attack the center, located near today's Prospect Park, in an area now known as Battle Pass. Their goal was to distract the Patriots and keep them stationary—neither advancing nor retreating—while the main body of the British forces executed a long, sweeping flanking maneuver, going through the Jamaica Pass around the American defenses on the Heights of Gowanus. This third group, led by Clinton and William Howe, would serve as the hammer, pounding the Americans from the left and the rear and cutting off escape.

Clinton's plan went into motion around 9:00 p.m. on Monday, August 26. First to march were troops under the command of Howe and Clinton, a force of ten thousand men who were to circle around the Americans' left flank. In an attempt to disguise their intentions, the British left their tents pitched and their fires burning in the field where they had been camped. British light infantry led the way, moving through the countryside as silently as possible and detaining any witnesses who happened to see the movement of the troops. By one account, they also forced Long Island residents to act as guides. Eighty-seven-year-old William Howard claimed that Clinton and two aides burst into his tavern around two in the morning "and asked for something to drink [and] conversed with him." When the small talk was over, Clinton announced, "Now you are my prisoner, and must lead me across these hills out of the way of the enemy." The octogenarian did as instructed, guiding Howe's troops through the largely unguarded Jamaica Pass.

Grant's forces marched out of camp an hour or two after the main force. Alerted by his scouts to the presence of the Pennsylvanians in the Red Lion, Grant waited for nearly three hours before marching on the inn. Around two o'clock in the morning, the guard at the inn changed, with untested militiamen replacing the veteran riflemen. Seizing the opportunity, Grant sent about three hundred men in for the attack. The terrified militia fled almost immediately. Grant's force captured their commander, Major James Bond, and several others. Fortunately, the Americans managed to get a message about the attack through to General Israel Putnam. Although he had commanded brilliantly at the Battle of Bunker Hill, on this occasion Old Put misread the British intentions and took Howe's bait. He rode down from one of the forts on Brooklyn Heights to the American camp, located next to the Vechte-Cortelyou farmhouse[9] near the present-day junction of Fifth Avenue and Third Street, and woke Lord Stirling, who was the commander of the forces in the area.

Thirty-three-year-old Major Mordecai Gist woke to the sound of signal guns, and the drummers beat a call to arms. He was in command of the battalion because Colonel William Smallwood was in Manhattan attending a court martial. It was his first day of battle and would prove to be one of the most harrowing and monumental days of his life. Gist organized his men, and under Lord Stirling's command, they marched toward the Red Lion Inn to confront Grant.

Stirling's true name was William Alexander, but he was known as Lord Stirling because he claimed to be a Scottish earl (a claim the House of Lords did not recognize). Described as an "overweight, rheumatic, vain, pompous, gluttonous inebriate," Stirling was chronically in debt before the war, as were many of the leading voices of the Revolution. Like Putnam, Stirling fell for Grant's ruse. He later wrote, "I fully expected, as did most of my officers, that the strength of the British army was advancing in this quarter to our lines." Stirling's officers included Major Thomas McDonough, who took command of the Delaware Regiment while John Haslet was away serving court-martial duty. Commencing in Brooklyn and throughout most of the war, these two regiments would fight side by side.

Believing Grant's men were the main prong of the British attack, Old Put sent over a thousand troops—including the Marylanders and the Delaware Regiment—to confront them. Gist recalled rousing the men

9. The Vechte-Cortelyou house was named for its orginal owners, a wealthy Dutch family who farmed the area. A 1933 reconstruction of the building, which used the stones from the original structure, is now the Old Stone House Museum in the Park Slope neighborhood of Brooklyn.

early: "We began our march to the right at three o'clock in the morning, with about 1,300 men, and about sunrise, on our near approach to the ground, discovered the enemy making up to it, and in a few minutes our advanced parties began the attack." As the first light of dawn came "with a Red and angry Glare," Gist positioned his men to meet the oncoming British army and they "immediately advanced and took possession of the ground and formed a line of battle. In the meantime, [the British] began warm fire with their artillery and light infantry, from their left, while the main body was forming in columns to attack us in the front." Clinton's plan was working: Grant diverted the Americans' attention from Howe's and Clinton's flanking action through the Jamaica Pass. Once through the pass, Howe and Clinton were to swing around and encircle the Marylanders and other Americans on Gowanus Heights.

After marching over a mile west to confront the British, Stirling deployed his men in an inverted V, something Frederick the Great of Prussia called the kettle. The arms of the V stretched outward in an attempt to envelop Grant's force as it pushed ahead. Grant initially pelted the Americans with artillery. The Marylanders were on the right flank on top of a hill near what is now Green-Wood Cemetery.

On top of the small hill, several companies of Smallwood's Mary-landers successfully withstood the British cannonade—exactly as Grant had hoped. One participant wrote that Lord Stirling "immediately drew up in a line, and offered them battle in the true English taste." The British advanced to within three hundred yards, and British ships in the bay bombarded the American line with cannon fire, leading former lawyer turned battle captain Nathaniel Ramsay to exclaim, "Both the balls and shells flew very fast, now and then taking off a head." He added, "Our men stood it amazingly well, not even one showed a dispo-sition to shrink. Our orders were not to fire till the enemy came within 50 yards of us: but when they perceived we stood their fire so coolly and resolutely, they declined coming any nearer, though treble our number." Captain Enoch Anderson of the Delaware Regiment wrote, "We gave them a fair fire,—every man leveled well. I saw one man tumble from his horse,—never did I take better aim at a bird, —yet I know not that I killed any or touched any."

To bolster the courage of the Americans, who were now vastly outnumbered, Stirling addressed his men. He spoke of Grant, who had little respect for the American troops facing him and had once boasted before the House of Commons that with five thousand men he could march from one end of the American continent to the other. Stirling shouted, "[Grant] may have 5,000 men with him now—we are not so many—but I think we are enough to prevent his advancing further on his march over the continent than that mill pond."

As the battle wore on, the two lines of men remained in position without advancing from sunrise until late in the morning, when the true nature of the British plan began to reveal itself.

Gist, commanding Smallwood's Battalion, then noticed a fateful pause: "Our men behaved well, and maintained their ground until ten o'clock, when the enemy [Grant's men] retreated about 200 yards and halted, and the firing on each side ceased."

The Marylanders realized to their horror that they were flanked. "We soon heard the fire on our left, and in a short time discovered part of our enemy in our rear." Gist continued, "Surrounded, and [with] no probability of reinforcement, his Lordship [Stirling] ordered me to retreat with the remaining part of our men, and force our way through our camp."

Clinton's flanking maneuver was unfolding like clockwork. Thanks to their hard marching and good reconnaissance, and to poor American positioning, Howe and Clinton had penetrated deep behind American lines. At 9:00 a.m., twelve hours after the attack commenced, two heavy cannon released massive blasts. This was the prearranged signal for Grant and the Hessians to unleash their assaults on the American right flank (Stirling) and the center (John Sullivan).

General Leopold von Heister and the Hessians approached the heart of the American lines on the Gowanus Heights under Sullivan's command. To dislodge Sullivan's men, the Germans assembled in an open field in front of the pass. The impressive show of force included three Hessian brigades that formed a line nearly a mile long. At the sound of Clinton's guns, the German onslaught began "with colors flying, to the music of drums and hautboys as if they were marching across Friedrich's Platz at Cassel. . . . They did not fire a shot, but pressed steadily forward until they could employ their bayonets." Surging ahead, the Hessians broke through Sullivan's men and ruthlessly butchered many of the hapless Americans. When they found groups of stragglers in the woods, they often circled around them, lowered their bayonets, and then slowly tightened the circle, often killing all those inside.

Less than a mile west of Sullivan's position, Gist and his men desperately fought back toward the Patriot forts on Brooklyn Heights. A British sergeant and "ten or fifteen grenadiers" taken prisoner by Maryland scouts brought in the alarming news "that the left and the main body of the Americans had been Defeated, and that they, themselves, had been scouring the field for stragglers," recalled Samuel Smith. This was their first real taste of close combat.

As the regiment broke down into files of men, it is very likely the companies became separated from the main body of the battalion. "When the regiment had mounted a hill, a British officer appeared as if alone, waved his hat, and it was supposed he meant to surrender. He clapped his hands three times, on which signal his company rose and gave a heavy discharge. The three companies in front broke. Captain Smith wheeled his company into [position], and was advancing, when he was ordered by Lord Stirling to form in line."

Gist recalled the incident from a different vantage point: "We soon fell in with a party of the enemy, who clubbed their firelocks, and waved their hats to us, as if they meant to surrender as prisoners; but on our advancing within sixty yards, they presented their pieces and fired, which we returned with so much warmth that they soon quitted their post and retired to a large body that was lying in ambuscade." One of the men from Ramsay's company added, "They entirely overshot us, and killed some men away behind in our rear. I had the satisfaction of dropping one of them the first fire I made."

With the enemy converging on all sides, Gist and about five companies of Marylanders pushed through their original bivouac area near today's Fourth Avenue and Third Street.

Heavy enfilading fire, also known as flanking fire, pelted the Marylanders from both sides until the Americans "came to the marsh [and a stone house], where [the main force] were obliged to break their order, and escape as quick as they could to the edge of the creek, under a brisk fire."

"During this interval," recalled Gist, the main force "retreated from our left into a marsh."

Stirling ordered the bulk of his men to plunge into the marsh at the present-day site of the Gowanus Canal and swim eighty yards across the swift current of Gowanus Creek to reach the relative safety of the American defenses on Brooklyn Heights. Compounding their difficulty, the Americans had destroyed the only other likely avenue for retreat—a bridge that crossed the marsh and creek—to prevent the British from using it. Another obstacle also stood in the way of the right wing of the American army's retreat: a stone house and its grounds occupied by hundreds of British troops led by one of Britain's greatest captains of battle, Charles Edward Cornwallis V (Earl, later Marquess, Cornwallis).

The son of an earl, Cornwallis was born in London and had a very aristocratic upbringing, including schooling at Eton and Cambridge. When he was eighteen, he became a member of the prestigious Grenadier Guards and found that he loved the army. While still a young man, he also became a member of the House of Lords, through which he gained connections that furthered his military career. His physical appearance was considered fairly unattractive. Thanks to a sports injury, one of his eyes looked unusual, and he was, by his own description, "rather corpulent" with a double chin. By contrast, his wife, whom he loved dearly, was known for her beauty. Eager for battle, he volunteered to serve in the Seven Years' War, in which he served with distinction and was noted for his gallantry in battle. He also volunteered for service in putting down the American uprising, even though he was one of only six lords in Parliament who voted against the Stamp Act. A soldier's soldier, Cornwallis led from the front and on several occasions had his horse shot out from under him. Almost recklessly brave, the earl was the perfect embodiment of his regiment's motto, *Virtutis fortuna comes* ("Fortune is the companion of courage"). Yet he saw to his men's needs, often generously paying for their equipment and provisions out of his own pocket. After the American Revolution, he led British forces in India to defeat Tipu Sultan. As a reward, he received a staggering fortune of tens of thousands of pounds sterling, which he gave to his men.

Howe had placed Cornwallis in command of the light infantry that had spearheaded the flanking maneuver. Knowing that Cornwallis and his men were positioned in the stone house, Stirling ordered a suicidal preemptive strike to buy time for the right wing of the American army to escape. "I found it absolutely necessary to attack a body of troops commanded by Lord Cornwallis, posted at the [Vechte-Cortelyou] house near the Upper Mills," Stirling recounted to Washington, "This I instantly did, with about half of Smallwood's [Battalion], first ordering all the other troops to make the best of their way through the creek." Gist recalled, "We were then left with only five companies of our battalion."

A single structure and the full weight of an entire dug-in British division separated the right wing of the American army from the fortifications at Brooklyn Heights.

Cornwallis's men trained their muskets and a light cannon on the advancing Marylanders.

"Fire!"

The fusillade dropped many of the men in their tracks, severing limbs and heads, killing several instantly. Undeterred, the men of Gist's companies formed into lines and charged into the hail of fire coming from the British soldiers in the Vechte-Cortelyou house.

That scene repeated itself several times as the Marylanders battled to allow their retreating countrymen to escape. "We continued the attack a considerable time," recalled Stirling, "the men having been rallied and the attack renewed . . . several times."

Gist noted that after the first attack "our little line became disordered we were under the necessity of retreating to a piece of woods on our right, where we formed and made a second attack." Keeping many of these men togther were the NCOs, such as towering Sergeant Gassaway Watkins. The Marylanders fearlessly surged again into a rain of deadly lead. Nathaniel Ramsay noted, "Our men fought with more than Roman valor."

During the battle, Stirling brazenly "encouraged and animated our young soldiers with almost invincible resolution," recalled Gist. The self-styled earl was buoyant, believing he and his men were on the point of driving Lord Cornwallis from the house, when heavy British reinforcements arrived. After the Hessians broke through Sullivan's defenses, they attacked the Marylanders. They linked up with Cornwallis's Highlanders and assaulted the Marylanders from the rear, while Grant's forces pushed in the front. Gist reflected, "Surrounded on all sides by at least 20,000 men, we were drove with precipitation and confusion."[10] Gist, Smith, Jack Steward, and Ramsay, best friends, found themselves in the fight of their lives, eerily living out Agamemnon's prophetic letter to the Independent Company of February 1775. Maryland's finest—rich and poor alike—lay dead and dying all around.

In their triumph, the British showed no mercy, taking few prisoners. One Redcoat officer noted, "The Hessians and our brave Highlanders gave no quarters; and it was a fine sight to see with what alacrity they dispatched the rebels with their bayonets, after we had surrounded them so they could not resist. We took care to tell the Hessians that the rebels

10. Gist's estimate of the enemy's strength is obviously too high. Written immediately after the battle, Gist's words are an artifact that conveys his sense of the overwhelming odds he faced. One of the Redcoats added, "The Americans fought bravely, and (to do them justice) could not be broken till they were greatly outnumbered and taken in flank, front, and rear."

had resolved to give no quarter—to them in particular,—which made them fight desperately, and to put to death all that came into their hands." Another of the Redcoats added, "We were greatly shocked at the massacre made by the Hessians and Highlanders after victory was decided."

Many of these brave soldiers, including brothers William and Samuel McMillan, bore the brunt of the vicious German and Highlander juggernaut. Born in Scotland and raised in Harford County, Maryland, the McMillan brothers were fierce supporters of the Revolution, and both served in the militia before becoming noncommissioned officers in Smallwood's Battalion. Caught in the vortex of the melee, William later wrote, "My captain was killed, first lieutenant was killed, second lieutenant shot through [the] hand." The Hessians also killed two corporals and two sergeants in the company, "one in front of me [at the] same time my bayonet was shot off my gun." McMillan described the harrowing nature of the battle, including a "perty severe fight." He went on to give the details of when things started to collapse, saying, "We were surrounded by healanders [Scottish Highlanders] one side, hessians on the other." Eventually, "my Brother and about—50 or 60 of us was taken."

Private John Hughes and Captain Barton Lucas, the commanding officer of the 3rd Company, barely escaped with their lives; in all, only seven of the sixty-man company survived. The remainder were killed or captured, including Gist's close friend William Sterrett. The entire Maryland Line, including Gist, thought that Sterrett was killed in action. A death notice appeared in the *Maryland Gazette*, and Gist wrote to express his sympathy to Sterrett's sister Polly, who later became Gist's wife. In reality, Sterrett was stripped of his belongings and taken prisoner by the Hessians. The Americans were cut off from the retreat by Cornwallis, and Gowanus Creek remained the only avenue of escape for any not crushed between the British and Hessian forces. The waters of the bay were at high tide, making the creek and adjoining marshes nearly impassable. The men had to wade and swim through waist- and often neck-deep water, while trying to evade the British fire. In the heat of the battle, one American looked back at Gist and claimed he and his determined band of Marylanders were all that stood between the British and the Continental Army's annihilation, "Major Gist [and his men] kept the ground, while the rest of the brigade crossed a creek. . . . The major and his party were drove, and I expected never to see them again."

Standing next to Smallwood, who had just returned from a court-martial held in Manhattan, and peering through his spyglass from a nearby hill located behind fortifications in the American lines, George Washington was visibly moved by the courage and great sacrifice of the Marylanders. According to one account, "Gen. Washington wrung his hands, and cried out, 'Good God! What brave fellows I must this day lose!'"

To cover the retreating Americans as they swam for their lives, Smallwood asked Washington for permission to bring up two cannons drawn from recently acquired reinforcements. Captain Thomas's Maryland Independent Company, including Lieutenant Jack Steward, had arrived in Brooklyn with Smallwood earlier that morning, and they, along with a regiment of Connecticut soldiers, provided covering fire.

According to sixteen-year-old Connecticut Private Joseph Plumb Martin, who maintained a valuable diary throughout the Revolution and who fought alongside the Marylanders in several battles, the men came "out of the water and mud, to us, looking like water-rats." Many Marylanders suffocated or drowned. Smallwood added, "Most of those who swam over, and others who attempted to cross before the covering party got down, lost their arms and accoutrements in the mud and creek, and some fellows their lives." In an effort to prevent more drowning, Captain Samuel Smith, in command of the 8th Company in Smallwood's Battalion, made the swim not just once, but several times. "He and a sergeant swam over and got two slabs into the water on the ends of which they ferried over all who could not swim."

Ramsay could not swim, but his great height of six-foot-three saved his life. He had to "hold up his chin to keep the water from running into his mouth." Ramsay's brother-in-law, Ensign James Peale, lost his shoes while swimming the morass. Another one of the Marylanders who survived near-drowning was orginal cadet Ensign Bryan Philpot.

His son later retold his father's ordeal: "[My father spoke] of the retreat after the battle in which he was obligated to swim a creek, and of the difficulty with which he escaped drowning from the struggles of a soldier who was also in retreat." He added, "[My father] describe[d] his feelings on first going into an engagement and [I have] heard him tell of a wounded soldier who was sitting by a tree by his side during a battle when a cannonball shot away the top of his head." Another soldier reported that the body of the decapitated man went flying through the air and knocked down one of the officers. Despite the omnipresent slaughter, some Marylanders managed to escape across the marsh and creek, including the intrepid Major Gist. He recalled, "A party retreated to the right through the woods, and Captain Ford and myself, with 20 others, to the left, through a marsh; nine only of us got safe in."

Many others did not make the crossing and were killed or captured—which was also a virtual death sentence. Smith summed up the depth and breadth of their sacrifice: "The men were surrounded, and almost all killed, for the Hessians gave no quarter on that day. The loss of the regiment was about 250; the residue got off, as best they could." The Marylanders lost many men whose names remain unrecorded. One known officer who lost his life that day was Captain Edward Veazey, an original member of Smallwood's Battalion who raised his own company. Another Marylander chronicled the carnage: "Captain Veazey is dead. Lieutenants Butler, Sterrett, Wright, Fernandis and deCoursey, with about 250 of our battalion are missing." The Marylanders had sustained some of the highest losses of any of the units that had entered the battle.

Those who escaped with their lives that day included William Chaplin, who was born in Colchester, England, and ran a plantation in Maryland. Chaplin, who still harbored loyalty to the Crown, was one of the lucky ones, as most of the men from his company were wounded or killed.

The Marylanders' brother regiment, the Delaware Blues, suffered fewer casualties during the battle, but its commander, Colonel John Haslet, reported that the regimental colors were brought back "torn with shot." With his ranks reduced, Stirling attempted to make his way off the battlefield but "soon found it would be in vain to attempt to make my escape, and therefore went to surrender myself to General De Heister, commander in chief of the Hessians." Cornwallis later praised him, noting, "General Stirling fought like a wolf."

The Marylanders' desperate, doomed charge on Cornwallis brought salvation for what was left of Stirling's command and the right wing of the American army, giving them a precious window of time in which to escape. It also tied up Grant's and Cornwallis's forces, which united could have been used to assault the American defenses on Brooklyn Heights. The Marylanders who participated in that unorthodox assault became known as the Maryland 400, or the Immortal 400. With their blood, the Immortals bought "an hour, more precious to American liberty than any other in its history." The Marylanders' stand chewed up daylight on the afternoon of August 27 and bought Washington time, preventing the British from uniting the various wings of their army to make a combined assault on the Brooklyn defenses during the day. Each hour that ticked by was an hour closer to darkness. Howe had a new army. This was their first battle, and night assaults were difficult for even the most experienced army in the eighteenth century.

Had Howe pressed the attack on the forts that afternoon, his victory likely would have been total. The war might have ended that day. It was one of the few times in the Revolution when all the circumstances were aligned for a crushing British victory. The British would have captured the bulk of the American army, including possibly even Washington and his top commanders. That could have snuffed out the Revolution, turning it into little more than a footnote in the history of the British Empire. However, a series of circumstances and actions gave Washington's forces another chance to survive.

Howe assumed he had time and the weather on his side. He had not only won a great battle: he was also convinced that he had trapped the bulk of the American army on Brooklyn Heights and that there was ample time to destroy it with minimal British losses. The Royal Navy was in position to prevent Washington's retreat across the East River, leaving the Americans effectively bottled up in their fortifications. Washington's army—and arguably the outcome of the entire war—remained at risk.

CHAPTER 10

ESCAPE FROM LONG ISLAND

After the Immortals' ultimate sacrifice, the British drove what was left of Stirling's brigade to the forts on Brooklyn Heights, "The enemy came within 150 yards of our fort, but were repulsed with great loss. We expected another attack today, but they are preparing, by their movements to give us a cannonade. . . . I hear the thunder of cannon and the roar of musketry, so I believe the attack has begun," wrote one of the few surviving Marylanders.

All night, stragglers from the Heights of Gowanus trickled into the American fortifications on Brooklyn Heights. The toll of the Battle of Brooklyn, also known as the Battle of Long Island, was staggering. By Smallwood's reckoning, 256 Maryland men and officers were killed or missing. The victorious British army sprawled out over a mile and a half before the American defenses, but it was exhausted after a night of marching and a day of battle. The men were tired and hungry. The British had defeated Washington's forward defense, but their victory could have been crushing. Perhaps mindful of the severe losses sustained on Bunker Hill, and of the delay caused by the Marylanders' stand, General William Howe made his fateful decision and ordered his men to halt instead of storming the American defenses. "It required repeated orders to prevail upon them to desist from the attempt."

Connected by over a mile of trenches, the five American forts that occupied high ground would have been difficult to take by direct assault. One British officer summed up the situation, noting, "We had no fascines to fill ditches, no axes to cut abatis, and no scaling ladder to assault so respectable a work. Lines were a mile and a half [in] extent, including angles, cannon-proof, with a chain of fine redoubts, or rather fortresses with ditches, as half a line the intervals; the whole surmount with a most formidable abatis finished in every part." Consisting of sharpened logs that faced outward, an abatis was the eighteenth-century equivalent of barbed wire. Men needed to pierce it with axes before any assault could go forward. While the defenses weren't insurmountable, overcoming them would take time and expose assaulting parties to fire. Howe looked upon his men as a precious resource that he didn't want to spend foolishly. After the battle at Bunker Hill, he wrote, "When I looked to the consequences of it, in the loss of so many brave Officers, I do it with horror—the Success is too dearly bought."

Rather than command a headlong frontal assault, Howe ordered his men to begin preparations for a formal siege. Half of his men acted as trench guards, while the other half started digging zigzagged trenches that methodically pushed toward the American lines. To finish off the Patriots, Howe planned to use his brother's warships in the East River to seal the fate of the American army. As Howe's coup de grâce unfolded, dark clouds rolled in. Cold rain fell in sheets, filling the trenches with ankle- to waist-deep water. Hail fell as lightning flashed, and a massive nor'easter pelted the American and British lines. American Private Joseph Plumb Martin recalled, "There fell a very heavy shower, which wet us all to the skin and much damaged our ammunition." The entire battlefield became a sea of mud. The rain hindered the work on the trenches and also created conditions for another timely weather event.

In the midst of the downpour, the strain of battle began to take a toll on the citizen-soldiers. John Hughes, a twenty-six-year-old Marylander from Frederick County who served in Captain Barton Lucas's 3rd Company, recalled that Lucas found the losses particularly difficult to bear. In an application for a pension[11] made after the war, Hughes

---

11. Beginning in the early part of the nineteenth century, surviving American veterans of the Revolutionary War could apply for a pension. The veterans would typically go to the local courthouse and swear under oath the details of their military service. The level of detail varied from cursory to exhaustive. At times, the local officials would also ask questions such as the names of the applicants' officers or the names of other men

stated "that at the Battle of [Brooklyn] his Capt. Barton Lucas became deranged in consequence of losing his company . . . all of whom except seven were killed or taken prisoner." Other nervous soldiers fired their weapons indiscriminately. "Troops fired off their Guns quite till Evening so that it seemed indeed dangerous to walk within our own lines," said one of the men.

From within the walls of a spacious mansion on Brooklyn Heights known as the Four Chimneys, George Washington convened a council of war and looked out upon his waterlogged troops from the windows of the estate. It had rained "so much that the Trenches, Forts, Tents, & Camp . . . overflowed with water." As the deluge continued and lightning arced across the sky, he asked his seven general officers from the Brooklyn Heights defenses what their next move should be. Washington's officers doubted whether an evacuation was possible. The East River was a mile wide and had swift currents. Not realizing that the storm winds had prevented the Royal Navy from sailing upriver and getting behind the American defenses in Brooklyn Heights, the generals believed their forces were vulnerable to attack by land and sea if they tried to cross over to Manhattan. In light of the dangers, General Israel Putnam argued that the men should remain behind their fortifications and fight.

Washington put an end to the debate by ordering an evacuation. Realizing the importance of secrecy and knowing that a single traitor could cause the downfall of the entire operation, he ordered that nobody be told the true nature of the plan outside a small circle of his principal lieutenants. All available boats were to carry additional reinforcements to Brooklyn, bringing his total force up to ninety-five hundred. Fortunately, these reinforcements included mariners and fisherman from Marblehead, Massachusetts, led by Colonel John Glover. Clad in short blue coats and white waterproof trousers, the Marblehead

---

in their units. Supporting affidavits from other veterans were sometimes attached. This book drew extensively on these raw, boots-on-the-ground stories of the Revolution.

Mariners were expert sailors, ideal for coordinating the amphibious evacuation. The remaining Marylanders along with Haslet's Delaware Regiment received the honor of forming the rear guard.[12] Smallwood recalled that his men "had but one day's respite" when Washington ordered them to "the advanced post at Fort Putnam, within two hundred and fifty yards of the enemy's approaches."

About 7:00 p.m., the evacuation began. Purposely keeping the men in the dark about the withdrawal, the officers ordered them to gather their arms and packs and told them that they were going to conduct a night attack against the enemy. Initially, the East River was swirling, and the tide was rough, making it impossible for boats to cross. Somehow, ninety-five hundred men and their equipment would have to pass over the East River under the eyes of the British.

Fortuitously, around 11:00 the wind changed and blew in a favorable direction for the Americans. In the beginning, only ten boats were available for the evacuation. They miraculously found more men, but the vessels would have to be stuffed to the gills, crammed with men and equipment in order to get everyone over before daybreak. When the boats were fully loaded, the gunwales rode only three inches above the water. After the shift in the weather, the river was "remarkably still, the water smooth as glass." An eerie silence prevailed upon Brooklyn. Using cloth-covered oars to muffle the sound, Glover and the Marblehead Mariners made countless two-mile round-trips across the river, delivering Americans to safety. When the wind became more favorable overnight, they put up sails as well to propel the boats as quickly and quietly as possible.

Near 2:00 a.m. the surreal silence was broken along the battlefield by a booming explosion. It is possible the detonation was an accidental discharge of a cannon that the Americans had spiked to prevent its use by the British. One eyewitness recalled, "The effect was at once alarming

12. Also in the rear guard was the 1st New York, with its 120 grenadiers, each of whom carried six hand grenades, which were about the size of a cricket ball and filled with gunpowder.

and sublime." When no further fire erupted, the ferrying operation continued.

An hour later, a misdirected order almost blew the entire evacuation. General Thomas Mifflin, a former Quaker from Pennsylvania who was the American army's first quartermaster general, ordered his rear guard out of position earlier than requested. Hundreds of men were about to flood the ferry site.[13] Still on the Brooklyn side, General Washington confronted Mifflin, saying, "Good God! General Mifflin, I am afraid you have ruined us by so unseasonably withdrawing troops from the line!" Fortunately, the British did not notice their absence, and the men returned to their positions without incident. The evacuation went on.

Shortly before sunrise, panic began to set in at the embarkation point. While many of the Americans had successfully made it across the river, all too many remained behind in Brooklyn. As light broke, it was difficult if not impossible to hide what was happening from the enemy. Crowds of men surged toward the remaining boats. Washington himself took control of the situation. One of his aides recalled that the commander in chief picked up a large stone, raised it over his head, and ordered the disorderly men to leave the boat. Otherwise, he would "sink it to hell." Word spread of Washington's leadership, and the retreat proceeded in a more orderly fashion.

On the British side, Howe's forces became suspicious. Around 4:00 a.m., Captain John Montresor, Howe's chief engineer and a veteran of the French and Indian War, led a patrol that stumbled upon empty American breastworks. In addition, a Tory woman sent her black slave to alert the British, but the slave was captured and detained by Hessian soldiers for several hours. Somehow, word of neither incident reached Howe.

Amazingly, the weather changed again. A thick fog blew in, masking the ongoing evacuation. One officer near the Marylanders recalled, "Those of us who remained in the trenches became anxious for our own safety. And when the dawn appeared there were several regiments

13. Today, the spot is near the base of the Brooklyn Bridge next to an elegant riverside restaurant.

still on duty. At this time, a very dense fog began to rise and seemed to settle in a particular manner over both encampments. I recollect this particular Providential occurrence perfectly [well]; and so very dense was the atmosphere that I could scarcely discern a man at six yards' distance."

What remained of Samuel Smith's 8th Company was very nearly left behind in the evacuation at Fort Putnam. Unaware of the timing of the planned retreat, Captain Smith's men stayed near the fortifications. "One of the corporals informed Captain Smith that he had been up and down the lines, and not a man was to be seen." Concerned, the captain sent out two lieutenants to continue the search. "On their return they reported that all the troops had gone, where they knew not." Smith ordered the company into the main redoubt, believing that the rest of Washington's army had abandoned them, leaving them behind "as a forlorn hope." His fears were allayed, however, when a lieutenant arrived and told him of the ordered retreat and that the rest of "the regiment was, by that time, in New York." Smith and his men hurried to the river, passing General Washington on the way. The general asked the young Baltimore captain "how it happened he was so late; and he answered he had received no orders until a few minutes past." Luckily, the Marylanders arrived in the nick of time. They climbed into the very last boat to leave shore, "and had scarcely got off from the wharf, when the British Light horse appeared on the hill and fired their carbines without doing any injury to [us]."

The Battle of Brooklyn was a disastrous defeat for Washington. He later estimated American losses at about one thousand men killed or captured, with the majority of the casualties being taken as prisoners. Many of those losses came from the Marylanders. More than half of Smallwood's Battalion was either killed or captured. Those that were captured were almost certain to die in the hulls of prison ships in New York harbor. The British and Hessians lost a small fraction of that number.

But as dawn broke on August 30, Washington had avoided a far worse fate. He had pulled off one of the greatest military retreats in history, giving the Americans a precious chance to regroup.

CHAPTER 11

MANHATTAN

On September 15, 1776, the American sentries on duty at Kips Bay, near today's Thirty-Fourth Street on the East Side of Manhattan, looked out into the dark, heavy gloom. As dawn slowly transformed the sky from black to gray, shadows began to take shape on the waters of the East River.

Nearly as one, the British frigates and other warships fired a seventy-gun broadside at the Patriot defenses, blasting them to bits. The Americans had a series of trenches and breastworks anchored on the high hill at Iclenburg, later known as Murray Hill. "All of a sudden there came such a peal of thunder from the British shipping that I thought my head would go off with the sound, recalled Private Thomas Plumb Martin. "I made a frog's leap for the ditch and lay as still as I possibly could, and began to consider which part of my carcass would go first."

Gradually as the scene unfolded, Martin and the other Americans saw, to their horror, what approached the Manhattan coast: an armada of flat-bottomed boats carrying British soldiers filled the horizon as far as the eye could see.

After a pause of more than two weeks following their decisive victory in Brooklyn, the British were finally making an amphibious landing at Kips Bay. Panicked by the sudden attack, the Americans began to flee. When word reached Washington, the general rode into the vortex of the battle in a vain attempt to stop the streams of men fleeing for their lives. It was William Smallwood's first time in the thick of actual combat since the French and Indian War. The portly, taciturn officer groused,

I have often read and heard of instances of cowardice, but hitherto have had but a faint idea of it, 'till now I never could have thought human nature subject to such baseness—I could wish the transactions of this day blotted out of the Annals of America,—nothing appeared but flight, disgrace, and confusion, let it suffice to say that 60 light infantry upon first fire put to flight two brigades of Connecticut troops.

Normally cool and deliberate, George Washington became unhinged. "Wretches, who, however strange it may appear, from the Brigadier General down to the Private Sentinel, were caned and whip'd by the Generals Washington Putnam & Miflin," recalled Smallwood, "but even this Indignity had no Weight they could not be brought to stand one Shot." In a related incident, William Beatty noted that "a New England Captain Was Dressed in Woman's apparel arm'd With a Wooden gun & Sword & [was] Drum'd out of the army for Cowardice."

Cowardice wasn't the only crime attributed to the American soldiers. Two Marylanders, William Arnold and Sam Clark, along with a member of the New York regiment, were accused of plundering the Manhattan mansion of Lord Stirling. When Washington found out about the incident days later, he ordered the three "to restore to the Quarter Master General, what they have taken, in failure whereof they will certainly be hanged." The two Marylanders were released, owing to insufficient evidence, but the New Yorker was sentenced to thirty-nine lashes.

Waves of British soldiers stormed ashore and fought against token resistance as they pushed inland toward their first objective: Murray Hill. In the midst of the unfolding disaster, Washington became catatonic in an open field with dozens of British soldiers only eighty yards away. Nathanael Greene remembered that the general became "so vexed at the infamous conduct of his troops that he sought death rather than life." Eventually an aide pulled the general from the field of battle.

With the British advancing into Manhattan, thousands of American troops abandoned their defenses in the southern portion of the city. After seizing Murray Hill with virtually no fight, an advance party of British light infantry got as far as what's now the site of the New York Public Library on Forty-Second Street. But rather than cut off the retreating Patriots or strike north, Howe stopped.

The reason for the temporary halt isn't completely clear, but according to legend, a local Quaker woman named Mary Lindley Murray may have played a role. Sympathetic to the American cause, Mrs. Murray is said to have invited Howe and the other officers to eat in her home in order to give the Patriots time to escape. She and her daughters reportedly used their charms to keep the officers entertained, while a maid kept watch from an upstairs window and let the women know when Washington's men had gotten away safely.

While Mrs. Murray's seduction may have played a role, some historians doubt that the invitation to eat—given by a mother of twelve in her fifties—was the entire reason for Howe's delay. A more practical consideration may have caused Howe to halt the army. According to General Henry Clinton, Howe issued an order to wait for reinforcements from a second wave of British and Hessian troops coming ashore. As soon as the second debarkation took place, Howe and Cornwallis resumed their pursuit of the Americans fleeing north. Washington called upon the Marylanders to make a desperate stand, this time around Ninety Sixth Street and Fifth Avenue near today's Central Park. The Marylanders dug in behind rocks and the hilly ground of McGowan's Pass, where the Post Road, the main artery for escape, ran between two hills before emptying into Harlem. "Washington expressly sent and drew our Regiment from its Brigade, to march down toward New York, to cover the Retreat. . . . [We took] Possession of an Advantageous Eminence near the Enemy upon the Main Road, where we remained under Arms the best part of the Day, till Sergant's Brigade came in with their Baggage, who were the last Troops coming in," reported Smallwood, "upon which the Enemy divided their Main Body into two Columns, one filing off on the North River endeavored to Flank and surround us, the other advancing in good order slowly up the Main Road upon us."

The Marylanders, led by Mordecai Gist and Smallwood, put up a stiff defense, allowing the last American regiment to escape into Harlem before retreating themselves in good order around dusk. Their resolute stand stopped the British light infantry's advance, and once again, the Marylanders were part of a critical rear guard that allowed the rest of Washington's army to escape. Nevertheless, the landing cost about 350 American casualties; most of those were taken prisoner. As before, the British gained ground but failed to trap Washington's army.

On Harlem Heights, Washington rallied his broken army. After digging in, the general sought to gain intelligence on the disposition of the British and sent out 150 rangers under Lieutenant Colonel Thomas Knowlton. The fearless thirty-seven-year-old veteran of the French and Indian War was beloved by his men and often led them in battle by enthusiastically bellowing, "Come on, boys!"

Infiltrating British lines on the morning of September 16, 1776, Knowlton's Rangers hit the pickets outside Howe's camp. The New Englanders fired several shots and retreated behind a stone wall. The British mobilized their troops and charged Knowlton, whose men unleashed over a thousand rounds into the incoming sea of Redcoats. Expending most of their ammunition, the rangers retreated back to Harlem Heights with the British only about five minutes behind them in hot pursuit.

Led by the light infantry, the three hundred troops chasing Knowlton were the vanguard of a larger main body of British infantry that surged toward the American defenses at Harlem. Washington's adjutant recalled how the British attempted to humiliate their American opponents: "The enemy appeared in open view and in the most insulting manner sounded their bugle horns as is usual after a fox chase. I never felt more such a sensation before; it seemed to crown our disgrace." Cocksure, the Light Bobs charged forward, foolishly leaving their flanks exposed. Washington saw the weakness and quickly devised a plan to entrap the advancing Brits: the Marylanders and other units would engage the light infantry's front and distract them while Knowlton and riflemen from Virginia would circle around their rear and attempt to entrap them. The hunters became the hunted.

Knowlton's Rangers and the Virginians used a ravine to obscure their movements as they crept up on the British left flank. Unfortunately, several rangers opened fire before the American encircling maneuver could be sprung; they soon found themselves hitting the British flank rather than the British rear. Knowlton and another ranger officer were killed in the unfolding action.

Upon hearing the sound of musket fire from the rangers (the signal to open up the frontal attack), the Marylanders sent concentrated musket fire tearing through the British light infantry, halting their advance. One participant noted, "Never did troops go to the field with more cheerfulness and alacrity; when there began a heavy fire on both sides. It continued about one hour, when our brave Southern troops dislodged them from their posts. The enemy rallied, and our men beat them the second time. They rallied again; our troops drove them the third time, and were rushing on them."

One Maryland officer noted, "The Marylanders, were ordered to march down the hill and attack the enemy, which they did [they made a bayonet charge]; and a smart contest ensued, in which the enemy gave way." Lieutenant William Beatty's Flying Camp was also involved: "The action was very sharp on both sides. . . . [One of the men] was wounded in the breast and the other on the back of his arm above the joint of his wrist and so down to his fingers. The bone is not broke." Men like Beatty, Jack Steward, Samuel Smith, John Eager Howard, and Gassaway Watkins likely took part in the battle, gaining valuable experience that steeled them for the long years of war that lay ahead. The Marylanders and other units forced the British to make a retreat through a buckwheat field that is today the grounds of Barnard College and Columbia University.

As the afternoon wore on, both sides poured reinforcements into the battle. The American line held, and eventually the British retreated back to their lines. Washington recalled the gory aftermath of the battle: "[From] the appearance of blood in every place where they made their Stand and on the fences they passed, we have reason to believe they had a good many killed and wounded." With the Marylander and American flanks now exposed, and wishing to avoid the fate of the enemy's light infantry, Washington wisely called off the attack. By about 3:00 p.m., the Battle of Harlem Heights was over; the victory, while small, gave a much-needed boost to the sagging morale of Washington's troops.

The lines remained static in front of Harlem Heights after the battle, with each side sending out patrols to probe the other's defenses and gain intelligence. On September 17, Maryland Lieutenant Jack Steward went behind British lines on a scouting mission accompanied by elements of another regiment. They attacked the British forward positions, and the two forces began to skirmish.

In the aftermath of the fight, Steward was brought before a court-martial on charges of "striking Sergeant [William] Phelps of Colonel [Gold Selleck] Silliman's regiment, and of threatening the life of Colonel Silliman." According to sworn testimony, Steward took Phelps to task for his performance in the battle, calling him a "damned coward." Steward struck Phelps and then argued with Colonel Silliman, who had arrived to break up the dispute. When Silliman ordered the arrest of the Marylander, Steward threw his hat on the ground and exclaimed, "I'll go to my tent—all you can do is to take my commission, but I am a gentleman, and will put it out of your power, for I will resign it, and in less than two hours will be revenged on you, God damn you."

Both men got off with a slap on the wrist: the court found Steward guilty of striking Phelps, but not of threatening Silliman. It determined Phelps was not guilty of cowardice. Neither man received punishment.

Despite the courts-martial, desertion was rampant. The army employed executions in an attempt to stem the tide of deserters. One sergeant from New England gave up hope, deserted, and attempted to shoot one of the American officers in the process. He was condemned to death for treason, and Delaware's Captain Enoch Anderson was ordered to take twenty of his men and shoot the man. "I drew near to the fatal spot," recalled Anderson; "—the prisoner was kneeling in front of the parapet, with a cap over his eyes. We came within twenty feet of him,—his every nerve was creeping, and in much agony he groaned. I groaned, my soldiers groaned,—we all groaned. I would rather have been in a battle."

At the last second, someone cried out, "A pardon, a pardon!" Amazed that he was to be spared, the condemned man cried, "Oh! Lord God, oh! I am not to be shot—oh! Oh!" The reprieve also had an emotional impact on the would-be executioners. Anderson wrote, "Such are the feelings of sympathy, that the tears of joy run down my cheeks. I was not above my poor boys, each also shed their tear. Gloomy as was the morning, the evening turned out crowned with pleasure." Not only was the man not executed, but Washington allowed him to continue serving as a soldier. He remained faithful to the Patriots for the remainder of the war.

With most of Manhattan in British hands, Washington and several of his generals wanted to torch the city rather than allow it to be used to garrison the British army. "I would burn the city and the suburbs," advised Nathanael Greene, who was gravely ill. "If the enemy gets possession of the city we never can recover the possession without superior naval force to theirs." Washington made the same case to Congress "but was absolutely forbid." Despite the congressional order, somehow a fire began on September 21 as the Americans retreated. Soon the city was engulfed in an immense column of fire and smoke. Chaos ensued as the residents attempted to flee. One eyewitness wrote, "The sick, the aged, women and children, half naked were seen going they knew not where. . . . The shrieks and cries of the women and children . . . made this one of the most tremendous and affecting scenes I ever beheld." Before the blaze was extinguished, more than six hundred houses, around 60 percent of the buildings in the city, had been consumed. As New York burned, Washington expected the British to attack Harlem Heights, but once again the Howe brothers' aversion to casualties led to another plan: an amphibious landing behind Washington's lines. Smallwood captured the dramatic moment of the British landings while writing a letter to the Maryland Convention: "I must break off abruptly, being ordered to march . . . the enemy landed thousand[s] of men. There is nothing left but to fight them." New York was surrounded by water, and nothing there was safe from the British navy.

CHAPTER 12

WHEN TWENTY-FIVE MEN HELD OFF AN ARMY

On the morning of October 12, 1776, a dense fog shrouded Long Island Sound, dampening noise and reducing visibility to near zero. Despite being in a war zone, local fishermen went about their business without realizing what lay hidden nearby. As the rising sun burned off the cloud cover, the stunned anglers suddenly found themselves among a sea of barges loaded with soldiers, horses, and cannon. Soon a frigate belched fire, providing shore bombardment for the Howe brothers' newest amphibious assault.

At first light, eighty British boats landed on Manhattan's Throgs Neck Peninsula in southeastern Bronx, the current location of Throgs Neck Bridge. A creek cut across the narrow peninsula at one point, making it more like an island at high tide. Ten days earlier, the Americans had stationed twenty-five crack riflemen led by Pennsylvania's Colonel Edward Hand to defend the area. The colonel and his men destroyed the bridge across the creek, creating a natural choke point and kill zone. When he saw the approaching juggernaut, Hand and his men dispatched a messenger to carry news of the landing to the American generals and steeled themselves behind a woodpile to await the enemy's advance. Against all odds, Hand's twenty-five men successfully held off four thousand British soldiers long enough for reinforcements to arrive.

Stymied at Throgs Neck, General William Howe ordered a retreat. But instead of immediately reembarking on their landing boats, he and his men camped on the tip of the peninsula for several days, giving Washington precious time to regroup. Eventually, Howe ordered his men back on their boats and headed three miles up the coast to Pell's

Point, near present-day Pelham Bay. Again, the Patriots were ready and waiting. The officers devised a unique strategy to take advantage of the terrain. They ordered their men to lie behind the numerous stone walls in the area. When the Redcoats approached, the first line of riflemen rose, fired a volley, and retreated. Believing the entire American force was on the run, the British mounted a bayonet charge. As the enemy approached, the second line of Patriots rose up and fired at point-blank range.

Pell's Point provides an example of the evolving style of war in the Revolution. As the war progressed, Marylanders were in the forefront of helping pioneer an American style of combat. That reflex to adapt flourished from the start and it remains evident to the present day. Tactically, the Americans tended to concentrate their firepower on a specific point in the battlefield where it had the greatest impact. They also developed defensive maneuvers that wore down the enemy, taking advantage of the terrain and making the best use possible of the militia and Continentals they had at their disposal. At the strategic level, the Americans used intelligence as a force multiplier, helping them position their troops to the best advantage. In addition, the Marylanders and the rest of the American troops relied on speed and flexibility, combined with judicious risk taking; they avoided needlessly wasting men's lives for operations that didn't produce results.

The British army had already mastered its style of combat when the war began. It had established rules for its soldiers to follow in battle—a European style of fighting. As the war progressed, it began to see the need to revise those rules, and it adapted. Both the American army and the British army were readjusting their forces, tactics, and strategy to fight the Revolution. A race ensued. The winner would be the army that could reshape itself faster.

Pell's Point also demonstrated the decisive impact elite units could have on the battlefield. The delaying tactics used by the skilled Patriot defenders killed and wounded around two hundred British and Hessians; but more important, these tactics gave Washington time to reposition his men. On the recommendation of his chief rival, General Charles Lee,

Washington moved the main body of his army from Harlem north to White Plains, leaving a group of twelve hundred men behind to reinforce the garrison at Fort Washington on the north end of Manhattan, at the highest point on the island. Lee had recently returned from Charleston, South Carolina, where he successfully repelled a British invasion.[14] Based on this success combined with his prior command experience, Congress held Lee in very high esteem, and he now appeared as an alternative for the position of commander in chief. The Marylanders once again formed part of the rear guard and were one of the final regiments to leave Westchester County before rejoining the army at White Plains.

Lee was one of the most bizarre and brilliant general officers in the American Revolution. He began his career in the French and Indian War and later saw action in Portugal and the Russo-Turkish War. Returning to America, he married the daughter of a Mohawk chief, who gave him his nickname Boiling Water, a reference to his quick temper. His mercurial temperament has led some biographers to surmise that he may have been bipolar. Physically, he was often described as gangly, with a head too big for his body. Lee was also fairly careless with his appearance and somewhat slovenly. Known to be somewhat coarse, Lee frequently used obscene language. A great dog lover and rarely seen without his train of dogs, the general once quipped that dogs, unlike men, were faithful. In 1773 he moved to Virginia and volunteered to join the Patriots. He

14. The bulk of the British army in the summer of 1776 was concentrated in New York, but a small expedition led by Sir Henry Clinton attempted to seize Charleston, South Carolina, on June 28, 1776, in an effort to roll back the Revolution in the South. The British had not yet devised a coordinated strategy to deal with the rebellion, nor did they have an accurate view of the scope or magnitude of the rebellion and the number of Loyalists and Patriot Americans—a flaw in strategy that persisted throughout most of the war. To take Charleston, Clinton first had to neutralize its harbor defenses at Fort Moultrie. The operation turned into a disaster when three ships ran aground in the shallow waters around the fort and the American garrison repelled a British landing force. The British navy shelled the fort to no avail; many of the cannonballs reportedly bounced harmlessly off the spongy palmetto log walls of the fort, inspiring South Carolina's nickname, the Palmetto State. After thirteen hours of intense combat, the British withdrew from Charleston and most of the South.

longed to be named commander in chief and viewed Washington as an incompetent rival.

Despite his prickly demeanor, Lee offered Washington a piece of excellent advice and recommended the move to White Plains because it was more defensible and contained a supply depot. The move saved the army, which was about to be enveloped by the latest British landing. Taking full advantage of the topography, Washington placed his troops on the high ground behind the Bronx River. He sent the Maryland and Delaware forces, as well as some Connecticut regimentals and some militia to Chatterton's Hill, a 180-foot-high crag on the right flank. There, approximately two thousand men hastily dug in and began constructing fortifications.

While bivouacked outside White Plains, the Marylanders were, at times, within sight of the enemy on the opposite side of the Bronx River. Captain Samuel Smith recalled that on one occasion, he "conversed with a British officer on the opposite bank." Smith asked about his friend, Major John André, with whom he had crossed the Atlantic prior to the war. The charismatic André was later hanged as a spy for his role in Benedict Arnold's treason. During the conversation, "the British officer advised him to retire, lest he might be shot by the [Hessian] Yagers, over whom he had no control."

This was a time of great sickness and hardship for the American army. During the retreats from Long Island and Brooklyn, it had lost the bulk of its baggage, including the tents. As a result, many soldiers became ill from exposure to the elements. One of the Maryland officers reported "near two hundred men unfit for duty and most them without any assistance from the Doctor."

By the time Howe had his entire army in place on October 28, the Americans had constructed a solid defense. Henry Clinton reported to Howe that he "could not from what I saw recommend a direct attack. . . . Their flanks were safe and their retreat practicable when they pleased." The two armies exchanged cannon fire for several days. Washington deployed a force of approximately fifteen hundred, including some of the Marylanders, to check the advance of the British. Smallwood approached his men "and asked how many would go with him, to draw the British out." According to a Maryland private, John Hughes, thirteen men volunteered. He continued describing the action:

[I] with Twelve others from [my] company went out to the British Breast Work, made of rails etc. to keep off the musket Balls, and fired upon the Sentinels. A Cannon Ball was immediately returned by the British, which struck a Fence Rail upon the Breast Work, and threw a half of the Rail against [my] thigh, and shivered the bone to pieces from the knee up. [I] was immediately carried off in a litter, and did no more actual service after this accident.

Howe put his army into formation. As the Marylanders gazed down from the top of Chatterton's Hill, the situation must have looked insuperable to the now battle-hardened veterans. "The sun shone bright, their arms glittered, and perhaps troops never were shown to more advantage," recalled one participant. Thirteen thousand strong, the British advanced. Smoke from artillery and shot filled the air. Captain Smith recalled, "A cannon commenced. . . . The enemy's object appeared to be to disarm our artillery."

Howe detached several thousand of his men and twelve pieces of artillery to attack Chatterton's Hill. However, in order to get there, they had to get across the Bronx River, which was running high following recent rain. They paused to "construct a rough bridge by felling trees and laying fence rails across them." Seeing the enemy temporarily halted, Smallwood led his men "more than halfway down the hill and opened fire, throwing the Hessians into disorder." When they finally made it across the river, the Hessians charged through burning fields ignited by the artillery fire. As they navigated their way through a hail of lead and flame, they held their cartridge boxes above their heads to keep them from exploding. Four thousand men, led by the Hessians, surged forward toward the Marylanders atop the hill.

One Marylander recalled the British approach: "The enemy advanced toward our lines in full view of headquarters, while a large body approached to the right, a warm engagement became and now continues with great fury." Despite the approaching onslaught, Smith could not help admiring the British advance. "It was a gallant sight to see them, steadily, without falter, march up a very steep hill," he wrote in his autobiography. "As the grenadiers ascended, however, they became the targets of their own artillery, which had to desist when the soldiers reached the top of the slope."

The Americans fired canister and grape into the oncoming enemy masses; the Royal Artillery responded with solid shot. One ball found its deadly mark. It "first took the head off . . . a stout heavy man and dash'd it open; then it took off Chilson's arm, which was amputated. . . . It then took Taylor across the bowels; it then struck Sergt Garret of our company on the hip—took off the point of the hip bone. What a sight that was to see . . . men with legs and arms and packs all in a heap." Marylander William Brooks recalled that "in this Battle he got his right leg broke and was sent from there to the hospital," where he spent two months recovering. Captain Smith, whose company was in the rear of the action, reported the lethal effect of British artillery: "A ball struck the ground, and, in its rebound, took off the head of Sergeant Westlay," after flying directly over Smith's shoulder.

The Americans repelled the first wave of the attack, which came up the east side. "[We marched] down the hill to attack the enemy . . . and a smart conflict ensued, in which the enemy gave way, but rallying again, and attacking the right of the brigade, lying again, and attacking compelled the militia aforeward."

Taking heavy casualties, the Hessians fought up the southern side of the hill. The militia panicked and "fled in confusion, without more than a random, scattering fire," reported Colonel John Haslet, who commanded the Delaware troops on the hill positioned near the Marylanders. Since Brooklyn, the two forces had typically deployed together and often the Delaware men were operationally under the command of the Marylanders. The British pelted the Marylanders and the Delaware

Regiment with a "very heavy fire of their artillery and musquetry for about half an hour."

At White Plains, Captain John Eager Howard of the Flying Camp was engaged in the battle. Now Washington sent Howard and his militia to the hill to cover the retreat of their fellow Marylanders serving under Smallwood.

Delaware Captain Enoch Anderson reported watching as "a soldier of our Regiment was mortally wounded in this battle. He fell to the ground;—in falling, his gun fell from him. He picked it up,—turned on his face,—took aim at the British, who were advancing,—fired,—the gun fell from him,—he turned over on his back and expired." Balls nipped Smallwood in the arm and hip, and scores of Marylanders went down under the fire.

Even the dependable Marylanders were forced to withdraw. "The Americans overpowered by their numbers, were compelled to save themselves, as best they could," recalled Smith. He himself "was so deeply engaged, that unapprised of their departure, he escaped with great difficulty—his men saving themselves by his orders." In the course of the retreat, Smith was struck in the left arm "by a spent ball" but continued fighting. Later Smith "stopped with two men, behind a stone [wall]; where they took deliberate aim at an advanced party of the enemy. On visiting the spot afterwards blood was found."

Eventually, he found Colonel Smallwood, who was wounded in the wrist, and was able to round up "about a hundred stragglers, and marched them within the lines." As he led his men into camp, they passed a New England regiment that was eating a meal. "A young private [from the other unit] rose and said, 'I guess you have been in the action?'"

"Yes," Smith replied.

"And maybe you have eat nothing today?" the private continued.

"No, not for twenty-four hours," answered Smith.

Hearing those words, "The men all rose and would eat no more, until we had satisfied ourselves," Smith said.

In the larger battle, both sides took heavy casualties. According to Gist's report, Maryland alone lost forty-six men and officers. A single

Hessian volley reportedly took out ninety-two Americans, but the Patriots remained steadfast. One of the British officers observed, "The rebels had excellent positions at White Plains. They had made their defenses better than usual, and maintained their posts with extraordinary tenacity."

After ejecting the rebels from the hill, the British went about improving the defenses and then continued the pursuit. Gist recalled,

> Since the skirmish the Enemy have been exceedingly busy in erecting a Breast work on the Eminence they took from us. Yesterday morning having got prepared to open it upon us, the General [Washington] ordered us to abandon our front lines, which in our present situation was rendered useless to us. The Enemy immediately took possession of them, and Judging that we were making a precipitate retreat, formed the line, and advanced upon us with a large column to bring on the attack, the artillery on each side keeping up a smart fire, and they soon found their situation disagreeable, and as if ashamed of the attempt they sneakily skulked behind a wood, and retired unseen to the lines in much haste.

Fighting and the harsh conditions that accompanied an army living in the field for several months continued to take a toll on the Marylanders. William Beatty wrote that the same day the Americans left White Plains "I being very unwell Crossed the North river for the purpose of going in the Country to recover my health and remained there for two weeks."

The Patriots reportedly inflicted more than three hundred casualties during the Battle of White Plains. When Washington ordered the entire army to retreat, they maintained order rather than fleeing as they had done at Kips Bay. The British had won the day, but at a heavy price. Washington and his men escaped the next day in a downpour, leaving the men at Fort Washington as the only American forces still on the island of Manhattan.

CHAPTER 13

FORT WASHINGTON

At an elevation of 280 feet above the Hudson River, the stout earthen walls of Fort Washington bristled with more than 140 Patriot cannon. Rocky slopes and a sheer cliff gave the citadel a false aura of impregnability. Nearly three thousand Americans, including a contingent of Marylanders, manned its ramparts. Against his better judgment, George Washington had left the troops behind to guard the fort that bore his name. He relied on the advice of General Nathanael Greene, who argued that it was necessary to hold the fort to prevent the British navy from approaching up the Hudson River. Although the fort had an impressive array of works, it was poorly designed.[15] There was no fuel, artillery casements, or a well within the fort. Water had to be hauled from the river below. A week earlier, American Adjutant William Demont, one of the war's worst yet least known traitors, had fled the fort and deserted to British lines, revealing to the enemy the fort's order of battle and its plans. This act of treason made it even more likely that the British would be able to overcome its flawed defenses.[16]

A group of Marylanders and Virginians, led by Colonel Moses Rawling and Major Otho Holland Williams, defended the northern slopes of the hill. Williams had spent his boyhood on a farm in a rural area of Maryland and then was apprenticed to be a clerk after his father died when Otho was only thirteen. He joined the Continental Army in 1775 as a first lieutenant and participated in the Siege of Boston, the Patriots'

---

15. The fort stretched for more than a mile from present-day George Washington Bridge.

16. For the British, William Demont served as commissary of prisoners after the fall of Philadelphia and as an officer during the war.

successful attempt to keep the British bottled up in that city, before being assigned to the defense of Fort Washington. Williams's inner circle of friends included Samuel Smith, Jack Steward, and Nathaniel Ramsay.

To crush Fort Washington, General William Howe gathered the bulk of his army, nearly thirteen thousand men. In the morning hours of November 15, the British converged on three sides at once. Three thousand Hessians, including Colonel Johann Rall, landed in the north, while General Hugh Percy pressed from the east and Charles, Earl Cornwallis hit the fort from the south. The Hessians scaled a steep grade on the north side of the fort, fighting and maneuvering around the obstacles the Americans had placed in their path, all the while facing a deadly hail of bullets. For more than two hours, the Marylanders and others kept the mercenaries at bay by holding a crucial pass. During the extended fighting, many of their rifles became clogged from overuse. At first, Washington had "great hopes the enemy was entirely repulsed." Eventually, however, the determined Hessian fighters made it to the top of the hill. Rall barked to his men, "All that are my grenadiers, march forwards!" The Hessians yelled, "Hurrah!" in response as the drums and horns sounded. As one, they surged toward the defenders.

Rall pushed back the Americans on the southern and eastern slopes to the fort; therefore, more than twenty-eight hundred Americans were now trapped in a fort devoid of water and vulnerable to bombardment from British ships on the Hudson.

After breaching the main ramparts, Rall sent a messenger with a white flag tied to a rifle to request the fort's surrender. He demanded that the men give up their arms and ammunition. He assured them that they would be allowed to keep their personal effects. The Americans had just thirty minutes to decide. While Washington sent messages from the other side of the Hudson River encouraging them to hold out, Colonel Robert Magaw, the fort's commander, didn't believe they could last much longer. Rather than see his men slaughtered, Magaw surrendered. The British took 2,838 prisoners along with 140 brass and iron cannon.

Among the captured was Major Williams, whose "Commission was stain'd ... by the blood ... from a wound ... received in the action."

One report from the battle stated, "Of the Maryland troops, Colonel Rowlings, Colonel Williams, and about two hundred of that battalion are prisoners. With their men they defended a pass against the Hessians for two hours, and killed two hundred of them."

Miraculously, a few men avoided both death and confinement, including Marylander Lawrence Everhart. He and a few more "escaped in a boat to Fort Lee, thence to Hackensack." In New Jersey, Everhart met Washington, who witnessed the capture of the fort from a distance. "Here [I] saw Gen George Washington in tears walking the porch."

Enraged after losing so many of their men in the battle, the Hessians stormed into Fort Washington and began slaughtering the Americans inside—despite their surrender. The British officers eventually put an end to the carnage, but the mercenaries' anger wasn't spent yet. As the prisoners exited the fort, a long line of Hessians and some of the Redcoats formed up on either side, forcing the Patriots to endure a gauntlet of abuse and humiliation. They hurled taunts, insults, and an occasional kick at the defeated men and robbed them of their few possessions. Many of the Americans didn't have shoes and were filthy after being confined to the fort, so they were prime targets for their jeering enemies. One of the British officers noted, "Their odd figures frequently excited the laughter of our soldiers."

A British officer ordered an American named Richard Thomas Atkinson to carry the American colors, a Gadsden flag bearing the words "Don't Tread on Me," out of Fort Washington. As he exited the structure and before entering the gauntlet, Atkinson furtively "lowered the colours" and gave them to another soldier. Rather than hand the colors over to the enemy, the soldier "put them within his breeches" and kept them until he was able to deliver them to Washington.

The taunting didn't stop as the Americans, including many Marylanders, headed for captivity. A first stop for many was the shops and churches of New York City which had been converted into temporary holding cells. There, Marylanders captured at Fort Washington rejoined their brother soldiers taken prisoner at the Battle of Brooklyn. For many Patriots captured during the war, imprisonment was little more than an extended death sentence. According to some historians, the British captured as many as thirty thousand Americans during the Revolution. Of those, some eighteen thousand, or 60 percent, died while being held prisoner. That's more than twice as many as those who died in battle. Those captured in the battles in and around New York faced some of the harshest conditions of all. While officers were sometimes allowed to stay in private homes, many of the rank-and-file prisoners were loaded onto prison ships in New York harbor. Ridiculously overcrowded, these filthy vessels bred disease, and in many cases the underfed prisoners on board didn't have the strength to overcome their illnesses. By most estimates, well over ten thousand Americans died on these ships alone. Many Marylanders endured the hellish conditions aboard the floating death traps and died forgotten. The majority of their emaciated bodies were unceremoniously tossed overboard like bags of garbage.

According to accounts from prisoners and guards, it was common for the enemy officers to mock the Patriots by asking them what their trade had been before the war. These professional soldiers, many born into families that had served in the military for generations, found it funny that Americans chose shopkeepers and farmers to lead their military. One Hessian officer recalled, "Among the prisoners were many colonels, lieutenant colonels, majors, and other officers who were nothing but mechanics, tailors, shoemakers, wigmakers, barbers, etc. Some of them were soundly beaten by our people, who would by no means let such persons pass for officers."

One of the British officers tried this tactic with Otho Holland Williams, who had commanded a regiment of Marylanders and Virginians at Fort Washington. When the Redcoat accosted him, Williams refused to be the butt of the joke. Instead, "he replied, that he had been bred in that situation which had taught him to rebuke and punish insolence, and that the questioner would have ample proof of his apprenticeship on a repetition of his offence."

Williams's response did little to endear him to his captors. Soon after this conversation, the British accused him of secretly corresponding with Washington and sent him to harsher accommodations as a result. He shared a room "about sixteen feet square that was seldom visited by the breath of heaven, and always remaining in a state of loathsome filth," with another American hero of the Revolution—Ethan Allen, who had been captured leading an attack on Montreal. "Their health was much impaired, for their food was of the vilest sort, and scarce enough to keep soul and body together, and to add to these discomforts, the anxiety that preyed upon their minds, was terrible in the extreme. The naturally fine constitution of Williams was much impaired, and he never recovered entirely from the effects of his imprisonment."

A Connecticut native named William Slade who was captured at Fort Washington kept a journal that chronicled the harsh treatment meted out by the British on a daily basis:

> *Sunday 17th.* Such a Sabbath I never saw. We spent it in sorrow and hunger, having no mercy showed. . . .
>
> *Tuesday 19th.* Still confined without provisions till almost night, when we got a little mouldy bisd [biscuit], about four per man. These four days we spent in hunger and sorrow being drided by everry one and calld Rebs.
>
> *Wednesday, 20th.* We was reinforsd by 300 more. We had 500 before. This caused a continual noise and verry big huddle. Jest at night drawed 6 ox of pork per man. This we eat alone and raw.
>
> *Thursday, 21st.* We passed the day in sorrow haveing nothing to eat or drink but pump water. . . .
>
> *Sunday, 22nd.* Last night nothing but grones all night of sick and dying. Men amazeing to behold. Such hardness, sickness prevails fast. Deaths multiply. . . .

A few lucky Marylanders managed to escape from these death traps. Baltimore native William Sterrett, who fought in Smallwood's Battalion and later became Mordecai Gist's brother-in-law, spent several months on the British prison ships in Wallabout Bay in Brooklyn. In April 1777 the commissary of prisoners, Joshua Loring, whose wife was Howe's mistress, visited Sterrett and tried to persuade him to swear allegiance to the British government, offering better treatment if he complied. He refused. The official "said I should continue in confinement and be subject to the distresses which were about to threaten us," Sterrett later wrote.

Duplicitously, the guards didn't enter Sterrett's name in their rolls, making it look as though Sterrett had taken the oath. In December the Americans tried to trade for Sterrett in a prisoner exchange, but because he wasn't officially listed as a prisoner, the British would not let him go. Through guile, the Marylander likely took the British oath of allegiance, made his way back to the American lines, and resumed serving in the Continental Army.

A few others also were able to flee and evade the enemy. Christopher Hawkins, a thirteen-year-old, ran away when he was sent to fetch laundry from town. He hitched rides, walked, and finally boarded a ship that took him back to his home in Providence, "much to the joy of my parents and not a little to myself." Ensign James Fernandis wasn't so lucky, languishing aboard a prison ship until a prisoner exchange released him in 1777.

Also among the prisoners captured in Long Island who escaped were the McMillan brothers from Smallwood's Battalion. William McMillan recalled that their harsh treatment began with their capture by the Hessians. "The Hessians broke the butts of our guns over their cannons and robbed us of everything we had," he recalled. "[They] lit their pipes with our money, caned us and gave us nothing to eat for five days, and then [they served us] biscuits from aboard ships, blue, moldy, full [of] bugs and rotten." Like some of the other prisoners, the McMillans were forced to serve as slave laborers and haul cannons for the enemy.

However, after holding them for a few days in the harbor, the British sent the McMillans and some other prisoners by boat to Halifax, Nova Scotia. After a miserable winter and a portion of the spring, the brothers broke out of their prison in April. "Ten of us run away from Halifax and had likely been taken two or three times by the British," stated William. The British weren't the only enemy, however. McMillan added, "Seven times we had likely been killed by the Indians if we had not had a man that could speak the Canadian language [French]." They trekked for miles though harsh wilderness, eating "grass on the rocks in the bays, shellfish, and snails," before they made it to Boston. "We suffered everything but death," said McMillan. Despite their ordeal, Samuel McMillan immediately rejoined the Continental Army, this time in a Massachusetts regiment, and William rejoined his Maryland brothers after recuperating for a time.

Some New York prisoners were returned from the ships to buildings in the city after the Continental Army fled. Many remained in converted churches, while some were held in a "sugar-house" on Liberty Street. An eyewitness who lived across the street from the sugar-house at the time recalled that it was a large building "with little port-hole windows tier above tier." In the unbearable summer heat, "every narrow aperture of those stone walls filled with human heads, face above face, seeking a portion of the external air." They fared little better in the winter. One, who was housed with a group of five hundred men, noted that approximately four hundred perished "from Exposure, bad treatment, Cold & Hunger."

Prisoners who requested medical help were often sent to their deaths. The British had a former French prisoner serving as a surgeon, despite the fact that he had absolutely no training and had been convicted of multiple crimes. A nurse in the prison revealed "that she had several times heard this Frenchman say that he would have Ten Rebels dead in such a room and five dead in such a Room, the next morning, and it always happened." When two Americans later took the "medicine" this Frenchman had been administering, it was found to be poison. After the war, the surgeon confessed that he had "murdered a great number of Rebels in the Hospital at New York, by poyson" and that when General Howe learned what he had done, the Frenchman got a pay raise. He also admitted to poisoning "the wells used by the American Flying Camp, which caused such an uncommon Mortality among them in the year 1776."

CHAPTER 14

THE CRISIS

In November 1776 "a thick cloud of darkness and gloom covered the land, and despair was seen on almost every countenance," remembered Ensign Peter Jaquett of Haslet's Delaware Regiment, which marched through rain and mud alongside Smallwood's Marylanders on their trek through New Jersey. The veteran captured the mood of the country, which had been reeling from defeats in Brooklyn, Manhattan, Fort Washington, and recently the capture of Fort Lee, which lay just across the Hudson River from Fort Washington.

Quickly following up on the decisive British victory at Fort Washington, General William Howe had sent Cornwallis and four thousand men across the Hudson. As the men climbed up an unguarded, steep cliff on the Jersey Palisades, Cornwallis quickly occupied Fort Lee, which George Washington had swiftly ordered evacuated after receiving word of the earl's approaching force. British troops seized the bulk of the Continental Army's equipment, including its shovels, picks, tents, cannon, and ordnance. Maryland Captain William Beatty noted, "Our army began to prepare for a retreat But before this Could be accomplished the Enemy landed above us Which Obliged Our army to make a quick retreat leaving all our Heavy Cannon & Stores & Baggage of all kinds behind, the Whole of Which fell into the Hands of the Enemy." The seizure of Fort Lee precipitated Washington's retreat across New Jersey toward the perceived safety of the wide Delaware River. It was also another blow to Nathanael Greene, who, as at Fort Washington, advocated holding the fortification.

*   *   *

The evening of November 20 was "dark, cold, and rainy," in Hackensack, New Jersey, but as the remnants of Washington's army and the Marylanders trudged through town, it was light enough for the local residents to recognize their sorry state. One inhabitant noted, "They marched two abreast, looked ragged, some without shoes on their feet, and most of them wrapped in their blankets." Washington's battered army had shrunk in size from an apogee of nearly twenty thousand men to only several thousand effectives. Even worse, it was now more poorly equipped than ever. The Americans had lost their tents and other equipment at Fort Lee and now had little in the way of shelter, cooking utensils, and other gear. Many of the soldiers, expecting a quick end to the war, had only summer clothing with them, and it hadn't stood up to the harsh conditions of camp life. Now winter was coming, and few of the American men were prepared for the coming hardship. One British officer sneered, "No nation ever saw such a set of tatterdemalions."

Pursuing the ragged Continental Army, Cornwallis halted his men on the far side of the Hackensack River. With his ranks swelled by reinforcements from Howe, his well-equipped force made a stark contrast to the weary Americans. But rather than attack, they simply moved into Hackensack after Washington left and then spent several days there resting and foraging.

While the British regrouped and raided local farms, Washington continued on to Newark. From there, he sent the sick and injured to Morristown, while the able-bodied continued on to New Brunswick. One of the Marylanders sent to Morristown was the tall Sergeant Gassaway Watkins. He later recalled, "Was taken sick in November, and sent to and left at Morristown, New Jersey. I put my clothing in the regimental wagon, and the driver carried all to the enemy. I travelled from Morristown to Annapolis without money or clothing and got to Annapolis in January, '77, and lay confined to my room until the last of April." He wouldn't rejoin the regiment until September 1777.

General Washington hoped to augment his dwindling force with additional recruits from New Jersey, but instead the army continued to shrink. One American officer stood by the side of the road and counted the passing men; he was horrified to discover they were down to three thousand. Many of those would leave when their enlistments expired on December 1, and still more would be heading home at the end of the month. Captain Samuel Smith recalled the dismal journey: "The rain fell in torrents, and the march was dreadful. Many of the men were exhausted and remained behind. The night was very dark; the road was made deep by the artillery and wagons which had passed. Every step was above the ankles [in mud]; and many to the knee." Beatty added, "This march being in the night the darkness of which together with the intolerable bad roads made this tour of duty very hard."

The remaining Marylanders and members of the Delaware Regiment circled around to hear the news. For days they had been fleeing Cornwallis. Now, they were halted, guarding a bridge, but the depleted units were showing the strain of so many recent lost battles. Major Mordecai Gist and Captain Smith had met with General Washington and "informed him that the [Maryland] Regiment and Delaware Regiment were reduced to 250 men, who were worn down with fatigue and guard duty." They requested that they be relieved by another unit.

Washington's reply would inspire the Marylanders through many hardships to come. "I can assign no other regiment in which I can place the same confidence; and I request you will say so to your gallant regiment." On hearing these words, the men "gave three cheers and declared their readiness to submit to every fatigue and damper."

The Marylanders had distinguished themselves as an elite unit and facilitated the retreat of the army on several crucial occasions. A core group of battle-hardened men, many of them close friends and original members of the Baltimore Cadets, were now helping hold the entire American army together. Some later moved to other units, providing strength and leadership skills gained through experience. General Alexander McDougall later summed up the situation, saying, "Even the bones of a regiment are of great moment in the forming of one."

Along with the rest of the army, the Marylanders suffered their share of hardships. Gist tallied up the Marylanders still fighting and reported, "[We] are badly off for Cloathes, having lost the principal part of their baggage." One officer traveled to Philadelphia in an attempt to purchase clothing for the men. After searching for four days, he wrote to the Maryland Council of Safety, "[I] am much afraid [I] shall not be able to procure [clothing] at present, particularly shoes and stockings, of which we are in great want, and unless they can be got will render many soldiers unfit for duty. I suppose between this and Christmas they may be procured, but at a most extravagant rate." Food was also in short supply. "A sufficiency of provisions we do not complain of," he wrote, "if a constant succession of beef and flour from day to day will do, and that sometimes without salt; and one day in the week we get salt pork. No kind of vegetables does the Commissary furnish us with, and such our situation we can get none." The shortages no doubt contributed to the growing assumption among the Maryland officers that few of the men would reenlist when their term of service ended in December.

Cornwallis followed the Americans—but in a measured way. While never far behind, the British general always seemed to be a day late. Cornwallis had orders to push the American army out of New Jersey but not to engage it in a major battle that might result in the loss of British troops. Hessian officer Johann Ewald, who commanded the unit of Jaegers (in English, "hunters"), asked to pursue the retreating Americans, but Cornwallis ordered him back, telling him, "Let them go, my dear Ewald, and stay here. . . . We do not want to lose any men. One Jaeger is worth more than ten rebels." From Cornwallis's statement and actions, Ewald concluded the British were interested in "ending the war amicably without shedding the blood of the King's subjects in a needless way."

Prior to the invasion of New York, the Howe brothers, General William and Admiral Richard, pursued a political solution. They believed in a minimal use of force whenever possible—as well as a minimal loss of life. In some ways, these beliefs mirror the modern (and sometimes flawed) tenets of counterinsurgency warfare. Howe eventually even offered a pardon to anyone who renounced the Patriot cause and swore allegiance to the Crown. Given the pitiful condition of Washington's army, it seemed like a prudent measure. Thousands of Americans flocked to British camps and pledged their peaceful obedience to the king.

Frustrated with the slow pace of the war and realizing the importance of destroying the Continental Army, Howe's top general, Sir Henry Clinton, asked for permission to sail to New Jersey and put an end to Washington's army once and for all. As an alternative, he suggested sending his men up the Delaware River to strike the American capital at Philadelphia and capture the Continental Congress. He saw the importance of envelopment and maneuver. Howe rejected both ideas.

From a strategic standpoint, the Howe brothers had a different aim from catching the Americans and crushing them. They wanted to keep Washington's army in retreat while they dispatched five thousand troops under Clinton to seize the port of Providence, Rhode Island, which would serve as an additional base for the British fleet because the waters around Manhattan typically froze solid during the winter.

This proved to be a crucial error, one that allowed Washington's army to escape once again. The Americans reached New Brunswick, a fateful milestone, on November 29. The enlistments for many of Washington's regiments, including the Marylanders of the Flying Camp, were up on December 1, dramatically reducing the size of the army. William Beatty remembered the exodus: "Two or three days after our arrival in Brunswick, being the first of December and the Expiration of the Flying Camp's troops time, our brigade marched to Philadelphia." Washington urged the men to stay, but most of the units whose enlistments had expired returned to their home states, as required by law—Washington's army was melting away and numbered only about three thousand men.

December 1776 marked a low point in the Revolution. Most of the Continental Army's twelve-month enlistments were about to expire by the end of the year,[17] and troops were becoming scarce as many headed

---

17. The enlistments of men who signed up on different dates expired at various times during the month of December 1776.

back home. Smallwood's men's enlistments expired on December 10, and his once proud battalion of nearly a thousand had dwindled to under one hundred. Samuel Smith noted the pitiful condition of the troops: "[Our] numbers by battles, sickness, and desertion, were reduced to ninety men and a few officers."

But from the bones of the old battalion, the new 1st Maryland Regiment and several other regiments were formed. Many of the remaining survivors of Smallwood's Battalion, including Gist, Jack Steward, and Nathaniel Ramsay, officially enlisted in the Continental Army for three years around December 10 and became part of the 1st Maryland Regiment. Other officers followed suit, and they were joined by many of the men from the Flying Camp, such as John Eager Howard and William Beatty.[18] Even though Otho Williams remained in captivity following the Battle of Fort Washington, he retained an honorary command and was even promoted while imprisoned. John Stone, formerly a captain in the battalion's 1st Company, temporarily led the 1st Maryland Regiment while Smallwood returned to Maryland to recruit new men. Smith, Gist, Colonel Stone, Ramsay, Steward, and a small core group of men were all that remained of the proud unit.

At New Brunswick, Cornwallis again caught up with the Americans. During the afternoon of December 1, Washington's forces had caught sight of British Light Dragoons on the far bank of the Raritan River outside town. Washington called upon a crack artillery unit led by twenty-one-year-old West Indian Alexander Hamilton. Like Gist, the brilliant young officer had raised his own artillery company and enforced discipline with the lash when necessary. The well-oiled unit caught the eye of Washington, who eventually made Hamilton his senior aide. Hamilton went on to be one of the most influential founding fathers of the United States, arguing the need for a strong national government

18. Most of the men in Smallwood's Regiment who reenlisted formed the 1st Maryland Regiment, the independent companies formed the 2nd Maryland, and the Flying Camp formed additional regiments. Congress mandated an army of eighty-eight battalions; Maryland was expected to furnish eight regiments but outfitted only seven. Rather than follow each regiment separately, this book follows the principal officers and enlisted men who were a driving force in each of these units.

after the war and helping to establish the nation's financial system. But on that cold December day, the young artillerist was helping defend the crossings and cover the American withdrawal from the town.

Enoch Anderson of the Delaware regiment recalled, "A severe cannonading took place on both sides, and several were killed and wounded on our side." The fight continued until "near Sundown," when the Delaware men received their orders to retreat. Unlike most of the army, the regiment had, until this time, managed to hold on to its tents. But this latest retreat left it as poorly equipped as the rest of the Americans. Anderson wrote:

> Colonel Haslet came to me, and told me to take as many men as I thought proper, and go back and burn all the tents. "We have no wagons," said he "to carry them off, and it is better to burn them than they should fall into the hands of the enemy." Then I went and burned them—about one hundred tents. When we saw them reduced to ashes, it was night and the army far ahead. We made a double quick-step and came up with the army about eight o'clock. We encamped in the woods, with no victuals, no tents, no blankets. The night was cold and we all suffered much, especially those who had no shoes.

Haslet's men and the Marylanders camped thirteen miles away in the town of Kingston. The next morning, the British crossed the river into New Brunswick. There, Cornwallis received orders to halt. Like the Americans, his army was also in poor shape. Many of the exhausted Hessians were barefoot, their shoes worn out from marching and fighting since August. To regroup, Cornwallis paused for several crucial days, letting Washington put additional distance between himself and the British. Arriving in Princeton, the Americans had "comfortable lodgings in the college," but their ranks were now down to twenty-five hundred men, with more leaving every day. With the British behind him, Washington faced another obstacle—the Delaware River. If the British trapped his men on its banks, his force could easily be annihilated.

To slow the advancing British, Washington left fourteen hundred men under the command of Lord Stirling in Princeton. The rest of the men continued on to Trenton, which lies on the bank of the Delaware River. The Delaware Regiment and some of the Marylanders marched in the rear of the main portion of the army, accompanied by the commander in chief himself. "We continued on our retreat; — our Regiment in the rear . . . —tearing up bridges and cutting down trees to impede the march of the enemy," recalled Anderson. "I was to go no faster than General Washington and his pioneers." They made it across the approximately four-hundred-yard-wide river around noon on December 2.

For five days, the American army crossed the wide river in boats by the light of huge pyres lit beside the river. Charles Willson Peale, a member of the Pennsylvania militia, described the setting as "the most hellish scene I have ever beheld, all the shores were lighted up with large fires, boats continually passing and repassing, full of men, horses, artillery, and camp equipage . . . made rather the appearance of hell than an earthly scene." Scores of the bedraggled troops filed past Peale. "A man staggered out of line and came toward me. He had lost all his clothes. He was in an old, dirty blanket jacket. His beard long and his face full of sores . . . had so disfigured him that he was not known to me at first sight. Only when he spoke did I recognize my brother James."

Ensign James Peale was one of the approximately one hundred survivors of Smallwood's Battalion.

Throughout the retreat, Washington repeatedly ordered General Charles Lee to join the forces in Pennsylvania. But Lee was moving at a snail's pace. For reasons known only to him, he stopped at a tavern in Basking Ridge, New Jersey, with a small guard. In the morning, still smarting from the decision to make Washington commander in chief, Lee sat down to write a letter to General Horatio Gates. "Entre nous, a certain great man is damnable deficient," he complained. "He has thrown me into a situation where I have my choice of difficulties: if I stay in this province, I risk myself and army; and if I do not stay, the province is lost forever. . . . In short, unless something which I do not expect turns up, we are lost."

Something unexpected did turn up—a group of British cavalry that included the fiery redhead Cornet Banastre Tarleton. The son of a merchant and slave trader, Tarleton squandered most of his inheritance on wine, women, and gambling, saving just enough to purchase his cavalry commission. His ruthless Light Dragoons became one of the most feared units of the war, and they faced off against the Marylanders on several occasions. On this day, they quickly surrounded the inn and killed or drove off the guards posted outside. Tarleton recalled, "I ordered my men to fire into the house through every window and door, and cut up as many as they could."

Begging for mercy, the female tavern owner ran to the door and shouted that Lee was inside. In response Tarleton promised to begin burning the building down unless Lee gave himself up.

After only a few moments, Lee himself came to the door, still in his dressing gown, and placed himself at Tarleton's mercy, saying that "he trusted he would be treated as a gentleman."

With no intention of trapping Washington on the banks of the Delaware, Cornwallis continued his leisurely pace across New Jersey. He left New Brunswick on December 7 and arrived in Princeton that afternoon, one hour after the American rear guard led by Stirling vacated the village. The British paused there that night, ransacking the college library.

Meanwhile, Washington had been rounding up as many boats as possible and bringing them to the Pennsylvania side of the river. Every boat, no matter how small, for miles up and down the river was pressed into service and kept out of the hands of the British. At the same time, the Pennsylvania navy piloted nine galleys up the Delaware to help patrol the river and prevent the British from crossing. In addition, Washington strategically placed his artillery to defend the key crossing points.

On December 8, the Redcoats and Hessians entered Trenton, and Howe and Cornwallis approached the river with some aides. According to a Hessian officer on the scene, no fewer than thirty-seven American guns opened fire. Despite the artillery, Howe refused to leave, displaying "the greatest coolness and calm for at least an hour." The officer added, "Wherever we turned the cannon balls hit the ground, and I can hardly understand, even now, why all five of us were not killed."

Once again, the Americans had escaped. One of the Hessian battle captains opined, "It became clearly evident that the march took place so slowly for no other reason than to permit Washington to cross the Delaware safely and peacefully." Historian Charles Stedman agreed, writing, "General Howe appeared to have calculated with the greatest accuracy the exact time necessary for the enemy to make his escape."

Safely on the other side of the Delaware, the Marylanders were assigned to guard crossing points along the river. Pennsylvanian Charles Willson Peale visited the Maryland camp and wrote that the men were "scattered through the woods in huts made of poles, straw, leaves, etc., in a dirty, ragged condition."

The British army now occupied much of New Jersey, its goal from the start. Howe wanted to push the American army out of New Jersey without sustaining many casualties and to capture its rich farms before the armies could pick them clean of livestock and forage. The British supply line stretched back more than three thousand miles to London, making it difficult to feed the men and horses. Initially, the British planned to compensate local inhabitants for the supplies they needed. However, instead of paying in hard currency, they issued IOUs that would often prove to be worthless or simply took what they needed. New Jersey was filled with Loyalists, many of them middle-class farmers with abundant fields and livestock. But instead of protecting its sympathizers in New Jersey, the Hessians ransacked the farms. "All the plantations in the vicinity were plundered, and whatever the soldiers found in the houses were declared booty." Some Loyalists and British also got in on the action. The American army wasn't innocent either, but Washington attempted to keep their marauding in check. Many of the colonists remained torn between their loyalty to the Crown and their desire for fair treatment. The plundering continued as long as the British occupied New Jersey and was a factor in swaying the allegiance of the locals.

During these dark days for America, a volunteer who carried a musket and a pen captured the mood of the country and also issued a call to arms. Radical and journalist Thomas Paine, the author of the widely read pamphlet *Common Sense*, wrote the first in a series of pamphlets called *The American Crisis* at this time. His immortal words are etched in the minds of many Americans while they are schoolchildren: "These are the times that try men's souls. The summer soldier and the sunshine Patriot will, in this crisis, shrink from the service of his country; but he, that stands it now, deserves the love and thanks of men and women." Paine ordered his pamphlet to be sold at no more than two pennies, or just the cost of printing, and it "flew like wildfire through all the towns and villages of the counties." Surprisingly for the eighteenth century, most of the American army was literate. The little book was also read aloud to small groups of privates and corporals, as well as townspeople, across the colonies. In the crisis and dark times, "people began to think anew. Thomas Paine's pamphlet caught that spirit and helped it grow. *The American Crisis* was more than an exhortation; it was a program for action. . . . Most important, he concentrated the mind of a nation on the single-most urgent task, which was to rebuild its army and to do it quickly," wrote historian David Hackett Fischer.

The pamphlet expressed the groundswell of actions that ordinary people individually and collectively took to change their circumstances.

Now encamped in Trenton with thirteen thousand men at his disposal, Howe was poised to strike Philadelphia and wipe out the Marylanders and what was left of the American army. In anticipation of a British assault on the capital, the Continental Congress fled the city. Eventually, it settled in Baltimore. However, instead of striking decisively, the British pursued a European, gentlemanly style of warfare and chose to encamp for the winter. To solidify their gains, Howe set up a series of fortified posts across New Jersey. He garrisoned British and Hessian troops in various towns, such as Perth Amboy, New Brunswick, Princeton, and Trenton. The decision proved fateful. Concentrated en masse, the British army was nearly invincible. But when it was separated and segmented in this way, any part was vulnerable to a focused American attack.

The strategic situation was also fraught with potential peril for the Patriots. A sudden cold snap could freeze the Delaware River, enabling the British to cross by foot. This fact, coupled with the unraveling of American financing behind the war effort and compounded by the enlistment problem, made the situation look grim. Washington wrote to his brother Samuel, "I think the game is pretty near up."

Yet in the midst of this despair, Washington glimpsed an opportunity. He decided on a bold gamble that might result in either a battlefied victory or the complete defeat of his army and the potential loss of the war.

CHAPTER 15

VICTORY OR DEATH—
THE GAMBLE AT TRENTON

Inside his tent on the banks of the Delaware River, General George Washington methodically wrote the same three words over and over on several small pieces of paper. He had decided on a daring plan: crossing the ice-choked Delaware River on Christmas night and mounting a surprise attack on the Hessian garrison there. Knowing that the assault could not hope to succeed if word of the plan reached the enemy, he detailed a Virginia brigade to serve as sentries around the Patriot camp. He ordered them "not to suffer any person to go in or come out—but to detain all persons who attempts either." The general himself selected the password for the night, and that was what he was writing on scraps of paper for distribution to the unit commanders. While the surgeon general of the Continental Army was visiting Washington, one of the slips happened to fall to the floor. "I was struck with the inscription on it," the physician wrote. "It was 'Victory or Death.'"

Contrary to the myth perpetuated by many children's books, the Hessians in Trenton were neither drunk nor idle. Their experienced commander, Colonel Johann Rall, the courageous hero of Chatterton's Hill and Fort Washington, kept his men in constant readiness and on patrol. A series of raids by Washington's army and the local militia in the prior days had put them on edge, and the men slept dressed and armed. Waiting for the Americans in Trenton were fifty Hessian Jaegers, twenty British Light Dragoons, and three Hessian infantry regiments led by Rall, Wilhelm von Knyphausen, and Friedrich Wilhelm von Lossberg, more than fourteen hundred men total. In addition, they had six artillery pieces. Rall realized the precarious nature of the Trenton outpost and frequently demanded reinforcements—to no avail. Unwisely, he decided not to entrench his garrison. Instead, he opted for flexibility and mobility, explaining, "I have not made any redoubts or any kind of fortifications because I have the enemy in all directions." In exasperation, he complained, "*Scheiszer bey Scheisz* [shit on shit]! Let them come. . . . We will go at them with the bayonet." British spies had warned of an impending attack on Trenton, but no one knew the exact day and time. The intelligence, combined with the raids, put Rall and his men in a perpetual state of alert and began to fray their nerves.

As the sun set on Christmas Day, Washington's army, including Mordecai Gist and the bedraggled remnants of Smallwood's Battalion, made its way toward the Delaware River. Once again, the unflappable John Glover and his Marblehead Mariners, who had orchestrated the brilliant East River crossing, led the amphibious operation to cross the river. Asked if the plan was doable, Glover confidently reassured Washington "not to be troubled about that as his boys could manage it."

Washington settled on a complicated plan to envelop Rall's garrison. Four independent columns would attack the town. He placed the Marylanders under the command of General Hugh Mercer, a Scottish army physician who had fled to Pennsylvania after the British defeated the Scottish, or Jacobite, uprising of 1745. They would be part of the main force, which would cross at McConkey's Ferry. Once ashore on the other side, the group of twenty-four hundred men would split into two columns. Farther south, two additional forces would cross the river below Trenton—one led by Colonel John Cadwalader of the Philadelphia Associators (a militia unit inspired by Ben Franklin in 1747 to defend Philadelphia) and the other by Brigadier General James Ewing, who commanded elements of the Pennsylvania militia. Although Washington did not know it, neither Cadwalader's nor Ewing's force would cross that night because the icy conditions made the river impassable.

The water had begun to freeze near the shore, and even sections in the center of the river were covered in ice. Yet the men followed their general without complaint. Henry Wells recalled that after the men reached the assembly point and before they boarded the boats, "our

General halted his Army and raising on his stirrups made us such an animating speech that we forgot the cold, the hunger and the toil under which we were ready to sink and each man seemed only to be anxious for the onset. The Snow & Slush ice covered the firm ice in the River, yet when our brave commander gave the word and turned his horse's head across the stream, no one complained or held back, but all plunged in emulous who should next touch the Jersey shore after our beloved."

By 11:00 p.m., a harsh storm pelted the men with snow, sleet, and biting wind as they crossed the Delaware in flat-bottomed ferry boats and Durham boats. The Durham boats were between forty and sixty feet long and unique to the region. They usually transported freight. Each of the boats could hold forty men—if they stood shoulder to shoulder as the small craft made the treacherous eight-hundred-foot journey. For the troops, many of whom could not swim, falling over the side would likely have meant death in the icy currents. At least one man did fall: Delaware Colonel John Haslet plunged into the icy river and was quickly fished out. Despite the risk of frostbite and hypothermia, the indefatigable Haslet and the Continental Army pressed on.

General Adam Stephen's Virginia Continentals were the first to make the dangerous crossing that night, followed immediately by General Mercer's brigade, which included most of the Marylanders. Marylander John Boudy, who was with Jack Steward and Gist, made the crossing "but thinly clad, and entirely barefoot all the while." He added, "The winter was now sitting in, and extremely cold." The Delaware Regiment and the rest of Lord Stirling's men came in the next group. Washington reported that the men experienced the "greatest fatigue" when "breaking a passage" through the solid ice. Much of the hard work was handled by the Marbleheaders, who manned the long poles used to propel the boats across the ice-packed river.

Miraculously, the Americans didn't lose a single soldier in the crossing. However, the storm had put them far behind their original timetable. Washington had planned to have everyone over the river by midnight, but his army wasn't reassembled on the far side of the Delaware until nearly four in the morning. Not knowing that the other troops hadn't made it across, Washington ordered his exhausted, shivering men to proceed at once on the nine-mile march to Trenton.

Through snow and sleet driven nearly horizontal by the punishing winds, the men and horses trudged through drifts and slid across the icy roads. As always, the Americans were poorly equipped, and few had clothing equal to the conditions. "Many of our poor soldiers are quite barefoot and ill clad," wrote one of the officers on the scene. "Their route was easily traced, as there was a little snow on the ground, which was tinged here and there with blood from the feet of the men who wore broken shoes." Another officer remarked that the men bore the hardship well. "It will be a terrible night for the soldiers who have no shoes," he noted. "Some of them have tied old rags around their feet; others are barefoot, but I have not heard a man complain." Boudy recalled, "Our Army was destitute of shoes and clothing — . . . It was snowing at this time and the night was unusually stormy. Several of our men froze to death." Not wanting to lose any more of his troops, Washington shouted encouragement to the men: "Soldiers, keep by your officers. For God's sake, keep by your officers!"

As they neared their goal, word came from General John Sullivan that the ammunition had become so wet from the storm that the Patriot guns would no longer fire. But by that time, Washington had little choice but to continue with the battle plan. "Tell General Sullivan to use the bayonet. I am resolved to take Trenton," he told the messenger. Throughout the night, the commander in chief remained determined and resolute; adversity brought forth his best qualities. "Press on! Press on, boys!" he shouted as he rode up and down the line encouraging his men.

Washington's plan called for the Americans to split apart and attack both sides of the city simultaneously. For once, things went according to plan. The Americans arrived on the outskirts of Trenton just before eight o'clock in the morning.

Thanks to the reduced visibility from the storm, they approached within two hundred yards before the sentries sounded the cry, "*Der Feind! Heraus! Heraus!*" (The enemy! Turn out! Turn out!)

Mercer's brigade, including the Marylanders, was moving down a hill along the west side of the town, entering the village through the house lots and alleys. Shots were fired, and the Americans charged, some yelling, "These are the times that try men's souls!" as their battle cry. The Hessians, disorganized, fell back from the onslaught that seemed to come from all around them. Small groups clashed throughout the city in the house-to-house fighting. Soon smoke from the cannons and muskets filled the streets and, combined with the continuing storm, added to the murk and confusion.

Very quickly after entering Trenton, Washington's army captured several Hessian artillery pieces. In the thick of the fighting, Rall ordered his men to retake the guns because their loss was considered a dishonor to the regiment.

With drums beating, Rall shouted, "All who are my grenadiers forward!"

By this time, the Americans had infiltrated the entire city, and marksmen took up secure positions in houses and behind fences from which they could pick off the enemy fighters. The American artillery was commanded by Bostonion Colonel Henry Knox, the corpulent former bookseller who had miraculously transported sixty tons of heavy artillery some three hundred miles from Fort Ticonderoga to Dorchester Heights overlooking Boston Harbor in the winter of 1775–1776. Knox concentrated his artillery and continued to pummel the oncoming Hessians. The mercenaries reclaimed their guns—but at great cost. Knox later wrote, "Here succeeded a scene of war, of which I had often conceived but never saw before." Another participant captured the macabre melee: "My blood chill'd to see such horror and distress, blood mingling together, the dying groans, and 'Garments' rolled in 'blood' the sight was too much to bear."

After his guns had been recaptured, Rall tried to rally his men. Acting on faulty intelligence, he assumed that his only escape route, a bridge across Assunpink Creek (a tributary of the Delaware River that flows through Trenton), had been blocked by the Americans. Elements of Rall's, Knyphausen's, and Lossberg's regiments attempted to make a stand, but Rall eventually ordered them to retreat through an orchard to the southeast. At that moment, two bullets struck the Hessian commander in the side. Mortally wounded, he "reeled in the saddle." His men attempted to evade the Patriot forces, but the Americans pursued them. On horseback, Washington led the attack, urging the Marylanders and his other troops forward, shouting, "March on, my brave fellows, after me!"

Hit from three sides, the Hessians, now leaderless, lowered their guns and their flags around 9:00 a.m. in a sign of surrender. Washington had just ordered another cannonade when the officer in charge of the field pieces informed him, "Sir, they have struck."

"Struck!" replied the general.

"Yes, their colours are down."

"So they are," he replied, spurring his horse forward to meet with the enemy. The two groups greeted each other and "after satisfying their curiosity a little, they began to converse familiarly in broken English and German."

Washington made sure the Hessian prisoners were treated humanely, stating, "[Prisoners] should have no reason to complain of our copying the brutal example of the British army in their treatment of of our unfortunate brethen." Through Washington's leadership, the Continental strategy and tactics generally aligned with principles of the Revolution. This democratic army of amateur citizen-soldiers followed a code of conduct that John Adams called a "policy of humanity." This policy governed everything from the way soldiers were supposed to treat civilians to giving quarter to enemy combatants who had surrendered—treating them with respect and not just executing them, as the British often did. To a large degree, these policies were followed in the northern department of the war (but not always in the South). Often these practices were diametrically opposed to the Crown's way of treating prisoners.

Word of the surrender soon spread to the men still positioned throughout Trenton. A huge shout shook the town as the triumphant Americans threw their hats into the air and cheered the victory. In short order, they found forty hogsheads of rum and cracked them open. One observer noted the drunken rabble: "With [Hessian] brass caps on it was laughable to see how our soldiers would strut, fellows with their elbows out, and some without a collar to their half-a-shirt, no shoes, etc." By the time Washington found out about the alcohol and ordered the casks destroyed, "the soldiers drank too freely to admit of Discipline or Defense." Washington had intended to continue his push forward and to attack Princeton and New Brunswick after Trenton, but these plans for a further offensive had be be scotched owing to the state of the army. The victorious yet drunken men rowed back across the icy Delaware. The blizzard continued to rage, and this crossing was even more treacherous than the first, costing the lives of three men. It was noon the next day before all the Americans got back to their camp, some having been awake and fighting against the elements and the enemy for fifty hours. The next morning more than a thousand reported unfit for duty.

The Americans had killed 22 Hessians, severely wounded 84, and taken 896 prisoner, while suffering few losses of their own. Equally important, they had captured "as many muskets, bayonets, cartouche boxes and swords," as well as the artillery, swelling their supplies. Washington ordered his men to treat the prisoners honorably. He even spoke to the Hessian commander, who lay dying in a nearby church. By Washington's report to Congress, the American casualties were "very trifling indeed, only two officers and one or two privates wounded." In actuality, more than that had perished from the harsh weather conditions.

The Americans had won a great victory, but they had little time for rest. Washington hadn't intended to fight again in Trenton so soon, but actions taken by John Cadwalader and his Philadelphia Associators forced his hand. Unable to make it across the river on Christmas night, the Associators and other units tried again on December 27 and successfully made it into Trenton. The Americans now had about three thousand men stranded on the New Jersey side of the river, where they were vulnerable to the approaching enemy. Making matters worse, the enlistment period for the bulk of Washington's men expired on New Year's Day. Washington mustered his oratorical prowess and appealed to the men to continue fighting. "My brave fellows, you have done all I asked you to do and more than could be reasonably expected," he began.

"But your country is at stake, your wives, your houses, and all that you hold dear. . . . If you will consent to stay one month longer, you will render that service to the cause of liberty and to your country which you probably can never do under any other circumstances."

Moved by the general's words and his "most affectionate manner," the majority of the men decided to continue fighting. Washington once again ordered them to load up on boats and cross the icy Delaware River on December 30.

On January 2, 1777, the American army girded for Cornwallis's counterattack, which it knew was on the way. The army camped on the banks of Assunpink Creek. Cornwallis was on his way to the city, leading a force of fifty-five hundred men with twenty-eight cannons; he left another force of about fifteen hundred men to guard Princeton. A bridge crossing the Assunpink was all that divided the two armies.

"Defend the bridge to the last extremity!" Washington ordered his officers in the hearing of the British nearby.

Colonel Charles Scott of the Virginia Regiment uttered a "tremendous oath," before agreeing, "To the last man, excellency."

On the other side of the creek, a small force of riflemen led by Pennsylvania's Colonel Edward Hand was skirmishing with the enemy, buying time for the rest of the Americans to dig in at the creek and cover the key crossing points, including an all-important narrow wooden bridge, one of only a few nearby ways to get over the creek. Behind them, the nearly frozen Delaware River cut off any hope of retreat—and they had no boats for crossing even if it had been possible. In front of them, a much larger force of British and Hessian troops was inexorably approaching. Spoiling for revenge, the Hessian officers ordered their men to take no prisoners. The Patriots' only hope was to hold their ground.

Though it had won a great victory in the very same place just a few days before, the American army now found itself in the grip of despair. "This was the most awful crisis," wrote one of the officers present, "no possible chance of crossing the River; ice as large as houses floating

down, and no retreat to the mountains, the British between us and them."
Another echoed the same sentiment, recalling, "If there ever was a crisis
in the affairs of the Revolution, this was the moment; thirty minutes
would have sufficed to bring the two armies into contact, and thirty
more would have decided the combat; and, covered with woe, Columbia
might have wept the loss of her beloved chief and most valorous sons."

As the Virginians, Marylanders, and other men in Washington's
army waited on the banks of the creek, the situation looked dire. With
the British bearing down on them, Washington's army was in grave
danger of being destroyed. One private summed up the situation: "On
one hour, yes, on forty minutes, commencing at the moment when the
British troops first saw the bridge and creek before them, depended
the all-important, the all-absorbing question whether we should be
independent States, or conquered rebels!"

On the bank of the Assunpink, Washington carefully arranged
his troops, including the Marylanders, so that his most trusted veteran
Continentals, with the invaluable artillery pieces, guarded the likeli-
est crossing places. He interspersed the less reliable militia among the
regulars to bolster their courage and prevent gaps in the line. At the
key bridge were Scott and his Virginians and the Marylanders led by
Gist and Stone. Before the battle began, Scott gave his men a few last
words of instruction:

> Well, boys, you know the old boss has put us here to defend this
> bridge; and by God it must be done, let what will come. Now
> I want to tell you one thing. You're all in the habit of shooting
> too high. You waste your powder and lead, and I have cursed
> you about it a hundred times. Now I tell you what it is, nothing
> must be wasted, every crack must count. For that reason boys,
> whenever you see them fellows first begin to put their feet upon
> this bridge do you shin 'em. Take care now and fire low. Bring
> down your pieces, fire at their legs, one man Wounded in the
> leg is better [than] a dead one for it takes two more to carry him
> off and there is three gone. Leg them dam 'em I say leg them.

Washington himself also stayed near the bridge. The men in Colonel Hand's harassing force could no longer hold their position and were falling back slowly to join the rest of the defense. As Hand's men approached the bridge, pursued by the enemy, the general's calm composure gave hope to the soldiers. One private later wrote,

> The noble horse of Gen. Washington stood with his breast pressed close against the end of the west rail of the bridge, and the firm, composed, and majestic countenance of the General inspired confidence and assurance in a moment so important and critical. In this passage across the bridge it was my fortune to be next to the west rail, and arriving at the end of the bridge rail, I was pressed against the shoulder of the general's horse and in contact with the general's boot. The horse stood as firm as the rider, and seemed to understand that he was not to quit his post and station.

The British attack on the bridge followed swiftly on the heels of Hand's arrival. Cannons fired a punishing volley from both sides of the creek. Cornwallis sent probing attacks up and down the line of the Assunpink, but the bulk of his assault fell on the bridge.

An officer in the Delaware Regiment recalled one of the assaults on the bridge: "The enemy came down in a very heavy column to force the bridge. The fire was very heavy, and the light troops were ordered to fly to the support of that important post, and as we drew near, I stepped out to the front to order the men to close up; at this time Martinas Sipple was about ten steps behind the man in front of him; I at once drew my sword and threatened to cut his head off if he did not keep close, he then sprang forward and I returned to the front. The enemy were soon defeated."[19]

The Hessian grenadiers made the first attempt to cross, making it about halfway before the American fire stopped them. One militiaman reported, "They continued to advance, though their speed was diminished. And as the column reached the bridge it moved slower and

19. After the battle, the Delaware officer did a roll call. Sipple had deserted and fled.

slower until the head of it was gradually pressed nearly over, when our fire became so destructive that they broke their ranks and fled." The Hessians lost thirty-one men in the attack, and twenty-nine surrendered.

But the defeat didn't stop the British forces, who again tried to mount an assault on the bridge. "Officers reformed the ranks and again they rushed the bridge, and again was the shower of bullets pushed upon them with redoubled fury," wrote one of the Americans. "This time the column broke before it reached the center of the bridge." Elated in their triumph, the Americans raised a cheer at the site of the British retreat. "It was then that our army raised a shout," recalled one man, "and such a shout I never since heard; by what signal or word of command, I know not. The line was more than a mile in length, and from the nature of the ground the extremes were not in sight of each other, yet they shouted as one man." Still the Redcoats were undaunted. "They came on a third time," noted one American artillerist. "We loaded with canister shot and let them come nearer. We fired all together again, and such destruction it made, you cannot conceive." With that failed attempt, the British withdrew for the night.

The three attempted assaults had left the bridge stained with gore. "The bridge looked red as blood, with their killed and wounded and their red coats," wrote one American. Another added, "Their dead bodies lay thicker and closer together for a space than I ever beheld sheaves of wheat lying in a field which the reapers had just passed."

While they held the bridge and the rest of the field, Washington's men were in grave danger of being encircled and destroyed by Cornwallis's larger force and the British force about to march down from Princeton. But with nightfall approaching, Cornwallis confidently postponed the main attack and opted to wait till the morning. According to legend, he rebuked one of his officers who insisted that unless they attacked immediately Washington would be gone in the morning. Cornwallis retorted, "We've got the old fox safe now. We'll go over and bag him in the morning."

1777

CHAPTER 16

PRINCETON

In the dead of night on January 2–3, 1777, just hours after the Americans' second victory in Trenton, a hushed order spread through the camp. As quietly as possible, the men passed the message from one to another: they were moving out once again.

Although the ragtag Patriot force had once again beaten back the British on the banks of Assunpink Creek, remaining near the Delaware would have been perilous. They found themselves backed up against the river with a much larger British force just a few miles away. Washington called together a council of generals to discuss the situation. If they attempted to retreat across the Delaware with the few boats they had available, it was likely that the British would attack before they made it to the other side, potentially destroying or capturing a large portion of the American army. If they stayed where they were, it was almost certain Cornwallis would attack again in the morning. Although they had a good position defending the bridge over Assunpink Creek, the enemy might use one of the fords up- or downstream and flank the Patriot army.

At some point in the debate, someone, perhaps Washington himself, suggested an audacious third plan. Instead of continuing their retreat, they would march north, moving as quietly as possible around the left flank of the British army. They could then strike at Princeton. That New Jersey town had a much smaller garrison of British troops, and with Princeton under American control, the army could move on to New Brunswick, where it could capture some much-needed supplies, including a massive war chest of seventy thousand pounds.

While this plan was appealing, it had a major flaw: a recent thaw made the muddy roads nearly impassable—especially for the artillery. But as night fell, the temperature dropped, freezing the sloppy roads solid. Washington seized the opportunity and roused the men to action. Because the desperate gamble could work only if the enemy remained completely unaware of their movements, the Americans left their camp-fires burning along the Delaware as they began the long, cold march. "Orders were given in a whisper; muskets were gingerly handled and footfalls lightly planted." They even went so far as to wrap the wheels of their cannons in pieces of cloth to prevent any noise from reaching the ears of the sleeping enemy.

Though exhausted from the battle of the day before, the Continental Army reached a creek two miles outside Princeton around daybreak; in its wake it left a bloody track of footprints on the icy ground. The frosty weather had transformed the landscape, coating trees, fences, and each blade of grass in sparkling ice. One American officer recalled, "The morning was bright, serene, and extremely cold, with an hoar frost that bespangled every object." There Washington split his force so they could surround the town from two sides, as well as hold the crossing at the creek in case Cornwallis decided to pursue them. The small group of Marylanders and the Delaware Regiment (at this time reduced to a handful of men commanded by John Haslet) were attached to Hugh Mercer's brigade, who, along with John Cadwalader's Philadelphia Associators, were in the vanguard of the attack.

Three British regiments and several troops of dragoons were stationed in Princeton. Most were under orders to march to Trenton in the morning to link up with Cornwallis's troops. Having set out from Princeton before dawn, Lieutenant Colonel Charles Mawhood, a veteran of the Seven Years' War, was shocked by the sight of the Marylanders and the rest of Mercer's men as they emerged from the woods. "We drew up on a woody eminence and looked at them for a considerable time," recalled one of the British soldiers. "Colonel Mawhood had two choices, either to retire back to Princeton, where . . . we might have defended the works about it, or push on to Maidenhead where the 2d Brigade lay." Mawhood with his intial force of approximately seven hundred men chose to fight. He ordered his troops to drop packs, fix bayonets, and form a line of attack.

Mercer and his men, including the "remaining fragment" of Smallwood's Maryland Battalion led by Mordecai Gist, "rushed without reconnoitering into a thick planted orchard and were soon surprised to find themselves in the presence of a well [drawn] up line of infantry, with flanking [picket] and two pieces of cannon."

In the ensuing battle, the British executed a vicious bayonet charge. As they surged forward, they shot Mercer's horse out from under him and bore down on the Americans. Terrified, Mercer's men fled, despite their officers' cries. Now fighting on foot and forsaken by his troops, Mercer drew his sword, but took seven bayonet wounds to the belly and fell. Similarly, Delaware's intrepid John Haslet, who survived nearly drowning in the icy Delaware during the crossing on December 25, attempted to rally the men until a bullet to the brain killed him instantly.

Now virtually leaderless, the remaining men of the brigade ran for their lives, pursued by the British. At that moment, Cadwalader's much larger force of twelve hundred Philadelphia Associators arrived on the scene and joined the battle. Cadwalader rode to the front of the line and ordered his men to begin firing when the Redcoats were "too far off." As they came forward, the Patriots reloaded but soon found themselves within range of the British, whom Mawhood had positioned "so that every man could load and fire incessantly." Inspired by the Associators, some of Mercer's men, including the Marylanders, halted their flight and resumed fighting. The few remaining officers—Gist and Steward among them—held the men together at this crucial moment. However, Cadwalader's front lines quickly broke and "threw the whole in confusion." The entire Patriot force was soon retreating in disorder.

Seeing the flight of his men, General Washington galloped toward the front lines. Each time he passed a group of men, he encouraged them to find their courage and stand their ground, waving his hat to them before moving on. He "expostulated to no purpose," initially failing to rally the men. Eventually, he rode to within thirty paces of the British lines, presenting a tempting target to the Redcoats. A tremendous volley rang out as enemy marksmen aimed for the general. One of Washington's aides covered his own eyes with his hat rather than watch, but when the smoke cleared, Washington still remained on his horse, calling on his men to join him in facing the enemy.

"Parade with us, my brave fellows!" he shouted. "There is but a handful of the enemy and we will have them directly."

His leadership inspired one officer to write home, "O my Susan! It was a glorious day, and I would not have been absent from it for all the money I ever expect to be worth." The letter continued, "I shall never forget what I felt at Princeton on his account, when I saw him brave all the dangers of the field and his important life hanging as it were by a single hair with a thousand deaths flying around him. Believe me, I thought not of myself."

The Patriot forces and Marylanders rallied, and with Washington now directing the battle, soon overcame hundreds of British soldiers, many of whom threw down their arms and ran. Seeing the Redcoats in flight, Cadwalader shouted, "They fly, the day is our own." Soldiers up and down the line soon echoed his cry and enthusiastically surged toward Princeton in pursuit of the enemy. Fighting alongside Cadwalader's ranks were about 130 Continental Marines, the predecessors of the U.S. Marine Corps. Like the Marylanders, the unit could trace its origins to a tavern. The men had only recently left their ships. After conducting a raid at Nassau in the Bahamas several months earlier, they were fighting in their first major land engagement, the start of an epic 240-year legacy.

Washington, urging his men to pursue the British, repeated the humilating battle cry that British troops had shouted when his men fled the field at Harlem Heights:

"It is a fine fox chase, my boys!"

As they progressed, a dismal sight met their eyes. The landscape, which had been glistening white with frost earlier, was now covered in gore. Because the ground was frozen, "all the blood which was shed remained on the surface."

Alerted by the sound of cannon and gunfire, the British troops remaining in Princeton had positioned themselves for battle in Nassau Hall in today's Princeton University. The Americans brought a cannon to bear and fired into the building, forcing the bulk of the Redcoats to surrender. Washington's desperate plan to escape Cornwallis's force at Trenton and seize Princeton had succeeded.

Although the Americans were as poorly equipped as ever, the victory raised the spirits of the men and the entire country. One Maryland private recalled the two victories at Trenton and Princeton: "Gen'l Washington . . . gained a victory, taking a great many prisoners, with the loss of but few men. My regiment and company was in this engagement, and done their duty. I remember, that this active and unexpected movement of Washington's raised the spirits of the soldiers and people."

For the British, the twin debacles at Trenton and Princeton ended the notion that the rebellion was nearly broken. Word of the victories spread worldwide and ended the assumption that amateur citizen-soldiers who just months earlier had been farmers, bakers, and blacksmiths could not defeat the most highly trained and experienced regulars in the world. Even Prussian King Frederick the Great sent his praise: "The achievements of Washington and his little band of compatriots between the 25th of December and the 4th of January, were the most brilliant of any record in the annals of military achievements."

Trenton and Princeton had changed the tempo of the war; now Washington seized the initiative. Instead of pursuing a defeated American army, the Redcoats heard rumors of new threats: an army of American troops (the corps formerly led by the recently captured Charles Lee) advanced from Morristown, and New Jersey militiamen harassed supply lines among the few fortified garrisons. Misinformation planted by Washington led the British to believe the American armies were bigger than their own. William Howe's plan of offering pardons to Americans to attempt to win over the population of New Jersey was also severely damaged. Hessian Jaeger Captain Johann Ewald summed up the mood:

"Thus had times changed! The Americans had constantly run before us. Four weeks ago we expected to end the war. . . . Now we had to render Washington the honor of thinking about our defense."

After holding the field at Princeton, Washington pursued small elements of Mawhood's routed troops about three miles toward New Brunswick. As he did many times during the Revolution, Washington called a council of war from the back of his saddle. He decided to give up the chase and also the prize: a war chest valued at seventy thousand pounds sterling, supplies, arms, and money stored in New Brunswick. Washington lamented that if he had only six or eight hundred more fresh troops they might have been able to take the town. But the men were exhausted.

Rather than push his luck and risk an engagement where he was outnumbered, Washington decided to continue on to the safety of the hills and broken wooded ground around Morristown, New Jersey, a small village containing "a church, a tavern, and about fifty houses of the better sort." It was a prudent decision: Cornwallis had surmised that Washington was headed toward New Brunswick and was preparing to fight. Morristown, by contrast, represented a temporary haven. It rested on a high plateau with steep slopes on two sides. A natural fortress, its only approach was from the east through small, treacherous passages. Notably, the earlier harvest from the rich farmland that surrounded the area could sustain the army. In addition, the town's location would allow the Continentals to move quickly if Howe advanced toward Philadelphia or the Hudson River.

Not long after reaching Morristown, Gist and the surviving Marylanders made the long trek home toward Baltimore. The officers needed to recruit men to refill the ranks. But first they had to crush an insurrection. Loyalists, including wealthy plantation owner James Chalmers, had revolted, creating an insurgency within the state. One of the Maryland delegates to the Continental Congress reported, "The Tories in Sussex [Delaware], Somerset and Worcester Counties, have been assembling for some days. They have 250 men collected at Parker's Mill, about nine miles from Salisbury, and 'tis reported they have three field pieces, which they received from the *Roebuck* [a British warship], with some men, with intention to seize the Magazine and destroy the property of the Whiggs."

Gist, William Smallwood, and a force of more than two thousand men marched to the Eastern Shore to quash the rebellion and imprison its leaders. The Maryland Assembly claimed that the region had set up "an armed force, and by erecting the standard of the king of Great Britain have invited the . . . enemy into their country." The size of the Patriot force dispersed the Loyalists, forcing them underground. Through the authority of the Council of Safety, Smallwood offered the local inhabitants (except the fourteen leaders of the revolt) a full pardon if they gave up their arms and took an oath of loyalty. Only 287 people accepted the deal. Smallwood's force captured a few of the leaders, but most, including Chalmers, got away and bided their time, waiting for the arrival of the British.

Eventually, some of these Loyalists formed the 1st Loyalist Maryland Regiment, a smaller mirror image of Smallwood's Battalion, which at its peak included 336 men. During this phase of the Revolution, they were busy aiding the British in whatever ways they could. For example, Chalmers served as a spy for the Crown and participated in "their ravaging and plundering Parties." He helped them secure horses and cows by seizing them from nearby farms. Another wealthy Eastern Shore landowner not only sold his own cattle to the British; he offered to let his neighbors keep their livestock in his fields "for protection" and then sold the lot of them to the British and "got for them a very large bagg of Gold." And Maryland Loyalist Robert Alexander, a former member of the Continental Congress, went so far as to offer his home to General Howe for use as a headquarters.

Another notable Maryland Loyalist, Dr. Alexander Middleton, served the British cause in a much more humanitarian way. He made plans to join the British army, but changed his mind when he saw the conditions in the Philadelphia prisons where the Americans were holding Tories. He spent some time treating the prisoners before a mob of angry

Patriots ran him out of town. Eventually, he met up with Chalmers, who made him a captain in the Maryland Loyalsts. Later, injuries forced him to resign his commission and flee to England with his family.

Men weren't the only ones who joined the Loyalist cause; Elizabeth Woodward claimed to have fought alongside her husband. She said that she was wounded in the leg while helping to fire shipboard cannon in a naval battle. Her fairly unbelievable tales also include helping her husband and twenty-two other men escape imprisonment. When the Patriots caught up with her, one shot her in the left arm, "but, undismayed, [she] took a loaded firelock and shot the rebel." By her account, she then stole the dead American's horse and sold it to one of the British officers. The Loyalist fervor in sections of Maryland continued to ferment for some time to come, but in the short term, Smallwood and Gist had helped tamp down the Loyalists' activities.

In December 1776 Congress had called on each of the colonies to raise regiments based on its population. Maryland was required to furnish seven regiments, and Smallwood and Gist set about recruiting the necessary men. Congress promised those who signed up twenty dollars in cash, plus "a suit of clothes yearly" and one hundred acres of land to be awarded when the war was over. Despite the bounty, officers found it difficult to sign up recruits. Initially, six Maryland regiments took the field, with the veterans from the cadets and Smallwood's Battalion forming the cadre of each regiment. Gist led the 2nd Regiment; Smallwood retained command of the 1st. Although he had been in British captivity in New York City, Otho Holland Williams also led one of the regiments—at least on paper. John Eager Howard accepted a commission as a major in the 4th Maryland Regiment, where he was joined by newly minted Lieutenant William Beatty, and captains Jack Steward, Nathaniel Ramsay, and Samuel Smith.

The new recruits from all socioeconomic classes and from towns and villages throughout the entire state of Maryland marched up toward Morristown, where scores of new American regiments from around the colonies coalesced. With so many men gathered in one place, the situation was ripe for an epidemic, and smallpox ran rampant among the troops. A devastating disease, smallpox began much like flu, with fever, nausea, and achiness. Symptoms got much worse within a week or two; the patient developed pus-filled sores and began bleeding from all orifices. In many cases, victims suffered from dehydration and secondary infections, and around a third of smallpox patients died of the disease.

At the time of the Revolution, no one had yet developed an effective vaccine for smallpox, so the only option for prevention was inoculation. This process involved incising a sore and then inserting the contaminated knife below the skin on a healthy individual. Sometimes this resulted in a form of smallpox that was less likely to kill the victim, but often the person being inoculated got just as sick as people who caught the disease in other ways. Nevertheless, Washington ordered inoculation for the Continentals and the civilians in the area, which helped prevent the epidemic from becoming worse. One of those inoculated was Marylander John Boudy, who recalled that "the whole Army, or nearly all, was inoculated for the smallpox."

It's likely that Dr. Richard Pindell, a Maryland surgeon who joined the 1st Maryland Regiment on January 1, 1777, performed some of those inoculations. The intrepid doctor, who enjoyed a good party and dabbled in gambling, went on to accompany the regiment throughout the rest of the war, recording many of its actions in his letters. The physician wrote that he joined the troops because he was "fired by the love of liberty." That passionate patriotism led Pindell not only to treat the injured and dying but also to rally the troops and even take command, leading men into the fight for brief periods of time in several key battles. Through the course of his six years of service, he "repeatedly rejected the most flattering and Lucrative offers, during the War, if I would leave the Service and enter into Private Practice, by which I could without Doubt have made an Ample Fortune." Instead, he remained fully dedicated to the cause, even though he frequently received only half the pay he had been promised and the army confiscated his two horses. Later in life, he suffered financial hardships until the Maryland legislature approved a petition that gave him "full pay of Col. of Dragoons for life."

Doctor Pindell was hampered in his care of the sick by a lack of knowledge. Most physicians at the time had little formal instruction and trained as apprentices under other physicians. Unaware of germs, bacteria, and viruses, surgeons operated with unsanitary instruments, leading to gangrene and other frequently fatal diseases. If a wound from a musket ball was not too deep, the surgeon attempted to remove the ball and then stop the bleeding, leaving the wound open to drain. If the ball had fractured bones in multiple places, the only real option for treatment was amputation. To perform surgery, available instruments comprised a wicked-looking assortment of probes and ball extractors. Sharp lancets and saws were used to hack off limbs, while tourniquets, when they were available, choked off the bleeding artery. The surgery involved plying the patient with a strong dose of liquor (when it was available) and then offering him a stick to bite. Orderlies held him down while the surgeon sawed through the bone as quickly as possible. Next he tied off the arteries and sewed the wound shut over the remaining stump. Unsurprisingly, only a little over a third of the men who had an amputation survived.

State-of-the-art medicine for the period included a witch's brew of herbal remedies such as Peruvian or Jesuit's bark, potassium nitrate, camphor, laudanum (opium), jalap, castor oil, Epsom salts, ipecac, red mercuric oxide, and sulfur in hog's lard. The colonies imported most of their drugs from England. As the Revolution progressed and embargoes worked their effect, medicines and other supplies became quite scarce, making it more difficult to treat patients. Field hospitals degenerated into scenes of horror. One of the American generals wrote, "Our hospital, or rather house of carnage, beggars all description, and shocks humanity to visit. The cause is obvious; no medicine or regimen on the ground suitable for the sick; no beds or straw to lie on; no covering to keep them warm, other than their own wretched clothing." Doctor Pindell and the other surgeons worked tirelessly to save as many men as possible, but in such conditions, it's little wonder that disease and infection killed many of them.

* * *

By the middle of May, forty-three new Continental regiments had gathered near Morristown; on paper, Washington had around eighty-seven hundred troops, arranged in five divisions consisting of two brigades each. William Smallwood, now promoted to brigadier general, took command of the 1st brigade, which included the 1st, 3rd, 5th, and 7th Maryland Regiments. The 2nd Brigade consisted of the 2nd Maryland Regiment, under Gist, along with the 4th and 6th Maryland, as well as their brother regiment under arms, the Delaware Blues. Like the Marylanders, the Delaware Regiment had a core of solid veteran officers, including Robert Kirkwood and Enoch Anderson. Born in 1746, Kirkwood graduated from Newark Academy (now the University of Delaware) and worked on his family's farm before becoming a first lieutenant in the Delaware Regiment at the age of twenty-nine. Later promoted to captain and brevetted to major at the end of the war, "Captain Bob" led the Delaware Blues and fought alongside the Marylanders in some of the war's most important battles. A man of steel, Kirkwood marched thousands of miles and took part in thirty-three battles for his country. His unit was often used for reconnaissance missions or as an indefatigable rear guard.

The 2nd Brigade was commanded by a Frenchman, Brigadier General Philippe-Hubert, Preudhomme de Borre, a taciturn officer with an abusive leadership style. Born in 1717, Chevalier de Borre had served with the cavalry in the French royal army fighting in Bavaria, Bohemia, and Flanders during the Seven Years' War. After being slashed by a sword four times in the head and once on the wrist, he never regained full use of his hand. In February 1777 he arrived in America with a ship packed with gunpowder, weapons, and fabric for uniforms. The Marylanders snapped up the supplies, but passed on de Borre's abrasive leadership and had little respect for him. The Marylanders, now welded together through several very difficult campaigns, had formed close bonds, and did not appreciate being led by someone other than their own, especially a foreigner.

Throughout the winter of 1777 and into the spring, even before most of the reinforcements arrived, Washington's army and the militia conducted what Europeans called a *petite guerre* (little war) against Howe's men, who occupied outposts throughout New Jersey. They fought numerous skirmishes and small battles all across the state. On several occasions, Washington called on the Marylanders for particularly dangerous operations. The Americans hit the routes of British foraging parties and even engaged in battles that involved several hundred troops. Twenty-one-year-old Marylander Private Joseph Nourse described one such attack on Quibbletown (now Piscataway, New Jersey). He wrote, "The whole of us, about 400, marched into the Enemies lines and attacked . . . but we were so disadvantageously posted that we could not stand our ground. We fought for ½ an Hour and then retreated." Although the Americans didn't accomplish any larger strategic goals with this attack and others like it, they were slowly grinding away at the British army while avoiding heavy casualties on their own side.

Washington was waging a war of attrition. The Americans inflicted casualties, interrupted the British source of supply in New Jersey, and forced the enemy to lose ground there. Howe's plans to reclaim New Jersey were unraveling because he could not protect the Loyalist population or those who were undecided between the Crown and the Patriot cause. He simply didn't have enough troops to maintain a series of outposts that allowed him to remain in control. This problem continued to plague the British throughout the war. Utilizing the strength and flexibility of the British navy, the Redcoats could occupy just about any American city on the East Coast, but seizing and holding ground that they had captured remained elusive because there weren't enough troops or Loyalists trained, equipped, and trusted by the British.

The *petite guerre* and the losses at Trenton took a toll on the British army throughout 1777. Thousands of British and Hessian troops were killed, wounded, or captured, or died of disease. The army's numbers fell from thirty-one thousand in August 1776 to a little over fourteen thousand by 1777. Howe was never able to replace the casualties, even with additional reinforcements coming from England. This drove and hampered British strategy throughout the war.

With the onset of summer, the skirmishing continued as Washington began moving his troops from place to place in an effort to counter anticipated moves by Howe. The two armies danced around each other, often retracing their steps in an effort to gain a superior position from which to fight. William Beatty recalled some of the remarkable sights he witnessed while marching through New Jersey, such as the Great Falls of the Passaic River located in Paterson and a deformed child "whose head was larger than half a Bushell [four gallons]" but whose body was about the size of a seven-year-old's, with useless hands and feet and "skin as white as milk." The child had an encyclopedic knowledge of the Bible and "could quote almost any scriptural quotations asked of him."

Washington frequently assigned the Marylanders to serve as a blocking force while the rest of the army withdrew from a particular location. An elite unit, the Immortals[20] were to occupy an exposed position and engage the advancing British forces, hoping to slow the enemy's march long enough for the rest of the Patriots to reposition themselves.

Because they often occupied forward positions away from the bulk of the army, a lack of uniforms and supplies continued to plague the Marylanders. One officer reported that the soldiers were "mostly Barefoot though they have Done more marching than any other division in the Army." He worried that the problems would "multiply Desertions among us Daily," but this fear never became a reality: only a handful of the men deserted. And when they did desert, General de Borre dealt ruthlessly and swiftly with them and anyone who assisted them. Deserters who were recaptured were typically shot, and Loyalists found aiding them were given a quick court-martial and executed. Lieutenant Beatty remembered, "The court passed sentence of Death on him which Genl DeBore ordered to be put in Execution by Hanging the poor fellow [Tory] on the limb of a sycamore close on the side of the road."

After Washington's retreat from New York, Howe had left some troops behind on Staten Island. These men regularly foraged for food in the

---

20. The term "Immortals" is used to describe the men of the regiment, an elite unit that made many sacrifices throughout the war, not just the men who who sacrified themselves at Brooklyn.

surrounding area, capturing livestock and causing consternation among the local residents. Based on some faulty intelligence, Washington believed that this force consisted primarily of inexperienced American Loyalists. A strike at Staten Island seemed to offer an easy opportunity for victory as well as the chance to earn the goodwill of the inhabitants by slowing and perhaps halting the British raids along the Jersey coast. The island also held a fort that controlled the Narrows, the southern waterway into New York Harbor and toward Manhattan.

Washington ordered Brigadier General John Sullivan to lead a raid on Staten Island in late August 1777. The New Hampshire native and former foreclosure lawyer had been captured in the Battle of Brooklyn but returned to duty in September 1776 in a prisoner exchange, and he played important roles in the battles at Trenton and Princeton. For the assault on Staten Island, his force would include "only those who were most active & best able to Endure a march" from the brigades led by Smallwood and de Borre. About a thousand men in all, his force consisted primarily of Marylanders and men from the Delaware Regiment. To throw off any enemy spies, Sullivan headed south out of camp before turning east. Smallwood's men led the way as the men crossed by boat to Staten Island.

The raid began as planned. Caught unaware, the surprised Loyalist troops took off running, allowing the raiders who intended to stop plundering to become plunderers themselves. They rounded up a number of prisoners and collected a considerable amount of arms and equipment. Before too long, Smallwood's men ran into a surprise of their own—the British 52nd Regiment of Foot. Equally stunned by the appearance of the Patriots, the British troops fled back into their fortifications on the island. Enoch Anderson from the Delaware Regiment recalled, "My line of march brought me near to a large brick house. Here I found some of the British. But a few only of them turned out—got round a haystack—fired one gun and then run."

The sight of enemy regulars running for cover convinced Sullivan's force that they had won the day. Abandoning any pretense of discipline, they ransacked the homes of the officers, grabbing whatever food and supplies they could find. One officer from de Borre's brigade later testified, "Our people [were] in a scattered, disorderly and dangerous situation; I made use of every effort to curb the licentiousness and stop the greedy grasp of our Soldiers, but found they had such a propensity to plunder that my exertions were ineffectual." Anderson said that, finding a house full of "lawful plunder," he sent his men inside to grab what they could while he remained outside and beat a drum to let them know when to come out.

While the Patriots were running amok and picking the area clean, the disciplined British regulars and their Loyalist allies regrouped behind their fortified walls. The Redcoats suddenly advanced on Sullivan's troops, who were no longer in any shape to engage with the enemy. Now it was the Patriots' turn to run. Anderson reported that Colonel Stone galloped past him, yelling, "Run, run, it's no disgrace!" The Marylanders bolted toward the crossing point, hoping to escape from the island back to New Jersey. "Here was great confusion," noted Anderson, "no commander—soldiers running at their will, and not boats enough; there being some unhappy error about the boats. I saw a boat coming over and kept my eye on it, and as it came nearer the shore, I came nearer to it. I kept my men in a solid body and I and my company entered the boat. We got safe over." The rear guard of approximately 150 men, led by Jack Steward, made several bold stands to allow the bulk of the Marylanders to escape. All Smallwood's men and most of de Borre's made it across. Captain William Wilmot, a wealthy Baltimore native and friend of Steward, described the action in a letter: "They came down on us with about 1000 of their heroes, and attacked us with about 500 of their new troops and Hessians expecting I believe that they should not receive one fire from us but to their great surprise they received many as we had to spare and had we had as many more they should have been welcome to them, they made two or three attempts to rush on us, but we kept up such a blaze on them, that they were repulsed every time."

Although he himself never surrendered, Wilmot saw Steward taken captive.

"What grieved me after seeing that it was not the lot of many of us to fall and our ammunition being expended, that such brave men were obliged to surrender themselves Prisoners to a dastardly, new band of murderers, natives of the land [Loyalists], when our ammunition was all spent Major [Steward] took a white handkerchief and stuck it on the point of his Sword, and then or'd the men to retreat whilst he went over to their ground, and surrendered, for he had never gave them an inch before he found that he had nothing left to keep them off with the enemy advancing fast to surround us," he wrote. "Even in that situation [I] found my self determined never to surrender and could do nothing else was obliged to run and strive to conceal myself which I did effectually, in a barn on some hay that was up in the roof of the Barn."

Terrified, the boatmen refused to go back to rescue what remained of the rear guard. Some of the troops were able to hide in the woods or swim to safety, but most of those who remained were taken prisoner.

The disastrous raid on Staten Island failed to meet any of its objectives. While only ten Americans were killed, the Patriots suffered the loss of numerous enlisted men and officers who were taken prisoner, including Steward. In all, the British captured three majors, one captain, three lieutenants, two ensigns, one surgeon, and 127 privates.

Following the ill-fated assault, Gist and Smallwood returned to Maryland for more recruiting—specifically militia. Sullivan and the rest of the officers and men rejoined Washington's army. The commander in chief wasn't sure about Howe's next move, but evidence pointed toward an attack on Philadelphia. Meanwhile, Steward and more than one hundred Marylanders were about to experience the horrors of internment aboard British barges and ships in New York Harbor.

CHAPTER 17

BRANDYWINE

In a well-ordered column, twelve men abreast, the Marylanders marched to the beat of the fife and drum. Each man wore a green sprig in his hat, an optimistic symbol of victory. Washington also thought the greenery would spruce up the appearance of the army, which lacked common uniforms. The commander in chief gave the army strict orders to stick with the rhythm: "[No] dancing along or totally disregarding the music, as too often has been the case." He added a further warning that anyone who stepped away from the carefully choreographed parade would receive thirty-nine lashes.

The Marylanders and the rest of George Washington's army once again were marching through the streets of Philadelphia on August 24, 1777, as part of a public relations maneuver. Despite being the young nation's capital, Philadelphia was known as a haven for Tories. Washington, who had the instincts of a showman, hoped to sway their allegiance with a show of strength and élan. He led the parade himself on his impressive great white charger. Then came the army. In all, it took more than two hours for the American troops to cross through the center of town. Bolstered by the shouts and claps of Philadelphians who crowded into windows and onto rooftops to watch, the men marched "with a lively smart step."

For months during the summer of 1777, Washington had been trying to divine William Howe's next move. The British general tried various feints and deceptions to draw the American army into battle. Although Washington dispersed smaller forces to guard against various possibilities, he refused to be drawn into an ill-conceived battle that was not on his terms. "We have such contradictory accounts from different quarters that I find it impossible to form any satisfactory judgment of the real motions and intentions of the enemy," he noted.

However, Washington was fairly certain that Howe planned to attack Philadelphia, eventually. As a countermeasure, the American general lined up defenses along the Delaware, the most convenient means of approach to the city. His guess seemed confirmed when the British troops loaded up on 228 ships in New York. Howe once again used naval superiority to his advantage to confuse and deceive Washington. Rather than turn into the Delaware as expected, he kept going. The American commander in chief was flummoxed. "I confess the conduct of the enemy is distressing beyond measure and past our comprehension," he admitted. Howe kept sailing for several more weeks, entering Chesapeake Bay and making his way back north before landing in an area known as Head of Elk, about fifty miles southwest of Philadelphia. He "must mean to reach Philadelphia by that route, though to be sure it is a very strange one," decided Washington.

With Howe's unconventional plan revealed, Washington prepared to meet the enemy. After the parade through Philadelphia, the Marylanders and the rest of the army marched to Chadd's Ford, which crossed Brandywine Creek. Filled with steep hills and ravines, Chadd's Ford offered a natural defensive position. The Americans held the high ground and most, but not all, of the important fords. They structured the defenses to force the British to battle their way across the Brandywine, funneling the Redcoats through the fords, which would act as kill zones. Preparing his troops for battle, Washington told them that if they defeated the Crown at Brandywine, "they are utterly undone—the war is at an end. Now then is the time for our most strenuous exertions." To fortify them for the coming fight Washington ordered the casks opened and gave each of the men an extra gill, about five fluid ounces, of rum. Liquor was an important component of eighteenth-century military life. The liquid courage could lift sagging morale. Washington also added another element of effective persuasion to minimize cowardice: any man fleeing the battlefield would be shot by American riflemen.

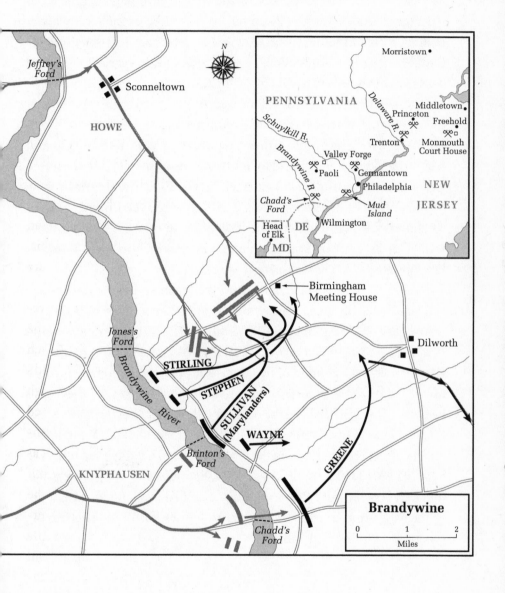

Jeffrey's Ford

Sconneltown

HOWE

N

Morristown

PENNSYLVANIA

Delaware R.

Middletown

Princeton

Freehold

Schuylkill R.

Trenton

Monmouth
Court House

Brandywine R.

Valley Forge

Paoli

Germantown

NEW

Chadd's
Ford

Mud
Island

Philadelphia

JERSEY

Head
of Elk

DE

Wilmington

MD

Birmingham
Meeting House

Jones's
Ford

Dilworth

Brandywine   River

STIRLING

STEPHEN

SULLIVAN
(Marylanders)

WAYNE

GREENE

Brinton's
Ford

KNYPHAUSEN

Chadd's
Ford

Brandywine

0   1   2

Miles

Washington spread his forces along a five-mile stretch of the creek to guard eight fords. The bulk of the Maryland forces fought under Brigadier General John Sullivan on the right side of the battle line at Brinton's Ford. The Delaware Regiment, detached from Smallwood's Battalion, guarded Jones's Ford. The men quickly prepared for a major battle, felling trees and hastily throwing up fortifications. Maryland officer William Beatty recalled, "As the Approach of the Enemy gave reason to Apprehend an Attack, the whole of the troops were ordered to throw up Breast Works in front of their respective camps." But Washington had made a crucial mistake. He left two fords to the north unguarded, either because he had inadequate intelligence about the area or because he didn't believe the enemy would travel the extra ten miles upriver to reach the crossings. On September 10 Sullivan even asked about fords farther upstream, but Washington's aides assured him these wouldn't be a problem. They were wrong.

Howe's spies informed him the northerly fords remained unguarded, and he decided on a near repeat of his strategy at the Battle of Brooklyn. In the early morning hours of September 11, 1777, sixty-one-year-old Prussian Lieutenant General Wilhelm Reichsfreiherr (Baron) zu Inn und Knyphausen led a column of five thousand to six thousand men directly up the main road to meet the bulk of Washington's army and the Marylanders at Chadd's Ford and the other nearby crossings. Knyphausen, like General James Grant at Brooklyn, led the unit meant to pin Washington down and to distract him from the flanking force. That force, led by Howe and Charles, Earl Cornwallis, included a slightly larger group of sixty-five hundred Hessians and Redcoats. They marched in a long looping route to the west before cutting back across to Jeffries Ford and attacking the rebels' flank from the north.

Marsch, schräg nach rechts! (Incline to the right!)
   Marsch, schräg nach links! (Incline to the left!)
   Halt!
   Angriff! (Charge!)

A Hessian officer barked orders in guttural German.

"The balls [were] plowing up the ground. The Trees crackling over one's head. The branches riven by the artillery. The leaves falling as in autumn by the grapeshot," recalled one Hessian who was near the Brandywine at Chadd's Ford as they were trying to pin down the Americans while General Howe and Cornwallis conducted their flanking maneuver.

As the battle unfolded and Knyphausen's force surged forward, Washington decided on an audacious strategy. He would go on the offensive and attack the enemy's left and right flanks as the Prussian was striking the American center. Washington ordered Sullivan and the Marylanders, who were on the extreme left, to cross the Brandywine and attack the Hessians' right flank. Samuel Smith of the 4th Maryland recalled, "Colonel [Nathaniel] Ramsay of the Maryland Line [Mordecai Gist's 3rd Regiment], crossed the river, and skirmished with and drove the Yagars" for a time. One soldier near the fight observed that the water of the creek was "much stained with blood."

Washington led from the thick of the action with soldiers falling around him. Even as enemy fire beheaded an artilleryman next to him, the general kept cool. According to legend, British Major Patrick Ferguson had Washington in his sights at one point, but didn't fire because his chivalrous nature prevented him from killing a man whose back was turned. Minutes after the encounter, an American rifleman wounded the honorable British officer.

Veiled in thick fog off to the west, Cornwallis's flanking force was closing in on its goal. A few sharp-eyed scouts reported the movement, and Washington had Sullivan send some units to investigate. However, the reports he received back were of a very contradictory nature, leaving the general unaware of the approaching menace. The troops led by Howe and Cornwallis had reached Jeffries Ford. Shortly after noon, they plunged into the waist-high water, marveling that the way had been left wide open though it could have been held with a hundred men. Soon they passed through the woods near the creek and swarmed into the nearby farmland. A young Quaker who lived in the area saw their arrival and wrote, "In a few minutes, the fields were literally covered with them. . . . Their arms and bayonets being raised shone as bright as silver, there being a clear sky and the day exceedingly warm." He noted Cornwallis's presence and panache: "He was on horseback, appeared tall and sat very erect. His rich scarlet clothing loaded with gold lace, epaulets, &c., occasioned him to make a brilliant and martial appearance." On the other hand, the Quaker wasn't impressed by Howe's appearance. "The general was a large, portly man, of coarse features. He appeared to have lost his teeth, as his mouth had fallen in."

By 1:15 p.m. Washington was realizing his fatal mistake and began pulling men away from the creek to meet the new British threat on his northern flank. At 2:30 Washington ordered Sullivan to stop his attack on Knyphausen and instead move north to face off against Cornwallis and Howe. The Marylanders, unfamiliar with the area, stumbled and ran through ravines, marshland, thickets, and fields trying to meet up with their countrymen and find the enemy. Sullivan recalled, "I neither knew where the enemy were, nor what route the other two divisions were to take, and of course could not determine where I should make a junction with them."

Eventually, Sullivan made it to the battlefield, but confusion again reigned as he attempted to position his troops. He first placed the Marylanders and others under his charge in front of a large wooded hill but soon noticed other American forces lined up behind him. Concerned, he "rode up to Consult the other General officers." Brigadier General Philippe-Hubert Preudhomme de Borre was temporarily in command of the Marylanders. With Smallwood and Gist both detached from the Maryland Line and organizing the militia, the Marylanders were left without two key leaders they had followed in the past. From the motions of the British force in front of them, the American officers could tell that Howe and Cornwallis planned a flanking action. To counter the threat, they needed to reposition Sullivan's men closer to the unit commanded by Lord Stirling, and they sent orders to that effect to de Borre. Strangely, de Borre promptly led the men in virtual circles.

Consequently, Sullivan and the Marylanders were still racing to get into position when the British attacked shortly after 4:00 p.m. Stone explained, "By the time we reached the ground they had to cannonade the ground allotted to us, which was very bad, and the enemy within musket shot of it before we were ordered to form the line of battle."

Immediately before the battle began, the Marquis de Lafayette came riding out of the woods to join the Maryland Line. Bestowed with the tongue-twisting name Marie-Joseph-Paul-Yves-Roch-Gilbert du Motier de Lafayette, the marquis was a wealthy French aristocrat who had dreamed since childhood of becoming a famous military commander. He volunteered to fight in America as a nineteen-year-old and had turned twenty just days before the battle. Washington had immediately taken a liking to the young man, making him an important liaison with France.

After their humiliating defeat in the Seven Years' War, the French burned for vengeance. Encouraging England's colonies to revolt against their mother country seemed like a good payback for the humiliating terms of the 1763 Treaty of Paris. Even prior to the Revolution, the French sent secret emissaries to survey the American landscape and sound out interest in independence. America also sent representatives to France to make the case for French involvement. They played up the mutual interest of both countries: here was an opportunity to settle old scores and redress the balance of power that had shifted in Britian's favor. American ambassdors, led by Benjamin Franklin, pushed for loans and the ability to purchase gunpowder and other supplies on credit.

While the French recognized that the Revolution was in their interest, they weren't convinced it was time for a formal treaty. They had concerns about the cost of the war and whether the Americans could win. In addition, King Louis XVI had to be careful about supporting the idea of rebellion against royal authority. Meanwhile, foreign fighters from France started offering their services to America. It actually became quite fashionable in Paris to seek a commission in the American army and the chance to win battlefield laurels. For most of the foreign fighters, the rose-colored view of war changed dramatically when they started fighting alongside the threadbare American army. But some French officers, like Lafayette, willingly risked life and fortune for the cause.

Shortly after Lafayette arrived at the Marylanders' position, "Lord Cornwallis's men suddenly emerged from the woods in very good order," noted Lafayette. They brought two twelve-pounders with them, and a bloody fight ensued. Lafayette was shot in the leg but still courageously attempted to rally the men. Also grazed by a bullet was John Boudy, who was fighting alongside Jack Steward. Boudy recalled that he "received a wound from a musket ball in his knee, which disqualified him from duty in the line till the Winter following."

One of the Patriot soldiers added, "The firing, while the action lasted, was the warmest, I believe, that has been in America since the war began." Henry Wells of the Delaware Regiment recalled, "During the fight, the wind favored the enemy and drove the Smoke directly in our faces which was one great cause of our discomfiture."

Less than an hour after it began, the battle turned into a rout as the Americans, led by de Borre, fled the battlefield. Lafayette explained, "The American fire was murderous, but both their right and left wings collapsed." Confusion grew, and some of the Marylanders accidentally began to fire upon their own men. It was the last time de Borre commanded American troops.

With men running for their lives, one Marylander proved unflappable. The most unlikely man trying to reestablish the American line that day went into action: Dr. Richard Pindell, their militant surgeon. It was the doctor's first pitched battle. "I rallied a considerable number of the retreating troops," he said, "formed them in Order, after they were driven from the field and keep command of them until an [officer] fell in and took command." He later explained, "I have done some military achievements that would have done Honour to those whose duty it was meet in Battle of the Bristled Bayonetts."

Back at Chadd's Ford, where Knyphausen's men briefly halted, bizarrely, "a total silence ensued." The general had ordered his men to stand down to await the outcome of the fight to the north. As time ticked away, "We began to be uneasy about General Howe for a great force of the rebels marched from the hills and woods before us toward him," wrote one of the British artillerymen. Those fears did not last long; within hours they began to see Sullivan's men "running in multitudes out of the woods. We now began again with all our artillery to play on the flying scoundrels; the fire was returned by them from all their batteries."

The fleeing Marylanders scrambled across the rocky terrain pursued by the British and the Hessians. The Redcoats brought their cannon with them and continued firing at the Americans. "We renew our fire from the artillery to scour the woods," reported one of the British soldiers. "They fly from all quarters." Colonel John Hoskins Stone of the 1st Maryland, a former lawyer and later a politician, said that he expected higher losses than actually occurred. "Never was a more constant and heavy fire while it lasted, and I was much amazed when I knew the numbers that were killed and wounded."

For many of the Maryland men, the rout at the Brandywine was seared in their memories. For African American Private Thomas Carney, a cordial twenty-three-year-old freeman likely from Queen Annes County, this was his first taste of battle. He was "well over six feet tall and noted for his great strength." This was also the first battle for Private James Gooding, who had recently rejoined the army after spending a good deal of time recovering from his smallpox inoculation. Another newcomer, Michael Ellis, reached the battle by a much more unusual path. During the early part of the war, he had been a sailor on a merchant ship captured by the British. He remained a prisoner on a frigate, but "when said frigate entered the Delaware River, [Ellis] made his escape and joined the Maryland Continental troops then at Brandywine." Marylander Jacob Allen also remembered the fight because he was "wounded in the hand and in the face," but recovered. Henry Wells of the Delaware Regiment was also injured. He later recalled, "We were led from the field into a Swamp, where the efforts of the horse were rendered ineffectual, from the nature of the ground. In the action

I received a flesh wound in the right haunch, the scar occasioned by which is plainly visible at this day."

Eventually, many Maryland officers and NCOs organized their men to make a stand and allow the remainder of the army to escape. Stone recalled, "We retreated about a quarter of a mile and rallied all the men we could, when we were reinforced by Greene's and Nash's corps, who had not till that time got up. Greene had his men posted on a good piece of ground, which they maintained for some time, and I dare say did great execution." Nearby, as the 4th Maryland, led by Smith, passed through a nearby cornfield, they "discovered a flanking party of the enemy." They exchanged fire, and one of the Marylanders "was shot in the heel." The men panicked again. "Some of the men left [Smith]; and [I] retired, almost alone to the top of a high hill, on which [I] halted, and collected nearly one thousand men; formed them into Companies; and remained until near sunset."

The late attempts to reengage in battle couldn't change the fact that the fight had already been lost. Smith decided to abandon his hilltop post and make his way to Chester, Pennsylvania, where he hoped to meet up with the rest of the army. Unfortunately, he didn't know the way. He found a local farmer, one of the many Quakers in the area, and asked him to guide the Americans to the right road. As a devout pacifist, the man initially refused. Smith pointed a pistol at the farmer and "assured him he was a dead man if he did not get his horse instantly and show the way to Chester."

"What a dreadful man thou art!" exclaimed the Quaker, who then saddled his horse and got ready to direct Smith to the road.

Before leaving, Smith offered a warning: "Now, I have not entire confidence in your fidelity, but I tell you explicitly, that if you do not conduct me clear of the enemy, the moment I discover your treachery, I will blow your brains out."

"Why, thou are the most desperate man I ever did see!" exclaimed the man, now truly frightened. He offered the Maryland officer his word and led him to the correct road. At that point, Smith thanked him for his help.

"I want no thanks, thee forced me!" replied the Quaker.

CHAPTER 18

WAYNE'S AFFAIR

A young girl's desperate shriek pierced the air. There in the house was her father's blue and buff uniform—the same uniform he had worn when leaving for war—but now it was soaked in blood.

"Oh my Daddy's killed, my dear Daddy's killed!" she wailed, tears streaming from her eyes.

The plaintive sound drew the attention of the house's other occupant. To his daughter's great relief, Lieutenant Colonel Persifor Frazer of the 5th Pennsylvania came rushing into the room. He wasn't dead, just one of the hundreds wounded at the Brandywine. With his home nearby, Frazer had taken the opportunity to stop in, pick up a few things, and see his family. However, the visit was short, and Frazer soon rejoined the rest of the Continental soldiers seeking to escape from General William Howe.

Another wounded American soldier wasn't so lucky and faced the stark reality of British imprisonment or service to the Crown. Michael Dougherty of the Delaware Regiment claimed, "I fought with desperation till our ammunition was expended and my comrades being compelled to retire, I was left helpless and wounded on the ground, and fell into the hands of the enemy." Because "confinement was never agreeable to me," Dougherty agreed to join the British cause, accepting the "King's bounty" and joining the 17th Regiment. This was not the last time Dougherty was captured, or the last time he turned his coat.

The battle was bloody with hundreds of dead and wounded— on both sides. Howe ordered his men to bury the dead and tend to the wounded, slowing their movement. As the bulk of Washington's army retreated east of the Brandywine toward Chester, Pennsylvania, Howe once again failed to vigorously pursue his defeated foe. Passing through Chester, Washington veered slightly north, then marched through Darby, Pennsylvania. His force then crossed a pontoon bridge that spanned the Schuylkill at Middle Ferry, near today's Market Street Bridge in Philadelphia.

Howe and Cornwallis pursued, and skirmishing broke out near White Horse Tavern on the outskirts of the city. Far from defeated, many of the Americans welcomed the chance to engage the enemy. Captain Bob Kirkwood of the Delaware Line recalled, "Every one Rejoiced, hoping to see [the British] in a few hours."

As the British approached the Americans, Hessian Colonel Count Karl von Donop decided to lead his Jaegers into battle personally. British light infantry followed the Jaegers. Surprised by the attack, Washington positioned his army poorly. Making matters worse, only a few roads provided an escape route.

Washington's adjutant general gloomily informed the commander in chief of the impending peril. "The order of battle is not complete. If we are to fight the enemy on this ground the troops ought to be immediately arranged." It looked as though the British army would have the opportunity to strike a crushing blow unless the Americans could gain the high ground on the far side of the valley. Hurriedly, the Americans rushed toward the more favorable ground, but the Hessians had already arrived and begun fighting the Patriots.

Fortunately for the Americans, weather once again intervened at the most opportune moment. "An extraordinary thunderstorm occurred, combined with the heaviest downpour in the world," wrote Hessian Captain Johann Ewald. Despite the torrential rain, the British forces weren't ready to give up their attack plans: the Jaegers and light infantry charged with sword and bayonet. Ewald and his men became enmeshed in hand-to-hand combat. The rain dampened the powder of both armies, caused their weapons to misfire, and forced an end to the melee. Marylander John Eager Howard, recently having rejoined the army after attending his father's funeral in Baltimore, recalled, "The inferiority of [our]

arms . . . never brought [us] into imminent peril as on this occasion."
But the weather once again gave the American army an opportunity to
retreat. William Beatty remembered, "Hard rain that took us to the Waist
& under the arms." Because the weather played the deciding factor in
the conflict, it became known as the Battle of the Clouds.

After putting enough distance between his army and the British,
Washington ordered General Anthony Wayne's two brigades, a comple-
ment of Continental dragoons, and four light cannon to link up with
Maryland militiamen led by Mordecai Gist and William Smallwood
traveling from Baltimore and get behind Howe's rear and harass him.
The general emphasized that "cutting off the Enemy's Baggage would
be of great matter." Washington ended his orders with a dire warning:
"Take care of Ambuscades."

Born to a family of Irish immigrants in Pennsylvania, Anthony
Wayne trained as a surveyor and worked in that capacity for Benjamin
Franklin, in addition to assisting with his father's tannery business. When
war broke out, the charismatic thirty-year-old recruited a militia regi-
ment, of which he became colonel. Commonly known as Mad Anthony,
Wayne earned a reputation for a hot temper. In the midst of battle, he
had an almost berserk manner and had been heard to call out to his men,
"I believe a sanguine god is rather thirsty for human gore!"

The British knew about Wayne's plans and that his encampment
was somewhere within a several-mile radius of Paoli Tavern, located
near present-day Malvern, Pennsylvania. They dispatched seventeen
hundred light infantry and a few dragoons to "surprise these gentlemen."
In a daring nighttime assault, the British ordered their men to unload
their weapons and march in silence—they would use only bayonet and
sword in the attack to preserve the element of surprise. As they began
the march, an electric mood enveloped the Redcoats: "the lads were all
in high spirits in hopes of a frolic."

Light rain fell while they marched toward Paoli. After a little more
than an hour, they came upon Wayne's camp around midnight. An outpost on the outskirts of Wayne's camp notified the general that the
British were bearing down on his sleeping men. Mounting his horse, he

rode through the camp and shouted, "Turn out my Boys, the Lads are coming, we gave them a push with the Bayonet through the Smoak."

As the British descended on the American bivouac, Wayne's British counterpart, General Charles Grey, shouted at his men, "Dash, Light Infantry!"

"HUZZAH!"

The guttural war cry echoed through the woods as hundreds of Grey's men hacked, slashed, and bayoneted their way into the American camp. Panic ensued.

Around the same time, Smallwood and Gist with a force of twenty-one hundred Maryland militia their way and three cannon were slowly working their way toward Wayne. The Redcoats had managed to load their muskets, and as shots rang out, the militia grew skittish. "One of our Men about the center of the Main Body was shot Dead by some of their Stragglers, which threw great part of our Line in great Consternation, many flung down their Guns & Ran off, & have not been heard of since," Smallwood wrote. The cavalry with him drew friendly fire: "The Rear taking us for British light Horse fired a Volley on us within 15 or 20 Foot, wounded several, and killed a light Horseman alongside of me in waiting for Orders." Smallwood stopped the friendly fire by dismounting and sardonically yelling out to the militia, "I should have been glad to have seen them as ready to fire on the Enemy as they now seemed on their friends."

Gist attempted to rally the poorly trained men but nearly died in the melee as he covered the rear of their retreat. He wrote to Captain John Smith of his own regiment, "My Horse received two Balls through his Neck but fortunately only fell on his Knees and Hams otherwise I must have received the Bayonet or fallen into their Hands." Smith, a fellow Baltimorean, was a close friend of Gist's and rose through the ranks of his unit. This incident did nothing to halt the terrified, fleeing Marylanders. Out of the original twenty-one hundred militiamen, more than a thousand deserted.

Wayne's men fought more bravely, but the attack diminished their ranks. The British sneak attack left nearly three hundred of them killed, wounded, or captured. On the enemy's side, only three were killed and eight wounded. The "Paoli Massacre" shocked Washington, who now maneuvered to avoid being trapped against the Schuylkill and Howe's army. But instead of attempting battle, the British general marched ten miles up the river and slipped into Philadelphia unopposed, capturing the American capital on September 26, 1777. In the eighteenth century, capturing the enemy's capital normally meant the end of the conflict. A year earlier, the loss of Philadelphia might have been a knockout blow to the rebellion, but with Washington's army intact and word of a British advance from Canada stalled near Saratoga, New York, Congress fled the city rather than surrender. The Marylanders and the rest of the Patriot forces steeled themselves for a counterattack.

On the morning of October 4, 1777, the Marylanders once again found themselves at the vortex of a major battle. Heavy fog and black smoke from burning fields of buckwheat created a hellish scene as the Marylanders assaulted the far right wing of the British army camped in Germantown. Visibility was measured in yards. One American reflected, "The fire of cannon and musketry, and other combustibles . . . made such a midnight darkness . . . that [a] great part of the time there was no discovering friend from foe."

The stage had been set a little over a week before when the British quickly seized control of Philadelphia without an urban battle, because the Americans had evacuated the capital. Washington wasn't willing to let the prize go without a fight. He began laying plans for an elaborate assault on Germantown, a small village about five miles north of the city that later became part of Philadelphia proper. General Howe had stationed about nine thousand of his men in the town. Washington, who had eight thousand Continentals and three thousand militiamen at his disposal, believed that he had the resources necessary to defeat Howe, the first step in his strategy for reclaiming the City of Brotherly Love.

Once again demonstrating a proclivity for complex battle strategies, Washington created a highly detailed plan that called for marching his troops in the dead of night from their camp at Methacton Hill. If all went as scheduled, separate pincer movements would converge on the British camp in the morning. Each unit would be required to travel between fourteen and twenty-five miles without alerting the enemy in order to reach its assigned location. Washington would lead a column of three thousand men, including most of the Marylanders, up the center on the main road from the west. Greene, General Adam Stephen, and Brigadier General Alexander McDougall would take the left flank with another six thousand men. The Maryland militiamen, led by Small-wood and Gist, would hold the extreme left pincer and march down an ancient Indian trail known as Old York Road. Each of the groups needed to be in position by 5:00 a.m. in order to begin the coordinated attack—something even the most drilled and experienced army would find difficult to execute. For Washington's group of militia and slightly more experienced Continentals, it was ambitious in the extreme.

From the very beginning, poor visibility hampered the assault. A thick fog rolled in, which, combined with the complicated system of roads and the moonless night, made it very difficult for the command-ers to navigate. The bulk of the Marylanders were unfortunately still under the command of John Sullivan, and the triple debacles at Long Island, Staten Island, and Brandywine—thanks to his inept leadership—remained seared in many of the men's minds. The Marylanders under Sullivan got lost, as did the other column of Continentals. Despite being behind schedule, Sullivan called a halt so that his men could rest and drink a bit of rum to fortify themselves for battle. They were soon back on their feet and in the correct position for the attack, but they had missed the 5:00 a.m. start time. The sun was already up, although it was difficult to see through the fog, which only grew thicker with the break of day.

Having received a warning about the American attack, the Brit-ish had posted pickets to keep watch for the approaching enemy. They soon spotted the advancing column, and the artillery opened fire, kill-ing several Patriots. With the fight already begun, Sullivan hurriedly ordered his men to assume battle positions. Almost immediately, he commanded the Marylanders to advance across an open field to meet an "encampment of the British Light Infantry in an orchard, where we found them formed to receive us," recalled Howard. He added, "A close and sharp action commenced." For around fifteen minutes the two groups shot at each other before "the British broke and retreated." In the thick of the action, William Beatty "survived the hottest of the fire" and miraculously was just grazed from "Dead ball on my thigh . . . but did no harm only made the [thigh] a little red." Also at the battle was Sergeant Gassaway Watkins, recently returned to the thick of the action after a long recovery from an illness that began in November 1776.

The commanding officer of the 4th Maryland Regiment, Colonel Josias Hall, who was on foot, sent John Eager Howard to order the Marylanders to withdraw. However, when Howard saw the situation for himself and found them "engaged from behind houses with some of the enemy," he reported back to Hall that he "judged it not proper to call them off, as it would expose our flank." Incensed, Hall demanded that Howard give him his horse, and he set off to deliver the orders himself. In his anger, the colonel failed to watch where his horse was going. It soon ran "him under a cider-press, and he was so hurt that he was taken from the field." Command of the regiment fell on the shoulders of the twenty-eight-year-old Howard. Sprinting through withering gunfire from the top windows of Cliveden, the house where the British officers had been staying, Howard led his men deeper into the British lines.[21]

Meanwhile, other American troops pushed through the morning mist and fog and soon clashed with British Colonel Sir Thomas Musgrave's 40th Regiment of Foot, which had been deployed to cover the Redcoat retreat. Hearing a rumor that the Americans were giving no quarter, Musgrave ordered his men to barricade themselves behind

---

21. Ironically, the very house that would bring death to many Patriots during the battle was the home of Howard's future bride, the beautiful Peggy Chew. Howard fell in love with Miss Chew after the war. Cliveden also hosted the young newlyweds' May 1787 dinner reception, attended by many dignitaries including George Washington. Gorgeous, charming, and animated, Mrs. Howard wielded significant sway over her husband, fondly calling him "Lord and Slave" and "good squire."

the heavy wooden doors of Cliveden. The home, which was owned by Loyalist Chief Justice Benjamin Chew, had sturdy walls made of quarried schist, which provided some protection from musket fire and artillery. As the Redcoats streamed into the house, "the rebels pressed so close upon their heels, that they must inevitably have entered the house at the same time, if he had not faced regiment about and given them a fire, which checked them enough for him to have time to get his regiment into the house and shut the door." Barring the mansion's doors, British troops turned the structure into an impenetrable fortress.

Firing from every window, the British showered a fusillade of musket balls on the Continentals attempting to storm the house. Bayonets ripped into those who broke through windows and doors. The ground around the Chew House became littered with American bodies. One participant later testified that he "was wounded at Germantown through the body, the ball extracted from the side of the back bone." The British even shot and killed an American officer who approached the house with a white flag to demand their surrender. Commanded by Lieutenant Colonel Thomas Musgrave, the six companies of British troops in the mansion stymied the American advance in the center of the battlefield. Darting from room to room, Musgrave inspired his men, yelling, "Hurrah to the King! Hurrah to the English."

Washington summoned a conference of officers. Most favored cordoning off the house and bypassing the strongpoint. The rotund Henry Knox, the Patriots' artillery commander, reminded the group of the military axiom about never leaving a fortified castle in the rear of an advancing army. Washington sided with Knox and pulled away three regiments from their successful advance on the British lines. Under Knox's direction, cannon pelted the house at point-blank range. After blasting Cliveden's doors, groups of Americans assaulted the house. "The Bravest [Americans] got to Doors & Windows . . . yet Col. Musgrave defended himself with so much Resolution & animated his People with so much Gallantry that they again fasten'd the Doors & from the

Windows kept up so well a directed fire that finally the Rebels were repuls'd with great Slaughter."

One Hessian described the carnage: "Seventy-five dead Americans, some of whom lay stretched in the doorways, under the tables and chairs, and under the windows . . . the rooms of the house were riddled by cannonballs, and looked like a slaughter house because of the blood spattered around."

The thirty minutes that were wasted attacking the Chew House gave Howe's men precious time to regroup.

Meanwhile, Greene's divisions thrust toward Germantown. One of the units, led by Scottish-born Virginia General Adam Stephen, blundered slightly off course, perhaps drawn by the sound of gunfire at the Chew House or perhaps misled by the general, who was later convicted by a court-martial of being drunk during the battle. In the fog, Stephen's men mistook some of the soldiers from Washington's column for the enemy and began firing. Not only did the friendly fire take many Patriot lives; it caused one American division to withdraw; leaving other parts of Washington's column vulnerable to attack. As men began to run out of ammunitions, panic set in, and the overly complicated battle plan fell apart.

On the extreme left flank of the battlefield about a mile from the Chew House, Gist and Smallwood's Maryland militiamen faced off with the elite of the British army: the Loyalist Queen's Rangers and the light infantry and grenadiers of the Guards Regiment.[22] As with the other columns, poor weather hampered the militiamen's progress. "We drove the enemy, when we first made the attack, but by the thickness of the fog, the enemy got in our rear," explained one of the men. "Therefore, [we] had to change our front, and then retreated until [reaching] a proper place." Gist added, "A thick foggy air prevaild throughout the

22. At that time in Philadelphia there were about three British and German battalions and seven Loyalist battalions.

whole of this Action, as if designd by Providence to favor the British Army which with the smoak of Gunpowder prevented our discovering the situation of their line."

Despite the poor visibility, the Marylanders at first experienced some success, driving the Redcoats and Loyalists from some of their earthen fortifications. Gist recalled, "A few Minutes after this attack began, our Division under General Smallwood Fell in with their right flank, and drove them from several redoubts." Before long, however, the militiamen's courage gave way. Seeing a group of Queen's Rangers approaching, Gist and his men mistook them for Hessian mercenaries. Alarmed, Gist ordered a small group into the cover provided by some nearby trees in order to counter the anticipated attack. Gist left to place another group on the left flank. When he returned to the woods, he "found that the whole had retreated." Even the officers were not immune to cowardice. Gist wrote that when the firing began, one of the militia colonels "was Immediately attack'd with some qualms of Sickness which obliged him to Retreat with precipitation to Maryland."

Despite the poor example, some among the militiamen fought bravely, including Captain James Cox of Baltimore.[23] On October 3, he had written to his wife to say, "We are still advancing Down toward the Enemie and Expect very soon to be foul of Each other which I hope may prove to our advantage." Unfortunately, his wife received the letter along with another, written three days later by her cousin George Welsh. "Your loving husband, and America's best friend, on the fourth instant, near Germantown, nobly defending his country's cause, having repulsed the enemy, driving them from their breastworks, received a ball through his body, by which he expired in about three quarters of an hour afterwards," wrote Welsh. General Smallwood also attested to Cox's courage, calling him a "brave and valuable officer."

23. Cox served in the Ancient and Honorable Mechanical Company of Baltimore, a militia company set up in 1763 to protect the city. The group lived on after the war, eventually claiming to be the oldest civic organization in the United States. The company named Baltimore's first sheriff and set up its first school and hospital, and many of the city's most famous citizens have been members.

But most of the poorly trained citizen-soldiers proved unreliable. Gist opined "The Weakness of the Human Heart prevaild," adding, "I suppose the Officer Commanding against us was acquainted by experience with this defect in Nature, who Immediately took the advantage of our Feelings and drove us from the Ground."

Unaware that his comrades on the other side of the battlefield were withdrawing, Greene continued the attack, reaching deep into the heart of the British camp. At that point, some of the men abandoned discipline and began plundering the enemy's stores. Their inattention left them open to counterattack, and every single man from the unit involved in the plundering was either killed or captured. With Cornwallis nearing the city, Greene began a retreat of his own.

Cornwallis pressed the rebels back and eventually linked up with the defenders at the Chew House. Colonel Musgrave and his men weren't finished yet. "Upon our troops appearing the 40th sallied out, and joined the pursuit," reported a British officer. Howard echoed the statement: "The enemy sallied out, one hundred or more and fired on our rear. Some of my men faced about and gave them a fire, which killed the officer in front and checked them."

The Americans retreated down the same winding country roads they had used for their approach the night before. William Beatty wrote, "Cornwallis Coming With a reinforcement & Some bad management on our side obliged us to retreat." Thomas Paine, fighting with Greene's army, marveled at the men's composure. He told Benjamin Franklin, "They appeared to me to be only sensible of a disappointment, not a defeat; and to be more displeased at their retreating from Germantown, than anxious to get to their rendezvous. . . . The retreat was as extraordinary. Nobody hurried themselves. Every one marched his own pace. The enemy kept a civil distance behind, sending every now and then a shot after us, and receiving the same from us."

Always leading from the front, Cornwallis urged his men to join the pursuit of the Americans, but the same weather conditions that had plagued the Patriots stymied them. One British officer recalled, "The British Grenadiers from the City of Philadelphia, who full of Ardour had run the whole way came up to join the pursuit, but the Fog which did not clear up 'till after the Enemy had begun to move off."

In all, 150 Americans died in the battle of Germantown, 520 were wounded, and 400 were captured. On the other side, the British lost seventy men, with 450 wounded and fifteen taken prisoner. "It was a bloody day," wrote Washington. "Would to heaven that I could add that it had been a more fortunate one for us." The Marylanders had also taken significant losses, including some among the officers; Colonel Stone and several other officers were wounded. The Americans lost many men and a chance to recapture a strategic city, but the fact that they nearly won a major battle resounded on the other side of the Atlantic, where the French were considering an alliance with the Patriots. An alliance with the French could prove to be decisive. Funding the Revolution was a huge challenge, and the American treasury was continually exhausted. Men weren't being paid or properly equipped with shoes, uniforms, and other basic supplies, and food was a frequent problem. Congress was looking to France for loans in hard currency to back up the paper money it was printing. Seasoned, drilled French troops would also be a welcome addition to the American forces, and the presence of French naval power could crimp the mobility, reinforcement, and supply of the British army.

It would also have an important indirect impact—turning the American Revolution into a global war that would force Britain to protect its far-flung empire, including possessions in India and the Caribbean. If that happened, the Crown would no longer be able to concentrate forces in North America and would have to disperse troops to its other outposts. Other nations would likely join the conflict, futher expanding the war. There was even a threat of invasion in England itself, which forced the country to keep a defensive force at home.

Weighing the possible risks of joining the Revolution, the French foreign minister said "nothing struck him so much" as the battle at Germantown.

CHAPTER 19

MUD ISLAND

South of Philadelphia near the present-day Philadelphia International Airport, a muddy expanse of marshland four hundred yards long and two hundred yards across at the widest point sits at the mouth of the Schuylkill where it meets the Delaware. In the 1700s, residents referred to the soggy wetlands as Mud Island. Atop the tiny island zigzagging ramparts made of cut stone and timber stretched the length of three football fields, amid fieldworks bristling with Patriot artillery pieces. Known as Fort Mifflin, the fortification boasted a maze of embankments and dikes, along with hundreds of wolf holes, shallow pits filled with sharpened spikes designed to gore any assault force.

During the fall of 1777, the Patriot fort became the site of one of the Revolution's longest sieges and greatest bombardments. It was of vital strategic importance. The British fleet needed to control the fort so it could resupply Philadelphia, and this need had a direct impact on General William Howe's plans to launch offensive operations against Washington's army. Royal Navy convoys attempting to reach Philadelphia would have to pass by the fort's guns and over the chevaux-de-frise. The chevaux-de-frise were a massive group of thirty-foot boxes constructed of huge timbers, lowered into the riverbed of the Delaware, filled with twenty to forty tons of stone to keep them in place, and topped with jagged iron-pointed spikes. The boxes were chained togther into a formidable barrier that could rip out the hull of any ship trying to cross.[24]

24. Part of the chevaux-de-frise, still in fine condition, was recovered from the Delaware River in 2007.

Washington ordered his men "to defend [Fort Mifflin] to their last extremity" and placed twenty-five-year-old Lieutenant Colonel Samuel Smith in charge of the facility, telling him, "The keeping of this fort is of very great importance, and I rely on your prudence, spirit and bravery for a vigorous and persevering defense." Smith commanded a detachment of approximately two hundred Marylanders, along with several hundred men from Virginia and Rhode Island. Rounding out the mix were Continentals from the 4th Connecticut Regiment, including seventeen-year-old combat veteran Private Joseph Plumb Martin, who described the island as "nothing more than a mud flat in the Delaware, lying upon the west side of the channel. It is diked around the fort, with sluices so constructed that the fort can be laid under water at pleasure. . . . On the eastern side, next the main river, was a zigzag wall built of hewn stone." One of the Hessians who was given the task of taking the fortification wrote, "The island, because of its swampy shore was unapproachable, and with double ditch and palisades, wolf holes, and stone walls would have cost many men if it had to be taken by assault."

Ironically, the man who had designed the fort was now in charge of destroying it. Howe's chief engineer, Captain John Montresor, a veteran of the French and Indian War who spent twenty years in the British army, had overseen Fort Mifflin's construction. Construction on the fort began in 1771. Montresor's grandiose plan would have cost forty thousand pounds, an enormous sum for the day, but the colonial General Assembly had allocated only fifteen thousand pounds for the construction of the fort. Less than a year after the initial work began, the project floundered. The fort remained partially constructed until 1776, when Benjamin Franklin and the Philadelphia Committee of Public Safety restarted construction on both Fort Mifflin and Fort Mercer, which was on the eastern shore of the Delaware.

The Patriots also had an engineer on their side. Washington assigned a twenty-eight-year-old French nobleman, Major François-Louis Teissèdre de Fleury, to aid Smith. De Fleury had studied engineering and served with the French army in Corsica. The general had a high regard for de Fleury, saying, "He is a Young Man of Talents and has made this branch of military Science his particular Study. I place a confidence in him." Smith and his engineer enjoyed a "perfectly good understanding and sincere friendship. . . . No jealousy, no underhanded practices—all was frank and conducive to the public service." Others described de Fleury as an excellent soldier and leader who could bring men and nations together.

Smith didn't get along nearly as well with his counterpart in the nascent Pennsylvania navy, Commander John Hazelwood. Hazelwood commanded a flotilla of "sinister black painted" galleys and floating platforms in the Delaware, a "mosquito navy." At the time, cannons were designated by the weight of the projectiles they could shoot, so a six-pounder, for example, shot six-pound balls. Some of the heavily armed British ships carried a thirty-two-pounder at the stern, four twenty-four-pounders, eight eighteen-pounders, and a crew of fighting sailors, several of whom were said to be Tory rowers pressed into service.

Taking Fort Mifflin posed a serious challenge to the British. Since the beginning of October, Montresor had carefully flanked the fort and constructed artillery positions to bombard it, including some on nearby Carpenter's Island. Pointing out the threat the island posed if the British constructed a battery there, Hazelwood shrugged off Smith's concerns: "A mosquito couldn't live there under my guns." When that's exactly what Montresor did, an alarmed Smith asked Hazelwood, with his fleet of vessels, to intercept British reinforcements heading to the island. Hazelwood acidly responded, "A shell would sink any of my galleys." Smith fired back a biting riposte: "Yes, and falling on your head or mine, will kill; but for what else are we employed or paid."

On October 10 Smith took matters into his own hands by leading a raiding party of about sixty men in the dead of night. He and his troops rowed over from Mud Island and crept behind the British guns. Using a tree line for concealment and protection, Smith's men started firing on the unsuspecting gun crews who soon put a white handkerchief on a ramrod and surrendered. However, several British officers refused to capitulate. In response, Smith "fired two shot on them & ceased on being told they would surrender, however they refused to deliver up the piece of Artillery." Eventually, under the barrel of a gun, the officers surrendered, and Smith took them prisoner. The raiders then spiked the British artillery, rendering it inoperable.

After the raid, Smith received an unexpected visitor: Jack Steward. Smith's friend, who had been captured by the British after the abortive Staten Island raid, escaped by quietly lowering himself into a small boat and rowing to New Jersey. While Steward had been imprisoned on a British hell ship in New York Harbor, Smith attempted to send money to the man with whom he had once fought a duel: he gave twenty-five pounds to a British officer who agreed to pass it to Steward. The officer "conveyed it to a Major Stuart" but not the Steward Smith intended, or so the story goes. It is possible Steward used the money to bribe his way off the prison ship; in any case, Smith was overjoyed to see his old friend and the supplies he brought to the fort.

The British continued to flank the fort, and from other positions, they shelled Mud Island. The shelling began to take a toll. On October 20 Smith wrote to Washington, "Yesterday a red hot ball entered our Laboratory, where were several boxes of ammunition . . . which blew up the barracks. Had it not been for the activity of Capt. Wells of the 4th Virginia and Capt. Luct, in putting out the fire, would have done much more damage." The Patriots, of course, were firing their own artillery back at the enemy. British Captain Lieutenant Francis Downman noted, "The rebels opened all their batteries and blockhouses upon us; their grape shot came so thick that we could not stand to our guns."

Another British soldier recalled what was perhaps one of the luckiest shots of the Revolution. From a range of five hundred yards, "they fired a 12-pound ball directly into the barrel of our 24-pounders, without damaging our cannon because it went in so accurately."

On October 23, nearly two weeks into the siege, the British fleet moved in to attack Fort Mifflin. The HMS *Augusta*, a man-of-war that carried sixty-four guns, and the *Merlin*, a twenty-gun sloop, closed in on the American position. Despite the superior firepower of the enemy, the Patriots manned their posts, landing direct hits on both vessels before they ran aground. Most of the crew members from the *Augusta* perished; those on the *Merlin* abandoned ship before they could meet a similar fate. By midday magazines on board the *Augusta* detonated, and the tremendous explosion broke windows in nearby Philadelphia. The resolute defense of Fort Mifflin bought Washington more time, but the siege was far from over.

Although the waterborne assault had failed, the British still had plenty of land-based artillery, as well as a floating battery. Their guns were soon hurling around fifteen hundred shots per day at the fortifications, and many of these shots found their mark. The action grew bloody on both sides. "Our men were cut up like cornstalks," recalled American Private Joseph Plumb Martin. "I saw five artillerists belonging to one gun cut down by a single shot, and I saw men who were stooping to be protected by the works but not stooping low enough, split like fish to be broiled."

Peter Francisco, a six-foot-eight seventeen-year-old also known as the "Giant of the Revolution," also played a part in defending Mud Island. A sea captain abandoned Francisco, who was born in the Azores, on the docks of City Point, Virginia, when he was only five years old. Locals took in the young boy, who spoke only Portuguese. They tutored him, and he later apprenticed to become a blacksmith, a profession chosen for him because of his massive size. He joined a Virginia regiment in 1777 and fought at Germantown and Brandywine before finding himself with the Marylanders in Fort Mifflin. He fought alongside them in multiple battles throughout the war.

According to eyewitnesses, Smith remained staunch throughout the cannonades. At one point he saw an aide ducking and asked, "What are you dodging for, sir? The King of Prussia had 30 aides de camp killed in one day!"

The aide replied, "Yes sir, but Colonel Smith hasn't got so many to lose!"

On October 26 an intense storm pounded the fort, turning the Schuylkill into a raging torrent and flooding the island under two feet of water. The misery continued as British Artillery pulverized the works. De Fleury assigned the men to rebuild the ramparts despite the weather. "[De Fleury] was a very austere man and kept us constantly employed day and night," recalled one of the men. "He always had a cane in his hand, and woe betided him he could get a stroke at." To avoid de Fleury, the soldiers hid in a ditch on the eastern side of the fort, where they built small fires to stay warm. "We would watch an opportunity to escape from the vigilance of Fleury, and run into this place for a minute or two's respite from fatigue and cold. When the engineer found that the workmen began to grow scarce, he would come to the entrance and call us out."

As the siege wore on, the supply situation grew worse. Nathanael Greene informed Washington, "The enemy are greatly discouraged by the fort holding so long and it is the general opinion of the best citizens that the enemy will evacuate the city if the fort holds out until the middle of next week." That was an exaggeration, but the British were growing frustrated. Hessian Captain Friedrich von Münchhausen, whose forces were arrayed on the other side of the river, summed up the situation beautifully: "I wish we would finally capture this cursed fort."

November 11, 1777, marked the beginning of the end for the Patriots in Fort Mifflin. Smith later explained, "I imprudently went into my Barracks to answer a letter from Gen. Varnum & a Ball come through the Chimney." The injured officer "rolled over and over, until he got to the front door." After a doctor saw to his injuries, he was evacuated from the island. It was Smith's last battle of the Revolution, and he spent most of his time recovering from his wounds in Baltimore. Attempting to fill his shoes, de Fleury rallied the men to continue repairing the daily damage done by the British bombardment. The day after Smith left, de Fleury wrote to Washington that "some of our palisade at the north side are broken, but we can mend them every night." However, he added, "the garrison is so dispirited that if the enemy, will attempt to storm us, I am afraid they will succeed." He continued, "They are so exhausted, by watch, cold, Rain & fatigue, that their Courage is very low, and in the Last allarme on half was unfit for duty."

Still, the men continued to hold the fort. On November 14, the forty-eighth day of the siege, General Greene wrote to Washington, who was several miles away with the main army, "The flag was flying at Fort Mifflin at sunset this evening." Despite the approach of winter, the British were preparing for a major assault, without ever letting up on their daily artillery barrage. In his message, Greene added that the cannon fire had been "very severe" during the day and that the British navy was "attempting to get up a two-and-thirty-gun frigate into firing range." To make the ship lighter and thus able to get farther upriver, the sailors removed the guns and placed them in a following sloop. However, luckily for the Americans, the wind and tide prevented the ship from approaching.

During the Americans' stout defense of Fort Mifflin, they received welcome news of a great victory at Saratoga. In the summer of 1777, the British had put a bold plan into motion. British strategists believed that the southern colonies were mostly loyal to the Crown and that the northern colonies were the seat of the rebellion. They thought they could stamp out the Revolution by sending down General John Burgoyne, a veteran of the Seven Years' War and an accomplished playwright who was currently in Montreal. Burgoyne and his seven thousand troops were to march south to seize Fort Ticonderoga in northern New York and eventually meet up with two other British forces near Albany, thus severing the northern colonies from their southern brethren.

Although Burgoyne captured Ticonderoga easily enough, he found further progress difficult. The area near the fort was filled with swamps and forests, and the Americans took every opportunity to slow down the

Redcoats. The Patriots destroyed bridges, left fallen trees on the roads, and otherwise sabotaged Burgoyne's force as well as they could. At the same time, the Americans went on a recruiting spree, calling up thousands of militiamen to join Major General Horatio Gates near Saratoga, New York. As a retired British soldier, Gates was well acquainted with the Cornwallis family. In fact, Charles Cornwallis's uncle Edward was one of Gates's early mentors. Gates had also served with Washington in the French and Indian War. Frustrated with the British army and lacking the money necessary to advance his career, he sold his commission as a major and bought a plantation in Virginia. He volunteered to serve in the Patriot army as soon as war broke out.

By the time Burgoyne made it to Saratoga in September, Gates had amassed a force of more than seven thousand men. The British general attacked and won a tactical victory because he remained in possession of the battlefield, but he suffered heavy casualties. Exhausted, Burgoyne chose to dig in and wait to link up with Howe—a union that would never occur. On October 7, 1777, at the Battle of Bemis Heights, the Americans captured a portion of the British defenses. Inspired by the victory, more militia streamed into Gates's camp, swelling his force to nearly twenty thousand in positions surrounding much of the British army. Burgoyne attempted a fighting retreat north, but the British situation was hopeless. "Gentleman Johnny," as Burgoyne was known, retreated to Schuylerville, the site of the first Battle of Saratoga. In a wine cellar, he met with his officers for a council of war. Baroness von Riedesel, who accompanied her husband, one of Burgoyne's principal battle commanders, recalled that Burgoyne spent the night singing and getting drunk while "amusing himself in the company of the wife of his commissary," his mistress. Above the merriment, the sounds of war still reverberated in the dank cellar. A British officer whose arm had been blown off by a cannonball wailed, and his shrieks "doubly gruesome . . . re-echoed in the cellar."

After several rounds of negotiation, Burgoyne and his men agreed to an armistice of sorts. In order to allow the British to save face, the document was called "The Convention of Saratoga," rather than a surrender or a treaty. Under the terms of the agreement, Burgoyne and his men would lay down their arms and would no longer fight against the Revolution. In return, the Americans agreed to allow them to return to England.

As the Americans played "Yankee Doodle," Burgoyne formally surrendered on October 17. Defiant to the end, many of the king's soliders broke their musket stocks in two as a final sign of resistance. But the cocksure Brits weren't headed home. Congress reneged on the terms of the surrender. Instead of going to England, Burgoyne's defeated army of more than six thousand troops headed south into captivity.[25]

Saratoga changed everything. For the Americans, the victory gave them the hope of ultimately defeating the British. More important, it also convinced the French that the revolutionaries had a chance to succeed. Playing to French stereotypes of Americans by donning a fur cap (while living in a mansion with a cellar stocked with a thousand bottles of French wine), Benjamin Franklin had been meeting with French officials. Eventually, he convinced them to ally with the American cause. Several months after the decisive victory at Saratoga, France signed two separate treaties with the United States: one that gave French goods most-favored-nation status in America and one spelling out the terms of a military alliance between the two countries. Each country agreed not to sue for peace with Britain without the consent of the other. The French also agreed not to seize any British territory in North America or Bermuda except any islands in or near the Gulf of Mexico that they might choose to attack. Initially, the treaty was defensive and allowed France to go to war at its choosing. But England declared war on France first a few days after the treaty was signed.

The alliance gave the Americans three things they desperately needed if they were to have a hope of winning their war: loans, troops, and naval support. From the British perspective, the French alliance

25. Howe secretly planned on sending the Hessians to Britain and retaining his British troops in America. Ironically, the march south and captivity were so poorly administered by the Americans that many of Burgoyne's troops escaped imprisonment and rejoined the British army.

transformed the Revolution from an attempt to suppress a colonial uprising into a global war. The British needed to defend not only the thirteen colonies, but Canada, the West Indies, and possibly even the British homeland itself from their French archrivals. Almost immediately, British troops began to leave North America to defend the rest of the Empire from France's military might.

When word of the treaties reached Washington, he was overjoyed. Although Washington preferred not to be touched, his friend Lafayette immediately embraced the general and kissed him on both cheeks in the usual French fashion. Washington wrote to Congress, "I believe no event was ever received with more heartfelt joy." And the army held a day of celebration in honor of the treaty.

Inevitably, the British did finally overcome the natural and artificial barriers that held them back and brought their vessels within firing range of Fort Mifflin on November 15. One Patriot soldier recalled, "This morning about 8 oClock the Enemy made a furious attack, by the River & land—the Ships came as near to the Fort as posable [possible] in the Main Channel." A fierce artillery battle ensued. The Marylanders and other Continentals on the island put up a valiant fight but were ultimately outgunned. "Mud Island was shot to pieces by the British ships," said one of the Hessian officers. "There was a ferocious cannonade, all their mounted batteries, cannons of the largest caliber, were not only dismounted, but buried in the rubble." He added, "Blood, brains, arms, legs, everything lay about." Several of the officers were killed, and several were wounded, including the intrepid de Fleury, who had been knocked out by a falling timber.

Around midmorning, the Americans decided to signal that they needed assistance. An artillery sergeant lowered the fort's flag, intending to raise a signal flag in its place. As the colors drew closer to the ground, the British cannon stopped firing and the troops began to cheer, believing that the Americans intended to surrender. But the

Patriot officers weren't ready to capitulate yet. "Up with the flag!" they all shouted. The sergeant obeyed, returning the flag to the top of the mast that served as a pole. The firing resumed on both sides, and as the sergeant stepped away, "he was cut in two by a cannon shot." By this time, "the fort exhibited a picture of desolation," wrote Martin. "The whole area of the fort was as completely ploughed as a field. The buildings of every kind hanging in broken fragments. . . . If ever destruction was complete, it was here."

Faced with the unrelenting loss of life and a fort disintegrating around them, the Patriots chose to evacuate. On the morning of November 16, under the cover of darkness, they rowed off Mud Island. Upon their departure, they left two items of note. First, as a final act of defiance, they did not lower their colors. "We left our flag flying when we left the island," recalled Martin. Second, a rebel soldier who had previously deserted from the German mercenaries supporting the British stayed behind. Münchhausen believed he "hid himself in order to desert to our lines." However, Martin attributed his staying to "having taken too large a dose of 'the good creature [alcohol].'" He added, "The British took him to Philadelphia, where, not being known by them, he engaged again in their service, received two or three guineas bounty, [and] drew a British uniform." But the two-time "deserter" didn't stay in British service. Once the Redcoats provided him with clothing and a little money, he deserted again and made his way to the Patriot camp at Valley Forge.

As the British took possession of the fort, a grisly scene awaited them. One of the Redcoat officers reported, "Colonel Osborn took possession of the island the following morning and found nothing but a charred camp and bloodstains." The Patriots had torched all of their buildings before departing, leaving only the commandant's house standing—and it was little more than a ruin. "The house of the commandant has so many holes that more than one thousand can be counted, and the floors are as blown up as when a herd of swine had been there."

The British "hauled down the Rebel Flag and hoisted an English Jack." They then immediately set to work repairing the damage that their six-week barrage had done. A light, "trifling snow" fell as they worked, just a taste of the cold winter ahead.

CHAPTER 20

VALLEY FORGE
AND WILMINGTON

In a scene repeated by thousands of men that winter, Joseph Plumb Martin winced as he placed his foot on the hard, frozen ruts of the dirt path he was following. Mile after mile, the stiff cowhide of his makeshift moccasins slowly ground through the skin on his ankles until every step was torture. Martin had made the rough shoes himself a few days earlier when his original pair fell apart on the trek to Valley Forge, Pennsylvania. Every morning, his feet and ankles hurt so much from the previous day that he could barely stand to put the moccasins back on. Yet he did so—and bore the pain of each excruciating step—because the other option was much worse. "The only alternative I had," wrote Martin, "was to endure this inconvenience or to go barefoot, as hundreds of my companions had to, till they might be tracked by their blood upon the rough frozen ground."

While the shoes lasted, they protected Martin's feet from the icy ground, but eventually, his ersatz footwear wore out. With no supplies for making new ones, Martin joined the rest of the Continental Army, which he described as "not only starved but naked." He added, "The greatest part were not only shirtless and barefoot, but destitute of all other clothing, especially blankets." Yet like the rest of the army, Martin continued marching, even when he began leaving bloody footprints behind him in the snow.

The torturous trek to Valley Forge marked the end of a long winding down. Since the capture of Mud Island on November 15, 1777, both armies had boldly remained largely inactive. During the period, some skirmishing took place, including the defense of Edge Hill (also known as the Battle of White Marsh), in which the Maryland militia won praise from George Washington, but British commander Willliam Howe seemed content to go into winter quarters rather than go on the offensive.

Unfortunately, when Washington's army arrived at its winter camp in Valley Forge, the problems that plagued it on the march only grew worse. The bitter cold, combined with the lack of supplies, caused innumerable cases of frostbite, hunger, and disease. Typhus, pneumonia, dysentery, and scurvy swept through the American camps, with as much as 30 percent of the army afflicted with one illness or another at any one time. The surgeons kept busy amputating limbs that had turned black from cold. The food was incredibly meager, often consisting of nothing more than "fire cakes," flour and water heated on hot stones. One physician with the army summed it up this way:

> Poor food—hard lodging—cold weather—fatigue—nasty clothes—nasty cookery—vomit half my time—smoke out of my senses—the devil's in it—I can't endure it. . . . There comes a bowl of beef soup—full of burnt leaves and dirt, sickish enough to make a Hector spew. . . . There comes a soldier, his bare feet are seen through his worn-out shoes, his legs nearly naked from the tattered remains of an only pair of stockings; his breeches not sufficient to cover his nakedness; his shirt hanging in strings; his hair disheveled; his face meager; his whole appearance pictures a person forsaken and discouraged.

Disgusted by the heart-wrenching, miserable conditions his troops endured, Washington did everything in his power to provide for his men. He pressed Congress to name Nathanael Greene as quartermaster general, and fired off numerous letters begging for food and clothing. In one, he predicted that "three or four days bad weather would prove our destruction," and explained that men had no soap, no shoes, very little clothing. Many couldn't even sleep because, as they had no blankets, they were forced to crouch near the fire at night. The general also expressed tremendous admiration for the men who were willing to undergo such deprivations. "Naked and starving as they are," he wrote, "we cannot enough admire the incomparable patience and fidelity of the soldiery."

Marylander John Boudy, who, unlike most of the men from his state, was briefly at Valley Forge, recalled, "Our army suffered excessively being destitute of clothing and provisions—so difficult were provisions to be procured, that they had to be collected by force." He added that he was sometimes part of foraging parties, which had "to make excursions forty and fifty miles and sometimes further, to collect provisions."

By the end of the terrible winter, nearly two thousand American soldiers perished.

Many of the Marylanders escaped the tragic fate of those at Valley Forge. Washington sent John Eager Howard and the bulk of the Maryland troops to Wilmington, Delaware. Wintering in town was far less difficult than wintering in the valley. William Smallwood and Mordecai Gist stayed in the Foulke house, where sixteen-year-old Sally Wister lived. She confided in her diary that she liked the looks of then twenty-nine-year-old Gist. She described him as "a smart widower," adding, "He's very pretty; a charming person." To a friend, she described his eyes as "exceptional; very stern; and he so rolls them about that mine always fall under them" and concluded, "He bears the character of a brave officer." For his part, Gist seemed more interested in a Miss Fostinam, writing to a friend that he wished to dance a minuet with her at the local tavern, but "I have been unhappily disappointed in my design." Despite being unlucky in love, Gist wrote to another friend, "I have the pleasure to Inform You that I share with the rest of my Brother soldiers, a tollerable state of Health. . . . my Spirits neither depressed nor elevated. . . . My time glides smoothly on, and each revolving Sun Shines out to make me happier in the defence of Virtue and my Country than the Haughty Tyrant that sits upon his Throne but to Enslave his subjects."

Gist did not agree with Washington's choice of Valley Forge as winter quarters, writing that it allowed the enemy to forage and harass the Continental Army at will and subjected the men to damp huts and disease. Ultimately, Gist did not have to endure the same suffering as most of his men during that bitter winter; he returned to Baltimore to recruit new men for the Maryland regiments. In Baltimore he quickly wed Mary Sterrett, sister to Lieutenant William Sterrett, an officer in the Maryland Line who was one of Gist's close friends. Apparently, Gist succumbed to love and romance, even though months earlier he had warned Jack Steward, "The enchanting pleasures of Venus can never stand in the competion with gods like Mars when the Soldier has Virtue enough to remember his Country."

The monotony and boredom of quarters in Wilmington brought their own set of challenges. The soldiers spent a great deal of time waiting, with little to do. Tempers began to fray, and fights broke out among the troops. Although normally coolheaded, John Eager Howard was involved in an altercation that resulted in a court-martial. He was charged "1st with wounding Capt. Lieut. Duffy with his Sward; 2d Abetting a riot in Camp; and 3d in front of his Men at his request assembled attempting the life of Capt. with a loaded firelock and fixed Bayonet being utterly subversive of Good Order and Discipline." The court acquitted Howard on the first and third charges. On the second, it ruled that "however Justifiable the Motives were by which Major Howard was first actuated his Conduct in that End was such as tended rather to promote than suppress a riot." Howard received a reprimand, as did Duffy, who was also found guilty of abetting a riot. After the incident, Howard reverted to his typical calm manner, but Duffy continued to be a problem. Years later, the army discharged him for "Scandalous and Infamous behavior unbecoming the Character of an officer . . . Being drunk; Rioting in the street; Abusing a French soldier; And acting in a seditious and disorderly manner."

One source of solace for the officers of the Maryland Line during the long winter was the unshakable Margaret Jane Ramsay. Her husband, Nathaniel, had been recently promoted to the rank of colonel, and the couple maintained a log hut in Valley Forge with some of the other Maryland officers (even though the bulk of the Marylanders wintered in Wilmington). Mrs. Ramsay played the role of hostess and entertained with refreshments such as coffee. Her brother remarked, "Maryland officers in the camp spent many agreeable hours sometimes accompanied by officers in other corps." The bonds of friendship forged in battle were strengthened during these times of shared sacrifice.

While the winter seems to have passed pleasurably for many of the officers, the Marylanders still faced their share of hardships. Beatty wrote that they "fared very well as to the quarters but the duty Was very hard & the troops Very bare of Clothing" until a British vessel shipwrecked nearby and the men captured "a valuable Prize of cloathing."

Petty disputes broke out, and Smallwood became "very unpopular, owing to his Stateliness and excessive Slowness of Motion." Smallwood didn't make any friends among the officers by announcing that they could speak with him only between three and six in the afternoon. "A pretty Condition he would be in, were the enemy to attack him in the morning," observed one of the men.

Disease also took a toll, and the Maryland ranks declined precipitously. The Marylanders didn't meet again with Washington until June 1778, and by that time only 269 of the 455 men in the 4th Maryland Regiment were fit for duty. During these trying times, desertion became a problem for the Maryland Line. During the winter, William Chaplin, who barely survived the Battle of Brooklyn, deserted to the British along with over a dozen of his fellow soldiers. A British newspaper reported the incident: "[Chaplin] and sixteen others deserted from Wilmington, and came in to Gen. Howe, at Philadelphia, where they took the oath of allegiance, were treated with great humanity by the British officers, and, at their own request, suffered to leave America." Chaplin and his fellow Marylanders left for England and were never heard from again.

For the troops in Valley Forge, endless drills under the direction of Baron Friedrich von Steuben occupied much of the long winter. The Prussian nobleman and officer entered Washington's service on the recommendation of Benjamin Franklin, who met von Steuben in France and mistakenly believed him to be a "Lieutenant General in the King of Prussia's service." In reality, he had been discharged from the

Prussian army as a captain in 1763, and at the time he met Franklin, he was serving as grand marshal to Josef Friedrich Wilhelm, prince of Hohenzollern-Hechingen in southern Germany. Volunteering to work without pay, the baron overhauled the Americans' training practices, setting up a model company of 120 soldiers that could then train other men. He imposed a strict camp layout and new sanitation standards that helped improve the health of the soldiers. According to legend, because he spoke little English, von Steuben relied on a translator to chew out the men, frequently yelling, "Over here! Swear at him for me!" when his insults in French and German failed to achieve the desired results. A dog lover, the colorful Prussian had an Italian greyhound name Azor who went everywhere his master did. Steuben collected his training advice in the *Revolutionary War Drill Manual*, which the Americans used through the War of 1812.

To serve a similar role in Wilmington, Washington sent one of von Steuben's assistants, Marquis François-Louis Teissèdre de Fleury, who had staunchly defended Fort Mifflin with the Marylanders. The training and the cold weather took a toll on the men, in terms of both their health and their morale, but through the baron's drill and training, the Marylanders and the American army were evolving and becoming a potent fighting force.

1778

CHAPTER 21

"A DAMNED POLTROON"

For nearly twelve miles, a seemingly endless train of wagons snaked across the hot, dusty roads of New Jersey. General Henry Clinton, who had replaced General William Howe as the commander in chief of the British forces, had ordered the evacuation of Philadelphia. He was moving his men to New York City, which was vulnerable to a naval attack by France, the French having entered the war on the American side. Clinton didn't have enough troops to hold both cities effectively. On June 18, 1778, more than ten thousand British and Hessian troops began the trek north to New York, accompanied by countless numbers of camp followers and Loyalists. The sheer size of the group made it extremely unwieldy, and the unrelenting heat and sandy roads slowed the lumbering column even further. On a good day, the long procession of scarlet crept only five or six miles closer to New York.

Back at Valley Forge, General George Washington had a decision to make: should he allow the British to escape to New York or should he take a chance at obtaining an impressive victory by attacking the troops on the move? The glacial pace of the British army made it seem an easy target; Washington was eager to prove that the Patriot victory at Saratoga in the fall of 1777 was not a fluke.

Ever a man of action, Washington decided that the potential gains from a victory outweighed the risks: he opted to attack before the enemy could reach New York. Command of the colonies' advance troops fell to Charles Lee, who had been back with the army for little more than a month. British cavalry led by Lieutenant Colonel William Harcourt and Cornet Banastre Tarleton had boldly captured the general at Basking Ridge,

New Jersey, in December 1776. The British had given Lee up in a prisoner exchange, but not before the garrulous Lee bragged about and freely revealed his strategies for how best to defeat Washington. Now he met his former captors on the ground near the courthouse in Monmouth, New Jersey, in what was the longest battle of the war.

On June 28, 1778, Lee set out with fifty-four hundred men to attack Clinton's rear guard near present-day Freehold, New Jersey. However, upon hearing of Lee's thrust, Clinton had quickly ridden back two miles and ordered six thousand of his best men "to face about and march back with all speed to attack the Rebels."

The battle began around midday in a three-mile-long, one-mile-wide area of solid ground hemmed in by swamps and rocky hills. It was a scenic location full of lush rolling farmland intersected by a series of creeks and ravines. Lee planned to surround Clinton's forces, but the strength of the opposition took him by surprise. After only an hour wilting in the blazing sun with temperatures soaring above one hundred degrees, the Patriots began a disorganized retreat.

Washington, meanwhile, was still leading the bulk of the Continental Army, including the Marylanders, toward the battleground when he began to encounter Lee's men fleeing from the field. The first sign of disaster was a panicky young fifer who carried the news. Soon larger groups of soldiers, many of whom were wounded and suffering from heat exhaustion, confirmed his story. Incensed, Washington questioned every officer he met about why Lee had ordered a retreat. Eventually, he met Lee himself in an encounter that has become legendary.

By some accounts, Washington simply looked Lee in the eye and asked, "I desire to know, sir, what is the reason—whence arises this disorder and confusion," to which Lee had no real reply. Other eyewitnesses insist that Washington's language was much more colorful. Lafayette reported that Washington called the younger general "a damned poltroon," and others described Washington's speech on the occasion as "a terrific eloquence of unprintable scorn." General Charles Scott, who later became governor of Kentucky, said it was the only time he heard Washington swear. "It was at Monmouth and on a day that would have made any man swear," Scott said. "Yes, sir, he swore that day till the leaves shook on the trees, charming, delightful! Never have I enjoyed such swearing before or since. Sir, on that memorable day, he swore like an angel from heaven."

No matter what his choice of words, Washington dismissed Lee and took charge of the battle. Eyewitnesses remember him riding up on his white charger, halting the fleeing men and inspiring them to turn and face their enemy. Lafayette later wrote, "General Washington was never greater in battle than in this action. His presence stopped the retreat; his strategy secured the victory. His stately appearance on horseback, his calm, dignified courage, tinged only slightly by the anger caused by the unfortunate incident in the morning, provoked a wave of enthusiasm among the troops."

Once again Washington called upon the Marylanders.

"If you can stop the British for ten minutes, till I form, you will save my army!" Washington sternly told Lieutenant Colonel Nathaniel Ramsay, second in command of the 3rd Maryland Regiment.

"I will stop them or fall," stammered Ramsay, one of the original members of the Baltimore Independent Cadets.

Washington gave the 3rd Maryland Regiment and a Pennsylvania regiment the task of delaying the British while the rest of the American army formed up. Normally under the command of Mordecai Gist, the regiment was detached, and Ramsay led it into the battle at Monmouth. Hastily, Ramsay ordered his men to hide in a wood near the road and await the arrival of the enemy, then just two hundred yards away. As the British troops approached their position, the Continentals opened fire. The Redcoats immediately charged into the trees, cutting down dozens of Patriots. Gist's second in command that day sacrificed himself and the unit to buy crucial time for the rest of the army to come to the field and save Lee's retreating troops. Interestingly, this was also the closest the Maryland Line came to fighting James Chalmers's Maryland Loyalists. The Tory regiment was guarding the British baggage train, a few miles away from where the Maryland Patriots fought so desperately. It was the last time the rivals were near each other. After more garrison-type duty for the Maryland Loyalist regiment, the British sent it to British West Florida, where it fought the Spanish in a doomed raid on Mobile in January 1781. After the Crown's defeat at the hands of the Spanish, what was left of the Maryland Loyalists returned to New York. At the close of the war, many of Chalmers's Loyalists made the great exodus from America to places in the British Empire such as Nova Scotia.

Otho Holland Williams had recently been released from British captivity in New York as a result of a prisoner exchange. During his captivity he had been promoted to colonel and given command of the 6th Maryland. The 6th, one of the newer regiments created in 1777, was "rather noted for its looseness of discipline and did not stand upon a mark with others of the line." Williams, a born leader, strategist, and organizer, whipped the regiment into shape, "making it equal, if not superior, in thorough discipline, to any in the whole army." Of this battle, Williams recalled, "Lt. Col. [Nathaniel] Ramsay of Maryland covered the retreat of his party and stood the attack of a body of horse." Brandishing his sword, Ramsay killed the first Redcoat who approached, but the British soon had him surrounded. A pistol shot grazed his right cheek and several other officers died. During the engagement, "Our Great good General [Washington] in person led the fight and was the whole time exposed to the fire of the Artillery," Williams added.

One of the dragoons charged Ramsay, but the Redcoat's pistol misfired, allowing the Marylander to attack with his sword, drag the cavalryman from his horse, and take his place in the saddle. His heroics ultimately failed to save him, however, as the dragoons eventually overpowered him and took him prisoner. Accounts of how Ramsay avoided death differ. One legend says that a British officer decided to spare Ramsay's life when he saw the American's Masonic ring. Another story claims that Ramsay covered himself in blood and mud and played dead until a merciful Redcoat officer saw through the ruse and decided to take him prisoner. In any case, by all accounts, Ramsay's captivity was not particularly arduous. The British took him to Long Island, where his wife, who had been accompanying him since the beginning of the war, joined him. The wealthy couple bought a house in New York and regularly entertained other officers who were "prisoners" and "endeavoured to make themselves as happy as their situation permitted."

Once again the Marylanders sacrificed themselves to buy precious time to set up a line on the high ground that bordered the battlefield. Washington placed his artillery units on both flanks, particularly the right, where he also positioned Greene's men. Lord Stirling (William Alexander) was on the left, with Washington himself commanding the troops in the center. Lafayette handled the second line of defense, which included the Delaware Regiment.

After the British scattered the Marylanders and other troops positioned in the trees, the Redcoats turned their attention to the left side of the American line. Failing to break through, the British and Hessians mounted attacks on the right flank, then the center. Charles, Earl Cornwallis, commanding the rear formations, personally directed the attack on the American position, including the Marylanders. The second line consisted of the light infantry, Brigade of Guards, and other famous regiments considered "the very flower of the rear division and of the army." For hours, British and American cannon fired volley after volley at each other. As the battle drew on toward evening on June 28, 1778, the heat began to take its toll on man and animal alike. Washington's own horse, a beautiful white charger, dropped dead from heat exhaustion. Like the horse, the men in the thick of the battle had grown incredibly fatigued from hour after hour of endless fighting in the punishing sun. However, Stirling brought forward some fresh troops, and the American lines stood firm, buttressed by Washington's commanding presence. Throughout the long winter at Valley Forge and Wilmington, they had drilled for countless hours under Baron von Steuben. Now those drills were paying off as Washington's army found the courage and tenacity to throw back repeated attacks.

It wasn't only the American men who fought tenaciously at Monmouth; legend says that women were involved as well. Mary Ludwig Hays, the wife of one of the Pennsylvania Continentals, began taking pitchers of water to the soldiers suffering from the heat, earning herself the nickname Molly Pitcher. According to Maryland Private Joseph Plumb Martin, she also assisted her husband, an artilleryman, in loading his cannon. Martin wrote, "While in the act of reaching a cartridge and having one of her feet as far before the other as she could step, a cannon shot from the enemy passed directly between her legs without doing any other damage than carrying away all the lower part of her petticoat. Looking at it with apparent unconcern, she observed that it was lucky it did not pass a little higher, for in that case it might have carried away something else, and continued her occupation." Some accounts say that later in the battle, when Mr. Hays became unable to carry on, likely owing to heat exhaustion, Molly Pitcher continued loading the cannon.

Around six o'clock in the evening, it was over; the British pulled back. Eager to press his advantage, Washington called forward his least exhausted troops to make an assault of their own. But it was not to be. The lateness of the hour and the approaching darkness forced Washington to scotch the attack until dawn. The Patriots slept in the field that night with their rifles and muskets close at hand. "The Whole of our army lay On their arms all night," recalled Captain William Beatty. Washington himself lay under a tree, using his cloak as a blanket.

When dawn broke the next morning, the refreshed Americans arose and prepared to resume the battle. However, the British were nowhere to be found. "The Enemy took the advantage of Moon Shine about 1 o'clock the Morning of the 29th and retreated to avoid the attack Intended to be made on them by daybreak," wrote Beatty. "They left a number of their Wounded Officers & Men at Monmouth Courthouse & Some prisoners they had taken." Washington would have to put off further battle until another day.

When they tallied the total killed and wounded at Monmouth, both sides reported similar losses. The Americans reported eight officers and sixty-one enlisted men killed, compared with four officers and sixty-one enlisted men killed on the enemy side. The British also noted, "Three sergeants, fifty-six rank and file died with fatigue," presumably due to the extreme heat. In addition, they lost 136 of their own men and 440 Hessians who deserted on the march.

Pursuing Clinton's retreating forces, the Marylanders and the rest of the army marched up to take positions around White Plains and the Bronx, New York.

A little more than a week after the Battle of Monmouth, a French armada dropped anchor off Delaware Bay. The fleet was commanded by a forty-eight-year-old general turned admiral, Count Jean-Baptiste d'Estaing. The nobleman's first career stuck in the minds of many of his men, who often still referred to him as "General." D'Estaing's flotilla included twelve ships of the line and four frigates, and it carried four thousand French regulars. Had they arrived eight days earlier, the battle could have been a decisive American victory and Clinton could have shared the same fate as Burgoyne, having been trapped between the American and French forces. It might have been the end of the war.

The fleet then moved toward Sandy Hook, New Jersey, and Washington saw a chance to trap and destroy the British fleet in New York Harbor. However, the hulls of the French ships were believed to be too large to get past the sandbar at the entrance to the harbor. With the operation in New York looking impossible, d'Estaing and Washington hatched a new plan to destroy the British garrison of six thousand men at Newport, Rhode Island. Sullivan and Greene would make an overland assault with more than ten thousand men, while the French attacked by sea. Here the weather favored the British. An unexpected storm and the British fleet commanded by Admiral Howe scuttled the amphibious portion of the assault. As a result, the Americans and French called off the entire operation, and d'Estaing retreated to Boston Harbor for repairs.

The Americans' intial joy over the French alliance wore off. Livid, Sullivan and other officers accused d'Estaing of betrayal. Washington wisely took on the role of statesman and took care not to ruffle French feathers. However, as the two forces began to work together, each was dismayed by the other. The French had expected that the American army had more men and that it was better outfitted. One of the French officers said of Washington's army, "I have never seen a more laughable spectacle. All the tailors and apothecaries in the country must have been called out. . . . They were mounted on bad nags and looked like a flock of ducks in cross belts." Washington, accustomed to being in sole command, found it irksome to have to run his plans by the French officers, and he mistrusted their motives. His perspective on the situation led him to assert a timeless truth: "It is a maxim founded on the universal experience of mankind that no nation is to be trusted farther than it is bound by its interest." Similarly, John Adams expressed frustration with the French involvement, saying that the French foreign minister kept "his hand under our chin to prevent us from drowning, but not to lift our heads out of water."

CHAPTER 22

LIGHT INFANTRY

Clad in a linen shirt and buckskin moccasins, and with numerous rings in his nose and ears, the aging Indian chief fought for his life as the ambush unfolded around him. Caught in a trap set by Lieutenant Colonel John Graves Simcoe, Marylanders and Stockbridge Mohicans fought hand-to-hand and tomahawk-to-knife against the British soldiers. Natives with multiple piercings and Mohawk haircuts grappled with uniformed Redcoats, dragging the British dragoons from their horses and cutting them down. Armed with rifles, tomahawks, and bows, the Mohicans fought bravely as they had on many other occasions, but this time they were unable to overcome their enemy.

"[I am] old and would die here!" the chief, Daniel Ninham, called out. He ordered his warriors to retreat, but he himself went on the offensive, attacking Simcoe. He wounded the colonel and, more important, bought time for some of his warriors and many of the Marylanders to retreat. Eventually, a British orderly killed the old man, bringing his courageous charge to an end.

During the Revolution, most Native Americans in the East fought for or were aligned with the British. In the Northeast the United States had to deal with the six nations of the Iroquois Confederacy: the Mohawk, Oneida, Onondaga, Cayuga, Seneca, and Tuscarora. Five of the six were united behind the Crown and mounted raids on American settlements near the frontier. Only the Oneida sided with the Americans. In the South the Cherokee were active and fought against the Americans for a time.

In a nearly forgotten chapter of American history, the Stockbridge Mohicans were a unique exception and fought for the American cause. After leaving their lands in 1734 for a variety of reasons including debt, the Mohicans had settled in a beautiful meadow surrounded by the bucolic Berkshire Mountains in Stockbridge, Massachusetts. Missionaries soon converted them to Christianity, and in 1775 the Stockbridge Mohicans joined the Patriot cause. Congress appointed Abraham Ninham, Daniel's son, who also served as a chief of the tribe, as an emissary to communicate with western Indians. In 1778 Abraham, Daniel, and about sixty warriors joined the Patriot light infantry led by Mordecai Gist.

In the fall of 1778 after the battle at Monmouth, George Washington moved the American army back up to White Plains, New York, in order to keep the British pinned down in New York. There the general ordered the creation of light infantry units, which had more flexibility and the ability to mount raids. In addition, they would counter the British light infantry operating in the area, harass their supply lines along the road network in today's Bronx and southern Westchester County, and hamper their efforts to forage. Light infantry was ideal for this role. In his general orders of August 8, Washington stipulated that each brigade would supply "a Corps of Light Infantry composed of the best, most hardy and active Marksman and commanded by good Partizan Officers." Already an elite unit, the Marylanders supplied many officers and men to the new corps. Other than ranger units, it was arguably the closest thing an American eighteenth-century army had to special-operations troops. The light infantry corps were some of the finest troops in the Continental Army: four regiments of veterans chosen for their "alertness, daring, and military efficiency." They traveled light and could strike quickly, since they were unencumbered by baggage and heavy artillery.

Gist commanded the light infantry, and Jack Steward led a detachment within it. On Washington's orders, they moved the light infantry up into high ground in Yonkers, where they were in a position to penetrate behind British lines and harass the enemy. Several dozen Stockbridge Indians fought alongside Gist's men. The light infantry skirmished, probing British positions through the scorching August of 1778. Fighting fire with fire and utilizing intelligence obtained from an American deserter, the British soon dispatched Simcoe, who commanded the Queen's Rangers, a light infantry unit descended from Rogers' Rangers of the French and Indian War, to destroy Gist's light infantry. Born in 1752 to a Royal Navy captain, Simcoe attended Eton College and Oxford University before pursuing a military career. Double-chinned, with a pronounced paunch and wild, untamable gray hair, he saw action in numerous battles in the Revolution, including the siege of Boston and the Battle of Brandywine, where he was wounded. He was working to create a regiment of Loyalist freed black slaves when he was offered command of the rangers. Under his leadership, the Queen's Rangers participated in many brutal engagements.

Attached to the Queen's Rangers were the notoriously brutal Banastre Tarleton and his legion of cavalry. Tarleton and Simcoe were perfectly matched as two of the most ruthless officers in the British army. Simcoe and Tarleton reconnoitered Gist and Steward's position and prepared an ambush on August 31, 1778. "Our light infantry, which is a few miles below us, have a little scratching," Marylander Benjamin Ford recalled, "[The British] rather worsted us yesterday, by ambuscading a small reconnoitering party under Major Steward; they killed six Indians and a white man or two and made prisoners of fifteen or sixteen Indians. Our little party behaved nobly, though surrounded by a much superior party." Ford's words downplayed the courage, valor, and horror of that day.

Once again Steward escaped death, thanks to the courage of dozens of Mohicans. In what became known as the Massacre of the Stockbridge Indians, Simcoe's men refused to provide quarter to some of the Indians, murdering them instead of taking prisoners.[26] Ford, who was by Steward's side, predicted, "It won't be long before Jack pays [the British] amply in their own coin, for their civility to him on this occasion."

On that long August day, Steward, Gist, and most of the light infantry escaped Simcoe's trap, but devastating losses forced what was

26. A plaque in the Bronx at Van Cortlandt Park East commemorates the ambush.

left of the Stockbridge Indians to return home to Massachusetts. Discharged by Washington's orders in September 1778, the tribe received a paltry thousand dollars for their service. They eventually lost their home at Stockbridge and relocated to upstate New York, where they settled with the Oneida.

Despite the setbacks and misfires, the French alliance was bearing fruit; the Revolution was morphing into a global war. In October 1778 the situation forced British commander Henry Clinton to release five thousand troops because they were needed for service in the Caribbean. There the Crown was pursuing a military campaign on the island of Saint Lucia, and it mounted a daring expedition to seize Spanish possessions in gold-rich Central America. Thousands of Clinton's men headed to Florida, and hundreds more to Halifax and Bermuda. In a two-year period starting in 1777, British losses totaled a staggering 15,664 troops in the western Atlantic. Replacement troops never made up the shortfall; in the four years following John Burgoyne's surrender at Saratoga in October 1777, Clinton received only 4,700 troops to replace losses of 19,200. Troop shortages plagued the British throughout the war, drove their military strategy, and restricted their ability to launch offensives. They needed to clear areas of Patriot troops, build new outposts, and hold them—but they never had sufficient resources to accomplish these goals.

In London, the disastrous defeat at Saratoga was refought in Parliament for most of 1778 and part of 1779. Major figures, including William Howe, expressed serious doubts that the war could be won now that the French had allied with the Americans. Major General Charles Grey, who led the Paoli Massacre that nearly killed William Smallwood and Gist, testifed, "With the present force in America, there can be no expectation of ending the war by force of arms." Sir John Wrottesley's assessment was even more dire: "If fifty thousand Russians were sent, they could do nothing . . . our posts [are] too many and our troops too much detached. . . . The chain of communication was too far extended."

For their part, the Americans also faced difficulty obtaining the number of troops they needed. The French never provided enough money to expand the war to the levels Washington desired. Lack of gunpowder, supplies, and money to pay soldiers hampered Washington's ability to launch large-scale offensive operations. The coming year proved to be largely a stalemate, with the British locked in New York and Washington's army in blocking positions outside the city and near West Point, preventing the enemy from breaking out. With neither side having the means to bring the Revolution to a decisive conclusion, the war dragged on.

1779

CHAPTER 23

DESPOTS

Throughout the second half of 1778 and into 1779, some of the most heated fights experienced by the Marylanders occurred not in battle, but in courts-martial held by the American army. Otho Holland Williams, released from captivity in February 1778, served in July 1778 on the court that heard charges against General Charles Lee, who was "charged with disobedience of orders in retreating unnecessarily, and in showing disrespect to the Commander in chief" at the battle of Monmouth. Williams and the rest of the jury found him guilty and sentenced him to be relieved from duty for one year. Williams noted that it was the "most important [trial] that has occurred so far," but it was far from the last, as courts-martial beset the Maryland Line for some time.

On January 5, 1779, a letter appeared in the *Maryland Gazette*, Baltimore's principal newspaper. Signed by John Eager Howard, Samuel Smith, and many other Maryland officers, it declared, "Captain [Edward] Norwood, (who is discharged from the service by a sentence of a court-martial on a disagreement with General Smallwood) during the campaigns in which he served with us, has ever conducted himself in such a manner as to command our warmest friendship and esteem as an officer and a man of honour."

For some time trouble had been brewing between the other Maryland officers and William Smallwood, whom they viewed as autocratic and petty, often retaliating harshly for the smallest slights. In the case related to the letter in the newspaper, Smallwood had discharged Captain Edward Norwood of the 4th Regiment for refusing to obey orders. Norwood didn't take his dismissal lying down. In addition to getting his fellow officers to sign a letter in his defense, he submitted a letter of his own to the *Gazette*. He charged that Smallwood had orchestrated his court-martial "for only saying General Smallwood was a partial man and no gentleman." He added, "I am sorry to say, such a system of despotism will appear to be springing up in our army that an officer who does his duty ever so exactly, and has neglected to pay a servile court to a haughty superior, holds his commission by a very precarious tenure."

In a country currently rebelling against its king, Norwood's charges of despotism resonated strongly. Incensed, Smallwood refused to let the matter drop and continued haranguing the officers who had supported Norwood. In March 1780 several officers, including Howard, sent Smallwood a note, which said, "Your scurrilous observations on the testimony we gave of our favorable opinion of Captain Norwood, discovers the malevolence and presumption, more than the probity and liberality of your mind." They added that other officers, "whom you took occasion to abuse in your ungentlemanly performance of 105 pages," would have signed the note as well except that they were "out of camp."

Smallwood seemed to single out Howard for revenge. He called for a court-martial against the young officer on three charges: disobeying orders on several days in January 1779, in one instance by not properly participating in a parade; "not furnishing the morning reports and weekly returns of his battalion at the time ordered and in a correct military manner"; and giving rum to servants as well as the combat troops. Gassaway Watkins, the imposing lieutenant from Howard County, Maryland, described the charges a little differently. "Was present when Colonel Hazen arrested Colonel Howard, for not keeping his men on the parade until they were frozen," he wrote in his memoirs.

The court delivered a mixed verdict. It said that Howard hadn't disobeyed orders, but that he hadn't remained with the part of his unit that participated in the parade. In addition it said that he had filed his reports on time but "in general the reports he furnished were incorrect and unmilitary." It also found him guilty of distributing the rum. Extraordinarily, George Washington personally intervened in the case, contravening the verdict of the court. He wrote that "painful as it is to him at all times to differ from a Court Martial in sentiment, he cannot concur with them in opinion where they find [Howard] guilty of disobedience of orders," although he did say that Howard had made mistakes in regard to the reports and the rum. Howard emerged from the incident with his reputation largely intact, while Smallwood remained as unpopular as ever. One possible reason for Smallwood's petty tyrannical escapades was the absence of his right-hand man, Mordecai Gist, a firm but fair leader who might have stopped the charges against Howard had he been in camp. Gist remained in Baltimore by the side of his dying wife, who gave birth to his son Independence only a few months after their marriage. He even disobeyed Washington's orders to return to the field, writing to the commander in chief, "It is with pain that I inform You of Mrs. Gist's extreme Indisposition whose life is dispaird of by her physicians and it is an additional wound to my sensibility that this melancholy circumstance compels me to act Incompatible with your Excellency's orders." A few months after he returned to the field, Gist became a widower for the second time in his life.

Unlike Smallwood, Williams was very popular with the other Marylanders. He maintained contact with Samuel Smith, who was recovering in Baltimore from his wounds taken at Mud Island, and through Smith with Nathaniel Ramsay, who was captive with his wife in British-occupied New York City. The friendship between Smith and Williams was deep. Jokingly, Smith referred to the letters from Williams as "like those from a favorite son." He went on to say that he would like to name his oldest son Otho.

At this time, some of Maryland's oldest soldiers were leaving the service because their three-year enlistments had expired. Many of the men had gone without pay, and they had households to maintain. Three years of battling the British and the elements, an economy in hyperinflation, and a war that seemed without end had worn down many of them. Among them was Lieutenant James Peale, who resumed his life as an artist.

The patriotic and the ardent—and those lucky enough not to be physically maimed—stayed. The core officers like Gist, Steward, Howard, and William Beatty become more important than ever. They provided the leadership, continuity, and experience that filtered down through their commands, and they worked desperately to fill their depleted ranks.

Filling Maryland's regiments remained a constant challenge. In 1778 the General Assembly passed a law that required Maryland to raise 2,902 recuits for service in the Continental Army, giving each county in Mayland a quota to fill. In 1776 and 1777, the men were nearly all volunteers, but now Maryland turned to a variety of machinations and even a draft to fill the shortfall of bodies. About a fifth of the men volunteered, while the bulk were militiamen or substitutes, and a small number were drafted by the state.

Vagrants were the first to be rounded up by the draft. Men were considered vagrant if they were free spirits without fixed domiciles and over eighteen years old. They were pressed into service by the local militia for at least nine months. If the vagrant signed on for three years, he would receive the standard enlistment bonus of land and money.[27]

A large source of manpower came from substitutes. The rich could avoid the draft by hiring men to serve in their place. The practice could be a shady business. Horror stories abounded as dishonest constables or militia leaders forced substitutes to enroll and then resold them to the highest bidder in another county. The racket yielded a small fortune before it was shut down by the state government.

Unlike the volunteers who filled the Marylander ranks at the beginning of the war, some of these new men did not want to be there. The officers and NCOs had to work with soldiers from diverse backgrounds and attempt to mold them into a fighting unit. The newcomers joined a core cadre of old soldiers and best friends who believed in the cause, fought for each other, and kept the Maryland regiments together under very difficult circumstances.

27. The amount of money and land depended on the year of enlistment.

* * *

In the spring of 1779, the Marylanders camped at Middletown, New Jersey, to thwart the British trade with the Tories in Monmouth County and along the Jersey Shore. Far removed from Continental bases of supply, the new recruits and veterans had to purchase their food, clothing, and other incidentals from a hostile local population. Men with hardly any money at all and no wages were forced to buy their own food. Combined with hyperinflation, this situation created widespread dissatisfaction within the Maryland ranks.

Hyperinflation ran rampant through the American economy and posed a grave threat to the American Revolution. The Continental Congress was printing its own money, but that money was rapidly becoming worthless. Over the course of three years, the value of the paper dollar tanked; by 1781 it took seven hundred dollars to purchase one British pound. Examples of hardship and pain abounded: "a bad supper and grog" and lodging cost $850, and one Continental officer noted that an "ordinary horse [was] worth $20,000; I say twenty thousand dollars!"

Several factors contributed to the depreciation of the Continental dollar. Foremost, Congress didn't have the ability to tax, and the states to this point had made no voluntary payments to Congress. In addition, several states were issuing their own currency, which competed with the Continental currency. In an effort to destroy the American economy funding the Revolution, the British engaged in economic warfare and launched a covert counterfeiting program; British agents distributed the fake dollars throughout the colonies, exacerbating the inflation problem.

Practically bankrupt because it didn't have hard coin to back up the paper it was printing, Congress largely depended on French money, but there wasn't enough funding to buy provisions to feed the army. Men weren't paid, clothed, or fed. The value of the dollar approached zero, and the miserable state of the American economy became a grave threat to the American Revolution.

Returning from Baltimore, Gist, recently promoted to the rank of brigadier general, complained to the Continental Congress, "We have the mortification to see the troops of every state provided with cloathing and other necessities at reasonable and moderate prices, whilst we alone have been obligated to purchase from private stores every necessity at the most exorbitant prices." The days of the smartly outfitted men of the Baltimore Independent Company were long over. The dissatisfaction was palpable and reached a boiling point on April 3, 1779, when Gist lost control of one of his companies and had to call on the assistance of the local militia. "Coll. Gist has requested of me to let Coll. Holmes know that he stands in need of assistance of the militia in order to bring his men into order, that one company hath mutiny'd at Middletown and are determined to go off to the enemy if not prevented and desires that Coll. Holmes assist him with about fifty militia tomorrow at Middletown." The incident foreshadowed additional mutinies that racked Continental regiments in January 1780, when nearly the entire Pennsylvania Line and a smaller portion of the New Jersey Line mutinied. The Maryland incident was significant because it was one of the first recorded mutinies, but the actual results seem to have been covered up. Very little correspondence related to the events exists, and what happened to the ringleaders remains unknown.

Shortly after the incident, Gist's men were replaced by Marylander Lieutenant Colonel Benjamin Ford and his men, but the newcomers didn't fare much better with the local population. At Shrewsbury, Ford's men shot up the local church steeple, which had a symbol of the British Crown at the top, and attempted to set fire to the church when they couldn't destroy their target with musket balls. (Christ Church at Shrewsbury retains the damaged orb and a musket ball embedded in the wood to this day.) Local insurgents later captured a dozen of Ford's men. The coup de grâce for the Marylanders' occupation of Monmouth County came in late April, when an eight-hundred-man raiding party originating in New York and led by British Major Patrick Ferguson attacked in force with the intent of destroying the Marylanders. An expert shot who had developed a novel breach-loading rifle before the war, Ferguson was a thirty-four-year-old, outspoken Scot.

With Ferguson hot on his heels, Ford beat a hasty retreat back toward the American lines, abandoning the militiamen as well as an advance guard of Marylanders. Captain William Beatty recalled that before the attack the Continentals had "continued very peaceable Spending our Spare time With a number of fine Ladies in this neighbourhood." With no warning, Ferguson attacked "in the morning before Sun rise," Beatty recalled. "We were very near being Cut off by a party of British under Major Ferguson But have little notice of the Enemies approach. We retreated about 7 Miles toward Monmouth Court House. I lost my Waiter & all my Cloaths except What I had On, Several Other officers Shar'd the same fate. Our loss in Men was 22."

After regrouping and moving north to the American fortress at West Point, the Marylanders would soon be doing the raiding.

CHAPTER 24

THE GIBRALTAR OF AMERICA— THE MIDNIGHT STORMING OF STONY POINT

The light infantry moved through the darkness. Though it was midsummer, the night was cold, and the wind lashed at their faces, as one by one the Marylanders and other Continentals stepped off solid ground and plunged into waist-deep, thick, green muck. Because the slightest noise could alert the British to their presence, resulting almost certainly in instant death, the men maintained silence. They were part of a twenty-man commando-like team called a "forlorn hope"—in today's lexicon, a suicide squad. Serving as the tip of a hundred-man spearhead assaulting one of the most heavily defended fortresses in North America, the men of the forlorn hope were determined to break through a formidable barrier and charge straight into British muskets and cannon, with little chance of cheating death.

Armed with heavy axes and muskets slung over their shoulders, the men had to cut a hole through the abatis—pointed, blade-like, wooden stakes that were waiting for them, poised to tear into the flesh and lacerate the limbs of any man who attempted to penetrate the British defenses. The heavy axes they carried were necessary to dismantle the first fortifications the rest of the assault force would encounter. Until the abatis was removed, the rest of the assault force would be unable to enter the fort. The forlorn hope would use the axes to slowly hack their way through the timbers while under constant fire from the enemy. If they made it through alive, they would have to begin the process again and chop through yet another row of thick abatis, which guarded a fortification bristling with guns.

Before the group had set out from the Springsteel farm, about a mile and a half west of the fort in Stony Point, New York, on the evening of July 15, 1779, General "Mad Anthony" Wayne had ordered, "Should there be any soldier so lost to every feeling of honor, as to attempt to retreat one single foot or skulk in the face of danger, the officer next to him is immediately to put him to death." The same fate would befall any man who spoke or discharged his musket. The officers carried spontoons—long, menacing, razor-sharp iron pikes on the end of wooden poles—which would be used without hesitation to fulfill General Wayne's order should the need arise.

At least one man disobeyed. His commanding officer later reported, "The column was ascending the hill. The man left his station and was loading his musket. [I] ordered him to return and desist from loading his musket. He refused, saying he did not understand fighting without firing. [I] immediately ran him through the body."

The remorseful officer who carried out the execution later confided the details of the atrocity to his commanding officer, who matter-of-factly explained, "You performed a painful duty, by which, perhaps, victory has been secured and the life of many a brave man saved. Be satisfied."

Despite the suicidal nature of the assignment, the men considered the forlorn hope a post of honor. It consisted of volunteers, "desperadoes led by officers of distinguished merit." The officer who led the forlorn hope and the advance guard attacking the left side of Stony Point was Marylander Major Jack Steward.

Steward's role in the Battle of Stony Point had begun several days earlier. Riding on horseback to the top of Buckburg Mountain, a nearly eight-hundred-foot-high hill west of the fort, Steward and the new commander of the light infantry, Wayne, surveyed the rocky strip of

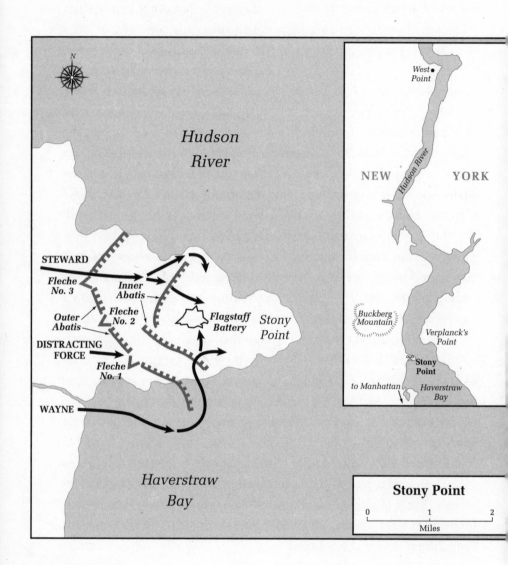

Hudson
River

STEWARD

Fleche
No. 3

Inner
Abatis

Outer
Abatis

Fleche
No. 2

DISTRACTING
FORCE

Fleche
No. 1

WAYNE

Flagstaff
Battery

Stony
Point

Haverstraw
Bay

West
Point

NEW   YORK

Hudson River

Buckberg
Mountain

Verplanck's
Point

Stony
Point

to Manhattan

Haverstraw
Bay

Stony Point

0   1   2

Miles

land that jutted out into the Hudson River below them. The ninety-acre peninsula rose about 150 feet above the water; rugged cliffs faced three sides of the stony outcropping. On the fourth side, it was well protected from assault by a marsh that effectively acted as a moat.

A month and a half earlier, on May 30, 1779, over six thousand British troops had left their posts in Yonkers and traveled up the Hudson River. They seized Stony Point, a key vantage. At that time the bluff held a partially completed American blockhouse, which the forty-man-garrison burned to the ground as they hastily retreated from the British. Only a few days after its capture, the British were at work "like a parcel of devils" as they constructed an imposing fortress outfitted with fifteen guns.

Directly across on the opposite side of the river stood another British fort, known as Verplanck's Point. The Redcoats immediately began fortifying both Stony Point and Verplanck's Point, both of which offered naturally dominant defense positions. Washington Irving described the twin fortresses as the "Pillars of Hercules," while the British called the site "the Gibraltar of America." The two bastions guarded the vital King's Ferry crossing point, which connected New England to the southern colonies. Approximately thirteen miles away lay West Point and the key to the American defenses on the Hudson. The two forts represented a potential dagger aimed at the American defenses at West Point, as well as a potential trap to lure Washington's army south, where it could be cut off from the rear by an amphibious assault from the Royal Navy.

To increase their field of fire, the British cut down the trees in the vicinity. With the resulting wood, they constructed two sets of abatis. One set of sharpened logs stretched across the back side of the peninsula, extending down to the waterline and facing west. Within the fortress, they constructed two separate belts of fortifications: the upper works, which the British described as "the table of the hill," and the lower works, which were near the marsh. In the lower works, the Royal Engineers built V-shaped fortifications called *flèches*, the French word for arrows. Beyond the *flèches*, the British placed troops and cannon that could pour enfilading fire on any American force assaulting the fort.

The British concentrated an enormous amount of firepower in Stony Point. They mounted fifteen pieces of artillery behind the fortifications. The heavy guns included a twelve-, an eighteen-, and a twenty-four-pound battery. To prevent an American assault, the British also arrayed several mortars, including one that could hurl a forty-eight-pound explosive ball and cut down an assault force like a scythe slicing through a field of wheat.

Guarding Stony Point were eight companies of the 17th Regiment of Foot (which included many veterans from the Battle of Princeton two and a half years earlier) and two grenadier companies of the 71st Regiment of Foot. Known as Fraser's Highlanders, the 71st was raised in Sterling, Glasgow, and Inverness in 1775 largely from Scottish clansman who flocked to fight in America. Staffed by several officers who were clan chiefs, the Highlanders had been in the thick of the fighting since Long Island. A detachment of Loyalists also helped man the British defenses, among them the Maryland deserter and traitor John Williams, who had previously served in the 4th Regiment. A number of other Americans who turned coat with Williams served at Stony Point, including the colorful opportunist Michael Dougherty, who fought with the Delaware Regiment in May 1777 and deserted a month later. After a few months' hiatus, he rejoined the regiment in August. Alongside the combatants, a number of woman and children and several African American slaves lived within the compound.

George Washington reacted swiftly to the threat posed by the fortifications and immediately began gathering intelligence for a potential assault. He assigned Wayne, the commander of his new light infantry force, to the task, writing, "The importance of the two posts at Verplanck's and Stony Point to the enemy is too obvious to need explanation. We ought if possible to dispossess them. I recommend it to your particular attention, without delay, to gain as exact a knowledge as you can of the number of the garrison, the state of the creeks that surround the former, the nature of the grounds and the vicinity of both, the position and strength of the fortifications."

Before Wayne took up his new post, Washington also wrote to Major Henry Lee. Known as Light Horse Harry Lee, he later became the father of the Confederacy's most famous general, Robert E. Lee. Altogether, Henry Lee had nine children by two wives. Before the war, he had graduated from the College of New Jersey and had worked as a lawyer. An excellent horseman, Light Horse Harry proved to be one of the greatest cavalry leaders of the Revolutionary War. An extreme disciplinarian, he discouraged desertion by having one recaptured deserter decapitated. When Washington found out about the incident, he ordered Lee to hide the man's body and not display it to the other soldiers.

This time, Washington wanted intelligence, and he wanted it immediately. He implored Lee, "I have now to request that you will endeavor to employ some person in whom you can confide, and at the same time is intelligent, to go into the works of Stony-point, or if admittance is not to be gained, otherwise to obtain the best knowledge of them you can, so as to describe the particular kinds of works, precise spots in which they stand, and the strength of the garrison. If you should succeed at this point, I must beg you will transmit me without delay a sketch of the work that I may be able to form an accurate idea of them."

For this daunting task, Lee tapped one of the great unsung heroes of the American Revolution—Allen McLane, a Philadelphia-born merchant's son who had moved to Delaware. Like Mordecai Gist, McLane had put his personal fortune on the line to fund his own company of men. Before Stony Point, McLane's irregular company was detached from the Delaware Regiment and served as foot soldiers or dismounted dragoons in Lee's cavalry. For most of the war, McLane operated as a lone wolf, acting as a scout and irregular leader, often behind enemy lines. He had a sixth sense about character and sniffed out the likelihood of Benedict Arnold's treasonous activities months before they even occurred, but tragically was rebuffed by Washington, who dismissed his concerns.

McLane was the perfect man to penetrate Stony Point and ferret out British secrets. Using his wits and guile, McLane, donning the hunting shirt and rifle of a common frontiersman, entered the fort through the front door under a flag of truce and boldly gathered intelligence in plain sight. He accompanied Mrs. Smith, a woman from the surrounding countryside who wanted to visit her son, one of six American turncoats stationed there.

Once McLane was inside the fort's defenses, an arrogant British officer approached to taunt the supposedly hick frontiersman. "What do you think of our fortress?" asked the Englishman. "Is it strong enough to keep Mister Washington out?"

"I know nothing of these matters," McLane replied. "I am but a woodsman and can only use my rifle, but I guess the General—General, mind you, not Mister—would be likely to think a bit before he would run his head against such works as these. . . . Trust me, we are not such dolts as to attempt impossibilities."

Meanwhile, with his keen eye, McLane noticed that the inner fort was incomplete. He reported this information to Lee, who in turn passed it on to Washington, who began formulating his plan.

Another valuable nugget of intelligence came from a British deserter who reported that the beach at Stony Point's right or southern flank was "only obstructed by a slight abatis." At low tide, the abatis did not reach all the way into the water, effectively opening a back door into the fort.

Armed with this new information, Washington dictated an assault plan to Wayne. He left no stone unturned and carefully brought the smallest details to Wayne's attention.

> My ideas for the Enterprise in contemplation are these: that it be attempted by Light Infantry only, which should march under cover of night and with the utmost secrecy. . . . The approach should be along the water on the south side, crossing the beach and entering the abatis. [The assault group] is to be proceeded by a vanguard of prudent and determined men, well commanded, who are to remove obstructions, secure the sentries, and drive in the guards. They are to advance the whole of them with fixed bayonets and muskets unloaded. These are

my general ideas of the plan for a surprise; but you are at liberty
to depart from them.

He then ominously cautioned Wayne about the need for secrecy: "Conceal the intended enterprise until the latest hour from all but your principal officers. . . . [If the enemy gains] a knowledge of your intention,
ten minutes previously obtained will blast all your hopes."

As the new commander of the light infantry, which had been in
existence for only several months, Wayne carefully assembled his force
for the assault. The Light Infantry Corps assembled for the attack on
Stony Point numbered approximately 1,350 men, including many Marylanders who were detached from their specific regiments to form this
elite fighting unit. They divided into two assault columns. From among
them, Wayne selected two special advance guard units to spearhead the
columns. Leading the men were officers handpicked by Washington
himself, including Major Jack Steward.

Standing shoulder to shoulder in parade formation, the light infantry
watched as Annapolis native Steward rode back and forth in front
of them on his stallion. The recruitment of men to fill the advance
guard units fell on the shoulders of the daring commanding officer.
Seeking volunteers for the forlorn hope, he called out, "I want no
men but the best, those that are willing to face death for their country." Men eagerly strode forward to join the suicide squad, and many
were turned down. Inspired by the major's words, Vincent Vass and
his messmate Samuel Arnold were among those who stepped forward
three paces. Vass later remarked that Steward "spoke very clever."
Steward's words must have hit home to encourage men to shrug off
the strong possibly of death.

Steward also sought volunteers for the remainder of his hundred-
man advance guards. Many Marylanders answered the call, including
John Bantham, a veteran of the battles of Brooklyn, White Plains,

Monmouth, and Germantown, and free African American George Dias (or Dice),[28] a cobbler by trade. Another Marylander who stepped forward may well have manufactured some of the supplies Dias used in his occupation. Baltimore native Elias Pollock (also known as Joseph Smith) was from one of five Jewish families who moved to Baltimore in the 1770s; he made a comfortable living manufacturing "black balls" used by cobblers like George Dias to blacken leather on the soles of the shoes.

Armed only with unloaded muskets, bayonets, and axes, Steward's advance guard, with the forlorn hope in the van, would make a frontal assault into the left side of the fortress. On the right flank were another 150-man advance guard and another twenty-man forlorn hope, led by French noblemen and engineer Lieutenant Colonel François-Louis Teissèdre de Fleury. He would hook around the abatis, going through the beach opening the British deserter had revealed.

In the center, Major Hardy Murfree would lead the only group of Continentals with loaded muskets. Their orders were to create a diversion, setting up galling fire to draw the British attention away from the flanks.

On the morning of July 15, the light infantry assembled. Wayne ordered them to appear "fresh shaved and well powdered." Mad Anthony had an audacious streak and a bizarre predilection for martial dress code. He once wrote, "I must acknowledge that I have an insuperable prejudice in favor of an elegant uniform and soldierly appearance, so much so, that I would rather risk my life and reputation at the head of the same men in an attack, clothed and appointed as I could wish merely with bayonets and a single charge of ammunition, than to take them as they

28. After he was wounded and escaped capture by the British in a later battle, the war never left Dias. Pension records state that, suffering from typhus, Dias was "now growing old, and having been wounded, his wound causes him much trouble. . . . The deponent states that he has no Property of any sort or kind whatever, which can yield him a farthing either now or hereafter that he is so poor he has not had a Bed to sleep on for three years and his whole personal property consisting of a few Instruments of his Proffesion, he carries about with him in a small bag."

appear in common with sixty rounds of cartridges. For good uniforms promoted among the troops a Laudable pride . . . which in a soldier is a Substitute for almost every other Virtue."

Around noon, Wayne's 1,350 men set out on a rugged, thirteen-mile march. Before departing, the men shed most of their equipment. Vass recalled, "We were to take nothing with us but our arms and our canteens." They set out on a torturous route over winding paths, "much of the journey through high mountains . . . and difficult defiles, obliging [the force] to move in single files the greater part of the distance." Vass recalled, "Off we went over the mountains, through deep morasses, rocks, there was to be no plundering. We surmounted every difficulty." In an effort to preserve the element of surprise, Wayne kept the assault force in the dark about their objective.

Late in the evening, the troops paused for a quick dinner. Wayne closed a letter to his brother-in-law and made a total commitment to the attack, leaving it up to fate to determine if he would live or die: "I am called to sup, but where to breakfast—either within the Enemies Lines in Tryumph or in an Other World."

About a mile from the fort the officers revealed to the men that their mission was to recapture Stony Point. Inserting a bit of competition into the endeavor, the officers told the men that the first five Americans to enter the inner redoubt, or the table of the fort, would receive rewards. A five-hundred-dollar prize would go to the first man to capture the flag. The second man in would be awarded four hundred dollars, the third three hundred dollars, and so on, on top of promotions for all. To further incentivize the troops, the officers would appraise all booty found in the fort and share it among the men. After the briefing, they used a common practice of the time to help them recognize friend from foe in pitch darkness: "we had white bits of Paper to fasten to the Crowns of our hats." To preserve secrecy, "Guards were placed at every house to prevent any person passing." The day before they had ruthlessly put to bayonet and sword any dogs in the surrounding area whose bark could betray the impending assault.

Nevertheless, their covert operation was jeopardized. The British had their own spies and discovered an attack was imminent. Lieutenant William Armstrong of the 17th Regiment of Foot later recalled, "I heard the company I commanded receive Orders to sleep in their Cloaths & Accoutrments, as two Spies sent out by Lt. Colo. Johnson, had come in and given intelligence. The Enemy was moving toward us." The British braced for an attack, but they didn't know if it would occur that night or the next day.

After Major Steward and his men tucked the white scraps of paper into their hats, Steward assigned the leadership of the forlorn hope to a man with whom he had served in combat, Richard Waters. In his own words, Waters "often courted Danger beyond his tour of Duty." Despite the extreme risk, leading the attack was considered an honor. Miffed that he hadn't been selected, twenty-something Pennsylvanian John Gibbon demanded that he should lead the forlorn hope. To settle the matter, "Lotts were drawn after ye order of battle was formed and the lott fell upon me," recalled Gibbon.

Gibbon's assault team crept toward the fort—as yet undetected by their adversaries. Behind him, a long line of infantrymen sloshed through the muck as quietly as they could, their unloaded muskets slung over their shoulders.

Approaching the British defenses, Steward and his light infantry passed Allen McLane and his men, who for the past twenty-four hours had stealthily moved closer to the British sentries in order to obtain intelligence.

As Steward's advance guard entered the marsh, they unexpectedly plunged into a deep, soupy morass. Their initial understanding was that the muck was only ankle deep, but they sank up to their waists and chests. Over the wind and rustling bushes, they heard a shout from a British sentry, then several more, coming from behind the abatis. Suddenly, the flash of powder illuminated the pitch-black night. The British drums beat the call to arms.

Upon reaching the abatis, the Marylanders and the other men of the forlorn hope swung hard. Their axes tore into the abatis, cutting a small opening.

Musket balls, followed by grapeshot, tore into the advance guard.

British Lieutenant William Armstrong ordered his men, posted in positions behind the abatis, to open up on the Americans. "[We] fired five or six rounds a man."

Despite the fusillade of British lead, Armstrong watched in horror as the Americans surged forward. "A large body of the Enemy then entering the opening of the inner Abatis, immediately in its front in which I had posted myself to defend."

Tearing their clothes and flesh on the sharpened branches, the men of the forlorn hope broke through, as their comrades fell around them. Cutting a narrow path, what was left of the group pushed on to attack the second abatis. The remainder of Steward's advance guard followed, making their way through the narrow lane cleared by the axes of Gibbon and his men. One Continental recalled maneuvering his body through the small breach made by the forlorn hope: "passing the abatis which was made of apple trees sharpened—the passage being narrow [I] was forced through and by this means had a sharp stick run through the fleshy part of his arm. Captain Shelton staid with [me] a few minutes until it was removed. [I] remembers this, for . . . [the] captain being deaf [I] had to catch him by the arm to let him know it." Over the din of battle, Lieutenant Colonel Henry Johnson, the British commander of Stony Point, was shouting orders at his men. Fatefully, he had ordered half of his force down toward the inner abatis, including Lieutenant John Ross: "[My commanding officer] desired me to fall in with his Company and to line the [outer or first belt] Abbatis; that I had just got within the Works." The fighting deteriorated into a hand-to-hand knockdown: "I receiv'd the Push of a Bayonet from a Man who knocked me down the Hill with the Butt end of his firelock."

Friend and foe became intertwined and were easily mistaken in the darkness.

"[One of my men] had done that by mistake," thought Ross.

"You damned Scoundrel!" he yelled. Soon afterward, Ross was taken prisoner by the Americans.

With most of his troops still in the front lines, Johnson had taken the bait of Murfree's North Carolinian diversionary force, which was putting up the "galling fire." That left his flanks open to the American assault, particularly his right flank, where the abatis didn't reach into the water. At low tide, enemies could maneuver around the barrier and make their way into the fort.

A three-pound artillery piece soon rained deadly fire at the wave of oncoming Americans led by Steward's forlorn hope. The cannon was mounted *en barbette*, on wheels and firing over a low wall as opposed to being in an encasement. The cannon fired sixty-nine deadly rounds into the Patriots. Thomas Pope, a Continental with Gibbon's forlorn hope, later said, "The Cannon was dischrg'd so neare my hed [head] it beate me back into the ditch, the report was so hard it disstroyed my hearing." Decades after the event he still had remnants "of the powder in my hand at this time."

British artillerists later confirmed that Steward's forlorn hope took the worst of it: "Seventeen out of the twenty, of which his Party consisted knock'd by the first fire from the three-pounder."

Despite the losses, Steward's advance guard continued moving ahead, soon flanking the British.

Confusion reigned among the Redcoats. "The rebels are in our rear!" one of Armstrong's men informed him. Suddenly, "Two Men, who having larges of White paper in their Hats, I sppose'd them to be rebels, came up close to me." Armstrong immediately ordered the company to "bayonet . . . and fire into our rear."

A musket ball then grazed the top of the young officer's skull and "rendered [him] insensible." Shortly after, the Americans took him prisoner.

In the confusion, Colonel Johnson continued delivering orders: "Face the damn rascals!"

But in the blackness of the night, the British had trouble telling who was who. A young lieutenant in the 17th Regiment recalled that as the Americans challenged him and his commanding officer, he replied, "Damn ye, who are you?!"

One of the Americans then lunged at Johnson, who "narrowly escaped from that party."

The men surged forward. Most of the Americans' clothes were "muddy to the neck" or "almost torn to rags." A hand-to-hand melee broke out as the column hacked through the second abatis and poured into the upper works. Bayonets, swords, and spontoons pierced flesh and bone.

At least two of the original members of Smallwood's Maryland Battalion were wounded in the battle. Lieutenant James Fernandis—who had nearly died in the battle against Cornwallis at Long Island and then almost rotted to death on prison ships in New York Harbor but was released in a prisoner exchange—carried a wounded Maryland officer on his back to safety, even though he himself was injured. The imposing Lieutenant Gassaway Watkins commanded a troop of men in Steward's advance guard. Also serving under Watkins at Stony Point was John O'Hara, an original member of Smallwood's Battalion. Pension records later recorded, "John O'Hara received a wound at Stony Point Battle in his right foot which caused him to be disabled through life."

The fight to take Stony Point relied on the efforts of more than one generation. Perhaps no family suffered more in the assault than the Coffmans. Joseph Coffman, who took part in the action, reported in his pension application that his "Father Joseph Coffman was a Captain in the Revolutionary service and killed in battle at Stony Point. That two of his brothers also were in the service and one of them, Benjamin Coffman, [was] killed by his side in battle at Stony Point."

The fire was so intense, recalled one Continental attached to the guard, that "[I] escaped receiving any wounds although [my] hat and cloaths were literally riddled."

On the right flank of the fort, Mad Anthony Wayne's assault was breaking through. Led by de Fleury, the men waded through ankle-deep water and skirted and hacked away at the edge of the outer abatis, entering the fort's right flank. The Frenchman's forlorn hope surged forward, and among this group one man stood literally head and shoulders above the rest. The hulking form of Peter Francisco, "the Giant of the Revolution," strode near the front of the line, his axe tearing through the side of the abatis by the water. Strapped to his back was a six-foot-long broadsword. A human tank, Francisco, with his friend Ansolem Bailey, fought "in the hottest of the fight and in the thickest of the Slaughter." During the attack, Francisco, wielding his broadsword, supposedly killed three grenadiers and suffered a nine-inch-long gash to the stomach.

Wayne was also wounded and came within inches of death. After a ball grazed his head, "spear in hand," he rose up on one knee, with blood streaming down his face, and shouted out, "Forward, my brave fellows, forward!" Lying in a pool of blood, Wayne briefly passed out, then awoke, begging his aides to carry him into the fort.

Fortunately for the Americans, the British gunboat *Vulture*, which had been assigned to guard the right flank of the fort and the critical beach opening to the abatis, was not there for the beginning of the assault. Owing to strong winds, it had sailed downriver.

In yet another stroke of fate, many of the British guns remained silent on the night of the attack, including a powerful howitzer that could have hurled a forty-eight-pound ball into the Americans assaulting the right side of the fort. The British had stored the ammunition in another area on the night of the assault, and most of their artillery, comprising primarily repurposed ship guns, was positioned for longer-range, daytime targets. As the Continentals closed in, Royal Artillerist John Roberts called out in frustration to one of his comrades that night, "For God's sake, why isn't the artillery here made use of, as the Enemy is in the hollow and crossing the water?"

Shortly after Roberts uttered those words, the howitzer fell into American hands. Wayne's men had quickly captured the battery, which could have devastated the assault party. One British officer recalled, "The Enemy were in Possession of the Howitzer Battery and were pushing for the Upper Work, upon which I was bent my Steps that way and fell over a Log of Wood and several People fell over me before I recovered myself, and I have great reason to believe the Enemy entered the upper Work at the Barrier."

Panic set in as the British manning Stony Point's forward defenses heard more voices and shouts behind their lines. Corporal Simon Davies of the 17th Regiment of Foot felt a sense of impending doom—they were surrounded. He turned to his commanding officer, Lieutenant William Horndon, who "told us we might continue firing if we choose it, as he should fire the cannon upon which we again directed our fire as before, and we were fired upon from the upper works."

In desperation, Horndon then directed two of his men to disguise themselves as Americans and try to break through enemy lines to look for a means of escape. Davies recalled, "He ordered two Men to turn their Coats [inside out] in order to examine if there was a passage out. But these Men found that the Enemy were also in front."

As a last resort he sent out an experienced sergeant to determine their options. When the sergeant was killed, the lieutenant "offered if we should stand by him, to turn the Gun around, and defend the Work or he would put himself at our head and lead us toward the shipping." Without options, Horndon bravely went into the lines by himself and surrendered Davies and the rest of his men to a Continental officer.

In a similar predicament, Lieutenant Roberts, attempting to evade the Americans who had recently captured his artillery, heard the advance party of Wayne's column yelling out, "Throw down your arms!" He saw that "[t]he enemy had not only turned the flank but got into our rear."

Hearing the shouts of the Americans in the fort, Roberts waded into the river, and began swimming toward the *Vulture*, which had by this time returned near the fort. "[I] forded a considerable way, I suppose near a half Mile, with all my clothes on, but hearing the *Vulture* sloop of war, which I could not see in the darkness of the night, fire a gun, I undressed myself and I swam." Exhausted and freezing, Roberts was the only British officer to escape from Stony Point.

Yelling, "The fort's our own!" the remaining men of the forlorn hope and the advance guard breached the fort's upper defenses on the table of the hill. The right column, led by de Fleury and Wayne, charged through a small opening in the defenses or over the parapets and reached the flag bastion first. Steward and his men were right behind them as the two assault wings converged on the top of the table.

Vincent Vass heard the "blares of Cannon and Small arms" as he charged through. Fighting his way to Stony Point's upper works, he had "received two wounds, a musket ball Scaled the bone of my hip, a buck shot entered my thigh." The friend who had volunteered for the forlorn hope alongside him was also injured. Vass recalled, "My mess-mate Samuel Arnold was wounded in the hip, we went up to Albany Hospital, & through mercy I got well, but my poor messmate died [as] mortification [gangrene] took place."

A Maryland marine was injured in the attack as well. Initially a member of the Continental Marines that sailed on the sloop *Liberty*, Peter H. Triplett dropped out of the corps and enlisted with the Mary-landers. After he "endured all the privations & hardships of the monu-mental winter of 1777–8 at Valley Forge," Triplett "was one of those who was placed on the Forlorn Hope under the Brave & Gallant General Wayne at the Storming of Stoney Point, where he . . . was wounded."

Another member of the forlorn hope, Thomas Craig, remem-bered the distinguished gallantry of de Fleury. Craig reported seeing de Fleury enter the fort and capture the flag. Vass also saw that "Colonel Flury [de Fleury] struck the colors with his hands." However, de Fleury exclaimed that he would not take the five-hundred-dollar bounty for capturing the flag. History records that several other men received the prize money, including a Sergeant Baker from Virginia, who had been wounded four times.

The British were enveloped and fighting for their lives as small pockets of men desperately attempted to re-form and repel the Americans. Vass said he heard the British cry out in the melee: "Quarters, quarters brave Americans! Mercy! Mercy! Dear Americans, quarter, quarter!" One young officer, a Loyalist American, found himself relying on the combat experience of one of his NCOs: "I was far too young for so important a situation . . . I acted, as many older officers no doubt had done before, and since—I obeyed the directions of an experienced sergeant, who also saved my life by shooting a man who had leveled his firelock at me within ten yards"

Within thirty-three minutes, it was over. The two sides lost nearly an equal number of killed and wounded—around one hundred men. The light infantry had captured 472 British and Loyalists. At 2:00 a.m. Wayne wrote to Washington: "Dear General,—The fort and garrison, with Colonel Johnson, are ours. Our officers and men behaved like men who are determined to be free."

For his daring actions at Stony Point, Marylander Jack Steward received a Congressional Silver Medal, a forerunner of the Medal of Honor—one of only eleven such medals awarded. De Fleury received a Congressional Silver Medal, and Wayne received a gold medal. Stony Point was one of the most decorated battles of the Revolution. As the war progressed, Congress also bestowed this extremely high decoration on one other Marylander, making the elite Marylanders one of the most decorated infantry units of the Revolution.

Shortly after the last British troops surrendered, twenty-four American artillerists who accompanied the assault force turned the captured guns against the Redcoats. Among the British were Lieutenant Colonel James Webster and Major Patrick Ferguson, both of whom played a pivotal role in events during the coming year. The Americans began shelling Verplanck's Point on the opposite side of the Hudson and relentlessly fired one hundred rounds per hour into the British garrison.

The British controlled the Hudson up to Stony Point and could land troops en masse at will, easily cutting off the fort. Washington didn't have enough men to hold Stony Point, so the Americans removed its guns and destroyed the fieldworks. They shipped the valuable munitions and supplies upriver to West Point, where Marylanders under Gist, Smallwood, and Howard helped man the defenses.

Before leaving Stony Point, Washington had one last matter to attend to—the deserters who had fought for the British. At 5:00 p.m. on July 18, justice was sure and swift. At a court-martial, headed by General Wayne, the turncoats from Stony Point "were tried, Deserting to the enemy; found guilty; and sentenced (two-thirds of the court agreeing thereto) to suffer Death." Virginia Continental George Hood recalled, "At daylight the Prisoners were all paraded and among them we found two American deserters: they were pick'd out, and Gen. Wayne soon made an example of them—We cut down the Flagstaff and erected a cross-piece for the Gallows, and hung them in sight of the British prisoners." All together five Americans who turned sides, including Marylander John Williams, swung from the makeshift gallows at Stony Point that day. After the executions, Hood and the rest of the men "all fell to work to destroy the garrison and bury the dead."

At least one Delaware soldier who had previously fought alongside the Marylanders before changing to the Loyalist side escaped the gallows: Michael Dougherty. Luckily for him, Dougherty was captured by his friends, the Delaware troops who had been part of Steward's advance guard. Dougherty said, "It was a great consolation, however . . . that the old Delawares were covered with glory and that as their prisoner, I was sure to meet the kindest attention." One of his brothers-in-arms bayoneted him during the night of the assault, but Dougherty's captors carefully dressed his wounds and nursed him back to health. "My wound, once cured, and whitewashed of my sins, my ancient comrades received me with kindness; and light of heart I marched forward with the [Maryland and Delaware] regiment destined to recover the Carolinas."

A week later, General Sir Henry Clinton reoccupied the fort, rebuilding and strengthening its defenses by enclosing the upper works. But the Patriot victory went a long way in 1779, boosting the flagging spirits of Americans in a year when little action occurred. Each victory or defeat affected morale and public opinion in America and in war-weary Britain.

CHAPTER 25

INTERLUDE

On August 19, 1779, the Marylanders took part in another raid that also helped lift the Patriots' flagging spirits. And once again, some of them served as part of a forlorn hope charged with destroying an abatis.

This time the target was the British outpost at Paulus Hook, New Jersey. Using the same tactics that had worked so well at Stony Point, Light Horse Harry Lee, with a troop of light infantry that included many Marylanders, mounted a surprise nighttime raid on the garrison, which sat directly across from New York City on a low-lying sandy peninsula, the site of present-day Jersey City. Practically as one, the men of the forlorn hope heaved their axes into the air and then lowered them, biting deep into the logs of the abatis that surrounded the British position. Quickly the men chopped their way through the enclosure, clearing a path to the blockhouses inside before the enemy had time to mount an effective defense.

The raiders, including two companies of Marylanders, streamed inside the opening. In a matter of minutes, they bayoneted fifty Redcoats and captured another 158 as prisoners. Only about fifty Hessians, who were holed up in one of the blockhouses, refused to surrender and continued firing on the Americans. With daylight approaching, the Patriots left the mercenaries where they were and began herding their prisoners back to the American lines. Given that there was a strong British garrison in New York City, the Americans had no intention of retaining the fortifications on Paulus Hook. Victorious, Lee and his men retreated north with their captives.

The two sides skirmished for the remainder of 1779, but Paulus Hook was the last engagement of note in the North, as Washington refused to be drawn into a large-scale battle with General Henry Clinton. The war lapsed as the cold winds of winter began to blow again.

During the winter of 1779–80, the Marylanders and the rest of the army returned to their former camps at Morristown, New Jersey. It was the worst winter the men endured. Even the saltwater inlets and harbors from North Carolina to Canada froze, and sleds, not boats, carried firewood across New York Harbor from Loyalists in New Jersey to British-occupied Manhattan. In the first week of January a heavy blizzard buried the Marylanders, who were living in tents or huts, under five feet of snow. Without proper clothing, shoes, and blankets, the men froze, many losing limbs or even their lives.

Making matters worse, the army was once again nearly out of supplies. George Washington wrote,

> The situation of the army with respect to supplies is beyond description alarming. It has been five or six weeks past on half allowance and we have nor more than three days bread at a Third allowance on hand, nor any where within reach. . . . Our magazines are absolutely empty everywhere and our commissaries entirely destitute of money or credit to replenish them. We have never experienced a like extremity at any period of the war. . . . Unless some extraordinary and immediate exertions are made by the States from which we draw our supplies, there is every appearance that the army will infallibly disband in a fortnight.

By early January, food became so scarce that they were "almost perishing." Washington noted in another letter, "They have borne their distress . . . with as much fortitude as human nature is capable of; but they have been at last brought to such dreadful extremity, that no authority or influence of the officers, no virtue or patience in the men themselves could any longer restrain them from obeying the dictates of their own sufferings. The Soldiery have in several instances plundered the neighbouring Inhabitants even of their necessary subsistence."

To deal with the situation, Washington called on the residents of New Jersey to supply a set amount of food for the army. If the people didn't comply, the officers in charge of collecting the food "delicately" let the people know that they would enforce the quotas. To obtain hard cash, the Americans begged for and received some loans from France, which took decades to repay. While this did much to alleviate the situation, hardship remained.

Poor conditions, hyperinflation, lack of pay and food, and the frigid winter caused nearly the entire Pennsylvania Line to mutiny. According to Marylander John Boudy, "The winter of this year was also very severe, and such was the sufferings of the Army for provisions and clothing that some regiments mutinied." Hoping to take advantage of the situation and turn the Continentals' coats, Clinton sent emissaries to the mutineers, who ignored them. At first, Mad Anthony Wayne negotiated with them. He discharged half the Continentals and provided the others compensation for back pay and extra clothing. But the whole idea of negotiating with disloyal men didn't sit well with Wayne. Instead, as Mordecai Gist had done months earlier in Monmouth County, Wayne called on New Jersey troops to quell the mutiny. With Washington's blessing, he rounded up several of the ringleaders and appointed a firing squad of fellow Pennsylvanians to execute their brother soldiers. Wanting to set an example, he ordered the men to fire at the mutineers from a range of ten feet. As a result, "the handkerchiefs covering the eyes of some of them were set on fire. The fence and even the heads of rye for some distance within the field were covered with the blood and brains." Astonishingly, one man survived. Wayne then ordered one of the firing squad members to bayonet the dying man, who was writhing in pain on the frozen field. He refused. Mad Anthony promptly pulled out his pistol and threatened to kill the soldier if he didn't follow orders. The man complied, driving his bayonet through the condemned man. Wayne then paraded the rest of Pennsylvania Line past the remains of the dead soldiers, driving the lesson home.

Astonishingly, one ringleader, a Marylander, escaped punishment and was later brevetted to the rank of general. "Gentleman Cadet" Henry Carbery, who served alongside Jack Steward in Captain Thomas's Maryland Independent Company at Long Island, was severely wounded by a bullet in the side of his body. Although most wounds to the body and side would have been fatal, amazingly, he recovered and transferred to the Pennsylvania Line in 1779. Carbery's troubles began in 1776 when his father, a Loyalist, disowned him for entering Smallwood's Battalion. According to Otho Holland Williams, Carbery thought the "northern army was going to be disbanded without pay or settlement of their accounts." With no family or money, and "put out of the army with nothing more to live on than a good military name," he encouraged scores of other Pennslyvania soldiers to march on Congress in Lancaster, Pennslyvania. When Wayne arrived to smash the mutiny, Carbery fled and escaped the fate of the ringleaders.[29]

Despite Wayne's and Washington's efforts, two hundred men from the Jersey Line mutinied shortly after the Pennsylvanians. Without hesitating, Washington assembled the ringleaders and executed most of them. The contagion was contained. Wayne snidely noted, "A liberal dose of niter [gun powder] had done the trick." No more large-scale mutinies within the Continental ranks occurred in 1780, but the root causes that inspired the mutiny lingered.

*   *   *

29. After the war the Gentlemen Cadet resurfaced in Baltimore and attempted to obtain a pardon. Congress appointed a special committee and issued a warrant for his arrest. He appeared in court, but the matter of states' rights versus the authority of Congress to issue an arrest order surfaced. Carbery emerged unscathed and would bravely serve in Maryland in several conflicts. He became its first adjutant general (commanding the militia and fulfilling other duties) and later the sixth mayor of Washington, D.C. He died with "a musket ball in his side that was never extracted."

At this time, a small but significant group of Americans set about declaring their own independence from Britain. Many of the luminaries on both sides of the Revolution, including Washington; Benjamin Franklin; John Hancock; Israel Putnam; Henry Lee; Horatio Gates; Nathanael Greene; Henry Clinton; John Graves Simcoe; Charles, Earl Cornwallis; and Marylanders Gist, Williams, Steward, and Nathaniel Ramsay, were Freemasons, members of a fraternal organization that traced its origins to the Middle Ages. Lafayette was also a member, and his Masonic beliefs were part of the reason he decided to join the Revolution. The key principles of Freemasonry are self-improvement and guidance by example. All Masons who entered the lodge were considered equals, a principle the Masons called "being upon the level." One Mason described the organization's philosophy this way: "What we have done for ourselves alone dies with us; what we have done for others and the world remains and is immortal." Prior to the Revolution, the local Masonic lodges in the colonies fell under the authority of the lodges in Great Britain. However, as the Revolution progressed, the brothers from America and Britain found that they needed to part ways.

Taking advantage of the seasonal lull in the war, Gist and Williams spearheaded efforts to set up an independent Grand Lodge and name a grand master for America. Even before the war, Gist had been one of the most powerful Masons in the colonies, having risen to the rank of "Worshipful Master." At a meeting in February, the American Masons established a committee to explore the idea of independence from the British lodge, and they unanimously elected Gist as president of the committee and Williams as its secretary. Gist penned a letter to the Masonic leaders in the colonies, in which he noted, "Unhappily, the distinctions of interest, the political view, and national disputes subsisting between Great Britain and These United States have involved us, not only in the general calamities that disturb the tranquility which used to prevail in this once happy country, but in a peculiar manner affects our society, by separating us from the Grand Mother Lodge in Europe, by disturbing our connection with each other, impeding the progress and preventing the perfection of masonry in America."

Using religious-sounding language, he begged them to "save us from the impending dangers of schisms and apostasy," by "pursuing the most necessary measures for establishing one Grand Lodge in America, to preside over and govern all other Lodges."

Gist succeeded in this effort, and urged Washington to become the first Grand Master of the United States Freemasons. Washington declined the position, and a single leader to unite the various lodges and orders was never chosen. Nevertheless, Washington remained active with the group throughout the Revolution, even taking time to celebrate the festival of Saint John the Evangelist (a holiday celebrated by the Masons that takes place two days after Christmas) with his Masonic brothers at Morristown. After the war ended, Gist wrote in a personal letter to Washington, "When we contemplate the distresses of war, the instances of humanity displayed by the craft afford some relief to the feeling mind; and it gives us the most pleasing sensation to recollect that, amidst the difficulties attendant on your late military stations, you still associated with and patronized the ancient fraternity."

Gist also applied for and received a warrant allowing him to establish a Masonic lodge among the members of the Maryland Line while they were in the field. They formed Army Lodge No. 27 with Gist as Worshipful Master and Williams as Senior Warden. The Masons believe that Smallwood, John Eager Howard, and even Johann de Kalb affiliated with this lodge during the time that the Marylanders were campaigning in the South. Following the war, Gist continued his involvement with the fraternal organization, becoming grand master of Ancient York Masons in South Carolina.

Eager to strike a blow against its rival, France had begun shipping men, money, and supplies to aid the Patriots and threaten British holdings in the Caribbean back in the fall of 1778. To counter this threat, the British built up their forces in the West Indies, shifting men away from the colonies on the mainland. In a largely forgotten chapter of the America Revolution, the British also went to war with Spain, France's new ally, which had declared war on Britain without recognizing the United States. In declaring war on Britain, Spain saw an opportunity to win back its recently lost territories of Florida (which at the time extended west along the Gulf Coast to the Mississippi River), the Bahamas, and Gibraltar. Britain also saw an opportunity and targeted Spain's holdings in Central America, focusing on the gold-laden Mosquito Coast of Honduras and Nicaragua. The narrow neck of land also was the principal overland access from the Atlantic to Pacific—a potentially lucrative prize. After some initial success, the campaign went sour for the British, with the net result of bleeding away more troops from North America. In addition, thousands of Crown soldiers who could have been sent to America went elsewhere, as the war morphed into a global conflict. Once again, lack of troops hampered British operations and had a profound effect on the American Revolution.

Despite a lack of reinforcements, General Clinton, at the behest of London, grudgingly implemented a new war strategy with his reduced forces. He planned to focus on the southern states, where much of the population included Loyalists and slaves. The British hoped an invasion in the South would force the Americans to deploy troops there to prevent a slave revolt as well as to guard the frontier from possible attack by the Indians, many of whom sided with the British. With the Patriot forces divided, Clinton believed he could easily conquer Georgia and move on to South Carolina.

Back in November 1778, Clinton had boldly put the plan into action and ordered three thousand of his men currently in New York to board ships bound for Savannah, Georgia. By December 29, 1778, the city had fallen to the British. But the fight for Savannah was far from over. The Americans laid siege, and in September 1779 they were joined by Count Jean-Baptiste d'Estaing's French fleet, which, after the debacle in Rhode Island in 1778, first sailed to Boston to refit and then moved off the coast of Georgia to participate in the attack on Savannah. However, the British dug in and, after a fierce battle, forced the French and the Patriots to withdraw with heavy losses.

Encouraged by the victory, Clinton moved more men from New York to the South. Eight thousand troops set sail in December and despite delays caused by hurricanes, landed with Charles, Earl Cornwallis thirty miles from Charleston, South Carolina, in February 1780. Benjamin Lincoln, the Massachusetts major general in charge of the Patriots' southern forces, ordered his men to take cover behind the fortifications in Charleston.

The focus of the war was moving south.

1780

CHAPTER 26

THE MARCH SOUTH

Concerned about the southern army's ability to withstand this coming British onslaught, George Washington decided to send some of his best troops to Charleston to reinforce Major General Benjamin Lincoln's forces while the bulk of the army would remain to the north to protect West Point and the gateway to the northern colonies. Once again, Washington called on his Immortals. They joined with the intrepid Delaware Regiment, in total twenty-one hundred men, to form the Maryland Division. The division consisted of two brigades, one led by William Smallwood and one led by Mordecai Gist. Many men were pessimistic about the prospects of survival and dubbed the entire unit a forlorn hope.

They left Morristown on April 16, 1780, becoming part of a campaign that kept them in the South for several years. Hundreds of the men did not live to return home. Captain Bob Kirkwood kept a daily journal of their odyssey and every day recorded the miles the Immortals marched. The majority within the Maryland and Delaware regiments traversed a breathtaking 4,656 miles—often barefoot—between the spring of 1780 and the spring of 1782. The state did not compensate them until 1783—and then paid only if they were lucky enough to have survived *and* to have jumped through the right administrative and judicial hoops. Wages ceased for most men in August 1780. Officers advanced some of the men money, but after the war men had to swear under oath and convince a Maryland judge that they were owed back pay.

To the dismay of Gist and Smallwood, the leadership of the Maryland Division once again lay in the hands of a foreigner, General "Baron"

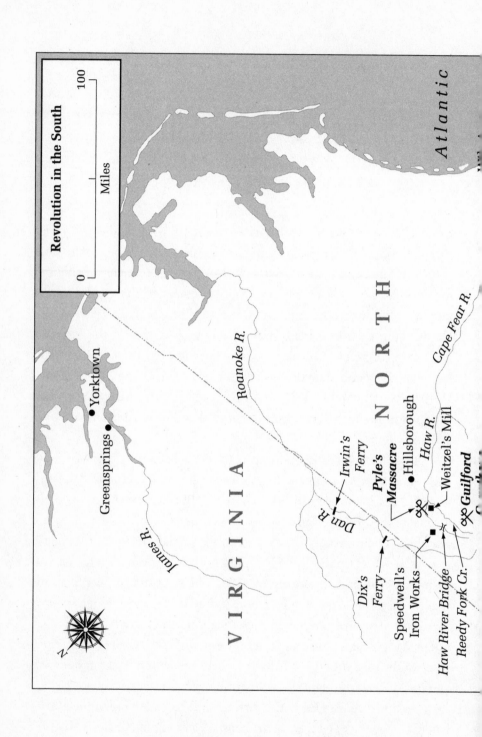

Revolution in the South

0   Miles   100

VIRGINIA

James R.

Greensprings •

• Yorktown

Roanoke R.

Dix's
Ferry

Speedwell's
Iron Works

Haw River Bridge

Reedy Fork Cr.

Dan R.

Irwin's
Ferry

**Pyle's
Massacre**

Weitzel's Mill

Guilford

N O R T H

Hillsborough •

Haw R.

Cape Fear R.

Atlantic

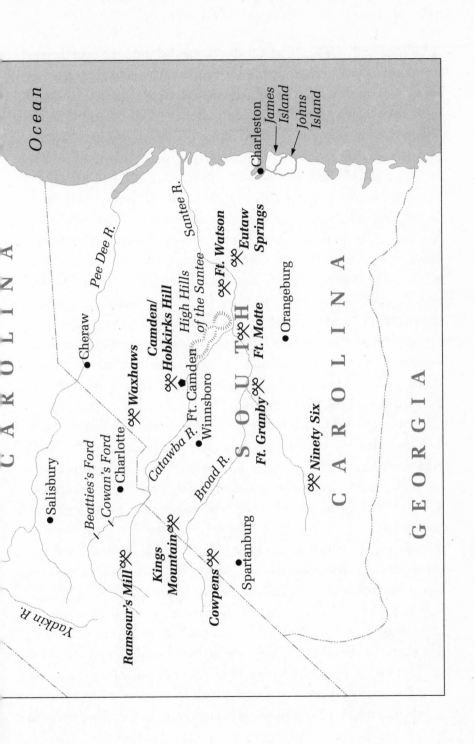

Johann de Kalb. De Kalb, who had commanded the Maryland division for months prior to their march south, was the Arnold Schwarzenegger of his day, described by his aide-de-camp as "a perfect Ariovistus, more than six feet tall." His endurance was the stuff of legend, and he regularly covered twenty to thirty miles per day on his own two feet, preferring walking to riding. This was all the more remarkable because in April 1780, de Kalb was fifty-nine years old. Well-disciplined and known for his "temperance, sobriety, and prudence," he regularly awoke before dawn and began working immediately. At nine, he indulged in breakfast, consisting only of dry bread and water, the only thing he ever drank. For lunch, he had soup and a bit of meat; for dinner bread again. At the end of the day, he "arrange[d] his portmanteau as a pillow and wrapping his great horseman's cloak around him stretch[ed] himself before the fire" to sleep. With his "patience, long-suffering, strength of constitution, endurance of hunger and thirst and a cheerful submission to every inconvenience in lodging," de Kalb was an excellent officer who endeared himself to his men, leading by example and willingly suffering the hardships of the lowest private.

Despite his Hannibal-like leadership style, like Von Steuben, de Kalb styled himself a "baron" and used an aristocratic prefix ("de") before his surname. General de Kalb was actually the son of Bavarian peasants. He left home at the age of sixteen and made his way to France, where he served as a lieutenant in an infantry regiment. Somewhere along the way, he changed his name from Hans Kalb to Johann de Kalb, which made him sound like a member of the nobility. He received several promotions, rising to the rank of major general, which conferred upon him the noble title of baron.

In 1767 the French had sent de Kalb to "inquire into the intentions of the inhabitants" in America. He reported back that the colonies were ripe for revolt, but France wasn't interested in sending soldiers to the as-yet-unbegun revolution at that time. Eager to participate in the war, de Kalb secretly returned to America with Lafayette and several other members of the French military who were seeking to serve the American cause. They arrived in June 1777. At that time, a stampede of Europeans had come to America in a similar manner, hoping for commissions in the army. Many did not obtain those commissions, but de Kalb eventually received the command of a division after some serious arm-twisting. Congress initially turned down de Kalb's request to be commissioned a major general, but the feisty Bavarian persisted and even threatened to sue Congress. Eventually he was accorded the same rank as Lafayette. Despite the rocky start with Congress, de Kalb sent the king of France favorable reports, which directly affected French funding for the war. It's not difficult to surmise that Washington let the baron command some of the Continental Army's most elite troops to make a favorable impression on the king of France. Now de Kalb was leading the Marylanders on the first leg of their legendary journey, racing the 150 miles to Head of Elk, Maryland, in just three weeks. Along the way, John Eager Howard stopped in Baltimore to sell some property to raise money for his upcoming expenses. He also left some funds behind "as a provision in case of my being taken prisoner." (Captured officers were expected to pay for their own imprisonment at the hands of the British.) At Head of Elk, the Marylanders boarded ships and sailed to Petersburg, Virginia.

As the Marylanders marched south, Henry Clinton and Charles, Earl Cornwallis's force, which had sailed from New York, laid siege to Charleston. Although Lincoln held on to the city for two months, he eventually surrendered to the Redcoats. On May 12, 1780, the Crown made prisoners of about six thousand American troops, including all the Continentals from South Carolina and North Carolina, and nearly all those from Virginia. Snared in the Crown's net were an additional one thousand American sailors and four American warships. It was the largest British POW haul of the war. At the time, it was customary for prisoners to be granted parole, that is, released on their oath that they would not fight again. However, the British denied Lincoln the traditional honors of war in accepting his surrender: the Americans were not allowed to march out with their colors or arms, and instead of granting parole, the British sent the rank and file to rot on prison ships.

A small group of Virginians led by Colonel Abraham Buford were riding toward Charleston to reinforce the city when it was captured. Realizing they couldn't add any value, Buford's Virginians quickly retreated, with the British cavalry in hot pursuit. Just before Buford and his men reached the North Carolina border, the British dragoons and cavalry, led by Banastre Tarleton, caught up to the Americans in the seedy South Carolina village of Waxhaws on May 29. The "battle," if one can call it that, went disastrously for the Americans. The British routed Buford and his men, who attempted to surrender. For a variety of reasons (Tarleton's excuse was that he had been thrown from his horse), the cavalry failed to honor Buford's white flag of truce. Tarleton's men brutally slaughtered 113 of the Virginians and wounded 150 more in an incident that became known as the Waxhaws Massacre. From the bloodbath, Tarleton earned the nickname Bloody Ban. For the next two years the incident had a huge impact on Whig, or pro-American, morale, and the term "Tarleton's quarter" came to mean that no prisoners would be taken. It also set the stage for bloody reprisals between the local Whigs and Tories. The survivors of the massacre, a little over a hundred men, all that was left of the American army in the South, rode like lightning north.

Confident that he had crushed the American army in the South, Clinton returned to New York, leaving Cornwallis behind to hold Georgia and South Carolina.

By this time, the Marylanders had landed in Petersburg, Virginia, and trudged 140 miles south to Hillsborough, North Carolina. After learning of Charleston's fall, de Kalb and company headed south into what was at the time some of the most rugged and wildest country of the thirteen colonies.

The Carolinas had few roads and were crisscrossed by numerous large rivers. Fording the waterways offered a challenge for offensive operations yet could provide good defensive positions and buy time for a retreating army. Control of the boats used on these rivers had a profound bearing on the campaign. In general, the terrain in the region was far different from that of the north. Near the coast, the Lowcountry consisted of a swampy, flat plain where prosperous, slaveholding plantation owners grew rice. Farther inland, rolling foothills gradually ascended into the Appalachians. The Backcountry, as this section was known, was home to less well-off farmers who raised corn and wheat in the shadow of the neighboring Indian nations. Farther west, some of the toughest men in America illegally occupied the land of western South Carolina and present-day Tennessee. The area fell behind the Royal Proclamation Line, which roughly followed the Allegheny Mountains and set aside the land to the west for the Native Americans; colonists were forbidden to settle there. In this forbidding place, these pioneers constantly battled not only the Indians but also the elements.

As they crossed the unfamiliar landscape, the Marylanders again faced a lack of food. Both armies picked the area clean, and Whig and Loyalist farmers often drove livestock out of harm's way before it could be seized by either army. Making matters worse, the frontier-like colonies had few towns and villages where provisions could be purchased. At the time, Charleston, the largest town, had only fourteen thousand inhabitants, including around five thousand slaves. The next-largest towns, Hillsborough and Salisbury, had only sixty to seventy houses each. In dealing with the constant hunger, the Maryland officers led by example. Otho Holland Williams recalled, "The officers, however, by appealing to their own empty canteens and mess cases, satisfied the privates that all suffered alike; and exhorting them to exercise the same fortitude of which the officers gave them example." As spring gave way to summer, the scorching heat wilted the men. Those that had uniforms withered away. Tens of thousands of ticks and fleas descended upon the men, feasting on their blood. Even the intrepid de Kalb groused, "The tick, a kind of strong black flea . . . makes its way under the skin and by its bite produces the most painful irritation and inflammation . . . my whole body is covered with these stings."

The Carolinas boasted a diverse population; former British Roundheads (those who supported Parliament during the English Civil War in the mid-seventeenth century), French Huguenots, and Scottish

Highlanders had fled to the Carolinas in order to escape persecution in their homelands years earlier. Settlements of Scotch-Irish, Catholic Irish, Dutchmen, and Swiss also dotted the landscape. In general, people settled close to others of the same nationality, forming independent communities that were divided religiously and politically. Some, like the Presbyterian Scotch-Irish, were devoted Patriots, while others, like the Scottish Highlanders, were fiercely loyal to Britain. The groups often erupted in violent conflict. Savage shootings and hangings became commonplace as the desire for revenge fueled feuds throughout the area.

With supplies running low, the Maryland Division continued marching toward South Carolina, foraging along the way. The lack of food convinced "a vast number of men to desert to the enemy," The men ate what they could find—often green corn and unripe fruit. On July 25 the half-starved cavalcade had reached Wilcox's Iron Works, where they were joined by General Horatio Lloyd Gates, who took over Lincoln's duties as commander in the South and assumed overall command of the Maryland Division and other units under de Kalb. Washington had wanted Nathanael Greene for the position, but Congress, without consulting the commander in chief, had appointed Gates, who still basked in the glory of Saratoga. Because of his age and disposition, some of the men referred to Gates as "Granny."

Initially, Granny's appearance improved the morale of the men, if for no other reason than his promise to supply them with plenty of "rum and rations." In the meantime, however, they continued to forage. Gates headed the Marylanders and the rest of his "Grand Army" toward Camden, South Carolina, the center of a web of British outposts that sprawled across the colony. Intelligence from Thomas Sumter and Francis Marion suggested the Grand Army might be able to attack and defeat the garrison at Camden.

Known as the Swamp Fox, Marion was an early pioneer of guerrilla warfare, leading the local militia in numerous quick, violent attacks on Loyalists and Redcoats. Unlike the swashbuckling composite character Mel Gibson depicted in the movie *The Patriot*, the real Swamp Fox was physically underwhelming: a frail, stubby fifty-year-old, hobbled by deformed knees and ankles. Reared on a plantation in South Carolina, he helped manage his family's land before serving in the French and Indian War and taking part in several battles against the Cherokee Indians. Although assigned to Lincoln's force in Charleston, he was away from the city when it fell to the British, having accidentally broken his ankle and gone to the country to recover. After Lincoln's surrender, he organized a small unit of men and set about terrorizing the enemy with hit-and-run attacks—despite his painful injury. Using principles he had learned from the Cherokee, Marion hid his men in the swamp and struck his targets hard, sowing terror throughout the region. To catch the slippery Marion, the British dispatched one of their most ruthless fighters—Banastre Tarleton. It was Tarleton who gave Marion his nickname: after pursuing the Patriot through twenty-six miles of Carolina swampland, Tarleton gave up the chase, exclaiming, "As for this damned old fox, the Devil himself could not catch him."

Thomas Sumter had also earned himself a colorful nom de guerre, the Fighting Gamecock. Born to Welsh immigrants in Virginia in 1734, Sumter joined the militia, which often battled with nearby Indian tribes. In 1761 he took part in the Timberlake Expedition, an adventure-filled foray into Indian country that brought him into close contact with the Cherokee. He befriended a chief named Ostenaco, and when Ostenaco wanted to meet the king, Sumter accompanied him to London, even though the trip left him bankrupt and landed him in debtor's prison. Eventually, he became a successful small businessman and plantation owner in South Carolina. When the Revolutionary War broke out, he received a commission as a lieutenant colonel of the 2nd Regiment in the South Carolina Line, but he resigned his commission and returned home after two years of fighting, hoping to live in peace. That dream was shattered in 1780, when British troops attacked his home, dragged his wheelchair-bound wife out on the lawn, and burned the building to the ground in front of her eyes. Incensed, Sumter struck back, attacking the British repeatedly and often taking risky gambles that paid off. One biographer wrote, "Fearless and inexorable, like a gamecock he struck with fiery gaffs, leaving death and carnage at every pitting. . . . Highly imaginative, the Gamecock was always the grand strategist, instinctively using both men and terrain to baffle the enemy. He was a daring tactician, leading raw militia in hand-to-hand fighting with British regulars."

With intimate knowledge of the Carolinas, Marion and Sumter advised Gates about the disposition of enemy forces. With limited troops, the British constantly struggled to maintain control over the territory they had seized. Making the best use they could of the region's topography, the British had established a series of outposts along the rivers and in small towns. While the main body of their forces remained in and around Charleston, they maintained small garrisons in George-town, Beaufort, Savannah, Augusta, Ninety Six, and Camden. As the most central of these posts, Camden was a key location, providing a crucial link between the Backcountry and the Lowcountry. If the British were to lose control of Camden, they would lose control of South Carolina.

With bands of horse-mounted partisans led by men like Marion and Sumter roving the countryside, keeping all these far-flung outposts in supply was a logistical nightmare for the British. Large wagon trains typically supplied many of the garrisons, but the trains were vulnerable to guerrilla raids. Armed with excellent intelligence gleaned from the population, the Patriots sallied from swamps and forests and ambushed the supply trains. The British never knew when and where these light-ning raids would fall. Besides attacking the supply network, small partisan forces tied up a large number of British troops and intimidated Loyalists, tamping down their support.

Gates headed directly for Camden, leading his men along a route that offered little in the way of food and plenty of opposition from Loy-alists who lived along the road. His plan, which he failed to share with his subordinates, was to set up a strong defensive position near Camden while partisan forces contined to harass British supply lines. Gates hoped that these attacks would either encourage the British to leave the area or convince them to attack his strong position. However, the actual battle went far differently from what the hero of Saratoga had envisioned.

CHAPTER 27

A "JALAP" AND
A NIGHT MARCH

Starlight shimmered through the pine branches, faintly illuminating the dusty road on the hot, humid, and moonless night of August 15–16, 1780. Led by the cavalry, the Marylanders marched Indian file with muskets slung over their shoulders. Behind them stretched the North Carolina militia and a winding baggage train nearly a mile long. The men trudged along the Waxhaws Road that linked to the Great Wagon Road, which ran through South Carolina and connected many towns, including the strategic British post of Camden, flanked on either side by an army of pine trees rooted in sandy soil.

The Marylanders had been journeying through the Carolinas for days, covering scores of miles. With their stomachs empty, the exhausted Continentals and militia of the Grand Army came to a halt and ate a hasty meal: loaves of bread, beef, and about four ounces of molasses for each man. For many, the meal was their last. In the short term, the sweetener produced an unexpected impact. Sergeant Major William Seymour of the Delaware Regiment explained, "Instead of rum, we got a gill of molasses per man served out to us, which instead of livening our spirits, served to purge us as well as if we had taken a jalap [laxative], for the men, all the way as we went along were every moment obliged to fall out of the ranks to evacuate."

Into the night the men marched south, confident of victory. Horatio Gates, the "hero of Saratoga," was rumored to have said, "I will breakfast to-morrow in Camden with Cornwallis at my table."

* * *

Earlier in the day, Gates estimated the strength of his army to be seven thousand men. Otho Holland Williams, now deputy adjutant general to Gates, knew the number was off by a significant amount and called for the regiments to report their strength. Each unit submitted its numbers; the rolls revealed 3,052 men "fit for duty." With the figures in hand, Williams soberly submitted the actual numbers to his superior.

Gates looked at Williams, nodding, and blithely dismissed the totals: "Sir, it will be enough for our purpose."

Gates's force still outnumbered Cornwallis's, but quantity didn't necessarily translate into quality. The bulk of the newly formed Grand Army consisted of militia, strengthened by a backbone of veterans from the Maryland and Delaware regiments. Many of these new troops had only recently been farmers and shopkeepers, and now they were facing highly trained British regulars.

On Gates's orders, William Smallwood and the Marylanders marched toward Camden, but the plan of attack didn't sit well with the senior Marylander. A North Carolinian militiaman "overheard Gates and Smallwood arguing about the battle plan." Williams recalled the consternation of his fellow officers as well: "Others could not imagine how it could be conceived that any army consisting of more than two-thirds militia, and which had never been once exercised in arms together, could form columns and perform other manoeuvers in the night, and in the face of the enemy."

Only a few miles away from the Marylanders, General Cornwallis was rallying his men and preparing them for a night march of their own—which set them on an unexpected collision course with the Grand Army. Cornwallis intended to seek out the Americans but had no idea how close they were. After the troops were mustered in, Cornwallis addressed his men: "Now, my brave soldiers, now an opportunity is offered for displaying your valour, and sustaining the glory of the British arms;—all you who are willing to face your enemies;—all you who are ambitious of military fame stand forward; where there are eight or ten to one coming against: let the men who cannot bear to smell gun-powder stand back, and all you who are determined to conquer or die turn out."

John Robert Shaw, a member of Cornwallis's own 33rd Regiment of Foot, recorded the earl's fiery speech and noted that nearly all the men turned out "except a few who were left to guard the sick and military stores."

The Redcoats were on the march.

Suddenly, the crackle of small-arms fire between the advance guards from both armies broke the silence of the hot August night. The two opposing forces that had unknowingly lumbered toward each other for several hours met.

In the darkness, a Frenchman, Colonel Charles Armand Tuffin, called "Colonel Armand," who had a checkered past prior to the war, led the American cavalry. In France, Armand had served in the Garde de Corps, the king's elite personal guard, but had injured Louis XVI's cousin in a duel—an incident that led to his exile to America. With Washington's permission, he had raised a cavalry legion. Around midnight, Armand's legion acted as a screening force, hit the vanguard of Cornwallis's army, took several casualties, retreated, and "threw the whole corps into disorder; which, recoiling suddenly in front of the column of infantry discovered the 1st Maryland Brigade. The Marylanders held the line and "executed their orders gallantly." The unanticipated collision shocked both armies. "The enemy, no less astonished than ourselves, seemed to acquiesce with a sudden suspension of hostilities," Williams recalled.

After taking a few prisoners, Williams determined that Cornwallis was leading the British. He then pressed the prisoners for additional information. The Brits revealed that Cornwallis commanded about two thousand troops, which lay about six hundred yards in front of the Patriots. Williams delivered the information to Gates, whose "astonishment could not be concealed."

On Gates's orders, Williams called a council of war. Hastily, Williams contacted each of the officers and asked them to assemble in an area behind the rear of the Patriot force. The first officer he approached was Baron de Kalb, who commanded the Maryland Division and the attached Delaware Regiment. When Williams told him the details of the troops that lay before them, de Kalb ominously replied, "Well, And has the general [Gates] given you orders to retreat the Army?"

Despite his misgivings, de Kalb remained silent during the council of war. As soon as they had all arrived, Gates communicated "the unwelcome news" of the enemy's position and then asked, "Gentlemen, what is best to be done?"

An uneasy silence hung over the meeting, and all the men "remained mute for a few moments." Gallant but headstrong, Brigadier General Edward Stevens, in charge of the Virginia militia, finally answered, "Gentlemen, is it not too late now to do anything but fight?"

De Kalb and the rest of the officers said nothing. With no additional advice offered, the men returned to their respective commands.

They had only a few hours to attempt to get some sleep before the morning's battle.

CHAPTER 28

CAMDEN

As the first rays of dawn poked through the pines on August 16, 1780, the Americans formed their battle line.

"Don't shoot until you see the whites of their eyes," officers repeated as the order went up and down the American lines.

A wall of scarlet appeared. "We see them a-coming, extending their lines as low as ours." Dawn soon gave way to the early morning sun, and Otho Holland Williams noticed what he thought was confusion in the enemy lines. He approached Horatio Gates, who "seemed disposed to wait events—he gave no orders."

Knowing the moment demanded decisive action, Williams pressed Gates for orders to attack.

The general sharply responded, "Sir, that's right—let it be done."

Galloping on his black charger, Williams "hastened to [General Edward] Stevens." His Virginia militia "instantly advanced with his brigade apparently in fine spirits." To aid in their assault, Williams asked for forty or fifty volunteers. The group of privates quickly assembled and the Marylander rode toward the front lines, ordering the men to act as pickets and slow the advancing enemy. "Take to the trees. Keep up as brisk a fire as possible!"

As the battle unfolded, Mordecai Gist surveyed the field: swampland, interspersed with conifers, lay on both sides of the Waxhaws Road, making it difficult for the British to flank the Americans. The terrain allowed the Redcoats to concentrate their smaller forces for a frontal assault on the Grand Army. But as Gates formed his men, he inadvertently made a disastrous error. The Americans' weakest forces, the

North Carolina and Virginia militia, were facing the seasoned British regulars of the 23rd and 33rd Regiments. The British army typically assembled its best units on its right flank, fighting "right-handed." Ideally, the American should have positioned his elite troops—the crack Maryland and Delaware regiments—across from the strongest British forces.

Stretching nearly a mile long on the right side of the Waxhaws Road stood the elite of the American army, Gist's 2nd Maryland Brigade, which included three Maryland Regiments, along with Captain Robert Kirkwood's stalwart Delaware Regiment. "[We] formed the line of battle . . . and lay on our arms until Break of Day," recalled Kirkwood.

Yelling "Huzzah!" the Redcoats fired a volley and charged across the sandy field.

Forgetting their orders not to fire until they could see the whites of the enemies' eyes, some of the militia responded almost immediately to the threat. One North Carolinian recalled, "I believe my gun was the first gun fired, notwithstanding the orders, for we were close to the enemy, who appeared to maneuver in contempt of us, and I fired without thinking, except that I might prevent the man opposite from killing me." Within seconds, a loud roar sounded up and down the line.

With bayonets gleaming, the Redcoats bore down on the Virginia militiamen, who "almost instantly collapsed. [In] a panic, they threw down their loaded arms and fled in utmost consternation." Within their ranks, only one regiment resisted the impulse to run. Unfortunately, the rest of the American left flank disintegrated. One of the participants noted that the urge to panic works "like electricity, it operates instantaneously—like sympathy, it is irresistible where it touches."

Williams, Gist, and Gist's friend Captain John Smith attempted to halt the fleeing militia, but the sight of British cold steel had broken the part-time soldiers. By contrast, the American right wing stood firm.

Smoke hung over the battlefield, obscuring the line of sight of both sides, and "the action became very Desperate; which continued for the space of a half an hour," remembered Kirkwood. Like a rock,

Marylanders held their line. "General Gist preserved perfect order in his brigade, and, with his small arms and artillery continued a heavy and well-directed fire upon the 33rd Regiment and the whole of the left division," Banastre Tarleton noted.

The 2nd Maryland Brigade, commanded by Gist, lunged forward toward the Volunteers of Ireland. The Volunteers had been formed by an Irish nobleman, Lord Francis Rawdon, a close friend of Tarleton. Described as "the ugliest officer" in the British army, Rawdon fought first at Bunker Hill and swiftly rose through the ranks, gaining the confidence of Cornwallis and his superiors. In the fall of 1777 he had been put in charge of raising a unit of Irish volunteers from the thirteen colonies. Now those volunteers faced their fellow Americans across the field of battle.

From horseback, opposite the Irishmen, John Eager Howard, who was emerging as one of the finest battle captains in the American army, shouted, "Fire!" With his commanding battlefield presence, he urged his men onward. One British officer recalled, "The enemy threw horrid showers of grape. . . . I commanded a company and lost more than half the number I took into the field, and the company next to me lost two-thirds. For half an hour, the event was doubtful."

Twice the Americans repulsed the Irishmen. Rawdon's troops began to falter. The combat veterans of the Maryland Line, "who had the keen edge of sensibility rubbed off by strict discipline and hard service, saw the confusion [of the militiamen] with little emotion," wrote Williams.

By this time, it was nearly impossible to see anything on the battle-field. "A dead calm, with a little haziness in the air, which preventing the smoke from rising occasioned so thick a darkness that it was difficult to see the effect of a very heavy and well-supported fire on both sides," recalled one observer. Despite the lack of visibility and the steadfastness of the Marylanders, Cornwallis sensed the tide of battle was beginning to turn. Outflanked but noticing his enemy had begun to stagger, the earl rode into the maelstrom "with great coolness, in the midst of a heavier fire than the oldest soldier remembers."

Cornwallis's intrepid leadership rallied his men, "Volunteers of Ireland, you are fine fellows! Charge the rascals—By heaven, you behave nobly!"

Johann de Kalb's courage equaled Cornwallis's, and he urged his men to hold their ground as he rode up and down the line. Suddenly his horse collapsed, killed by a British ball.

British infantry assaulted Gist's brigade on the left flank. In his coup de grâce, Cornwallis committed Tarleton's cavalry to battle.

Despite the gaping hole in Gates's line, de Kalb continued to fight. Disregarding the loss of his horse, the sixty-year-old Bavarian refused to yield ground. De Kalb's aide remembered that as the British closed in on the commander of the Maryland Division, "[de Kalb] fell into the hands of the enemy, pierced with eight wounds of bayonets and three musket balls. I stood by the baron during the action and shared his fate, being taken by his side, wounded in both arms and hands."

Williams shifted from Smallwood's 1st Brigade back to Gist and de Kalb, who were fighting for their lives. He summoned Benjamin Ford, who was commanding a regiment: "[I] called upon the [regiment] not to fly and was answered. They have done all that can be expected of them. We were outnumbered and outflanked. See the enemy charge with bayonets."

The Marylanders were being flanked on three sides by the British. At this crucial moment, Williams and Gist looked for Smallwood, "who, however, was not to be found."

Gist continued to fight, along with the other Marylanders. One of Gates's aides, Major Charles Magil, described the actions of Marylanders:

The men, to their Immortal Honour made a brave defense, but were at last obliged to give ground and were almost all killed or taken; Gist's Brigade behaved like heroes, so did Smallwood's. But their being more to our left afforded us no opportunity of saving them. . . . Gist's Brigade charged with bayonets, which first made the enemy give way . . . but we owe all misfortune to the militia; had they not run like dastardly cowards, our army was sufficient to cope with them.

Tarleton's charge, combined with the British infantry attack on the American line, resulted in a melee that was staggering in its intensity. "Rout and slaughter ensued in every quarter." The entire American line collapsed.

Gist attempted to rally his men and withdraw in good order while indirectly helping what remained of Gates's Grand Army to escape. According to Tarleton, "Brigadier General Gist moved off with about one hundred continentals in the body, by wading through the swamp on the right of the American position, where the British cavalry could not follow; this is the only party that retreated in a compact state from the field of battle."

De Kalb fought on though mortally wounded. The baron cut down a Redcoat with his sword before collapsing. British soldiers began to strip the dying Bavarian of his gold-embroidered uniform. Cornwallis rode into the scene and immediately put a stop to the filching. Compassionately, he said, "I am sorry, sir, to see you, not sorry that you are vanquished, but sorry to see you so badly wounded."

In his weakened condition, de Kalb allegedly looked at Cornwallis and nobly responded, "I thank you sir for your generous sympathy, but I die the death I always prayed for: the death of a soldier fighting for the rights of man."

As in their flight for survival at Brooklyn, the Marylanders scrambled through the swampy waters that flanked the battlefield, fleeing for their lives. Tarleton and his Legion were fast on their heels, cutting down the fleeing Continentals and militiamen with saber and pistol.

In the midst of the flight, a Continental rushed up to John Eager Howard and informed him of a wounded Maryland officer. Howard surged into action and helped extricate the injured man from the field of battle. One Maryland officer later reflected on the courage of Gist and Howard and his fellow Marylanders: "I saw in particular, such coolness and personal bravery in General Gist, Colonel Howard, and some others. . . . I am confident upon equal ground we could have fought, and I think subdued an equal number of the British troops." He added that Howard was one of the last to leave the field, accompanied by African American Thomas Carney, "who bore his part under Howard."

Unlike Howard and Gist, General Horatio Gates disgraced himself by being one of the first officers to leave the field of battle. Reports also indicated that Smallwood was not visible on the field. In his letter to the Maryland government, Smallwood glossed over his flight, putting the chain of events in the most favorable light: "I retreated with the shattered remains of the Maryland Division by way of Waxhaws, hence to Charlotte, where I intended to have made a stand."

For more than twenty miles, the men ran for their lives. Chaos ensued. Williams recalled, "The cries of the women and the wounded in the rear, and the consternation of the flying troops, so alarmed some of the wagoneers, that they cut out their teams and taking each horse [fled the battlefield]."

One of the worst single defeats of the entire American army was over in an hour. Now the southern colonies of the United States lay open to the British.

Before the battle began, Gates had commanded the Grand Army's heavy baggage train with approximately two hundred wagons to evacuate the battlefield, but the drivers ignored the order. As a result of their disobedience, the camp followers and women who had accompanied the army were now at the mercy of the British. Most strikingly, the American cavalry, which had been ordered to guard the baggage train, was now plundering it. The dragoons started breaking into trunks, pulling out clothing, food, and coins that belonged to the Maryland officers. They eagerly broke into their gin cases, opening the bottles and passing them around.

As Cornwallis's commissary general surveyed the battlefield, he also noted the detritus of war. "The road for some miles was strewn with the wounded and killed who had been overtaken by the legion in their pursuit. The numbers of dead horses, broken wagons, and baggage scattered on the road formed a perfect scene of horror and confusion: Arms, knapsacks, and the accoutrements found were innumerable; such was the horror and dismay of the Americans."

With little time to gaze upon the plundering, the Marylanders and militiamen fled. Wagoners who had lightened their loads by tossing the contents of their wagons on the side of the road sped past them, nearly running them down. Continentals and militiamen streamed north, searching out their comrades and evading Tarleton's pursuing cavalry. Nearly as dangerous were the local Tory sympathizers, who took advantage of the opportunity to pounce on the hapless and disorganized Patriots. Cornwallis's victory stoked the confidence of the Tories, who now openly turned against their fellow colonists. Many of the Americans had thrown away their arms in their flight and were easy prey for the British sympathizers who were "every day picking them up, taking everything from them which was of value."

In terms of modern counterinsurgency, Cornwallis's strategic victory was affecting the war's true center of gravity, which was the civilian population. Their allegiance could—and did—easily shift between the Crown and the United States over the course of the war. Loyalist Americans now felt emboldened by the victory.

Civilians weren't the only ones whose allegiance was affected by the shocking defeat at Camden. Nearly 130 Continentals and militiamen also changed sides and aided the British, "capturing some, plundering others, and maltreating all the fugitives they met," according to Williams. Those captured were offered a stark choice: languish in the bowels of a prison ship until their likely death or enlist in the British army with the possibility of survival or even escape. For many, it was about survival. Others were simply opportunists who wanted to be on the winning side because of the potential wealth it could bring.

One of those compelled to join the British was Maryland Private James Gooding, who reported, "[I] was wounded through [my] belly and through [my] thigh. [I] lay in Camden about three months." After healing from his wounds, he deserted the Loyalists and rejoined the Patriots, serving in the light infantry under Howard. Another turncoat was the infamous soldier of fortune and Delaware Continental Michael Dougherty. "Our Regiment was cut up root and branch . . . my unfortunate self wounded and made prisoner," he recalled. Once again, allegedly, his aversion to prison "persuaded and listed [*enlisted*] in Tarleton's Legion." He later lamented, "What a mistake! I never before had kept such bad company."

Facing incarceration in a British prison ship or death if they were captured, Gist, John Gunby, Howard, and many other members of the original Baltimore Independent Cadets ran for their lives. Gist and Howard assembled some of the larger groups of retreating Marylanders. Together they made the long journey toward Charlotte.

The fleeing soldiers were "a great number of distressed with families." Williams's pen described "the disorder of the whole line of march . . . [its] compound wretchedness—care—anxiety, pain, poverty, hurry, confusion, humiliation, and dejection would be characteristic traits in the mortifying picture."

One of Gist's officers, Lieutenant Gassaway Watkins, "was pursued by Tarleton's horse, jumped a fence eleven logs high, and was two nights and days without eating without seeing anyone and slept in the woods."

The men found insufficient food in Charlotte. So Gist ordered them north toward Salisbury. The route was so fluid that Robert Kirkwood barely noted the flight in his journal. "I can give no account of our marches on the Retreat untill we came to Salisbury, where we arrived on the 21st." Nearly starving and living on whatever they could find—primarily peaches and watermelons—the men avoided local Tories and marched for nearly two hundred miles. Initially, the senior officer in the field was Smallwood, who claimed to assume command of the stragglers.

They joined Gates. After fleeing the battlefield, Gates had ridden for three and a half days, covering a remarkable distance for even the most experienced rider.

The tattered remains of the army filtered into Hillsborough. Sergeant Major William Seymour, a stalwart veteran of the Blues, recalled, "The fugitives from Camden came in daily, but in a deplorable condition, hungry, fatigued, and almost naked. . . . [The men needed to be] completely refitted with clothes, tents, and blankets."

It is impossible to determine American losses exactly; however, estimates say at least 650 of the Continentals were killed or captured. The Marylanders had sustained over 50 percent casualties during the Battle of Camden. But slowly, the remnants of the Grand Army trickled into Hillsborough, even up to two or three weeks after the battle. As they had done so many times before, the Marylanders re-formed and were able to help rebuild the army.

One bright spot occurred when Francis Marion freed a number of Continental troops. The Swamp Fox described the gallant action in his own words: "Attacked a Guard of the 63rd and Prince of Wales Regiment with a number of Tories. Took 22 regulars [British] and 2 Tories prisoner and retook 150 Continentals from the Maryland line."

Cornwallis was riding high after his decisive victory in Camden. In Europe and at Henry Clinton's headquarters in New York, the war appeared to be finally turning a corner in favor of the Crown. The Dutch, reacting to the string of British wins, stopped supplying the Americans with gunpowder, supplies, and equipment. Even in Paris the victories had a chilling effect. In the two years of war since the alliance was signed, there had been few tangible battlefield results except the two botched operations under Jean-Baptiste d'Estaing. Some questioned how long France would remain at war and whether it separately tried to make peace with Britain despite the treaty. The war was driving France toward bankruptcy, and an understanding with Britain was considered an honorable way to exit the war. There was a serious possibility that France would pull out its troops and end its funding. Perhaps the greatest threat to independence came several months later when Russia and Austria proposed a peace conference to mediate an end to the war.

The year 1780 looked even darker than the fall of 1776 for the new nation. "Reconciliationists" in Congress had begun calling for talks with Great Britain. American morale was at a low point, and many believed the war would come to an end with some sort of accommodation rather than the complete independence that the Patriots wanted. Their last hope was to win some significant battles in 1781. If the British could simply maintain the status quo, continuing to consolidate their gains in South Carolina and grow additional Loyalist units without any major battlefield losses, their ultimate victory seemed certain.

Cornwallis and Britain appeared to be unstoppable. One officer wrote of Cornwallis: "His army is his family, he is the father of it. There are no parties, no competitions. What may not be expected from a force so united, a leader so popular and patriotic? The great confidence the army place in him will enable him to carry the world before him."

General George Washington had a unique relationship with the men of the Maryland Line. After the Battle of Brooklyn, in which the Marylanders launched several bayonet charges that held off the British, allowing elements of the American army to escape, Washington called upon them numerous times to make decisive contributions in major battles. The Marylanders fought in both the North and the South, frequently turning the tide of the conflict.

Source: https://commons.wikimedia.org/wiki/George_Washington#/media/File:Portrait_of_ George_Washington-transparent.png

In 1774 the intrepid Mordecai Gist, an early agitator for revolution, was elected the commanding officer of the Baltimore Independent Cadets, "gentlemen of honour, family, and fortune." The independent company included many best friends who formed a cadre of officers in some of the greatest regiments in the Revolution.

Source: Benson Lossing, Pictorial Field Book of the Revolution

One of the most important small unit engagements in American history was the Marylanders' epic stand in front of the Old Stone House in Brooklyn. Buying precious time, their bayonet charges and holding action allowed a portion of the American army to escape. More than 250 of the men of the Maryland Line were either killed or captured by the British.

Source: Alonzo Chappel

Hanging from the venerable American Legion Post 1636 in Brooklyn, New York, is a corroded sign memorializing a mass grave. Nearby, perhaps beneath a garage or a paved street, lie the Marylanders' undiscovered bodies. The exact location of their grave is a mystery to this day. Their remains lie intermingled in what should be hallowed ground. Many other Marylanders were captured and likely perished on prison ships in New York Harbor.
Author Photo

Cornwallis was bunkered in the Old Stone House in Brooklyn in August 1776 when the Immortals made their preemptive strike against the position. It was rebuilt near the end of the nineteenth century using stones from the original house.
Author Photo

General Charles, Earl Cornwallis, arguably one of Britain's greatest generals during the Revolution, first engaged with the Marylanders at the Old Stone House in Brooklyn. A fearless leader and an adaptable tactician, Cornwallis faced Washington's Immortals in numerous battles throughout the war.

Source: https://commons.wikimedia.org/ wiki/File:First_Marquis_of_ Cornwallis.jpg

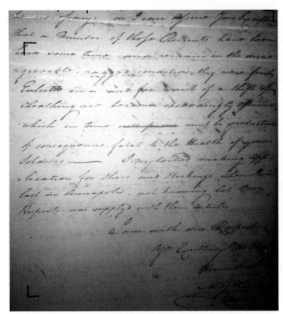

Letter from Mordecai Gist. Much of the research for *Washington's Immortals* came from unpublished primary sources: pension files, letters, and diaries. In the words of the participants, these unpublished sources capture a largely unknown, boots-on-the-ground, side of the Revolution.

Source: Myers Collection New York Public Library

GENERAL HOWE.

Lord General William Howe was in charge of the British land forces fighting in the early years of the Revolution. He had a reputation for gambling and whoring, frequently bringing his married Loyalist mistress, derisively known as "the Sultana," to public events. Although a member of Parliament and distantly related to the king, he had some sympathy for the Patriots and would have preferred a diplomatic resolution to the conflict.

Source: Library of Congress

WASHINGTON CROSSING THE DELAWARE

After fighting in New York and New Jersey, the Marylanders sustained heavy losses of those killed, captured, and wounded. Worn down by heavy fighting, a small number of Marylanders participated in the crossing of the Delaware.

Source: Library of Congress

The Battle of Trenton, a turning point in the war, led to a decisive military victory and the capture of hundreds of Hessian soldiers. It raised the sinking morale of the country.
Source: Library of Congress

A forgotten battle of the Revolutionary War, the Second Battle of Trenton involved an epic stand at the Assunpink Creek, where the Marylanders and Washington's Army blunted multiple British assaults.
Source: Library of Congress

Instead of retreating after the against-all-odds stand at the Second Battle of Trenton, Washington boldly went on the defensive and attacked the British at Princeton, another American victory.
Source: Library of Congress

Ironically, some of the most beautiful places in America, including the bucolic area around Pennsylvania's Brandywine Creek, are fields of battle where many Americans sacrificed their lives.
Author photo

This monument honors the men who fell in the massacre at Paoli, where British light infantry forces overran an encampment occupied by soldiers under the command of General "Mad Anthony" Wayne. Mordecai Gist and William Smallwood marched Maryland reinforcements into the area and fought in part of the melee.
Author photo

British forces occupied the Chew House, located in Germantown, Pennsylvania, and turned it into a fortress. The quarried schist structure still stands today, its edifice pockmarked by musket and cannon balls.

Source: Library of Congress

Humble, charismatic, and known for his prodigious memory and dignified manners, John Eager Howard was one of Maryland's most outstanding officers. He would later marry Peggy Chew, whose former home (pictured above) figured prominently at the Battle of Germantown.

Source: National Park Service

THE TAKEING OF MISS MUD ILAND.

One of the longest sieges of the American Revolution involved the bombardment of Mud Island. The Patriot fortress blocked naval passage to British-occupied Philadelphia. Marylander Samuel Smith commanded the garrison there, and his forces participated in a raiding party to destroy British guns, as well as in the destruction of several British warships.

Source: Library of Congress

A great regimental commander of the war, Marylander Samuel Smith, a brilliant, charismatic leader, maintained close personal relationships with John Eager Howard and several other Maryland officers. During the Revolution, leadership went hand-in-hand with deep ties of friendship and family, and this eighteenth century band of brothers forged unbreakable bonds that carried the Continental Army through the darkest days of the war. Smith defended Fort Mifflin on Mud Island, where he was seriously wounded. He would later emerge as the victorious commanding officer who defended Baltimore in the War of 1812.

Source: National Park Service

At the Battle of Monmouth, the longest battle of the Revolution, Washington once again called upon the Immortals to help check the British advance. Marylander Nathaniel Ramsay and his regiment held off the British long enough for Washington to reform his men, but Ramsay was eventually surrounded and taken prisoner. According to legend, a British officer spared Ramsay's life upon seeing his Masonic ring. His wife, Jenny, a camp follower and the center of social life in the regiment, joined Ramsay in captivity.

Source: Wikipedia—Emanuel Gottlieb Leutze, located in the Roger W. Heyns Reading Room of the UC Berkeley Library

A view of Stony Point overlooking the Hudson River. At the time of the Revolution, the British had heavily fortified the point, featuring multiple rings of defenses.
Author photo

THE BATTLE OF STONY POINT.

Among the most brilliant raids of the Revolution was one that occurred at Stony Point, New York. The Marylanders, many of whom were part of the light infantry, a precursor to special operations forces, conducted a spectacular assault, resulting in the capture of hundreds of British prisoners. The main thrust of the American attack involved a "forlorn hope" (in today's parlance, a suicide squad), men equipped with axes to cut through a sharpened log barrier known as an abatis. One of the main groups was led by Marylander Jack Steward, who was decorated by Congress for his effort.

Source: Library of Congress

A veteran of the French and Indian War who was well acquainted with both George Washington and the Cornwallis family, Horatio Gates was a contender for Washington's position as commander in chief of the American forces. He led his men to a resounding and important victory at Saratoga, New York, but his poor strategic decisions at Camden, South Carolina, resulted in a spectacular loss for the Americans. His military reputation never recovered after the debacle.

Source: National Park Service

A rugged frontiersman, Daniel Morgan ran an independent wagon team during the French and Indian War, earning the nickname "The Old Wagoner." Animated by a fierce hatred for the British, he organized a company of Virginia riflemen at the start of the war, playing a pivotal role at the Battle of Saratoga. Recognizing Morgan's brilliance as a military tactician, Greene placed him in command of the Flying Army. At the Battle of Cowpens in South Carolina, he employed multiple lines of defense to great effect, decisively defeating Banastre Tarleton and his Legion.

Source: National Park Service

One of the great commanders of the war, Maryland native Otho Holland Williams joined the Continental Army in 1775. Unusually, he was promoted while in captivity and then released in a prisoner exchange. Williams went on to lead Maryland forces in many battles in the South. Most notably, he conducted brilliant rearguard and screening actions during Greene's epic, yet largely forgotten, race to the Dan River.

Source: National Park Service

Utilizing a defense in depth, which was quite novel for the time, Morgan led his forces, including the Marylanders, to victory over the British at the Battle of Cowpens. During the battle, William Washington, who would fight alongside the Marylanders throughout the South, dueled Banastre Tarleton. Washington narrowly escaped death after his sword broke in half, but his courageous African American orderly saved his life. Tarleton and nearly two hundred of his men escaped.
Source: William Ramney https://en.wikipedia.org/wiki/Battle_of_Cowpens

The son of a slave trader, Banastre Tarleton was a British cavalry officer with a reputation for ruthlessness, earning him the nicknames "Bloody Ban" and "The Butcher." As Cornwallis's right hand in the southern campaign, he pursued the Marylanders throughout the Revolution, frequently facing them in battle. He lost two fingers at the Battle of Guilford Courthouse but later pursued a political career after the war ended.
Source: Library of Congress

The terrain at Cowpens played an important role in the battle. The Greene River Road bisected the field, and it was flanked by ravines and creeks. General Morgan used the landscape to his advantage, delivering a crushing defeat to the British.
Author Photo

A distant cousin to George
Washington, William Washington,
an officer with the Continental Light
Dragoons was influential in several
battles, particularly the Battle of
Cowpens. Known as a bold and fierce
commander, he fought alongside the
Marylanders at several engagements
throughout the Southern Campaign.
He was wounded and taken prisoner
at the Battle of Eutaw Springs.
Source: National Park Service

Arguably Washington's most able
general, Nathanael Greene led the
southern army, including the
Marylanders. He characterized his
strategy in the South this way: "We
fight, get beat, rise and fight again."
His battlefield strategy ultimately
accomplished the goal of largely
clearing the Carolinas of
British forces.
Source: National Park Service

Elite regiments at the core of the army, the stalwart Maryland Line kept the American Army together during 1780 and 1781, including during the Battle of Guilford Courthouse. Cornwallis won the engagement, but lost more than a quarter of his men. The battle had an enormous impact on the war and compelled Cornwallis to advance north into Virginia.
Source: U.S. Army National Guard

The overlooked battle and siege at Fort Ninety Six involved a sapping tunnel dug under the fort as well as a forlorn hope assault. Even in the heat of battle, a deep bond formed between two assault members in the forlorn hope: Captain Perry Benson and free African American soldier Thomas Carney, who saved Benson's life after he was severely wounded during the attack. Both men maintained their friendship long after the war.
Author Photo

After nearly six years of continuous war, many Marylanders, including Mordecai Gist, witnessed the surrender of Cornwallis's army. They had come full circle. In their first battle, the Marylanders had been "cut to atoms" by Cornwallis's guns at Brooklyn, and they faced their nemesis on the battlefield multiple times before his final defeat at Yorktown.

Source: U.S. Capitol

General Washington resigned his commission in front of Congress at the Maryland State House in Annapolis at the conclusion of the war. Many of the officers of the Immortals were present to hear him say, "Having now finished the work assigned me, I retire from the great theatre of action... and take my leave of all the employments of public life." Hearing of Washington's plan to resign instead of becoming a dictator, King George III proclaimed, "If he does that, he will be the greatest man in the world."

Source: U.S. Capitol

CHAPTER 29

"LAY THEIR COUNTRY WASTE WITH FIRE AND SWORD"

The Patriot militiaman lay on the ground, clutching his right arm. Wounded in a skirmish, the hapless man looked dully at his shattered limb.

The life-threatening wound was just the beginning of his horrific ordeal. The available medical treatments of the day were as likely to kill patients as to cure them. But in the backwoods of Carolina, even these barbaric treatments were unavailable. Instead, wounded men bit down on a leather strap or a stick, grimacing against the pain while their comrades held them down during "surgery."

In this case, with the bone "very much shattered," everyone knew the soldier's arm must be amputated if he were to have any faint chance of survival. With no doctor available, a blacksmith hacked off the limb "with a shoemaker's knife and a carpenter's saw. He stopped the blood with the fungus of the oak, without taking up a blood vessel."

Scenes like these repeated over and over again as Loyalist militiamen pushed their way north, skirmishing with their countrymen along the way. The victory at Camden had a galvanizing effect on the Tories, emboldening them to rise up against their Whig counterparts. By this time, the number of Loyalists in the British army in America had swelled dramatically. In the early years of the war, the British didn't consider the Loyalists reliable and didn't make them a major factor in their strategy. The global war had bled the Crown's troops from North America, and the British had a dramatic need to fill the shortfall. They raised thousands of provincials in New York, and by 1780 nearly nine thousand Tories were serving in the British army. However, the policy was coming into effect a little too late. Throughout the war, the British consistently struggled to find enough troops to garrison areas that they had taken. Had the British actively recruited Loyalists from the beginning of the war, they would have had more troops to man outposts and protect the Loyalist population in areas they had cleared.

Despite the success at Camden, Cornwallis reported to General Henry Clinton that the "whole country" along the border with North Carolina and northeast South Carolina was in "an absolute state of rebellion." Bands of guerrillas nipped at the British forces and slowly waged a war of attrition in some ways similar to the *petite guerre* in New Jersey in 1777. They also terrorized British sympathizers in a campaign of intimidation. The British had a hard time protecting the local Loyalist population outside Charleston. A vicious civil war roiled the countryside; both sides employed brutal methods and gave no quarter. In a series of more than a dozen small battles, Cornwallis estimated that he lost nearly a tenth of his fighting force that had landed in Charleston in February 1780.

Cornwallis was convinced that to pacify South Carolina, he had to invade North Carolina and stamp out insurgents who were coming across the border. Over the summer of 1780 he laid plans for seizing North Carolina and began contacting Loyalist leaders and stockpiling supplies. He prepared to march with twenty-two hundred men from Camden to Charlotte, North Carolina.

Backcountry militia forces, loyal to the Crown, grew quickly, often terrorizing Whigs by plundering and torching the homes of those who served Francis Marion and Thomas Sumter. They hanged combatants and roughed up civilians. The war raging in the backcountry of the South was very different from the war in the North, but, as in modern war, the militiamen had an oversized impact on the population—influencing it, intimidating it, or even protecting it—and they went places regulars had trouble entering.

Many Loyalist militiamen coalesced around Lieutenant Colonel Patrick Ferguson, whom the Marylanders first encountered when his raiding force landed at Monmouth County, New Jersey, back in April 1780. On September 1, Ferguson joined Cornwallis at Camden. "Major Ferguson joined us from Camden again with the disagreeable news that we were to be separated from the Army, and act on the frontier with the militia," recalled Anthony Allaire, an American Loyalist volunteer. Ferguson's task was to act as a screening force, protecting Cornwallis's left flank from rebel partisans who had been congregating west of the Appalachian Mountains. Ferguson's Loyalists represented the left wing of Cornwallis's plan to invade North Carolina. Flawed from the beginning, this plan lacked a backbone of British regulars integrated into Ferguson's troops and instead relied entirely on militiamen. It was a rare strategic blunder for Cornwallis—and one that proved disastrous.

Next, disastrously for the British, British General Sir Henry Clinton had issued an edict requiring paroled prisoners to join the British militia or be considered traitors to the Crown. The proclamation roiled the population, which was split between Whigs and Tories. Whigs, on the defense, found themselves in the position of having nothing to lose from fighting against the British. This announcement—combined with confiscations of property from Americans found working against the Crown's interests, and with various atrocities like that committed at Waxhaws—spurred many to oppose the Crown rather than to join the Loyalist militias like Ferguson's.

With nearly a thousand Tory militiamen, Ferguson moved north from the British stronghold at Ninety Six, which helped secure the backcountry of South Carolina and acted as an anchor in a series of posts in the southern part of the state. He and his group attempted to snuff out the insurgency by force and boldly proclaimed, "If they do not desist from their opposition to the British arms, we would march over the mountains, hang their leaders, and lay their country waste with fire and sword."

He made an appeal to the Loyalists of North Carolina, issuing a call to arms for their self-defense that included a heavy dose of propaganda:

Gentlemen: unless you wish to be eat up by an inundation of barbarians, who have begun by murdering an unarmed son before his aged father, and afterwards lopped off his arms, and who by their shocking cruelties and irregularities, give the best proof of their cowardice and want of discipline; I say, if you wish to be pinioned, robbed, and murdered, and see your wives and daughters, in four days, abused by the dregs of mankind—in short, if you wish or deserve to live, and bear the name of men, grasp your arms in a moment and run to camp. . . . If you choose to be pissed upon by a set of mongrels, say so at once, and let your women turn their backs upon you, and look out for real men to protect them.

Ferguson's words didn't do much to rally support, but they thoroughly pissed off a group of Americans known as the Overmountain Men. These rugged, independent Americans had defied the king and settled beyond the Royal Proclamation Line of 1763, which established everything west of the Appalachian Mountains as Indian territory. Considered illegal squatters, this mixture of Scottish and Irish immigrants (along with a few Germans and Welsh) inhabited what is today the extreme northeast corner of Tennessee, where Tennessee, North Carolina, and Virginia meet. Virginia Governor Lord Dunmore called them a "dangerous example" for their rebellion against the Crown.

True pioneers, hardened by years of living on the frontier, they fought constantly for their survival against both the elements and the Indians in the area. That hard living had shaped the men's bodies, and to their foes, they seemed truly intimidating: "[They] appeared like so many devils from the infernal regions, so full of excitement were they as they darted like enraged mountains up the mountain. . . . They were the most powerful-looking men, [I] ever beheld; not overburdened with fat, but tall, raw-boned, and sinewy with long matted hair—such men as were never before seen in the Carolinas."

As one backwoodsman later bragged, "We were formidable. . . . Our equals were scarce, and our superiors hard to find."

Ferguson's foolhardy boast about hanging their leaders and laying waste to their country stiffened the resolve of the Overmountain Men, who intended to destroy the Scottish-born officer. To separate friend from foe, the men used a password and countersign for identification. Ominously, the countersign was "Buford," a reference to the Waxhaws Massacre.

Ferguson marched toward Tennessee to screen Cornwallis's army, which was heading for North Carolina, and had quickly occupied Charlotte without a fight. When he received word of the approach of the Overmountain Men, he withdrew to Kings Mountain, where the Loyalist militia set up a defensive position. The British officer expected to be reinforced by Cornwallis, who was encamped roughly twenty-five miles away.

A downpour pelted the Overmountain Men on October 7, 1780, as they rode in rows toward Kings Mountain. Their officers reminded them to keep their weapons dry. Many of them removed their shirts to wrap around their Deckard rifles. These rifles, made by a German immigrant, were among the best available at the time, able to shoot accurately at a distance of 250 yards, a feat unmatched by other weapons during the Revolution.

As the Overmountain column came to a brief halt, Colonel Isaac Shelby, the effective commander of the group, turned to another officer and said, "I will not stop until night. I will follow Ferguson into Cornwallis's lines." Three officers took their places at the van of their respective regiments, as they trundled forward again into the streaming rain. By noon the rain had stopped, and a cool breeze brushed the faces of the marching men. When the three regiments were passing a house owned by a Tory, a girl suddenly rushed out and questioned some of the men. "How many are there of you?"

"Enough to whip Ferguson if we can find him," the men responded.

The girl pointed to a ridge several miles away. "He's on that mountain."

With the new information, the officers agreed to a simple plan: envelop the mountain and annihilate the Loyalists.

Around 3:00 p.m. on October 7, 1780, an order came down from the officers: "Dismount and tie your horses. . . . Tie up greatcoats, blankets, etc. to your saddles."

Militiaman James Collins, only a teenager at the time but a trusted courier, recalled that the men rode into battle armed to the teeth with locally forged weapons: "We got swords, butcher knives, and war spurs made by the blacksmiths." The teenager also remembered the moments leading up to the battle: "We were paraded and harangued in a short manner of the prospect before us. The sky was overcast with clouds, and at times a light mist was falling; our provisions were scanty and hungry men were like to be fractious; each one felt his situation; the last stake was up and the severity of the game must be played; everything was at stake—life, liberty, property, and even the fate of wife, children, and friends seemed to depend on the issue: death or victory was the only way to escape suffering."

As the men assembled, the officers invited the faint of heart to leave. But peer pressure influenced the men, who "could not well swallow the appellation of 'coward.'" All of them received general orders: "Fresh prime your guns, and every man go into battle firmly resolving to fight till he dies."

The men silently moved toward their positions around the mountain where Ferguson's Loyalists were camped. According to Ferguson's morning report, the Loyalists numbered 1,125 men, with the only British national being Major Patrick Ferguson. Nine hundred Overmountain Men surrounded the Loyalists.

About ten minutes before the final column could get into position, the Overmountain Men attacked. "The orders were at the firing of the first gun for every man to raise a whoop, rush forward, and fight his way as best he could." Collins recounted the furious assault as the men let out bloodcurdling shouts. "We were soon in motion, every man throwing four or five balls in his mouth to prevent thirst"—and also to be in readiness to "reload quick." The Overmountain Men weaved through the trees and boulders as they charged up Kings Mountain.

Foolishly, Ferguson did not entrench on top of the mountain. Instead, he formed up battle lines. As the Loyalist Americans fired down on the Overmountain Men, their volleys tended to overshoot the charging Patriots. Collins recalled, "Their great elevation above us proved their ruin: they overshot us altogether, scarce touching a man except those on horseback, while every rifle from below seemed to have the desired effect."

The Loyalists, however, repelled Collins and his group twice. One Patriot soldier recalled, "The fight seemed to become more furious. Their leader Ferguson came into full view, within rifle shot, as if to encourage his men." Collins and the men charged for a third time. The Loyalists' ranks began to melt away. Sensing victory, the officers roared, "Hurrah, my brave fellows! Advance!"

The Loyalists began crying for quarter as the pocket of resistance at the top of the crest started to collapse. The final phase of the battle lasted about twenty to thirty minutes. Ferguson spurred on the men from his white charger, waving his gleaming sword as he rode from one end of the line to the other, but despite his efforts to rally his troops, white flags of surrender began to appear.

The Overmountain Men chose not to accept the surrender of those who called for quarter. Many of the rebels yelled, "Give them Buford's play!" Disregarding the white flags, the Overmountain Men slaughtered the Loyalists. As one rebel recalled, "[We] continued to fire without comprehending in the heat of the moment what had happened; some had heard at Buford's defeat, the British had refused quarter . . . and were willing to follow that bad example." Several of the officers attempted to intercede and, knocking guns upward, shouted, "Don't shoot! It is murder to kill them now for they have raised the flag!

"Cease firing! For God's sake, cease firing!"

Collins recalled the carnage: "The poor Tories appeared to be really pitiful; the dead lay in heaps on all sides, and the groans of the wounded were heard in every direction."

Their leader shared the fate of his men, as did one of Ferguson's mistresses, Virginia Sal, who had accompanied him into the battle. The beautiful redhead was struck in the head by a bullet.[30] Surveying the scene, Collins spotted Ferguson's bullet-riddled body and noted, "It appeared that almost fifty rifles must have leveled at him at the same time; seven balls had passed through his body; both his arms were broken and his hat and clothing were literally shot to pieces."

Reports indicated that 157 Tories were killed; 163 were badly wounded. The Overmountain Men captured 698 men as prisoners.

On the day after the battle, the families of the Loyalist Americans gazed on the horror of the battlefield. "The next morning, which was Sunday, the scene became really distressing; the wives and children of the poor Tories came in, in great numbers; their husbands, fathers, and brothers lay in great heaps while others lay wounded or dying," Collins recalled. The victors hastily buried the dead. They covered the fallen with old logs, tree bark, and rocks, leaving them vulnerable to the beasts of the forest. Collins observed, "The hogs in the neighborhood gathered into the place to devour the flesh of men. . . . Half the dogs in the country were said to be mad and were put to death." Collins returned to the battlefield several weeks later to witness the haunting remains of Ferguson's militia. "All parts of the human frame lay scattered in every direction."

Savagely, the Overmountain Men stabbed and beat many of the Tories they had taken prisoner before subjecting them to a long march into captivity. Lieutenant Anthony Allaire noted in his diary, "Several of the militia that were worn out with fatigue, and not able to keep up, were cut down and trodden to death in the mire." Allaire was lucky. He and several of the captured militiamen escaped and began a two-hundred-mile journey to the British stronghold at Ninety Six, avoiding Rebel patrols along the way.

By October 7, 1780, Ferguson and his entire force had been either killed or captured. The victory of the Overmountain Men served as a turning point in the South. The colonists now saw the "invincible" British as vulnerable to defeat. Yet the victory came at a price. "State

30. Ferguson had two mistresses, known as Virginia Sal and Virginia Paul. Virginia Paul escaped the battle alive but was held prisoner by the Overmountain Men. Documentation corroborates the existence of the two women, and ground-penetrating radar revealed a second body buried under Ferguson's on Kings Mountain.

legislatures, especially the one in North Carolina, seemed to think the war could be won by militia alone, and there was no longer a need to build states' Continental Regiments."

Even in Maryland, the issue of militiamen versus Continentals remained a problem, as did the short enlistment period. Men would train up, gain esprit de corps with their comrades, and then be sent back to civilian life. "Just as such soldiers begin to learn the common duties of a military life, their times expire," wrote Gist, "and they return disgusted to their former State as Citizens, by which means an Army becomes enervated, disagreeable sensations arises in the Breasts of our Officers, they feel a conscious inferiority for want of proper Commands and lose that emulation necessary in a military life. This gives place to a relaxation of Discipline, which must ever be followed by misfortune and Disgrace in Action."

Gist warned that, as in any war, politics played a major role in the army's success or failure, and he called on the legislature to set aside personal goals in favor of the cause. He wrote, "The Independence of the United States is as fixed as fate; yet if we neglect to support it with Dignity or to aim at national Glory, if we cease to sacrifice private Interests to public Good, the Blessing will corrupt at our touch and like an affectionate love, worn out by Injuries, grow into a hated Monster."

Most of the responsibility for Ferguson's defeat lay on Cornwallis's shoulders for dividing his army and allowing one wing to be destroyed. Seriously ill, Cornwallis spent more than a dozen days riding in the back of a wagon. Believing that the opposing force numbered more than three thousand, he retreated from Charlotte to Winnsboro, South Carolina, ending his first invasion of North Carolina.

Cornwallis didn't return to the colony for four months. Sir Henry Clinton perfectly summed up the importance of the American victory: "[Kings Mountain] unhappily proved the first link in the chain of evils that followed each other in regular succession until they at last ended in the total loss of America."

CHAPTER 30

WASHINGTON'S BEST GENERAL

Despite the debacle at Camden, American partisans led by Thomas Sumter and Francis Marion continued to nip at Cornwallis's troops, striking his outposts and ambushing his supply lines. The backbone of the southern army, the Maryland Continentals, continued to rebuild as reinforcements streamed south. Their role as veteran, elite troops that formed the nucleus of a new southern army was more important than ever.

When Congress finally learned the full extent of the disaster at Camden, it offered Washington the opportunity to appoint a new commander of the southern army to replace Horatio Gates. Several men vied for the position, including William Smallwood, who self-ishly bucked the chain of command and appealed directly to his contacts in Congress. According to Nathanael Greene, Smallwood also "intimated the great difficulties he encountered and the exertions he had made to save a remnant of General Gates's army."

As backroom politics swirled around the selection of a new southern commander, Smallwood and Mordecai Gist reorganized the remaining Maryland Continentals, beginning the process of rebuilding the tattered army. They compressed the two Maryland brigades, the 1st and the 2nd, into a single regiment of two battalions. The 1st, 3rd, elements of the 5th,[31] and 7th Marylanders became the 1st Battalion; the 2nd, 4th,

---

31. Most of the 5th, nearly one hundred men and two cannon, were detached prior to Camden and fought with Sumter. Nearly all these men were either captured or killed.

6th, and the Delaware Regiment became the 2nd Battalion. Within their ranks were key officers and a core group of enlisted men who had survived all the battles since Brooklyn.

Colonel Otho Holland Williams and Major John Eager Howard were given joint command of the regiment. Gist and Smallwood did not join their new Maryland Line; instead, they went back to Baltimore to recruit more men to rebuild the southern army.

Once the Marylanders were formed into a new regiment, Gates had the foresight to re-designate a portion of them as light infantry and dubbed the unit the Flying Army. It consisted of two companies of one hundred men each from Maryland, along with one company from Delaware. The foot soldiers were accompanied by Lieutenant William Washington's Continental Light Dragoons. A distant relative of George Washington, the twenty-eight-year-old was described as "six feet in height, broad, strong, and corpulent." His peer, Light Horse Harry Lee, wrote that William Washington's "military exploits announce his grade and character in arms. Bold, collected and persevering, he prefers the heat of action . . . than the drudgery of camp and watchfulness of preparation." Perhaps Daniel Morgan characterized William Washington best: "War was his game, and he was good at it." Severely wounded in the Battle of Brooklyn, William Washington fought through most of the major campaigns of the war and actively battled his archenemy Banastre Tarleton in the south.

George Washington wisely chose his most able general, Nathanael Greene, to command the southern army. Greene had rehabilitated his reputation following the disasters at Fort Washington and Fort Lee. Throughout the long winter in Valley Forge, the army was in desperate need of supplies and food. To take this heavy burden off his shoulders, Washington had appointed Greene to the role of quartermaster general. A combat general who despised a chairborne command, the Rhode Islander was loath to accept the position. But when he became quartermaster general, Greene's business and organizational acumen emerged and worked miracles on a broken American supply chain that was often out of money and matériel. Washington praised Greene's efforts, writing that the army "in March 1778 was in great disorder and confusion and by extraordinary exertions You so arranged it, as to enable the Army to take the Field the moment it was necessary, and to move with rapidity after the Enemy when they left Philadelphia. From that period to the present time, your exertions have been equally great, have appeared to me to be the result of system and to have been well calculated to promote the interest and honor of your Country."

In addition, the former Quaker had devoured numerous books on military tactics, enabling him to provide Washington with excellent advice on numerous occasions.

The general quickly assessed the situation in the South. His first move as commander was a controversial decision to divide the American army. Greene explained, "I'm well satisfied with the [army] movement, for it has answered thus far all the purposes for which I intended it. It makes the most of my inferior force, for it compels my adversary to divide his, and holds him in doubt as to his own line of conduct." Logistics decided the fate of both armies. As Napoleon later declared in an iron maxim of war: "An army marches on its stomach." Challenged by lack of supply, Greene would have had great difficulty supporting his army if it were all assembled in one place. By dividing his army, he was able to feed his men. In addition, his action served to divide the British army, which would have been most potent if united. On Greene's orders, the Maryland and Delaware troops began marching south toward Charlotte, North Carolina, on October 7, 1780.

1781

CHAPTER 31

THE RAGTAG ARMY

The condemned man slowly walked in front of the southern Patriot army, which had assembled in parade formation to witness the execution. As the deserter approached the tree, a thick hemp rope was placed around his neck. On Nathanael Greene's orders, the man was hanged in sight of his brothers-in-arms. The Marylanders stared in silence while the last vestige of life left the dead man's body, as it swung back and forth in the cold Carolina air.

The poorly equipped southern army Greene had inherited was in shambles; morale and discipline were awful. Desertion was rampant. Greene noted, "The officers have got in such a habit of negligence and the soldiers so loose and disorderly that it is next to impossible to give it a military complexion." He addressed the problem immediately by making an example of the deserter. The execution had an instant effect on discipline; one private summed up the mood in the camp: "new lords, new laws."

Demonstrating solid leadership, Greene tackled multiple problems at once. He sent Polish volunteer and engineer Thaddeus Kosciuszko to find and construct a suitable base camp for the army, a "camp of repose," where the men could refit. Born in 1746 in the Polish-Lithuanian Commonwealth, Kosciuszko graduated from a military academy before traveling to France to study drawing, painting, and architecture. In 1776 he sailed to America to aid the Patriot cause, and the Continental Congress soon put his civil engineering skills to use.

In late December 1780 Kosciuszko selected a spot on the banks of the Pee Dee River in the northeast corner of South Carolina, near the town of Cheraw. Here the army could regroup, clean its weapons, and drill. Planning to go on the offensive, Greene next sent his quartermaster general, Lieutenant Colonel Edward Carrington, to explore and map the major rivers of North Carolina, from the Yadkin to the Catawba. He also directed Carrington to begin to build or collect flatboats that could be used to ferry the army across the various waterways for their upcoming operations against British commander Charles, Earl Cornwallis.

After the disaster at Camden, replacements had filtered in from several states, including several hundred troops from Maryland. The ragtag American force now numbered about fifteen hundred militiamen and approximately 950 Continentals, the bulk of whom were Marylanders. Its ranks continued to swell and ebb as groups of militiamen came and went. The unpaid militiamen often needed to deal with issues at home, such as running their farms and businesses and protecting them from vindictive Tory neighbors or the British. The bulk of the American army, several thousand troops, still remained in and around West Point pinning down the British garrison in New York. In the North, the strategic stalemate of 1779 continued. Since neither side had adequate forces to defeat its adversary, the war raged in the South.

On December 3, 1780, one of the greatest battle captains of the Revolution rode into the camp of repose: Brigadier General Daniel Morgan. Born on July 6, 1736, Morgan was a man of the frontier. A quintessential American, he ran away from home in his early teens and eventually settled in the wilderness of Virginia; his rugged individualism determined his destiny. A born leader with a commanding presence and high intelligence, Morgan rose from a menial farm laborer to a foreman and operated an independent wagon team for the British during the French and Indian War; later, this job earned him the nickname The Old Wagoner. He also saw action in the war that ignited a deep and burning hatred of the British after an incident where he struck a British officer and received several hundred lashes as punishment. At the start

of the War for Independence, Morgan had organized a group of riflemen from the backcountry of Virginia. They fought in Boston and later
in Canada during the bloody assault on Quebec. When the American
commander of the Quebec assault, Benedict Arnold, went down with
a bullet to the leg, Morgan took charge and led the troops through
the rest of the battle. In the Battle of Saratoga, Morgan also played
a pivotal role, leading the regiment of Virginia riflemen in a crucial
counterattack that cut off the British retreat from the battlefield. But
failing health forced him to take a leave of absence from June 1779 to
June 1780. The wounds he suffered at Saratoga contributed to his ailing
constitution, which plagued him throughout the entire war. Congress
recruited Morgan, although he was only partially recovered from his
service in Canada and Saratoga, back into the army and commissioned
him a brigadier general. Greene wisely appointed him commander of
the Flying Army.

When Greene assigned Lieutenant Colonel John Eager Howard to
the Flying Army (Otho Holland Williams remained behind with Greene
and the bulk of the army), he gave Morgan a stalwart confrere. Together,
they proved to be nearly invincible. Howard's battalion comprised three
sixty-man Maryland companies, formed from what was left of the regiments that previously fought at Camden, as well as the Delaware Blues
and two companies of Virginians. Captain Richard Anderson led the 1st
Maryland Company, which included one platoon of the 1st and 7th Maryland Regiments. Captain Henry Dobson commanded the 2nd Maryland
Company, a mixture of veterans from the 2nd, 4th, and 6th Maryland
Regiments. Lieutenant James Ewing, who had been with the Marylanders since the beginning, assisted Dobson in command of the company.
The third sixty-man company, led by Lieutenant Nicholas Mangers and
Lieutenant Gassaway Watkins, was composed of veterans from the 3rd
and 5th Maryland Regiments. Watkins had also been with Smallwood's
Battalion since its inception, enlisting on January 14, 1776. He had fought
at Long Island, White Plains, Germantown, and Monmouth, and had
barely survived a brush with Banastre Tarleton's cavalry at Camden.

The intrepid Captain Bob Kirkwood led the Delaware Blues, which included fifty-one privates, three sergeants, three corporals, an ensign, a lieutenant, and a captain—sixty Continentals in all.

Two Virginia companies rounded out the infantry, which included many Continental soldiers who survived the Waxhaws Massacre.

About one hundred Light Dragoons under Lieutenant Colonel William Washington rode with the force. On December 16, the Flying Army left Greene in Charlotte and marched southwest. The Marylanders and the rest of the combined force pushed toward Ninety Six to link up with the North Carolina militiamen under the command of General William Lee Davidson. Greene gave Morgan a free hand to conduct operations "either offensively or defensively, as your own prudence and discretion may direct—acting with caution and avoiding surprises by every possible precaution."

Meanwhile, the bulk of Greene's army, including many of the Marylanders, remained on the Pee Dee River near Cheraw, South Carolina. Through spies and reconnaissance patrols, Cornwallis received intelligence that Greene had split his army, and he immediately recognized the threat Morgan's Flying Army posed. Greene's strategy forced the earl to do exactly what the American wanted: divide his army into not two but three parts. Cornwallis sent Major General Alexander Leslie to defend Camden, and he directed Tarleton to secure Ninety Six and then crush Morgan. With its heavy baggage and cannon, Cornwallis's main army was to move slowly northwestward from Winnsboro, South Carolina, into North Carolina and attempt to destroy any remaining elements of Morgan's force. Cornwallis hoped to crush the Flying Army between the two British pincers.

Tarleton would first strike Morgan with a task force that totaled approximately eleven hundred men. Tarleton's cavalry was reinforced with two hundred men of the 7th Regiment of Foot, the Royal Fusiliers. They had seen action in 1775 in Canada, where they had suffered a brutal defeat, but they re-formed and fought in numerous battles over the next few years. A battalion of Frasier's Highlanders the 71st Regiment of Foot also augmented the force, along with two three-pound artillery pieces known as grasshoppers. In addition, fifty men of the 17th Light Dragoons joined them. The Marylanders had faced the 17th at Camden and the 71st at Stony Point.

Cornwallis's orders to Tarleton were clear: "Dear Tarleton, If Morgan is still in Williams' or anywhere within your reach I should wish you to push him to the utmost . . . no time is to be lost."

Tarleton wrote back, "My Lord . . . I must either destroy Morgan's corps or push it before me over the Broad river, toward King's Mountain." Cornwallis confirmed the plan, responding, "Dear Tarleton . . . You have understood my intentions perfectly."

Perceiving that Morgan did not intend to attack Ninety Six, the hard-driving Tarleton immediately set out to neutralize his adversary. Unable to assault Ninety Six because he didn't have the manpower to attack a large, fortified enemy force, Morgan requested permission from Greene to advance into Georgia and attack British outposts. "Here we cannot subsist, so we have but one Alternative. Either Retreat or move in Georgia." He warned of dire consequences of retreating. "The spirit which now begins to pervade the People and call them into the field will be destroyed. The Militia who have already Joined will desert us, and it is not improbable that a regard for their own safety will Induce them to join in the Enemy." Morgan understood that the population and the militia would gravitate to whichever side was winning.

Not knowing the threat closing in on The Old Wagoner from Tarleton in the south and Cornwallis in the east, Greene ordered Morgan to move north to a position near the Saluda and Broad Rivers, near present-day Columbia, South Carolina. Morgan was to conduct raiding parties against the British supply lines that supported the network of outposts across South Carolina and "harass their rear if they should make a movement this way."

Morgan attempted to defend a ford at the Pacolet River, but Tarleton outmaneuvered him and crossed six miles below. Tarleton's task force, over one thousand strong, moved at lightning speed, quickly but quietly closing the ground between them and their quarry. Employing the same tactics George Washington had used at Long Island and

Trenton, Tarleton kept the fires in his bivouac lit as a ruse while his men went on the march at night in pursuit of Morgan. Tarleton was now just one day behind Morgan.

On January 13, Greene sent a letter to Morgan responding to Morgan's request to enter Georgia by asking for more details on Morgan's plan and passing on some intelligence: "Col. Tarleton is said to be on his way to pay you a visit . . . I doubt not that he will have a decent reception and a proper dismission."

The British were closing in on the Americans. Morgan faced a stark choice: cross the Broad River or make a stand.

CHAPTER 32

HUNTING THE HUNTER

Casting an imposing shadow, General Daniel Morgan strode with confidence and determination beside the rows of blazing campfires. The fearless veteran of numerous military campaigns stood a full six feet tall. Morgan didn't wear many of the trappings of a typical eighteenth-century military officer, and he carried only a simple sword. As a result, the men felt an affinity with Morgan: he was one of them.

Like all the other men in the Flying Army, the Marylanders stared transfixed at their general. His personal battle history was etched deeply across his body. On his left cheek, he bore an angry scar from a ball that entered his neck, passed through his mouth, took out most of his rear teeth, and exited his upper lip. It was at that moment, the night of January 16, 1780, according to legend, one of Morgan's aides lifted the general's shirt, exposing the leather-like scars on his back. Morgan told the Continentals that at one point during the French and Indian War, he had knocked down a British officer who assaulted him with the flat portion of a sword. For the offense, Morgan's superiors condemned him to four hundred lashes, "of which only three hundred and ninety-nine were inflicted. I counted them myself," The Old Wagoner continued, laughing, "and am sure that I am right, nay, I convinced the drum-major of his mistake . . . so I am still their creditor to the amount of one lash."

The unforgettable scene demonstrated Morgan's unwavering commitment to the cause. His resolve was put to the test in the upcoming battle, which afforded little opportunity for retreat. Tactically, the Flying Army's back was up against a river. With the British poised to pounce should he make himself vulnerable by attempting a crossing, he had little choice other than to fight. Recognizing the do-or-die nature of the undertaking, the general told his aides, "Here is Morgan's grave or victory." Morgan then informed the men that they would fight the next day on the ground where they bivouacked—Cowpens.

Earlier in the day, Morgan had surveyed the ground near present-day Spartanburg. Approximately five hundred yards long, the Cowpens was an open meadow dotted by only a few lonely trees, thanks to the thousands of cattle that grazed there every spring before being driven roughly a hundred miles southeast to Camden and the coast. A collection of oaks, hickories, chestnuts, and maples ringed the field, and nearby springs and creeks provided plenty of water. Although the ground was largely even, a few low rises, including one small hill that would later be known as Morgan's Hill, swelled the landscape. A landmark ground familiar to all the backcountry men and militia, the wide plain served not only as a roundup for cattle but also as a local rallying point. Prior to Kings Mountain, it had been the final staging area for the Overmountain Men.

The Green River Road cut across the Cowpens, running in a general northwesterly direction. A ravine made it difficult to approach from the west, and one of the numerous creeks flowed along the road to the east. This arrangement suited Morgan perfectly, for it meant that the British would be unable to flank his troops. However, the topography would also make escape difficult for the American forces, a fact that Morgan hoped would encourage his men to fight to their utmost. He later wrote, "As to retreat, it was the very thing I wished to cut off all hope of. I could have thanked Tarleton had he surrounded me with his cavalry. It would have been better than placing my own men in the rear to shoot down those who broke from the ranks. When men are forced to fight, they will sell their lives dearly."

The Marylanders settled in on Cowpens for the night, lighting campfires and eating their evening meal of bacon and cornmeal. The brief pause gave the weary Americans at least some opportunity to rest and prepare for battle. Banastre Tarleton's men, on the other hand, arrived at the battleground exhausted and hungry, having been on the march since 3:00 a.m.

That night, as Morgan walked among the ranks, spirits ran high in the American camp. Marylander John Eager Howard related, "The [militia] were coming in most of the night, and calling on Morgan for ammunition, and to know the state of affairs. They were all in good spirits, related circumstances of Tarleton's cruelty, and expressed the strongest desire to check his progress."

Vengeance weighed heavily on many of the men's minds. The Marylanders, along with their Kirkland's Delaware men, had incurred devastating losses at Camden. Private Henry Wells recalled, "Two of my Cosins fell into the hands of the enemy at Camden, and [one] died from the Severity of their treatment—the other lived to be exchanged, but returned with a shattered Constitution."

Morgan weighed his options. That evening, with the arrival of additional militia units, the general decided to fight. He first called a council of war with his officers. Morgan drew a rough map to illustrate his simple, yet brilliant, battle plan. He based it on an understanding of his opponent—an ancient, well-proven tenet of war. "I knew my adversary," said Morgan, and "was perfectly sure I should have nothing but downright fighting."

The general knew his enemy, and he knew the terrain. But more important, he knew his men and how to employ them, especially the fickle militiamen. Morgan was a common man with an uncommon ability to understand a complex problem and devise an ingenious tactical solution. He proposed a defense in depth, which was novel for the time. He would seek to delay the advance of the attacker and buy time by having his men fall back to prepared positions as the enemy advanced. This allowed them to inflict additional casualties and exact a high price from the advancing British. The technique is particularly effective against an adversary that can concentrate its forces and focus them on a single point in the battlefield. Given its profound simplicity, it is remarkable that Morgan was the first officer known to employ defense in depth during the Revolution.

The general's first line consisted of skirmishers, handpicked men who were crack shots. They would position themselves about 150 yards in front of the militia. He told the riflemen to aim for the officers to soften up the British as they came forward. The second line consisted of militiamen, who Morgan knew were capable of only limited fighting. He asked them to fire three shots and withdraw through holes in the Continental line, where they would re-form and prepare for a counterattack.

The third line consisted of the Maryland, Delaware, and Virginia Continentals. They would remain concealed behind a small ridge until their time to face the oncoming British. At that point, the militia, along with Lieutenant Colonel William Washington's cavalry, would lead a counterattack and envelop the British.

Upon hearing the plan during the council of war, William Washington concluded with certainty that there would be "No burning, no flying: but face about and give battle to the enemy, and acquit ourselves like men in defense of their baggage, their lives, and the interests of the country."

After the council of war, Morgan went from campfire to campfire, and told the groups of men about their role in the battle plan. In one of those groups was South Carolina volunteer dragoon Thomas Young, a veteran of Kings Mountain. Still only a teenager, the militiaman burned with the desire to avenge the death of his brother, who had been murdered by Tories. "I shall never forget my feelings when told of his death," Young wrote in his memoirs. "I do not believe I had ever used an oath before that day, but then I tore open my bosom, and swore that I would never rest till I had avenged his death. Subsequently a hundred Tories felt the weight of my arm for the deed." About Morgan's visit that night, Young reflected:

> It was upon this occasion that I was perfectly convinced of General Morgan's qualifications to command militia than I had ever before been. He went among the volunteers, helped them fix

their swords, joked with them about their sweethearts, told them to keep in good spirits, and the day would be ours. And long after I laid down, he was going about among the soldiers encouraging them and telling them that The Old Wagoner would crack his whip over Ben in the morning, as sure as they lived.

Late that night, Morgan exhorted the militia, "Just hold up your heads, boys, three fires . . . and you are free, and when you return to your homes, how the old folks will bless you, and the girls kiss you for your gallant conduct."

In anticipation of battle, many of the men didn't "sle[ep] a wink that night." Nevertheless, Morgan ordered militia to actively patrol the area in front of his army for Tarleton. About two hours before daybreak, a scout galloped up to Morgan with news that Tarleton was about five miles away and bearing down fast on the Flying Army. With Andrew Pickens at his side, Morgan rode through the men, who were huddled in blankets for protection against the frost that lightly coated the South Carolina countryside.

Morgan's stentorian voice pierced the silence of the morning.

"Boys, get up, Benny's Coming!"

CHAPTER 33

COWPENS

The first low purple rays of dawn cut through the morning mist on January 17, 1781. "The enemy came in full view. The sight . . . seemed somewhat imposing; they halted for a short time. We looked at each other for a considerable amount of time," remembered one participant.

With the temperature in the low twenties and a sprinkling of frost coating the ground, the Patriots clapped their hands together to keep them warm and prepare for the British onslaught.

Three hundred yards in front of them, the Redcoats began dropping excess equipment and forming into lines as they readied themselves for battle. To size up the force facing him, Banastre Tarleton commanded his legion's dragoons to charge the American riflemen. The Patriot officers ordered their men not to deliver their fire until the enemy was within fifty yards.

"Aim for the men with the epaulets," they ordered.

Less than an hour before the British reached the battlefield, Sergeant Lawrence Everhart—the former Maryland infantryman who had made a daring escape from Fort Washington and was now riding in Lieutenant Colonel William Washington's cavalry—and twelve of his men had trotted down the Green River Road into the predawn darkness on a special reconnaissance operation, three miles beyond American outposts. Their mission was to determine Tarleton's exact location. For more than a mile, the cavalrymen rode silently through frostbitten trees dotting barren fields, when suddenly they collided head-on with Tarleton's advancing legion, over a thousand strong. Stunned by the oncoming enemy onslaught, the Marylander and his men wheeled their horses and bolted in the opposite direction, with Tarleton's advance guard in hot pursuit. The British rode the "fleetest race horses which [they] had impressed from their owners in this Country, and which enabled them to take Sergeant Everhart and one of the men." The rest of the group barely outpaced Bloody Ban's advance guard and upon their return urgently relayed to General Daniel Morgan "information of the approach of the Enemy."

After shooting Everhart's horse out from under him, a Loyalist quartermaster, an acquaintance of Everhart's, took him prisoner and brought him before one of the British officers. "Do you expect Mr. Washington and Mr. Morgan will fight this day?" asked the officer.

"Yes, if they can keep together only two hundred men," Everhart replied.

"Then it will be another Gates' defeat," asserted the unknown officer.

"I hope to God it will be another Tarleton's defeat," said Everhart.

Fixing him with a piercing glare, the officer replied, "I am Colonel Tarleton, sir."

Tarleton ordered his men forward. The British columns advanced across the frozen field toward the first line of Americans, the skirmishers, screaming, "Huzzah! Huzzah! Huzzah!"

BOOM! BOOM!

Two three-pound grasshoppers fired into the American line. The piercing sound of fifes playing the "Scottish and English Duties" and drums beating out a rhythm reverberated over the din of battle. The British infantry broke into a jog, crossing nearly the length of two football fields in three minutes.

On the other side of the battlefield, Morgan thought to himself, *"They are running at us as if they intend to eat us up."* Riding up and down

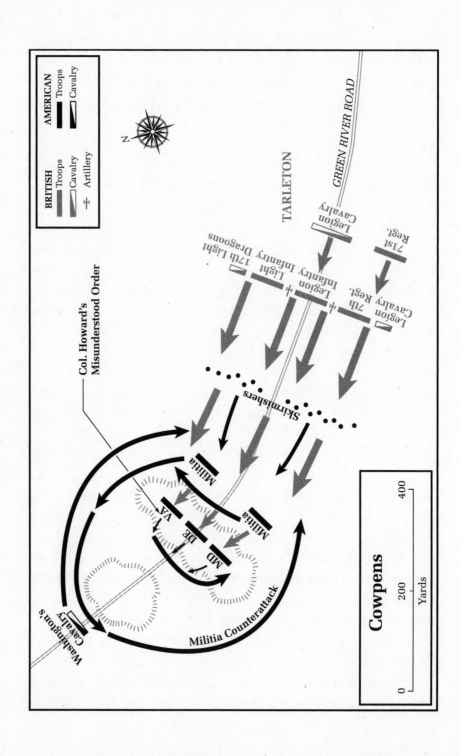

Cowpens

BRITISH
Troops
Cavalry
Artillery

AMERICAN
Troops
Cavalry

N

GREEN RIVER ROAD

TARLETON

Legion
Cavalry

71st
Regt.

Legion
Cavalry Regt.

7th

Legion
Infantry

Light
Infantry

17th Light
Dragoons

Skirmishers

Col. Howard's
Misunderstood Order

Militia

Militia

VA
DE
MD

Washington's
Cavalry

Militia Counterattack

0   200   400

Yards

the lines, he encouraged his men: "They gave us the British halloo! Boys, give them the Indian halloo, by God!"

Veteran militiaman Thomas Young recalled, "[Morgan] galloped along the lines, cheering the men and telling us not to fire until we could see the whites of their eyes." The militiamen maintained the order "with great firmness."

Leading with bayonets, the British rushed forward. "The British line advanced at a sort of trot. . . . It was the most beautiful line I ever saw," said Young.

One militiaman remembered, "When they came near enough for us to distinguish plainly their faces, we picked out our man and let fly."

Another militiaman remembered seeing one of his men set his sights on a British officer. "[He] fixed his eye upon a British officer; he stepped out of the ranks, raised his gun, and he saw the officer fall."

"POP! POP! POP!"

The British pushed past the skirmishers, then faced a devastating hail of well-aimed shots from the militiamen in the second line. With the Americans firing from killing range, or about fifty yards, "the effect of the fire was considerable; it produced something like a recoil."

The militia fire took a devastating toll. Lieutenant Roderick Mackenzie, a Highland light infantry officer, reported, "Two-thirds of the British infantry officers had already fallen, and nearly the same proportion of privates."

Despite their exhaustion from a night march that began at 3:00 a.m. and not having eaten since the previous day, the British continued to charge. A gap appeared in the American lines. According to plan, the militiamen had fired their three shots and were withdrawing. To the British, it appeared to be a rout.

The Redcoats "rent the air with their shouts and quickened their advance."

Tarleton's taut battle lines became uneven, as several units surged forward ahead of the others to bear down on the Maryland and Delaware Continentals. "The British approached the Continentals, and casualties mounted. The fire on both sides was well supported and produced much slaughter."

As the militia exited through the line of Continentals, British dragoons from the 17th Light Dragoons came around the rear of the left wing of the rebel force. The fighting was brutal, as British sabers hacked and slashed at the Americans. One militiaman received "seven wounds on his head and two on his shoulders. . . . The wounds on the head opened the skull to the brains."

Unwittingly, the British were moving directly into Morgan's carefully laid trap.

Exhausted, they finally reached the crest of a small ridge. To their surprise, they saw Commander John Eager Howard's Continentals lying in wait.

Badly bloodied by the skirmishers and militia, the British Legion infantry were stunned to see the dauntless, blue-jacketed Continentals armed with bayonets. Despite their exhaustion and depleted ranks, the British closed ranks and charged. Musket balls went whizzing through the air, some striking bone and flesh. The smell of burnt powder wafted on the breeze. Maryland officers Enoch Anderson, Henry Dobson, and Gassaway Watkins, and Delaware's Robert Kirkwood, shouted out the commands that many of the men had drilled for years.

"Prime and load!"

"Shoulder!"

"Make ready!"

"Take aim!"

"Fire!"

When the Continentals fired, "it seemed like one sheet of flame from right to left."

Kirkwood's Delaware Blues, attached to the Marylanders, bore the brunt of the British attack, suffering 25 percent casualties. British bayonets wounded one-third of Captain Kirkwood's men in the hand-to-hand fighting.

Both sides maintained their positions "with great bravery; and the conflict between them and the British troops was obstinate and bloody."

Howard and Morgan moved up and down the lines encouraging the men. Maryland Private Andrew Rock recalled, "[I] saw [Morgan] frequently at the battle of Cowpens."

As the two sides slugged it out, exchanging one volley after another, Tarleton laid out his trump card. He ordered his cavalry into action. The fearless leader recalled that he "thought the advance of the 71st Regiment of Foot into line, and the movement of the cavalry in the reserve to threaten the enemy's right flank, would put a victorious period to the action. No time was lost performing this maneuver."

William Washington's cavalry met the threat and broke up Tarleton's horsemen. Nevertheless, the American line stood in danger of being enveloped. Howard observed, "I had but about 350 men, and the British about 800 that their line was extended much further than mine, particularly on my right, where they were pressing forward to gain my flank."

Disaster then struck. Howard ordered Captain Andrew Wallace of Virginia to wheel right, but Wallace misinterpreted Howard's orders. Instead, the men turned their backs on the British and began marching to the rear. Morgan, alarmed at the unexpected reversal, galloped up to Howard. In a loud tone of voice, Howard pointed at his men and "soon removed [Morgan's] fears by pointing to the line and observing that the men were not beaten and retreated in that order."

The botched order profoundly changed the course of history. Seeing the backs of the Continentals, the British surged forward to deliver a knockout blow. Delaware Lieutenant Anderson recalled, "Thinking that We Were broke, [the British] set up a great Shout, Charged us With their bayonets, but in no order."

The Continentals were marching toward the small knoll that history has called Morgan's Hill. As the men reached the hill, Howard issued an order:

"Battalion! Halt! To the Right About,—Face!"

They did an about-face in lines, which Howard described as "perfectly formed." Each company and platoon then unleashed a devastating fire. As Howard recalled, "The enemy pressed upon us in rather disorder, expecting the fate of the day was decided. They were by this time within 30 yards of us. . . . My men, with uncommon coolness, gave them an unexpected and deadly fire."

The coup de grâce came when a messenger from Colonel Washington handed Howard a note: "They are coming on like a mob. Give them a fire and I will charge them."

Just then, Morgan galloped upon the scene. Waving his sword, he shouted at the men, "Form, form, my brave fellows! Give them one more fire and the day is ours. Old Morgan was never beaten." Delaware Private Henry Wells vividly remembered that the "powerful and trumpet-like voice of our Commander drove fear from every bosom and gave new energies to every arm."

Emboldened by Morgan's words, "We then advanced briskly, and gained the right flank," James Collins, a seventeen-year-old veteran of Kings Mountain, recalled. The Americans fired a devastating volley. In the "close and murderous" fire, nearly half of the Redcoats fell. Stunned, some of the British troops "threw down their arms and fell upon their faces."

Howard ordered the Continental drummers to beat out a familiar cadence—charge bayonets. "The order was obeyed with great alacrity," Delaware Lieutenant Enoch Anderson remembered. As the Continentals surged forward into the Redcoats, they were "in amongst them With the Bayonets, Which Caused them to give ground and at last to take To The Flight, But We followed them up so Close that they never could get in order again until We Killed and took the whole of the infantry prisoners."

Sergeant Major William Seymour, who was near Anderson, added, "Officers and men behaved with uncommon and undaunted bravery, but more especially, the Brave Captain Kirkwood and his company, who that day did wonders, rushing on the enemy without either dread or fear."

The fighting remained close in. Marylander John Bantham "received three severe wounds on my right side by bayonet." Another Marylander, Cudbeth Stone, was injured "in the thigh by a ball of a musket passing through it."

As their world closed in on all sides, the Scots of the 71st Regiment broke. Washington's cavalry swooped in and hit their left flank and rear.

The American militiamen also joined the envelopment. Coming over Morgan Hill, they charged into battle "seeing the fortune of the day had changed." Firing erratically, the Scots fell back "in a panic" and "a total rout ensued."

A tide of screaming Continentals descended on the vulnerable British artillery. The three-pound grasshoppers were left alone to fend for themselves. John Eager Howard ordered Marylander Captain Nathaniel Ewing to take one. Within earshot, Marylander Captain Anderson also heard the command from Howard. Only a few yards from the artillery piece, which was leveled at them, Anderson saw that the artillerist was "about to put a match to it. At this critical moment, [Anderson] ran up, and, with the assistance of his spontoon, made a spring, and lit immediately upon the gun." In one of the more bizarre and colorful exploits of the Revolution, Anderson had pole-vaulted onto the artillery piece. He then disabled the match-wielding artillerist with his spontoon.

Several yards away, the British artillerists were valiantly defending another cannon to the death. Howard personally intervened. "I saw some of my men going to bayonet the men who had the match . . . who appeared to make it a point of honor not to surrender his match. The men, provoked by his obstinacy would have bayoneted him on the spot, had I not interfered, and desired him to spare the life of so brave a man. He then surrendered his match." The entire unit continued fighting "[till all] were either killed or wounded."

In an attempt to change the course of the battle and rescue the guns, Tarleton first tried to gather his reserve dragoons, and then personally charged into the melee. But the Marylanders stopped the dragoons cold. In a flurry of sabers and pistols, Maryland Private Andrew Rock "received a severe cut with a saber from one of the British cavalry upon his left arm."

Private Henry Wells was struck across the shoulder by one of Tarleton's men "with his Sword with Such violence that the colar of my coat, my vest, and my Shirt were each cut through, and the flesh & skin Slightly scratched and bruised, so much so that there was a considerable not [knot] or welt on my Sholder."

After seizing the guns, Howard and his men enveloped the last pockets of British resistance. They galloped toward the 71st, which had broken into squads that formed into small compact groups. Calls rang out for "Tarleton's quarter." However, once again, Howard's humane mercy helped avert a massacre.

Howard yelled, "Surrender! Lay down your arms!"

Several officers delivered up their swords. One 71st Grenadiers officer, Captain Duncanson, gave Howard his saber. "Upon getting on my horse, I found him pulling at my saddle, and he nearly unhorsed me." Seeing the terror in the British officer's eyes, Howard asked him "what he was about."

The Englishman stammered that "they had orders to give no quarter and they did not expect any; and as [Howard's] men were coming up, he was afraid they would use him ill."[32]

The British resistance melted away as "men surrendered and those that could ran." Thomas Young recalled, "[They] broke, and throwing down their guns and cartridge boxes made for the wagon road, and did the prettiest sort of running."

Sensing that the battle was slipping beyond his grasp, Tarleton attempted to rally about two hundred of his dragoons and mount a suicidal charge into Howard's men. His courage proved fruitless as his men decided to "forsake their leader and left the field of battle."

Coming in at full gallop, and screaming, "Buford's Play!" the watchword of Waxhaws, William Washington's dragoons descended on Tarleton's fleeing men. Their sabers cut into the infantry scrambling to leave the field.

Desperate to halt the flood of his men exiting Cowpens, Tarleton and his subordinates went to extreme lengths. "Some officers went so far as to cut down several of their men, in order to stop the flight."

32. According to Howard, he received "messages from him [Duncanson] many years afterwards, expressing his obligation for my having saved his life."

In a last gasp, Tarleton gathered a small group of horsemen who charged into the maelstrom. "Fourteen officers and forty horsemen were, however, not mindful of their reputation, or the situation of their commanding officer. Col. Washington's cavalry were charged, and driven back into the continental infantry by this handful of brave men."

Leading his troops from the front, as was his custom, Washington rushed ahead of his men by "perhaps 30 yards." The Virginian sped between Tarleton and the Marylanders. Several British officers, including Tarleton himself, by some reports, "saw the American commander and wheeled about and made a charge at him."

The two officers drew their weapons and faced off on horseback. "Tarleton made a thrust at him, which he parried." However, the slashing stroke snapped Washington's sword in two.

Seizing the opportunity, one of Tarleton's officers then attempted to strike the Virginian. But Washington's African American orderly saved his life. "The officer of the left . . . was preparing to make a stroke at him, when a boy, a waiter, who had not the strength to wield his sword, drew his pistol and shot and wounded this officer, which disabled him."

A third officer attacked Washington. The Redcoat retreated ten to twelve steps, then turned around and fired a pistol. Intended for Washington, the shot missed its mark and struck the colonel's horse. Greene's biographer later wrote, "The noble animal that bore Washington was destined to receive the ball that had been aimed at its rider."

Seeing that their attempts to kill Washington had not succeeded, Bloody Ban and his dragoons fled. As they were leaving the field, Tarleton's men attempted to kill some of their prisoners. They shot Lawrence Everhart in the head at point-blank range, leaving a deep hole over one of his eyes. Remarkably, the Marylander survived the traumatic wound and remained lucid enough to talk to Washington. Minutes afterward, he asked Everhart who had attempted to execute him. "[Everhart] pointed out to me the man who shot him, and on whom a just Retaliation was exercised, and who by my order, was instantly Shot, and his horse as well as I can recollect, was given to Everhart, whom I ordered in the Rear to the Surgeons," recalled Washington.

Quickly mounting another horse, Washington led his men in pursuit of Tarleton.

As the British ran in all directions, the Patriots, including the Delaware and Maryland Continentals, began picking up prisoners. One of the British Legion dragoons attempting to flee was former Delaware Continental Michael Dougherty, who had turned traitor for the *second* time and was picked up by his own men for the *second* time. He later reported that he "should have escaped unhurt, had not a dragoon of Washington's added a scratch or two to the account already scored on my unfortunate carcass." After wounding the legionnaire, amazingly, Kirkwood took back the turncoat soldier of fortune, "My love for my country gives me courage to support that . . . I love my comrades and they love Dougherty."

Tarleton's prized baggage train also fell into their hands. Galloping on horseback and pushing ahead of the Marylanders, South Carolinian dragoon and veteran of Kings Mountain Thomas Young attempted to purloin what he could. "[I] resolved upon an excursion to capture some of the baggage. We went about twelve miles and captured two British soldiers, two Negroes, and two horses laden with portmanteaus. One of the portmanteaus belonged to a paymaster in the British service and contained gold."

As Young was plundering the baggage, several of Tarleton's dragoons suddenly intercepted him.

[I] put spurs to my horse, and made down the road. . . . Three or four dashed through the woods and intercepted me. . . . My pistol was empty, so I drew my sword and made battle. I never fought so hard in my life. . . . In a few minutes, my finger on my left hand was split open; then I received a cut on my sword arm by a parry which disabled it. In the next instant, I took a cut from a saber across my forehead. . . . The skin flipped down over my eyes, and the blood blinded me so that I could see nothing. Then came a thrust on the right shoulder blade, then a cut on the left shoulder, and at last, a cut on the back of my head—I fell upon my horse's neck.

Severely wounded, Young blacked out, and mercifully, Tarleton's men took him prisoner. The dragoons then continued their flight south away from Colonel Washington's pursuing cavalry and Kirkwood's infantrymen. Despite their casualties, the American foot soldiers set out immediately on a forced march, a feat they repeated several times in the coming months. Although exhausted after marching dozens of miles since the battle, Kirkwood's men continued picking up British prisoners. Sergeant Major William Seymour related, "[We were] instrumental in taking a great number of prisoners. . . . Very Well pleased With Our day's Work."

On the field of battle, the victorious John Eager Howard was holding seven swords belonging to British officers who had personally surrendered to him. Arriving on the scene, General Morgan complimented him, "You have done well for you are successful; had you failed, I would have shot you."

Howard quickly retorted, "Had I failed, there would have been no need of shooting me."

All around them, the Continentals and militiamen were busily looting the prisoners' knapsacks and personal belongings. The booty was most welcome. One of the participants noted the dismal state of the Flying Army: "Our poor fellows, who were almost naked before, now have several changes of clothes." The clothing transformed the Patriots. Many now wore British green and scarlet.

Overshadowing the glory, the cries of the wounded and dying echoed across the battlefield. American losses were relatively light, perhaps ten killed and fifty-five wounded. British casualties are hard to ascertain but numbered around one hundred killed and two hundred wounded; all together about seven hundred of Tarleton's force headed into captivity. The wounded strained the limited medical resources of the Continental Army. Indomitable Maryland surgeon Dr. Richard Pindell was on the scene, triaging life and death. Pindell performed a panoply of field medicine, from bandaging wounds to sawing off limbs too damaged to save. Pindell described the understaffed conditions: "I was left on the field in care of the Wounded, not any Aid or Force Except a Lt. Hanson . . . and our two waiters." Eventually, working his way through the cries of the wounded and dying, Pindell dressed Marylander Lawrence Everhart's vicious head injury. Despite Bloody Ban's reputation for cruelty, he sent his own medical staff to assist Pindell, who cared for the wounded and dying of both sides.

Without even waiting for Kirkwood's light infantry or Washington's cavalry to return, Morgan sent the Virginians and their prisoners marching north. The Flying Army took a different route to the northeast, where it eventually linked up with the remainder of Greene's army, including the bulk of the Marylanders. The American officers knew that Cornwallis, less than fifty miles away, wanted to avenge Tarleton's loss and rescue the captured men.

CHAPTER 34

"To Follow Greene's Army to the End of the World"

Encamped in the Carolina Backcountry, Charles, Earl Cornwallis stood with his dress sword thrust into the ground, his hand firmly gripping the pommel. He listened intently as Banastre Tarleton recounted the disaster at Cowpens. His attempts to suppress his anger failed as he leaned forward on the blade, snapping it in half.

The earl swore loudly that he would destroy Daniel Morgan and retake Tarleton's men no matter what the cost.

Cornwallis was obsessed with catching the southern army, and for good reason: if he could destroy Nathanael Greene and Morgan, he would eliminate the major threat in the South and cut the line of supplies coming from Virginia to aid partisans in the Carolinas. Control of the South would largely revert to the Crown.

George Washington and the bulk of the American army, about six thousand poorly clad and badly fed men, remained encamped north of New York City in and around West Point. Capturing New York remained Washington's obsession, but even if French reinforcements had seized the fortified city, he recognized that the ultimate outcome of battle might be defeat for the Americans. Stalemate reigned, as neither side had enough troops to go on the offensive and break the logjam. However, an American traitor nearly broke the impasse wide open: Major General Benedict Arnold, the true hero of Saratoga.

Short, muscular, and overbearing, the American general was described as an "evil genius" by some of his men. Arnold walked with a limp—his leg should have been amputated at Saratoga, but he refused the surgery and painfully hobbled around for the rest of his life. At

Saratoga, General Horatio Gates had initially relieved Arnold of command, but instead of standing down, Arnold guzzled some rum and rode back into battle like a madman, turning the tide at several critical points. British commander John Burgoyne credited Arnold with the victory, but Gates got the glory at home. Next Arnold requested a court-martial to clear his name over accusations that he used his authority in a variety of business schemes to profit from the war. After Arnold was acquitted of all but two minor charges, Washington put him in command of the crucial American defenses at West Point, New York. Festering with his grievances, Arnold contacted the British, and over the course of many months, fed information on American troop positions and defenses to Samuel Smith's former friend, Major John André, who at the time had been courting the beautiful Peggy Chew, who was also the object of John Eager Howard's affections. The plot had been exposed, and André had been captured behind the American lines and hanged as a spy. In September 1780 he left his post and boarded the British sloop *Vulture*, anchored off Stony Point, after word reached him that the plot had been exposed.

Upon learning of Arnold's treason, Washington moved more troops into the area and shored up the fortress's defenses, effectively nullifying the threat. But Arnold, paid handsomely with a pile of British cash, a pension, and a commission as brigadier general, remained a thorn in the United States' side. General Henry Clinton turned him loose in Virginia, accompanied by a force of about sixteen hundred troops. If Arnold could link up with Cornwallis, Clinton hoped the combined army could take and hold Richmond and the significant cities in Virginia.

Humiliated by the defeat at Cowpens, Tarleton offered his resignation until a court-martial inquiry could resolve the matter. But Cornwallis could not afford to lose an officer of Tarleton's skill and assuaged his pride. "You have forfeited no part of my esteem as an officer by the unfortunate event on the action of the 17th," he stated.

Although Tarleton had lost his light corps at Cowpens, new reinforcements under the command of Major General Alexander Leslie coincidentally arrived that very day. The reinforcements included the Brigade of the Guards, commanded by one of the most colorful characters of the war, Anglo-Irish Brigadier General Charles O'Hara. O'Hara had served many years in Senegal, where he was lieutenant colonel commandant of the African Corps, which consisted entirely of military convicts, often men found guilty of repeated desertion who were pardoned by the Crown in exchange for lifelong service in Africa. There his features became ruddy and sun-darkened, contrasting with "teeth as white as ever." His appearance matched his leadership style, and one admirer summed him up as "the most perfect specimen of a soldier and a courtier of a past age."

Despite his sterling appearance, O'Hara had a checkered past. A gambler and a professional soldier of fortune, he was a notorious debtor.

Like Cornwallis, he was fearless in battle and beloved by his men. They would gladly follow him into hell.

With little baggage, the American army was able to march faster than the British. To keep pace, Cornwallis took a bold and daring gamble: making his entire army a light corps. It was a huge risk that was unheard of for any British commander in the American theater.

The general ordered a huge bonfire. Establishing a precedent for his men to follow, he threw his own personal accoutrements in first, followed by wagons, tents, china, beds, and even the rum. It all went into the pyre, which burned any impediment that would slow the army down.

O'Hara detailed the extreme measures: "Lord Cornwallis sett the example by burning all of his Wagons, and destroying the greatest part of his Baggage, which was followed by every Officer of the Army without a murmur." Cornwallis's powerful gesture of shared hardship emboldened and inspired his men.

Unimaginable adversity lay ahead for the British. Greene had hoped to lure Cornwallis away from his base of supply hundreds of miles away in Charleston, South Carolina. Cornwallis was pushing the army to its very limits. O'Hara described the troops: "Without Baggage, necessaries, or Provisions of any sort, for Officer or soldier, in the most barren, inhospitable unhealthy part of North America, opposed by the most savage, inveterate perfidious cruel Enemy, with zeal and with Bayonets only, it was resolved to follow Greene's Army to the end of the world."

Cornwallis spent one more day readying his army and ordering each man to have "one pair of spare soles." Then he set his sights on Morgan and the prisoners. Tramping across the barren North Carolina countryside, his twenty-five-hundred-man army, now without baggage, was bearing down on Morgan. Wisely, The Old Wagoner had sent the POWs north on a different route with the Virginia militia, keeping them out of Cornwallis's hands, while he continued moving northeast with the plan of eventually reuniting with Greene.

Cowpens had a dismaying effect on the local population, intimidating the Tories. As word spread of Morgan's great victory, those supporting the British feared for their lives. Roving bands of American partisans, led by men like Thomas Sumter and Francis Marion, prowled the countryside. The advance of Cornwallis's army also scattered many Patriot families, as they took to the roads to avoid the British troops. The flight of both Tories and Patriots depopulated the area, and food and forage became scarce. What was left was plundered—by women. "The sources of the most infamous plundering" came from Cornwallis's female camp followers.

Greene hoped to wear down Cornwallis and perhaps find an optimal time to strike. But at the present, his army was in no condition to face Cornwallis in a stand-up fight. Despite being a northerner, Greene knew the topography better than many of his southern subordinates, and, more important, better than his enemy. A voracious reader and a quick study, Greene thoroughly understood the maps developed by his quartermaster general, Lieutenant Colonel Edward Carrington. Mastering the terrain, he would turn North Carolina's creeks and rivers against his opponent. In Cornwallis's obsessive pursuit, Greene also sensed an opportunity. "I am not without hopes of ruining Cornwallis, if he persists in his mad scheme of pushing through the Country," he said.

Cornwallis drew ever closer to Morgan. On January 24, 1781, the British general covered thirty miles. Four days later just ten miles separated him from his adversary. Morgan wrote to Greene, "Cornwallis will push on." Now, only the Catawba River lay between the two armies. And Morgan was "filling up all the private fords . . . with every obstruction imaginable." The Catawba could be forded at several locations. Unfortunately, Morgan didn't have enough men to defend all the crossing points in strength. But fate and the weather intervened. Dark clouds rolled in, and a violent thunderstorm turned the Catawba into a swirling maelstrom, preventing Cornwallis's crossing for several days.

Hunkered down over 120 miles away, Greene's army and the bulk of the Marylanders bivouacked in Cheraw, South Carolina, pelted by the foul weather. Maryland Captain William Beatty remembered that "a very Heavy rain fell Which rais'd the river Pee Dee and small Creeks so much that the troops Were Obliged to draw Corn in lieu of Meal." Despite the privation and abysmal conditions, the officers maintained discipline, and "a Soldier Was shot for Desertion."

News traveled slowly, and nearly a week passed before word arrived of Morgan and John Eager Howard's victory at Cowpens. Greene ordered a party. The men soon became inebriated on cherry bounce, a concoction of rum and cider. In the celebration, Otho Holland Williams, Beatty, and a large contingent of Marylanders swilled vast quantities of the elixir. Williams floridly captured the drunken moment in a letter to Morgan: "Drunk all your health, swore you were the finest fellows on earth, and love you, if possible more than ever." They topped off the evening by firing a *feu de joie*.

A man of action, Greene boldly decided to assess Morgan's situation for himself; he rode with only a couple of cavalry and a guide more than a hundred miles through Tory-infested country, somehow avoiding British patrols. To this day, Greene's exact route to Morgan remains a mystery. Mud-spattered and exhausted, Greene and his small group arrived at Morgan's camp on January 30, 1781.

Known as a decisive commander who rarely leaned heavily on consultations with his subordinates, Greene unexpectedly called a council of war.

CHAPTER 35

"SAW 'EM HOLLERIN' AND A SNORTIN' AND A DROWNIN'"

Perched on a log next to the raging waters of the Catawba, General Nathanael Greene discussed the situation with his commanders: William Washington, Daniel Morgan, John Eager Howard, and General William Lee Davidson, who led the North Carolina militia. One of these commanders would not live out the next day.

For about twenty minutes they considered how best to slow Cornwallis. They knew the waters of the mighty river separating the two armies wouldn't stay high for long. And Greene related that "the enemy was determined to cross the river." To buy time, they decided to use Davidson's militia to hold the main crossing points. Greene's mastery of local geography was a key factor in developing their strategy, and his audience was surprised "that tho' Genl. Greene had never seen the Catawba before, he appeared to know more about it than those who were raised on it."

Shortly after the commanders sat down, the advance elements of the British army, about five hundred strong, suddenly appeared atop a hill on the opposite side of the river. Cornwallis and his staff passed in front of them and moved from one station to another, viewing the American leaders with their spyglasses. Greene and Cornwallis stared at each other across the swirling waters, the only thing protecting the Patriots.

Greene had ordered Howard to march most of the Delaware and Maryland Continentals north to Salisbury. A few Marylanders stayed behind with the militia to bolster the ranks of the citizen-soldiers.

With the time bought by the rain, Greene and Morgan arranged their slim forces to defend the crossings. Lacking the numbers to mount a vigorous defense on all the possible fords, the Americans played a guessing game, allocating their meager forces where they believed Cornwallis would cross. Two hundred fifty North Carolina militiamen held Cowan's Ford, a key crossing point.

One of the men defending the ford was fifteen-year-old schoolboy Robert Henry, who had survived a bayonet wound at Kings Mountain. "We went up the river to John Nighten's, who treated us well by giving us potatoes to roast, and some whisky to drink. We became noisy and mischievous. Nighten said we should not have any more whisky," remembered the schoolboy. Fortified with drink, Henry and his band fell asleep on the evening of January 31, 1781.

Henry and his fellow militiamen were still slumbering the next morning, February 1, when the British started crossing the ford. However, the noise of the horses plunging through the water alerted one of the militiamen, who then kicked the dozing sentry into the water and began yelling, "The British! The British!"

One of the first to cross was the earl. "Lord Cornwallis, according to his usual manner, dashed first into the river, mounted on a very spirited horse, the brigade of guards followed, two three-pounders next, the Royal Welch Fusiliers after them," recalled Sergeant Roger Lamb.

The swift waters of the Catawba swept many of the Redcoats downriver. The militia's muskets and rifles then went into action. One of the officers shouted, "Fire away, boys! Help is at hand!"

Robert Henry later stated, "[I] fired and continued firing until I saw that one on horseback had passed my rock in the river." He added, "I saw my lame schoolmaster loading his guns. I thought I could stand it as long as he could and commenced loading. [The schoolmaster] fired and then I fired, the head and shoulders of the British being just above the bank. They made no return fire."

What the militiamen's bullets failed to achieve, the swollen river accomplished for them. The fire and the water together nearly took out the British high command. Major General Alexander Leslie's horse threw its rider into the river, and Brigadier General Charles O'Hara's stallion "rolled with him down the current nearly forty yards."

Courageously, many members of the militia fired from positions near the water's edge. "There wasn't many on 'em, but I'll be darned if they didn't slap the wad to his Majesty's men suicidally! For a while; for I saw 'em [British] hollerin' and a snortin', and a drownin' . . . until his lordship reached the off bank."

Cornwallis's horse was hit several times, but it carried the British commander to the opposite shore, where the courageous stallion collapsed.

Shouting commands, the earl urged his men forward as the Patriots' defenses melted away. Robert Henry heard his schoolmaster spur him on:

"It's time to run, Bob!"

In the melee, General Davidson attempted to rally his men.

Struck in the chest by a ball, the militia leader died instantly as he approached the action near the water's edge at Cowan's Ford.

The skirmish cost the British dearly, as Henry reported a large number of British casualties: "not less than one hundred." He added, "The river stunk with dead carcasses" as many bodies lodged in a fish trap downstream, "several of whom appeared to have no wound, but had drowned. We pushed them into the water, they floated off, and each went to his home."

Some Marylanders, including Captain Gassaway Watkins, fought alongside the militia. Watkins went through his own epic ordeal in his flight for survival:

> In February, the day that General Davidson was killed, I left camp with orders from General Greene and was with the retreating militia, two miles from the battleground. At 12 o'clock that night, I stopped at a house on the road, cold, wet, and hungry, but got nothing to eat. There were at least a hundred persons in that house. My dress [uniform] was noticed by an old man of the country, who asked to speak with me in private. He told me

there were enemies as well as friends in the house and offered his services to me. I started in a few moments after and told him that I wanted [his help]. He was faithful. We rode all night and got to the foard. About 10 o'clock the next morning, the trees came tumbling down, one after the other down the Yadkin. The old man said it was impossible to cross. I was satisfied there was nothing to stop the enemy and the wish of my general to bring his troops to a point near action, so I immediately pulled off my coat and boots, put the dispatches in the crown of my hat, tied it on my head, took leave of my friend, who with tears in his eyes wished me well, and with difficulty crossed the river. My guide and my friend expressed his joy by throwing up his hat, and I returned it with gratitude. About 7 o'clock I got to headquarters, received by Generals Greene and Morgan.

Most of the militiamen and the Marylanders successfully made a fighting withdrawal from the fords and continued their long and arduous march toward Salisbury. "We marched all night in the rain and mud, and a most fatiguing march it was. We arrived . . . four miles short of Salisbury, at sunrise on the 2nd & halted to get dry and for the men who had fallen out of the ranks from fatigue, to come up," wrote Delaware Sergeant Major William Seymour.

The army was in bad shape. Seymour related, "[We were] in a most dismal condition for the want of clothing, especially shoes, being obliged to march, the chief part of them barefoot." As they marched, some left a trail of bloody footprints.

Incessant, frigid rain was turning the roads into a quagmire of muck and filth. Soaked to the bone, the soldiers found every step miserable. Delaware Lieutenant Thomas Anderson, attached to the Marylanders, recalled "every step being up to our Knees in Mud . . . it raining On us all the way."

In these deplorable conditions, the army skirmished and marched nineteen hours a day in miserable sleet and rain. Greene described the death march: "More than one-half of our number are in a manner naked, so much so, that we can put them in the least amount of duty. Indeed there is a great number that have not a rag of cloths except a piece of blanket (in the Indian form) around their waists."

The weather and the march were literally killing Morgan, who became gravely ill with debilitating sciatica. One doctor on the march found him lying on a bed of leaves under a blanket, "rheumatic from head to toe." Besides the fevers and other ailments Morgan was "violently attacked with the piles [hemorrhoids]." Morgan could hardly mount a horse, yet he continued to lead his men, checking positions and urging them forward.

Greene and Morgan soon evacuated Salisbury and headed north for the possible safety of another river, the Yadkin. With less than six hours of sleep, the Marylanders were covering up to thirty miles a day in an attempt to outrun Cornwallis, who was stubbornly pursuing them.

Ever the logistician, Greene wisely ordered boats—craft of all makes and sizes—assembled at the Yadkin to be pressed into service and made ready to facilitate the army's crossing. Plowing through the muck and sludge, the still largely barefoot Marylanders made it to the river, which was swollen with rain.

Both Greene and Cornwallis looked to the river with hope. For the British general, it seemed the perfect opportunity to pin down the Americans and destroy them. But the Patriot commander knew that the raging waters of the Yadkin represented his salvation. Performing another minor miracle, Greene's quartermaster general, Lieutenant Colonel Edward Carrington, had the boats waiting when the Flying Army arrived.

Quickly, Greene, Morgan, and Howard steered the men onto the ad hoc flotilla. Most cast off just in time; the vanguard of Cornwallis's army hit the Flying Army's rear guard as some of the last men were clambering aboard their craft.

Once again the Flying Army had escaped Cornwallis's grasp. Having gathered all the boats available for miles up and down the river, Greene and the Marylanders were as safe on the far side of the Yadkin as if Cornwallis were a hundred miles away. Smugly, Greene, Morgan, and Howard set up camp near the river, to the consternation of Cornwallis, who could see his adversary only dozens of yards away. Greene designated a small log cabin close to the riverbank as his headquarters. Because it was one of the few visible targets, the British artillery began to target it, and several balls landed nearby. One allegedly sheared some of the wooden shingles off the roof. Unflappable, Greene refused to allow the British bombardment to interrupt his work. One observer noted, "His pen never rested, but when a new visitor arrived . . . the answer was given with calmness and precision, and the pen immediately resumed."

With his quarry nearly in his grasp, the earl ordered his army to look for a ford farther upstream. Greene noticed the movement of the British troops and astutely wrote, "[F]rom Cornwallises pushing disposition, and the contempt he has for our Army, we may precipitate him into some capital misfortune."

CHAPTER 36

THE RACE TO THE DAN

After crossing the Yadkin, the Marylanders, pummeled by sleet and rain, struggled through forty-seven miles of mud and muck. The Flying Army eventually reached Guilford Courthouse and reunited with William Beatty, Jack Steward, Otho Holland Williams, and the rest of their brothers in Nathanael Greene's main army. A blustery day, February 7, 1781, marked the first time both wings of the southern army had been united since Christmas.

At Guilford, Greene called another council of war. Painting a grim picture, he laid out the facts: Few militia reinforcements had arrived. About five days after Greene's men had crossed the Yadkin, the waters had receded enough for Cornwallis to cross, and he was now in close pursuit. Greene summed up the stakes: "If I should risk a General Action in our present situation, we stand ten chances to one of getting defeated, & if defeated all of the Southern states must fall." He pressed Morgan, Howard, Williams, Steward, and his other senior officers for their opinions on the army's next course of action. The consensus: "avoid a general action at all Events."

The time wasn't right for a fight with Cornwallis; the Americans simply didn't have the numbers. Frantically, they requested additional reinforcements, writing to Virginia Governor Thomas Jefferson, "Great god what is the reason we can't have more men?"

Greene's lieutenants agreed that they must press on to the Dan River, where they might acquire additional reinforcements from Jefferson and Continentals led by Baron Friedrich von Steuben. As he had done at the Yadkin, Greene prepared to have boats ready and waiting.

He had several crossings to choose from: the fords of the upper Dan and two lower crossings, one at Dix Ferry and the other at Irwin's Ferry about six miles south. He chose the lower fords and ordered his quartermaster general, Lieutenant Colonel Edward Carrington, to round up anything that could float and carry men.

Before he left, Greene spent hours surveying the ground around Guilford.

In preparation for the march north to the Dan, Greene once again divided his army. With men and munitions in short supply, deception would have to take the place of muskets. Seven hundred veterans of the light troops, with the Marylanders and William Washington's and Henry Lee's cavalry at their core, would serve as a screening force or a decoy to lure Cornwallis away from the ferry point Greene planned to use for the rest of the army. Unfortunately, the light corps was without the services of Daniel Morgan, who was spent from the long marches. Racked by pain and fever, he had retired to his home in Winchester, Virginia. Greene lamented, "Great generals are scarce. There are few Morgans to be found."

Command of the light troops fell on the shoulders of one of Greene's great field commanders, Marylander Otho Holland Williams. If everything went as intended in the complicated plan, Williams would lure Cornwallis upriver away from the rest of the army, which could then safely cross to the other side. Hopefully, Williams could then double back and cross the Dan after the main portion of the army had made it across. But there was a strong possibility that Cornwallis's larger army would trap Williams's smaller corps with the Dan at its back and crush it.

Their ranks depleted by Cowpens and the arduous march to Guilford, the light troops, principally made up of Marylanders and Delaware troops under John Eager Howard's command, received badly needed reinforcements. Williams ordered the 1st and 2nd Maryland Battalions to furnish twenty-five and thirty men respectively to bring each company back up to sixty men and backfill the heavy losses Kirkwood's Delaware Regiment had sustained.

Given the task of deceiving Cornwallis, the light infantry endured yet another difficult trek. Since leaving their base camp in December, many of the light troops had fought and tramped the equivalent of the distance from Washington, D.C., to New York City in sleet, snow, rain, and frost, sleeping completely exposed to the elements. For those who somehow survived, the Maryland and Delaware Continentals had remarkably traversed nearly five thousand miles on foot over a two-year period. Sergeant Major Seymour recorded in his journal one ball-busting leg of the journey:

> We marched from here on the ninth . . . taking the road toward the Dan River, which we reached on the fourteenth, after a march of 250 miles from the time we left our encampment at Pacolet River. By this time it must be expected the army, especially the light troops, were very much fatigued both from traveling and want of sleep, for you must understand that we marched for the most part both day and night, the main army of the British being close in our rear so that we had not scarce time to cook our victuals, our whole attention being on our light troops.

Williams's men remained constantly on the move—often within a whisker of destruction. Eliminating bridges and skirmishing on nearly a daily basis, Williams sent Light Horse Harry Lee and William Washington to harass and slow down the vanguard of Cornwallis's army. The light troops marched onward, and Cornwallis pursued them, taking the bait. Williams reported to Greene on February 14, "Accident informed me the Enemy were within six to Eight miles of my Quarters. I detached Col. Lee with a Troop of Dragoons & put the rest of the light troops in Motion to cross the Haw River at a Bridge."

Lee ambushed leading elements of Banastre Tarleton's force and described charging into them. "The enemy was crushed on the first charge: most of them were killed or prostrated; and the residue, with their captain attempted to escape." For Lee the ambush was personal; earlier they had killed Lee's unarmed teenage bugler in cold blood.

With orders to administer "Tarleton's quarter" Lee's men tracked down the British captain and several of his dragoons. After cutting him on the face, neck, and shoulders with their sabers, the Americans took the British cavalry officer captive. Raging because his men had not killed the captives on the spot, Lee then prepared to hang the officer for slaying the American bugler. The Brit pleaded for his life, insisting that his men were intoxicated and disobeyed his orders when they killed the boy.

Angrily, Lee threw a pencil and piece of paper into the British officer's hand and ordered him to "note on paper whatever he might wish to make known to his friends," before his execution.

The lynching never took place. More of Tarleton's men arrived on the scene, forcing Lee and his men to flee.

Tarleton and Cornwallis trailed hot on their heels. It was an exhausting and grueling march, and Greene admitted that in the past four days, he "had not slept four hours." But Williams's decoy was working.

The crossing of the Haw was bittersweet, though. Greene reported, "North Carolina militia have all deserted us, except about 80 men. Majors and captains are among the deserters." He cautioned Williams, "You have the flower of the army. Don't expose the men too much, lest our situation should grow more critical."

As Greene neared the ford on the Dan with the bulk of his army, Williams direly noted that the British were close on his tail, but he was willing to sacrifice himself to enable the army to cross. "My [Dear] General, At Sun Down, the Enemy were only 22 miles from you and may be in motion or will most probably be by 3 o' Clock in the morning," wrote Williams. "Their intelligence is good. They maneuvered us from our Strong position . . . and then they moved, with great rapidity. . . . I'm confident we may remain in the State, but whither it will not be at the risk of our Light Corps whither we shall not be wasted by continual fatigue you have to determine. What do you make of that?"

Washington and Lee continued their desperate rear guard. "More than once the legion of Tarleton and the van of O'Hara were within musket shot." Never far behind, "[the British army] was in full view of the troops of Lee as the latter ascended the eminence, on whose summit they entered the great road to Irwin's Ferry."

Racing down "deep and broken" roads encrusted with frost, "the light troops resumed their march with alacrity." Relentlessly, Tarleton and the 33rd Regiment of Foot pushed to close the gap between them and Williams's Marylanders. The two armies covered the final forty miles of road to Irwin's Ferry with just minutes separating them. With victory in sight, the British closed in on Williams's troops and hoped to pin their backs against the Dan and destroy them.

On February 14, at 2:00 p.m., an express message from Greene to Williams arrived, relaying glorious news: "The greater part of our wagons are over and the troops are crossing. The stage is clear." In a series of brilliant actions, Greene had moved his exhausted troops across the Dan. Williams relayed the dispatch to his men, who let out a cheer and "became renovated in strength and agility; so powerful is the influence of the mind over the body." With a second wind, the exhausted men covered forty miles in twenty hours of straight forced marching.

Williams's light corps arrived at Irwin's Ferry on February 14 and began crossing under torchlight. Boats carried the Marylanders and other men across while the horses swam alongside.

Several hours later, the British army arrived. The race was over. Tarleton offered a rare compliment: "Every measure of the Americans, during their march from the Catawba to Virginia was judiciously designed and vigorously executed." Having survived a race against time and death, Marylander William Beatty summed up the march: "Notwithstanding the Enemies Superior Strength & the Close pursuit they gave us Our Retreat Was So Well Conducted that We lost nothing in it but Some extent of [territory]."

Behind the safety of the Dan, Greene went about rebuilding his army with new reinforcements largely made up of militiamen. He prepared to recross the Dan and do battle with Cornwallis in North Carolina at a small crossroads town that he had surveyed several weeks earlier.

CHAPTER 37

GUILFORD COURTHOUSE—
"A COMPLICATED SCENE
OF HORROR AND DISTRESS"

On March 15, 1781, Light Horse Harry Lee rode out to the front of the first line of Patriot soliders assembled near the courthouse in Guilford County, North Carolina, in present-day Greensboro. Lee appeared "in a great rage for battle," as he brandished his sword, still bloodied from an earlier skirmish with Banastre Tarleton's legion. The twenty-five-year-old cavalry leader's rousing battle cry reverberated throughout the American ranks: "My brave boys, your lands, your lives and your country depend on your conduct this day—I have given Tarleton hell this morning, and I will give him more of it before night."

Soon the sound of fifes and Highlander pipes carried across the light breeze that accompanied Lee's words. Forming the front line, Robert Kirkwood's Delaware Blues, militia, and cavalry—all together nearly a thousand strong—stared across the rain-soaked, recently plowed cornfield at the "scarlet uniforms, burnished armor, and gay banners floating in the breeze" as Cornwallis's army assembled in formation over four hundred yards in front of them. On the Ides of March, March 15, 1781, in the damp, cold morning air, the Americans took their carefully plotted positions in the defense and prepared for what proved to be one of the most decisive battles of the war.

Continental artillery began the battle by firing into the British ranks. The Redcoats answered: they quickly unlimbered several six-pounders and thrust them to the front of the British line. The men felt and heard the ominous thunder of cannon. Lee shouted, "You hear damnation roaring over all these woods, and after all they are no more than we." He implored his men, noting that "it would be sufficient if they would stand to make two fires."

As Lee spoke these words, he rode into position on the southern flank. Behind him lay two additional lines of defense backstopped by the elite 1st Maryland, modeled after Morgan's ingenious Cowpens defense in depth, or "collapsing box" defense, designed to bleed the advancing army as it approached each line.

Nathanael Greene had spent only about a week on the north side of the Dan River. After gaining additional troops, he recrossed with about 4,440 men—including the army's backbone, the elite Maryland and Delaware Continentals. He intended to pick a fight with Cornwallis. "We marched yesterday to look for Cornwallis. . . . We are now strong enough."

The Rhode Islander faced challenges of his own, similar to those faced by Gates eight months before. Unreliable militia made up nearly half his troops. In a blunt letter, Daniel Morgan had summed up Greene's chances: "If [the militia] fight, you will beat Cornwallis; if not, he will beat you, and perhaps cut your regulars to pieces, which will be losing all our hopes." He further advised, "Put the rifleman on the flanks, under enterprising officers who are acquainted with that kind of fighting and put the militia in the center with some picked troops in the rear, with orders to shoot down the first man who runs."

Greene knew the field of battle. Weeks earlier, he had walked the grounds of Guilford Courthouse for hours; the topography made it an ideal killing ground. Cornwallis would have to approach from the west by moving across an open field. With flanking difficult, the British would largely have to push down the main road that ran through the mile-long battlefield. A ditch and densely wooded ground covered with oak and conifer trees shouldered the main thoroughfare on both sides. Moving northeast, the British would have to fight across an open vale. The courthouse sat in cleared ground on top of a precipitous slope—an ideal defensive position.

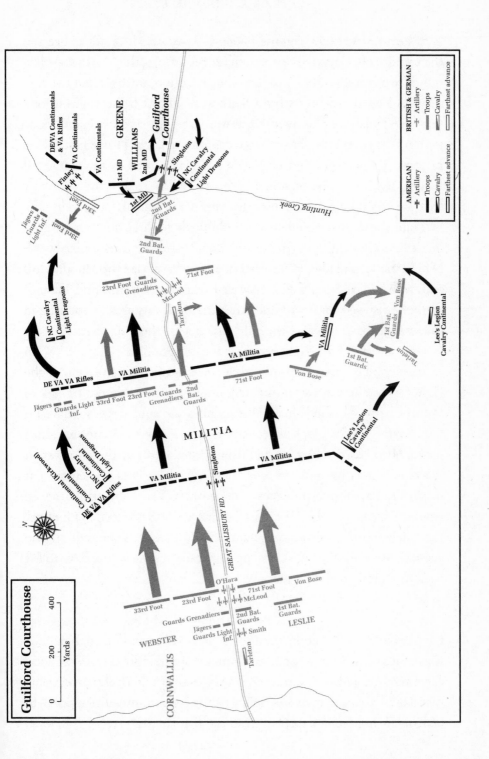

Guilford Courthouse

0   200   400

Yards

CORNWALLIS

WEBSTER

33rd Foot   23rd Foot

Guards Grenadiers

Jägers   Guards Light
Inf.

O'Hara

71st Foot
McLeod

2nd Bat.
Guards

Smith

Tarleton

Von Bose

LESLIE

1st Bat.
Guards

MILITIA

VA Militia

GREAT SALISBURY RD.

Singleton

VA Militia

Lee's Legion
Cavalry
Continental

NC Cavalry
Continental
Light Dragoons

Continental (Kirkwood)

DE VA VA Rifles

VA Militia

71st Foot

VA Militia

Von Bose

1st Bat.
Guards

Tarleton

VA Militia

1st Bat.
Guards

Von Bose

Lee's Legion
Cavalry Continental

Jägers
Guards Light
Inf.

DE VA VA Rifles

VA Militia

23rd Foot

Guards
Grenadiers

2nd
Bat.
Guards

NC Cavalry
Continental
Light Dragoons

23rd Foot   Guards
Grenadiers

Tarleton

McLeod

71st Foot

2nd Bat.
Guards

2nd Bat.
Guards

Hunting Creek

33rd Foot

Jägers
Guards
Light Inf.

Finley

33rd Foot

1st MD

1st MD

2nd MD

WILLIAMS

GREENE

*Guilford
Courthouse*

Singleton

NC Cavalry
Continental
Light Dragoons

DE/VA Continentals
& VA Rifles

VA Continentals

VA Continentals

AMERICAN

Artillery

Troops

Cavalry

Farthest advance

BRITISH & GERMAN

Artillery

Troops

Cavalry

Farthest advance

N

Greene devised a defense in depth based on Morgan's advice and the terrain. He placed his least experienced troops, the North Carolina militia, front and center on his first line in front of the open field behind a fence. Positioned on its right flank were 110 of Robert Kirkwood's seasoned Delaware Continentals, as well as eighty-six of William Washington's dragoons. On the opposite flank stood Light Horse Harry Lee, his cavalry, and two hundred Virginia riflemen, who were veterans of Kings Mountain. The men had orders to fire two shots and withdraw past the second line of defense, the Virginia militia. After piercing the first line, the British would need to fight through three hundred yards of dense brush and gullies to the second line. More than five hundred yards behind the second line on the eastern edge of a vale lay the Marylanders and the rest of the attached Delaware Regiment. Virginia Continentals further bolstered this third line. After the Redcoats cleared the woods, they would have to cross the vale and charge the Continentals, who were in position on a slight rise near the courthouse.

After all the hardship and fruitless weeks of chasing Greene to the Dan, Cornwallis's army was ragged, hungry, and nearly out of supply. When Cornwallis shed most of his supplies and equipment to make his entire army a light corps, he relied on foraging in the Carolina countryside. But North Carolina had been picked clean by the two armies. His troops ran low on provisions, forage for the horses (the equivalent of gasoline for modern armies), and powder. Only a decisive victory would make the unbelievable shared sacrifice worth the cost. At Guilford, Greene had thrown down the gauntlet. Twelve miles separated the two armies. If Cornwallis didn't take up the challenge, he would have to fall back to Wilmington for resupply.

On March 15 around noon, the artillery from both sides began their duel. Casualties were light in the twenty-minute bombardment, yet the solid cannon shot could be devastating. One North Carolina militiaman wrote that one of his unit's men was "killed by the last cannonball, supposed to be from a six-pounder thrown from the British artillery. . . . [The] ball struck him in the head, as he was resting on one knee to keep himself steady, which made his posture coincide with the parabolic curve of the descending ball, it tore out the spine the whole length of the body."

As soon as the guns went silent, Cornwallis ordered his army forward. In a red line that stretched nearly a mile, the British advanced. After pushing through some underbrush and woods, the Redcoats entered the muddy field and headed toward the North Carolina militiamen behind the rail fence. Moving at a fast trot, the British charged toward the Americans with fixed bayonets. Sergeant Roger Lamb, a British soldier with the 23rd Regiment of Foot, recalled, "[We were] in excellent order in a smart run. . . . When [we] arrived within 40 yards of the enemy's line it was perceived that their whole line had their arms presented, and resting on a rail fence. . . . They were taking aim with the nicest precision."

Elements of the British horse headed forward at full gallop. Their "armor which was burnished very bright [caused such] a flash of light to be thrown back on the American horses, as they approached, that it frightened them and caused a momentary disorder." When the British drew near, the Americans opened up. The volley was "most galling and destructive, causing one half of the Highlanders dropt on the spot."

One North Carolina militiaman described the carnage: "After they delivered their fire, which was a deliberate one, with their rifles, the part of the British line at which they were aimed look like the scattering stalks of a wheat field, when the harvest man has passed over it with his cradle."

The fire stunned the disciplined British regulars. "At this awful moment . . . a general pause took place; both parties surveyed each other with a most anxious suspense."

In a display of intrepid leadership, British Lieutenant Colonel James Webster ended the hesitation, shouting, "Come on, my brave Fuzileers[!]"

Inspired by Webster's words, the Royal Welsch Fusiliers surged forward. As they closed to within yards of the rail fence, it was now bayonet time, and the American militia didn't want any part of it. Before being overrun, some of the citizen-soldiers fired their two shots. Others fired one—or not any at all—and then broke into a run toward the

Virginians behind them, dropping weapons and canteens. The stampede toward the second line, as at Cowpens, opened up a hole, allowing the panic-stricken militiamen to retreat to the rear of the battlefield. One officer described the rout: "[The men] broke off without firing a single gun and dispersed like a flock of sheep frightened by dogs."

Conversely, another participant noted the valor of some of the men: "Some made such haste in retreat as to bring reproach upon themselves as deficient in bravery, while their neighbors behaved like heroes."

As the British broke through the first line, the American flanks stubbornly held. The riflemen hit the British with enfilading fire, slowing their advance. Holding out as long as possible, Kirkwood and the others fired multiple deadly volleys before retreating in good order. Fighting tree to tree, Kirkwood's men and the others on the flanks, including Washington's and Lee's troops, fell back toward the third line, where the Marylanders were waiting. The protracted fighting withdrawal took the lives of many British and Hessians. Delaware Continental William Seymour recalled, "Riflemen and musketry behaved with great bravery, killing and wounding great numbers of the enemy."

Bloodied and hungry, the British and their Hessian allies tramped through dense woodland. Pushing through the thick and tangled vegetation between two farmers' fields and fighting through the flankers, Cornwallis's men covered three hundred more bloody yards. There they hit the second line, manned by the Virginians. Combat deteriorated to the squad and platoon level. Sharp skirmishes flared amid the trees, gullies, and rugged terrain of the battlefield. Many of the firefights became intense. One Virginian claimed his men "fired away fifteen or eighteen rounds, & some, twenty rounds per man." Colonel Otho Holland Williams, now in overall command of both the Maryland regiments, recalled the Virginians' stand: "[They] continued their opposition with such firmness . . . during which time the roar of musketry and the cracking of rifles were almost perpetual and as heavy as I have ever heard."

The British officer corps took a beating. A musket ball pierced Brigadier General Charles O'Hara through the thigh, yet he still led his men onward. Looking around at the thinned ranks, Tarleton claimed, "All [the] officers were wounded."

The Virginians put up such a stout defense that the British advance stalled. After having had two horses shot out from under him, Cornwallis personally interceded and valiantly moved to the front of the line. British Sergeant Roger Lamb remembered the scene:

> I saw Lord Cornwallis riding across clear ground. His Lordship was mounted on a dragoon's horse (his own having been shot), the saddlebags were under the creature's belly, which much retarded his progress, owing to the vast quantity of underwood that was spread over the ground; his Lordship was evidently unconscious of the danger. I immediately laid hold of the bridle of his horse and turned his head. I then mentioned to him, that if his Lordship pursued in the same direction, he would in a few moments have been surrounded by the enemy, and, perhaps cut to pieces or captured. I continued to run alongside the horse, keeping the bridle in my hand, until his Lordship, gained the 23rd Regiment, which was at that time drawn up in the skirt of the woods.

It took nearly an hour and a half from the start of the battle for the British to reach the Marylanders in the third line. John Eager Howard, second in command of the 1st Maryland Regiment, saw the British emerge from the tree line and survey the position of the Continentals: "The first [Maryland] regiment under Gunby was formed in a hollow, in the wood, and to the right [west] of the cleared ground about the Courthouse the Virginia brigade under Genl. Huger were to our right. The second [Maryland] regiment was at some distance to the left of the first in the clear ground, with its left flank thrown back as to form a line almost at right angles [to the] 1st regt."

As the British emerged from the woods and entered the vale in front of third line, Greene was feeling optimistic about his prospects; his best troops, including the Marylanders, stood rested and waiting.

He was "flattering himself with a happy conclusion, passing along the line exhorting his troops to give the finishing blow."

With bayonets gleaming in the sunlight that shone through the clouds on that blustery March day, about six hundred of Cornwallis's bloodied men re-formed and looked upon the Marylanders. Spotting several American artillery pieces, the British charged across the open field toward the green men of the 2nd Maryland. Lieutenant Colonel Benjamin Ford, one of the original members of Smallwood's Battalion, directly commanded the 2nd, which was composed largely of raw recruits with a sprinkling of veteran officers.

Confusion immediately descended within the ranks of the inexperienced troops as Ford ordered them to maneuver and face the British advance, led by the wounded Brigadier General Charles O'Hara and Colonel James Stuart. One American officer described how the commander of the 2nd Maryland attempted to position his men: "Ford ordered a charge that proceeded some distance."

But not all the men moved when ordered. Otho Holland Williams, Ford's immediate superior in charge of the Maryland Brigade, explained, "The Second has but 8 comm'd officer to 6 comp'ys and has a large portion of State troops [militia]. I can give no better reason why that regiment refused to charge when it was ordered." The 2nd suffered from a deficiency of officers in the lower ranks. Drawn from levies all around the state of Maryland, the group didn't share the strong bonds of community or the years of experience of the 1st Maryland. Williams countermanded Ford's order to charge after he saw their confusion and reordered the line to face the British onslaught.

Halting the charge did little to calm the nerves of the untested troops. As the Redcoats advanced, they loosed a deadly volley, killing the 2nd's second in command, Major Archibald Anderson, and wounding several other Marylanders. The death of a senior officer likely had a chilling effect on the raw recruits' morale. To their dishonor, the 2nd

Maryland broke and ran. The Guards captured the two American artillery pieces under the command of Captain Anthony Singleton.

The near-rout of the Marylanders almost led to Greene's capture. Seeing the 2nd Regiment flee, the American commander attempted to rally the broken troops. British soldiers passed within thirty yards of the southern commander, but Greene was saved by "Col. Morris calling to me and advertising to me of my situation. I had just time to retire."

Although trees, smoke, and "unevenness of the ground" obscured the 1st Maryland's view of the battlefield, word of the breakthrough reached Howard. "Capt. Gibson, Deputy Adjutant General rode to me and informed me that a party of the enemy, inferior in numbers to us, were pushing through the cleared ground and into our rear, and if we would face about and charge them, we might take them."

Howard rode over to the 1st Maryland commander, Colonel John Gunby, who issued an order: "Face about."

Led by veterans Gassaway Watkins and William Beatty, the 1st changed direction, fired, and reloaded their muskets as they surged toward the Guards' flank. Howard remembered, "[We] immediately engaged with the Guards. Our men gave some well-directed fire, and we then advanced and continued firing."

As the two elite units closed to within yards of each other, the Marylanders' line erupted with a tremendous volley of fire. "They fired at the same instant, and they appeared so near that the blazes from the muzzles of their guns seemed to meet," recalled one participant. The Marylanders' shots had an immediate and deadly impact on the Guards, who "were thrown into confusion by a heavy fire."

In the melee, someone shot Gunby's horse out from under him, and the officer from Maryland's Eastern Shore found himself pinned underneath the animal. Howard immediately took command and urged his men forward into the Guards' left flank. Howard's close friend Captain Gassaway Watkins, Jack Steward, and other veterans from the original Maryland 400 interspersed within the 1st Maryland's ranks kept the men fighting as a cohesive unit.

The piercing sound of a bugle broke through the din of battle. In a scene reminiscent of Cowpens, William Washington's cavalry swooped down upon the Guards, slashing and hacking with their sabers. "The swords of the horsemen were upon the enemy, who were rejoicing in victory and safety," as one Continental described it, "and before they suspected danger, multitudes lay dead."

In the thick of the action, six-foot-six, 260-pound Peter Francisco cleaved several British soldiers with his six-foot broadsword. He later attested, "[I] was wounded in the thigh by a bayonet, from the knee to the socket of the hip, and, in the presence of many, [I] was seen to kill two men, besides making many other panes which were doubtless fatal to others."

Stunned by Washington's cavalry, the Redcoats reeled. As at Cowpens, Howard, sensing an opportunity, ordered the men to charge with bayonets. Letting out a yell, the Marylanders, including Private Thomas Carney, surged forward. The African American Continental "bore a conspicuous part as a soldier . . . when the Maryland troops came to the charge, he bayoneted seven of the enemy."

The 1st Maryland tore into the ranks of the elite 2nd Guards Battalion. The Marylanders, with their core group drawn from the elite of Maryland society, pitted themselves against British officers of noble lineage. Both units had a proud history and had engaged in many of the major battles since Long Island.

Under the onslaught, the Guards buckled. The melee broke into desperate hand-to-hand combat. Williams later described the bitter fighting: "They bayoneted and cut to pieces a great number of British Guards." Fists, swords, and bayonets lacerated flesh and bone. The fighting swirled around fifer James Nowell, who had recovered from "an accidental wound in one of his legs from a bayonet in ye encampment [at Elizabethtown, New Jersey]" only to have his bad luck continue. In the firefight, he again suffered wounds to the leg.

In a microcosm of the fighting between the two elite units, two officers dueled valiantly. The acting commanding officer of the Guards, Lieutenant Colonel James Stewart, attacked Baltimore native Captain

John Smith of the 1st Maryland. According to legend, Smith and Stewart had dueled prior to the battle. A close friend of John Smith recounted the melee:

> Smith and his men were in a throng, killing the Guards and grenadiers like so many Furies. Colonel Steward [*sic*], seeing the mischief Smith was doing, made up to him through the crowd, dust, and smoke, and made a violent lunge at him with his small sword. The first that Smith saw was the shining metal like lightning at his bosom he only had time to lean a little to the right, and lift up his left arm so as to let the polished steel pass under it when the hilt struck his breast, it would have been through his body but for the haste of the colonel and happening to set his foot on the arms of a man Smith had just cut down, his unsteady step, his violent lunge and missing his aim brought him with one knee upon the dead man, the Guards came rushing up very strong, Smith had no alternative but to wheel round to the right and give Steward a back handed blow over or across the head on which he fell; his orderly sergeant attacked Smith, but Smith's sergeant dispatched him; a 2nd attacked him Smith hewed him down, a 3rd behind him threw down a cartridge and shot him in the back of the head, Smith now fell among the slain but was taken up by his men and brought off, it was found to be only a buckshot lodged against the skull and had only stunned him.

One of Smith's men fighting next to him was Marylander James Gooding, who had been gut-shot in Camden, was captured, and later "deserted from the British." The Continental private's hand was disabled by "a cannon's being thrown off its conveyance. Being placed between two pieces of cannon his hearing has been much injured since."[33]

33. During the war, Gooding claimed he trusted Smith with his military pay and land grant. In his pension application Gooding swore under oath, "He never received any land and entrusted Captain John Smith to receive his pay, who retired with it to South Carolina and never paid him a cent."

In a decisive move, Howard's men recaptured Singleton's cannon. Tarleton summed up the pivotal moment: "The Maryland brigade followed by Washington's cavalry moving upon them before they could receive assistance, retook the cannon, and repulsed the guards with great slaughter." Howard recounted, "I observed Washington's horse, and as their movements were quicker than ours, they first charged and broke the enemy. My men followed very quickly, and we pressed through the guards."

Exposed and now flanked by the 1st Marylanders, the Guards faced nearly certain destruction, which would open a critical hole in the center of Cornwallis's line. Howard thought, *"The whole were in our power."* Tarleton later reflected, "At this period, the events of the action was doubtful, and victory alternately presided over each army."

At that crucial moment, Cornwallis emerged from the woods and, immediately understanding the dire nature of the scene unfolding before him, ordered a desperate gambit. He commanded Lieutenant John McLeod, who had dragged his two three-pound grasshopper artillery pieces nearly a mile, to fire grapeshot into the Marylanders and cavalry, despite the fact that it would also hit the Guards. The iron balls tore into the flesh of Continentals and Redcoats alike. The draconian measure tipped the battle toward the British.

The grape had a devastating effect on the Marylanders. As Washington's horsemen wheeled to the rear, Howard's men now found themselves in a dangerously exposed position. "Columns of the enemy appear[ed] in different directions. Washington's horse having gone off, I found it necessary to retire, which I did leisurely, but many of the guards who were lying on the ground and who we supposed were wounded, got up and fired at us as we retired."

Through the grape and musket fire, the Marylanders withdrew. Seeing the Continentals' backs, the 23rd and 71st Foot and the cavalry rallied and charged "with greatest alacrity."

Possibly rattled by his near capture and the disintegration of the 2nd Maryland, Greene was unwilling to risk the entire army. He ordered a general withdrawal.

Greene the planner had a prearranged line of retreat toward the north-east. Using the Reedy Fork Road as an escape route to the prearranged encampment at the ironworks at Speedwell Furnace, Williams organized the army's retreat: "The artillery horses being shot, we were obliged to leave four six pounders in the field which was our only considerable loss. The General ordered the troops to retire which was executed with such good order and regularity."

Forming a solid line of infantry, Cornwallis ordered all his units forward to pursue the retreating Americans, who put up a spirited rearguard defense. In one incident, a Virginian fired a ball that took out the kneecap and femur of Lieutenant Colonel James Webster, who was leading his brigade forward. Exhausted, with his ranks reduced by more than a quarter, Cornwallis was in no position to pursue Greene.

Henry Lee's cavalry was one of the last American units to leave the field. As they galloped off, Peter Rife, one of Lee's cavalrymen, encountered two Irishmen in a scene that demonstrated the humanity of the men and the absurdity of war:

There were two Irishmen, one of whom belonged to the British and the other to the American army. Of course Mr. Rife did not know their names; but, for the sake of convenience, we shall call the one belonging to the British O'Bryan, and the other Jimmison. O'Bryan had been badly wounded; and, from the intensity of his pain, without thinking or caring where he went, he had strayed off so far from corps to which he belonged and toward the Court House, that he was near the road by which the Americans retreated. Being within a few steps and recognizing in Jimmison a countryman, he called to him, and begged for mercy's sake to give him a drink of water. He held in his hand a long round staff, resembling that on which the Ensign carries his flag, and had on the top of it a sharp iron, like that which we commonly see on top of a flag staff [a spontoon]. Jimmison happening to have some water in his canteen, stepped up very kindly and gave him a drink. When he turned to go away, and before he had got any distance, O'Bryan, so frenzied with pain and thirst, as Rife supposed, that he did not know what he was doing, threw his staff, with all his remaining strength, at his benefactor, and the iron point struck him, but inflicted only a slight wound. Jimmison then turned back and drove his bayonet into O'Bryan's heart, which at once put an end to his life and his misery. Having done so, he turned toward Martinsville and overtook his company just as they were entering the village.

The British pursued the Marylanders and the rest of Greene's army only a few miles. Greene's men retreated to their camp thirteen miles away at Speedwell Furnace, where Greene ordered them to construct fieldworks. Cornwallis had led 1,924 men into battle. Of those, 93 had been killed, 413 had been wounded, and 26 were missing. Pinned down with over a fourth of his army dead or wounded, Cornwallis could neither retreat nor advance but spent a miserable night in the hellish, blood-soaked fields of Guilford Courthouse.

Clouds soon enveloped the sky as "a violent and constant rain" that lasted "40 hours" darkened the region, soaking the field of battle and the wounded Americans and British alike. Charles O'Hara, the colorful leader of the Brigade of the Guards, who had bullet wounds to the chest and thigh, described the suffering: "I never did, and I hope never shall again, experience two such days and Nights, as these immediately after the Battle, we remained on the very ground on which it had been fought cover'd with Dead, and Dying and with Hundreds of Wounded, Rebels, as well as our own. . . . [The torrential downpour] made it equally impractical to remove or administer the smallest comfort to many of the

Wounded." One officer who did receive medical attention was Tarleton; in a grisly scene, a surgeon amputated several of his fingers to treat a wound suffered in the battle. Tarleton later often waved the stump at his men and told them that he had given the missing fingers for king and country.

Cornwallis's commissary general Charles Stedman vividly remembered, "The night was remarkable for its darkness accompanied with rain which fell in torrents. Nearly fifty of the wounded, it is said sinking under their aggravated miseries, expired before the morning. The cries of the wounded and dying, who remained on the field of action during the night exceeded all description. Such a complicated scene of horror and distress, it is hoped, for the sake of humanity, rarely occurs, even in military life."

While neither the British nor the Americans realized it at the time, Guilford Courthouse altered the course of the war. It changed the strategy of both sides: it halted a potentially disastrous pending Patriot attack on New York, stopped the British conquest of the Carolinas, and set the stage for a stunning defeat of a British army at Yorktown.

During the spring of 1781, George Washington remained obsessed with defeating Henry Clinton in New York and argued with his French counterpart General Jean-Baptiste Donatien de Vimeur, comte de Rochambeau, that New York had to remain the objective.

Before the disastrous defeats at Charleston and Camden, the French had decided on a major escalation of the war. They sent Rochambeau with more than five thousand troops to Newport, Rhode Island, in the summer of 1780. Born in 1725, the count had joined the French cavalry after the death of his older brother, climbing to the rank of brigadier general during the French and Indian War. Prior to this assignment, Rochambeau had been placed in charge of an aborted French invasion of Britain in 1779; the troops for that invasion were diverted to North America. The grizzled, thirty-seven-year veteran of many wars bore a distinctive scar above his eye and was known for his mercurial demeanor.

According to his aides, the general didn't trust anyone, not even his subordinates, whom he considered to be "rogues and idiots." However, Washington's temperament melted the Frenchman's taciturn personality.

Washington pushed Rochambeau toward a final showdown in New York, an epic battle he thought would destroy the main British army in North America and end the war. The count sniffed out a disaster waiting to happen that would likely cause the destruction of the French and Amercian armies. For five years Clinton had prepared Manhattan's defenses, and he was hoping for an American attack. This was the chance he had been waiting for to bring the elusive American and French armies into a major battle and defeat them. As in Savannah, the Crown would be behind excellent defenses. It looked as if time and money might actually be on the side of the British, and it behooved Clinton to let Washington attack rather than take a great risk himself. Time was running out on the French alliance and funding for the rebellion.

In the spring of 1780, instead of attacking New York, Rochambeau saw an opportunity to pick off not Cornwallis, but a force of thirty-five hundred men that, under General William Phillips and later Benedict Arnold, had been raiding Virginia. Through tact, charm, and wisdom, he sowed the seeds of the allies' southern strategy. Secretly, he called on Admiral François-Joseph-Paul de Grasse to sail from the Caribbean for the Chesapeake with the objective of trapping Phillips's and Arnold's forces. The British troops were separated from larger forces in Charleston and New York and could potentially be destroyed.

The pyrrhic British victory at Guilford Courthouse, in no small part caused by the damage the Marylanders inflicted and their role in keeping Greene's army togther, compelled Cornwallis to move his battered army to Wilmington, North Carolina, instead of following Clinton's orders to hold South Carolina.

Eventually, the earl decided to move north and invade Virginia, putting his army—and the outcome of the war—at risk. Simultaneously, Greene and the Marylanders marched back into South Carolina.

CHAPTER 38

HOBKIRK'S HILL

In the thick, sticky darkness of the South Carolina night on April 22, 1781, the Marylanders heaved massive sections of logs into place as quietly as possible. Just yards away, the Redcoats slumbered in Fort Watson, near the current location of Summerton, South Carolina, unaware that the Americans were erecting the means of their destruction. Slowly, the giant pile of green logs grew. For days, the Marylanders, Henry Lee's cavalry, and Francis Marion's irregulars had toiled, felling trees, hacking timber, and assembling the pieces of what became a forty-foot-tall tower.

More than a week earlier, Nathanael Greene had decided to take action. On the heels of the battle for Guilford Courthouse, Charles, Earl Cornwallis's damaged army was refitting in Wilmington, North Carolina. Greene knew it would be some time before Cornwallis could take the field, but he did not know whether the British general had moved north toward Virginia or south toward the Carolinas after the battle at Guilford Courthouse. Taking the initiative, and following Washington's axiom "Don't be drove," Greene returned to South Carolina, where the British had various outposts scattered from Ninety Six to Augusta to Fort Watson, Georgetown, and Camden. By moving his army rapidly, he hoped to dispatch each of them. And by cutting off certain choke points, he could put the others out of supply.

Greene split his force into two groups. He formed a smaller task force from Lee's Legion and a Maryland company of Continentals under Captain Edward Oldham, who had been with the Marylanders since the beginning, having joined the Flying Camp as a first lieutenant. He made his way up the ranks to captain. Oldham received high praise from his fellow officers. Lee wrote, "To the name of Captain Oldham, too much praise cannot be given. He was engaged in almost every action in the South, and was uniformly distinguished for gallantry and good conduct. With the exception of [Robert] Kirkwood, of Delaware . . . , he was probably entitled to more credit than any officer of his rank in Greene's army—a distinction which must place him high on the rolls of fame."

Greene ordered Oldham and Lee to head toward Wilmington in an attempt to deceive the British about their true line of march. Once confident the ruse had succeeded, the Marylanders and the horsemen abruptly changed direction and headed south to join the Swamp Fox, Francis Marion. Their combined forces would hit Fort Watson, a crucial spoke about fifty-five miles south of Camden that guarded the supply chain connecting Charleston to Camden. Simultaneously, Greene and the main army marched on Camden, the linchpin in the defensive network of posts.

Garrisoned by eighty regulars and forty Loyalists, Fort Watson sat atop a thirty-foot mound surrounded by three rows of nasty abatis. The Marylanders and other troops surrounded the fort on April 15, 1781, and began considering how they would compel those inside to surrender the garrison. They approached the defenders with a white flag and demanded their unconditional surrender—and were rebuffed. Next, Oldham and Lee cut off the fort's only source of water, but the defenders countered by digging a forty-foot well within Watson's stout walls. A stalemate ensued. The British thumbed their noses at the Americans, knowing they lacked entrenching tools, heavy artillery, and the time for a protracted siege. Then, in a display of quintessential American ingenuity, Colonel Hezekiah Maham came up with a novel solution: The Patriots would build a large tower out of trees from the area. By climbing the structure, the men could shoot down into the enemy fortifications, while the thick logs protected them from return fire.

On the night of April 22, the Americans carried the Lincoln Log–like sections of the tower to within rifle range of the fort, where they erected the Maham tower, as their log structure came to be known. Manned by some of Oldham's riflemen, the tower loomed over the walls of the fort, and at first light the riflemen started picking off the defenders inside. Concurrently, two forlorn-hope assault parties, one made up of Marylanders and the other of Marion's men, hit the abatis.

The lethal fire from the tower prevented the defenders from manning the fort's walls. And the tower, combined with the ground assault from the forlorn hope, caused the garrison to capitulate soon.

While Fort Watson was small, its loss had a major impact on the war in the South, a fact recognized by Francis, Lord Rawdon, the British officer who currently commanded the defenses at Camden as well as the Crown's eight thousand troops that garrisoned the forts dotting the South Carolina and Georgia countryside. The loss of Fort Watson meant that Rawdon's supply lines were cut, putting the crucial post at Camden in jeopardy.

On the afternoon of April 19, while some of the Continentals and the militiamen were constructing the Maham tower at Fort Watson, Greene and many of the other Marylanders arrived at the outskirts of Camden. The American commander had found the outpost too heavily fortified for a direct assault. Several stout redoubts, which arced around the town and connected with interlocking defenses, and a central stockade would have gored his men. Less than two miles from his adversary, Greene gazed on the fortified town. He did not possess the numbers to invest in a siege; instead, he waited for the British to attack.

Greene hoped to lure Rawdon out of his defenses to attack the Americans' numerically stronger forces on favorable ground. To that end, he employed a series of probes to provoke Rawdon. On the night of April 20, under cover of darkness, Captain Bob Kirkwood and his crack light infantry hit Logtown, a grouping of seedy cabins situated on the outskirts of Camden. Kirkwood's men quickly seized most of the hamlet, but a "scattering fire was kept up all night." At dawn a sharp firefight took place. "[We] had a smart schirmaze [skirmish], beat in the Enemy, about two hours afterwards had a Very agreeable Sight of the Advance [fortifications of Camden] of the Army."

The next day, the Delaware Blues and William Washington's cavalry mounted a raid on the western side of Camden and "Burnt a House in one of the Enemy's Redoubts." The raid yielded scores of cattle and horses. The pinprick-like raids posed only a minor problem to the British—until the fall of Fort Watson.

The stalemate broke on April 24. Rawdon, "the ugliest officer in the British Army," listened intently as a teenage Maryland drummer boy divulged priceless information that changed the course of the entire campaign. The boy, who had fought hours earlier alongside his brothers in the American line before deciding to change sides, revealed Greene's order of battle to the twenty-six-year-old Rawdon and gave him the crucial information that Greene would soon be reinforced by Thomas Sumter and Francis Marion.

To make matters worse, Rawdon had recently gotten word of the fall of Fort Watson. The loss of the outpost, combined with the Swamp Fox's running amok in the countryside and ambushing his supply train, cut Camden off from Charleston. Rawdon needed to act quickly before food supplies gave out. If Camden fell into American hands, the posts within the network would either wither on the vine from lack of supply or face destruction if Greene concentrated his forces on any one of them.

The British had only about a week's worth of supplies stockpiled in Camden. In what was one of the most daring assaults of the Revolution, Rawdon audaciously decided to attack Greene. Outnumbered two to three, the Irish scion took drastic measures to beef up his force, combing Camden for every warm body he could find.

On the chilly morning of April 25, 1781, at ten o'clock, Rawdon marched out of Camden to attack. "By arming our musicians, our drummers, and in short everything that could carry a firelock, I mustered above nine hundred for the field, sixty of whom were dragoons. With this force and two six-pounders we marched, about ten o'clock yesterday morning, leaving our redoubts to the care of the militia and a few sick soldiers."

Just a few miles away from Rawdon's oncoming onslaught, Greene sipped a cup of tea while his fifteen-hundred-man army leisurely washed their clothes and cleaned their weapons. The Marylanders and the rest of Greene's troops manned defensive positions about a mile and a half outside Camden on a sandy ridge known as Hobkirk's Hill. Timber and thick, lush underbrush coated large portions of the knoll, while the Great Wagon Road bisected the center of the embankment. In a reverse of the alignment of the troops at Guilford Courthouse, the Rhode Islander posted the Marylanders up front to the east of the Great Wagon Road with the Virginia Continentals on its western side. The militiamen stayed atop the hill in reserve with Washington's cavalry. Greene's army waited for Lord Rawdon to make the next move, completely unaware of how soon it would come.

To deceive the Americans, Rawdon's troops raced south, "filing close to the swamps," and then quickly turned east into a wooded area to mask their movements. Rawdon's scratch force consisted of infantry, cavalry, two artillery pieces, and even a company of fifty walking wounded designated "convalescents." They tramped along a meandering stream toward the left flank of the American lines, which was manned by the Marylanders and Kirkwood's Company. In a shocking American intelligence failure, the British remained unseen by Greene's sentries until they hit pickets about three hundred yards in front of the Marylanders.

The Volunteers of Ireland, who had tangled with the Marylanders at Camden, charged into pickets occupied by Maryland and Virginia Continentals. Kirkwood's Blues served as a reserve behind the pickets and quickly moved into line with the Continentals. Moving from tree to tree, the Americans kept the Volunteers at bay long enough that the main line could form behind them.

Hearing the sharp firefight in their front, Captain William Beatty and the other officers roused the men from their camp duties and ordered them to fall into the line. Many of the men "were still washing [their clothes] and never joined us," bemoaned Howard.

Confused and stunned, the Marylanders formed and received the British bravely. Advancing on a narrow front as they attacked the Marylanders, the Volunteers of Ireland charged at a slight angle because Rawdon's long column of men was moving westward. As the British assaulted the Americans, the Redcoats were pelted with "heavy showers of Grape." The artillery had a chilling effect on the British advance; as Seymour remembered, "[It] put the enemy in great confusion, having killed and dangerously wounded a great number of them."

Smoke and thick vegetation obscured the line of sight for both sides until they were nearly on top of each other. One Continental described the sights and sounds of the battle as a "universal blaze of musketry from left to right throughout our whole line for an hour, every officer exhorting all the bravery and energy of his soul."

The American artillery and musket fire checked the British advance. "The Enemy were staggered in all quarters, and upon the left retiring." Greene the brilliant strategist morphed into Greene the tactician—a role he never filled well. Sensing the tide of the battle turning in his favor, Greene ordered an attack. Instead of receiving Rawdon's assault and counterattacking, he rolled the dice on an all-out assault "to charge bayonets without firing." William Washington, serving as part of the reserve, would circle around Rawdon to hit him from the rear.

Everything was coming together for a crushing American victory, and then it all started to fall apart.

The intrepid Beatty, one of the original Boys of '76, who had risen to the rank of captain, led the advance companies of the 1st Maryland in the charge. As he and others, including Thomas Carney and Gassaway Watkins, bravely surged forward, a musket ball struck Beatty in the head, killing him instantly. Greene later praised the young officer as "an ornament to his profession," and poignantly noted that "the promising young youth who was engaged to marry an amiable girl" would never see her again. The death of a prominent, much-admired battle captain many likely viewed as bulletproof caused "confusion and [the men] dropped out of line." The disorder spread through the companies around Beatty as more men went down. Fatefully, Colonel John Gunby ordered the regiment to fall back and re-form. The order created a disastrous chain reaction. As the men retreated, a huge hole formed in the American line, dooming the American counterattack.

Simultaneously, the 2nd Maryland charged forward, but soon faced enfilading fire from Rawdon's men. A ball traveling at nearly seven hundred feet per second crushed the elbow of the 2nd's commanding officer, Lieutenant Colonel Benjamin Ford. The regiment fell back in chaos. Ford's men carried him from the field.

Despite the mounting losses, John Eager Howard and Jack Steward continued to surge forward until Howard received the order from Gunby to fall back, which he obeyed. Soon the Eastern Shore native, "exerting himself," attempted to rally his men. The Marylanders briefly re-formed and fired a few shots before they fled for their lives up the hill. Rawdon's men continued to surge forward with the American guns in their sights. In his fifth year of war, militant surgeon Richard Pindell, riding Lawrence Everhart's horse, which he had obtained at Cowpens, once again tried to rally the men as he had first done at Brandywine. "I aided the officers in repeatedly rallying and keeping in order a great number of the retreating troops," he recalled. "After the officers were exhausted and worn down, I kept them together by my own personal exertions."

Captain John Smith and his company, made up of about forty-five Irish Marylanders, stood in the way of the oncoming British horde. In the midst of the charge, Greene galloped up to Smith and "ordered him to fall into the rear and save the cannon."

Smith, recovered from the head wound delivered by Lieutenant Colonel James Stuart at Guilford, swiftly moved into action. The matrosses, the assistant gunners who tugged on heavy ropes that hauled the guns, had abandoned their posts at the sight of the tide of Redcoats. Seizing the thick hemp ropes with one hand and holding their muskets in the other, Smith's men slowly dragged the guns off Hobkirk's Hill. Suddenly, at full gallop, British dragoons charged Smith's men. Smith and the other men dropped the ropes, formed, aimed, and fired their weapons at the oncoming horsemen—dropping many and forcing their withdrawal. Rawdon's infantry rumbled forward, and Smith's band received them and "fought like bulldogs" and "repeated [this] several times until they got within two or three miles from the field of action."

William Washington's cavalry finally appeared on the field. Instead of attacking Rawdon's rear as directed by Greene, his cavalry inexplicably took a circuitous route behind Logtown and fell upon a group of Redcoats. The Virginian paroled or captured two hundred British troops. Not one to kill unarmed prisoners of war without cause, he was bogged down and delayed by their number. However, Washington arrived in the nick of time to help save the guns. Even Greene had a hand in the action and was seen dismounting and helping pull the ropes. The guns were saved. On the other hand, Smith and his men were not. After taking heavy losses, Smith surrendered and was stripped down to his shirt and his commission, which "hung around his neck in his bosom."

With the guns safe, Greene continued his general withdrawal, retreating several miles to the old Camden battlefield. Here amid the bones of the fallen and debris of the previous summer's battle, he prepared to receive Rawdon, whose exhausted troops had the strength to pursue the Americans only a few miles.

Greene soon sent Kirkwood and Washington back to the hill to save the wounded and pick up any stragglers. Using a bit of guile and bluff, Washington and the Delaware Blues attempted to lure the British dragoons off the hill into an ambush. The ruse didn't work, and as soon as the Brits realized the subterfuge, they retreated. Kirkwood and Washington brought the American wounded back to the old Camden battlefield, and Doctor Pindell once again went to work tending the wounded, while many of them lay dying. Rawdon's losses amounted to 38 killed, 177 wounded, and 43 missing. Outnumbered two to three, he had won a remarkable tactical victory. However, by vacating the city after the win, he gave up the key British post in South Carolina; the relinquishment had strategic consequences that affected the rest of the war.

Along with the death of Beatty, Williams recorded American losses as follows: 18 enlisted killed in action, 108 wounded, and 136 missing. While many of the missing found their way back to American lines, some willingly went into the hands of the British. Rawdon dryly noted, "A number . . . finding their retreat cut off, went into Camden & claimed protection as Deserters."

After lingering for nearly two months, original Baltimore Independent Cadet Benjamin Ford succumbed to wounds sustained in the battle. As usual, Doctor Pindell tended to the men severely wounded in the battle, including his close friend Ford. "The dye is cast," he wrote. "We were yesterday reduced to the disagreeable necessity of Amputating one of our Dearest Friends, who since he has reached this place has suffered one continued scene of pain . . . the bones exposed and the arm became swelled."

The loss of two core officers took its toll, as Williams noted: "Ford died a few Days hence of the wound he received before Camden. Have not enough officers left to command the small band of veterans still left."

The manpower shortage led to some unconventional ideas, including the recruitment of African Americans from the South. A leading figure in this area was Lieutenant Colonel John Laurens, a prominent South Carolinian whose father was an ambassador to France. He petitioned George Washington about the idea, which included emancipating slaves after their service in the American army. The Marylanders also had a hand in the project, and Jack Steward asked the Maryland government to let him command a regiment of African Americans. In addition, Otho Holland Williams discussed the idea with his good friend Samuel Smith in Baltimore: "Williams had asked in his letter to Col. Smith why, if white men could not be got, Negroes were not enlisted; there is talk of raising such a regiment, and [Jack Steward] wants the command. [There is doubt] that Steward can wheedle the legislature into giving it to him." Despite being personally torn on the subject, Washington scotched the idea owing to the sensitive nature of slavery in the South.

Condemned to death by Rawdon, Captain John Smith stared at the dank walls of the Camden jail. Several British witnesses had attested "that Capt. Smith had killed Col. Stuart of the Kings Guards in cold blood two hours before the battle on his knees begging for mercy." By chance, a British deserter informed Greene of Smith's plight, and Greene, standing by his officer, fired off an angry missive to Rawdon.

Under the protection of a flag of truce, a messenger delivered the letter, which said, "Nothing can be more foreign from the truth than the charge. Captain Smith no doubt did his duty in the action but has too noble a nature to be guilty of such a base conduct as you mention, nor did I ever hear an insinuation of the Kind in the army."

Persuaded by Greene's letter, Rawdon rescinded Smith's death sentence and paroled the wealthy Baltimore native. Ten days after the battle, Rawdon gave up on trying to destroy Greene after several failed attempts to attack, because each time Greene retreated and took up a superb defensive position. Out of supply after the fall of Fort Watson, Rawdon torched Camden, leaving it a heap of ashes, and evacuated the city, bringing with him "all the most obnoxious loyalists." Dozens of American wounded remained behind and under the care of the paroled John Smith, whom Rawdon appointed "commandant of the place, in charge of the sick and wounded."

Guilford Dudley, a North Carolina militia officer who barely survived Camden, had breakfast with Greene days after the battle. He remembered that Greene wore "a smile of complacency" when he heard the news. Greene himself laconically summed up the experience: "We fight, get beat, rise and fight again."

Having accomplished their strategic objective, the Marylanders left the smoking ashes of Camden and pushed deeper into South Carolina to destroy Rawdon's outposts one by one. Their next target was the crucial outpost of Ninety Six, located on the Georgia border. They were not accompanied by Smith, who honored his parole and began the long journey on foot to Charleston. There he placed himself in the hands of the British but feared to "feel the Effects of British tiriny," as he wrote to Williams before setting out. He lived out the remainder of the war in British custody. He never experienced mistreatment from the British, but ironically felt the wrath of his fellow Americans. On the road to Charleston, this original member of Smallwood's Battalion was tortured and attacked by thugs claiming to be Whigs, who "stripped him, bound him and inflicted on him a barbarous castigation on the bare back."

CHAPTER 39

NINETY SIX

The sappers' pickaxes and shovels dug into the hard South Carolina clay as they burrowed closer to the Star Fort in early June 1781. Sweating profusely while they worked under the dim flicker of candlelight, the Patriots added several yards to an underground tunnel that stretched back to American lines. This tunnel, designed to break through the stout and heavily defended walls of the British-held fort at Ninety Six, South Carolina, was the latest tactic the Polish chief engineer, Thaddeus Kosciuszko, had pulled from his arsenal of siege-warfare methods. Taking the fort was strategically important because it protected a great bastion of Loyalists and supported the British fort at Augusta, Georgia. Cornwallis acknowledged, "[Ninety Six] must be kept at all events & I think no reasonable expense should be spared—besides Georgia depends entirely upon it."

Named because it was ninety-six miles from the Indian settlement at Keowee, an important trading post, the town of Ninety Six was home to a garrison of 550 Loyalist troops led by Colonel John Harris Cruger. Born into a wealthy New York family, Cruger commanded a battalion of Loyalists from New York and New Jersey. Participating in the capture and siege of Savannah, he moved to South Carolina but was captured by partisans at a dinner party celebrating the king's birthday. Fortunately for him, he was released in a prisoner exchange and was sent to Ninety Six with his men to improve its defenses. To the original palisade wall, he and his men had added a deep ditch surrounded by an abatis, and on two sides of the town they constructed additional works. To the west, new defenses protected Ninety Six's water supply—one of the fort's greatest vulnerabilities was its lack of a water source within its walls. To the east was the Star Fort, an impressive works with sharp angles designed to maximize the defenders' line of fire and keep assault parties from approaching the fort's walls. A trio of three-pound guns was also on hand.

After the battle for Hobkirk's Hill, Nathanael Greene had split his force and began mopping up the Carolinas. Forces led by his commanders Francis Marion, Thomas Sumter, and Harry Lee—often accompanied by a small contingent of Marylanders—routed the British from their smaller outposts at Fort Motte, Granby, Watson, and Orangeburg. After the evacuation of Camden, only the exterior British posts at Ninety Six in South Carolina and Augusta in Georgia remained, although the Redcoats still retained control of Charleston and Atlanta. In 1781 Greene had yet to win a major battle in the South. The American, however, was winning strategically, forcing the British to abandon their outposts and lose influence and control over territory as well as over the Loyalist population that they were trying to protect and keep on the side of the Crown. The British were being forced to retreat and retrench farther toward their main base in Charleston.

Now Greene and the main army set out to take Ninety Six. To achieve this objective, Greene brought with him 850 Maryland and Delaware Continentals plus approximately two hundred militiamen. The Patriots outnumbered the Loyalists nearly two to one, but given the strength of the defenses at Ninety Six, Greene felt that his troops were insufficient for a direct assault. Instead, they settled in to lay siege to the town. Helping him in planning was Major Joseph McJunkin, a wounded Patriot officer who had been taken captive by the British, "carried to 96 & put in Jail with prisoners of War." Just a few days before Greene arrived, the Loyalists in Ninety Six paroled McJunkin. He recalled "[m]eeting Greene near 96 & being anxious that he should capture that place."

Inexperienced in siege warfare, Greene first directed Kosciuszko to begin constructing entrenchments about seventy yards from the Star Fort. The Loyalists soon moved one of the three-pounders into position and began to fire a devastating barrage. Supported by this cover,

Loyalists from New York sallied forth from inside the Star and pounced on the Patriot working party constructing the trench, putting them to the bayonet. African American slaves then emerged from the fort to retrieve the Americans' pickaxes and shovels.

Stung by this first failure, Greene moved his sappers back about twelve hundred yards from the Star and again began construction of parallel trenches designed to get them closer to the walls of the fort. It took ten days to get back to the point where they had first begun digging. The fort's defenders became masters of the counterattack, and the excavation parties were frequently interrupted by sorties from the strongpoint. Despite the Loyalists' seemingly relentless assaults, the Patriots persisted, and their tunnels inched closer to the fort. Greene's men continued digging until they were within thirty yards of the walls, where they constructed a Maham tower. Ordinarily, the tower would have allowed Greene's riflemen to shoot down into the fort, but Cruger's Loyalists countered the threat by piling sandbags on top of their existing fortifications, leaving slits through which they could fire back at the Patriots. They also attempted to set the tower on fire by launching heated cannonballs—but to no avail—as the tower was constructed of green wood. In response, the Patriots shot flaming arrows into the town, forcing Cruger to order teams of workers to tear the roofs off all the buildings within. As June progressed, the scene was beginning to look more desperate for the besieged; the Loyalists were now so harried by Greene's men that they could counterattack only at night.

After having successfully attacked Augusta, Lee and Andrew Pickens arrived at Ninety Six on June 8, bringing with them a number of Loyalist prisoners whom they paraded in front of the fort. Instead of disheartening those inside, the pathetic spectacle backfired: the sight of their fellow soldiers as POWs steeled their resolve. They continued to defend the town, more determined than ever to resist.

Hoping to take advantage of the brutal Carolina summer temperatures, Greene sent Lee's men to attack the defenses that surrounded the town's sole water supply, a small creek. Their sappers immediately began digging trenches on the west side of town. The Loyalists responded by stepping up their nighttime attacks. Despite these efforts, it soon became very difficult for the Tories to get access to the water. They sent slaves to the creek under the cover of darkness, but the supplies they were able to bring back couldn't satisfy the needs of the town. Still, the tenacious Loyalists held on.

On June 11 a messenger brought Greene the news that two thousand British reinforcements had landed in Charleston and were on their way to Ninety Six, led by Lieutenant Colonel Francis, Lord Rawdon. Greene ordered Thomas Sumter and Francis Marion to delay the Redcoat advance, but the two officers misjudged the route Rawdon intended to take. As a result, the Redcoats bypassed the Americans, marching unhindered straight for Ninety Six.

The defenders inside the fort also soon learned that relief was coming; this knowledge greatly fortified their resolve, despite the tremendous hardships imposed by the Patriots. On June 17 a Loyalist messenger approached the town casually on horseback. He chatted easily with Greene's forces, posing as a friendly local who was merely curious about the standoff. In this way, the messenger gradually made his way toward the front lines, where he suddenly spurred his horse and took off, galloping directly toward the gate, while shouting and waving a letter above his head. Somehow, the messenger managed to evade fire and make it safely behind the walls of the fort. Almost immediately, the Loyalists let up a great cry of celebration, and the sound of a *feu de joie* was heard from within the fort, sending the Patriots a clear message that the Redcoat reinforcements were on their way.

Now nearly out of time, Greene had all but exhausted his options. He first attempted to set the fort on fire, but the Loyalists discovered his plan and thwarted the effort. Next he attempted to blow a hole in the defenses with explosives, but again the defenders rebuffed the attempt. Having tried everything else, Greene began laying plans for an assault on both sides of the fortifications. To attack the east side, he would send two groups of assault forces. The first, a forlorn hope, would cut through the abatis and then fill the ditch that ringed the town with bundles of sticks. The second group would then charge through the gap in the abatis and rush up to the walls carrying long, hooked poles. They would then use these poles to remove the sandbags from the top of the wall, leaving the Star Fort vulnerable to fire from the Maham tower. Now protected by this covering fire, the first group would then climb over the defenses and begin their attack on the defenders within. On the west side, the plan was much less complicated: they would simply assault the stockade en masse, relying on their numbers to force their way through and into the town. Greene hoped the enemy troops would be trapped between the two assault forces.

As dawn broke on June 18, the Americans put their plan into effect. At noon they fired a signal gun. The men in the Maham tower and in the advance trenches opened fire on the Star Fort, as the Marylanders in the forlorn hope charged across the open field. Led by Lieutenant Edward Duvall, the group of Marylanders, including Captain Perry Benson, Captain George Armstrong, Thomas Carney, and many others, rushed toward the fort "amid the thunder and smoke." They leaped into the ditch surrounding the fortifications, and axe-men began cutting through the abatis. "Through every loophole and crevice the fatal balls of the rifle poured down, and the projecting and re-entering angles hemmed them in between two walls of fire. Above bristled a deadly array of pikes and bayonets. As the abatis yielded to their efforts, they became at every instant more and more exposed. Officers and men fell around them on every side."

Captain Armstrong of the 1st Maryland Regiment was killed. Lieutenant Duvall was wounded, as was Captain Benson, whom Thomas Carney "carried . . . on his shoulder to the place where the surgeon [Doctor Pindell] was stationed." Benson never forgot that Carney saved his life, and the two men became lifelong friends.[34]

34. After the war, the men would also visit each other when they were nearby. Benson would rise to the rank of general in the Eastern Shore militia during the War of 1812. He stopped the British landing and attempt to seize Saint Michaels, Maryland. Benson would also be one of eastern Maryland's official delegates to receive Lafayette when he triumphantly returned to America in 1824. It's highly likely that Thomas Carney was there as well.

For forty-five minutes, the men fought in the ditch, breaking through the abatis as the hookmen struggled to pull down the sandbags and breach the Star Fort's walls. Lieutenant Samuel Selden, commanding the Virginians in their forlorn hope, was also wounded "in an attempt to remove some bags of sand the enemy had placed on the Breast works," and the group sustained many casualties. The high number of killed and wounded convinced Greene to call off the attack. Despite the galling fire, most of the wounded were brought back to the safety of the American lines, including Selden, who had been hit in the arm: "a [musket] ball entering his wrist, shattering the bone of the limb nearly to his shoulder." Usually in cases like this, the accepted remedy of the time was for the surgeon to amputate the arm while his assistants held down the patient. But Selden refused to be restrained, choosing instead to hold the doomed limb steady himself. "To this end Selden would not submit. It was his right arm he was about to lose. He sustained it with his left during the operation, his eyes fixed steadily upon it, nor uttered a word, till the saw reached the marrow, when in a composed tone and manner he said, 'I pray you Doctor, be quick.'"

Also wounded in the forlorn hope was John Bantham, an original member of Smallwood's Battalion. This was actually his second forlorn-hope mission, the first being Stony Point. At Ninety Six, he "got his skull bone broke." Another member of the 400 who enlisted in July 1776, Briant Munrow, took a wound severe enough that he "had a furlough to go home till recovered of his wound." Gassaway Watkins, who had taken command of the company formerly led by Captain Beatty, also took part in the assault. For these Boys of '76, the last five years had been some of the hardest of their lives: marching thousands of miles, starving, and surviving smallpox and numerous other maladies, several subzero winters, and British bullets. But these men of iron from the Maryland Line and their brother regiment the Delaware Blues led by example and kept the army together. They were slowly clearing South Carolina of the British even after they had been defeated in battle.

* * *

Lee and Bob Kirkwood's company assaulted the stockade on the opposite side of the Star Fort and seized it according to plan. All seemed to be going well, until the Loyalists sent out a group of thirty men to attack the gathering assault forces. In a bloody, vicious fight, the two groups beat at each other with clubbed muskets and bayonets. Eventually, two of the Patriot commanders fell, and the rest retreated. At that point, 127 of Greene's men had been killed or wounded, with another twenty missing, while the Loyalists lost eighty-five. With Rawdon now just thirty miles away, Greene had no choice but to abandon his position and move on. Morale in his army sank to an all-time low. Lee reported, "Gloom and silence pervaded the American camp; everyone mortified. Three days more and Ninety Six must have fallen; but this short space was unattainable. . . . Greene alone preserved his equanimity; and highly pleased by the unshaken courage displayed in the assault, announced his grateful sense of the conduct of the troops."

Greene marched his men northeast, toward Charlotte, North Carolina. After dispatching a few men to reinforce Ninety Six, Rawdon followed in hot pursuit. About forty miles into the chase, his men caught up to Greene's rear guard—Lee's Legion and Kirkwood's infantry. This time, however, the Americans prevailed. For more than two weeks, the Redcoats had been marching through the oppressive Carolina heat and humidity in their woolen uniforms. The arduous journey had already claimed more than fifty of Rawdon's soldiers. The Redcoats were also short on food and salt, and the spent troops proved no match for the Americans, who were relatively well rested following their siege of Ninety Six. Rawdon quickly pulled his forces back to the fort. He ordered the evacuation of the town and commanded the Loyalist troops to follow his own men back to Charleston.

Sensing an opportunity, Greene sent Lee and Kirkwood orders to get in front of the enemy and cut them off. Now it was the Delaware troops' turn to fall victim to exhaustion. In the twenty-three days after the failed attack at Ninety Six, the infantrymen marched an astounding 323 miles. Rawdon, joined by some reinforcements, holed up in the town of Orangeburg, South Carolina. For having been constantly on the move, the army was remarkably upbeat. Williams noted, "Army in good spirits thou a little like my old my coat grown old . . . [I] have seldom taken off my sword or boots to sleep and horse is constantly saddled." Greene called in Marion and Sumter with a view to attack the Star Fort again, but his troops were out of food and nearly spent. "Never did we suffer so severely as during the few days' halt here [in Orangeburg]. Rice furnished our substitute for bread, which, although tolerably relished by those familiarized with it . . . was very disagreeable to the Marylanders and Virginians, who had grown up in the use of corn or wheat bread." With few beef cattle available, the men turned to a food supply that was much more abundant—frogs. "Even alligator was used by a few; and very probably, had the army been much longer detained up on that ground, might have rivalled the frog in the estimation of our epicures."

Knowing that his men were in no condition to fight, Greene gave up his plans to capture the fort at Ninety Six. Instead, in July 1781 he led the bulk of his men to the high hills of the Santee, an oasis of defensible high ground. It offered plenty of grain, cool breezes, and—most important—a place to rest and recuperate. Lord Rawdon was also headed for a rest—but in his case it was much more permanent. The strains of war had taken their toll on his health and, although only twenty-seven years of age, he was deemed no longer fit for combat and sent back to Britain.

Their time in the hills gave Greene and the Marylanders the rest they needed. Additional troops had filtered in, and Greene now had twenty-four hundred men under his command. George Washington ordered Greene to resume offensive operations in South Carolina and to continue to take out the remaining British outposts outside Charleston. This also limited the enemy's ability to send reinforcements from Charleston to Cornwallis in Yorktown. A British force of two thousand led by Rawdon's replacement, Lieutenant Colonel Alexander Stewart, came out of Charleston to meet them. Stewart, a career officer, rose from the rank of ensign to major general after the war.

At this point in the war, a bizarre phenomenon became apparent: many of Greene's troops were British deserters, but a large portion of Stewart's men had formerly fought for the Patriots. "We fought the enemy with British soldiers, and they fought us with those of America," noted Greene.

As Greene's army marched south, his men were still poorly clothed and poorly equipped. "Hundreds of my men were naked as the day they were born. Their bare loins were by galled their cartridge boxes while a clump of rags or a tuft of moss alone protected their shoulders from being chafed by their guns."

Greene's army camped near Eutaw Springs, an area where an underground river briefly appears aboveground near present-day Eutawville, South Carolina, about fifty miles northwest of Charleston. Stewart's men had difficulty finding Greene because the locals had "rendered it impossible [to scout], by waylaying the bye-paths and passes through the different swamps." Famished and unaware that their enemy was nearby, Stewart's men began collecting provisions from the surrounding area.

CHAPTER 40

EUTAW SPRINGS

On the evening of September 8, 1781, shots rang out somewhere near the front of the long column of Patriots. Nathanael Greene's army, which had been marching since four in the morning, instantly became more alert. Stationed at the rear, the Marylanders couldn't see what was happening at the front of the line—they could only hear the gunfire.

Suddenly, dozens of British soldiers burst out of the brush on the side of a road. Believing themselves under attack, the Marylanders opened fire. The Redcoats were stunned to come upon their enemy so abruptly. They had been on a foraging mission and were carrying large sacks filled with sweet potatoes and other vegetables they had claimed from nearby fields. Unprepared for battle, the Brits struggled to load their muskets, but the Patriots quickly overpowered them. Delaware's Sergeant Seymour wrote, "Most of [them] we either killed, wounded, or captured."

The foraging party had set out at dawn that morning on Lieutenant Colonel Alexander Stewart's orders. While they carried their muskets, their primary goal for the day was to collect food. Shortly after their early morning departure, a pair of American deserters informed Stewart that Greene was nearby and on the move. Stewart immediately sent out some scouts—fifty cavalry and 140 light infantry, led by Major John Coffin. Just a few miles down the road, the cavalry ran into what they believed to be a party of militia and charged. In fact, they had run headlong into Greene's column, led by Lee's Legion. Greene's force responded with heavy fire, killing or capturing a number of Redcoats. When Coffin realized his mistake, he broke off and hurried back to inform Stewart that Greene's army was on the way.

Meanwhile, the sound of the gunfire alerted the rest of the foragers that something was wrong. They split into smaller groups to make their way back to camp. Unfortunately for the British, many of those groups stumbled into the column of marching Patriots on the way. All in all, about half of the foragers were killed or captured, and the other half remained cut off from Stewart's army until after the battle, reducing the number of troops he had at his disposal to just fourteen hundred.

The Redcoat colonel "determined to fight them, as from their numerous cavalry a retreat seemed to me to be attended with dangerous consequences." With the Americans only four miles away, British drummers beat a call to arms. Stewart hurriedly arranged his defensive lines. His troops had pitched their tents in an eight-acre clearing surrounded by a palisade and some sparse woods. A large brick mansion owned by the Patrick Roche family and several smaller outbuildings also lay on the property, providing excellent cover for the British troops. As on many Revolutionary War battlegrounds, a road—in this case, the main thoroughfare to Charleston—bisected the property.

Greene marched his men about three miles before calling a halt so that they could take one last action to prepare themselves for battle—drinking from the casks of rum carried by the army's wagons. Otho Holland Williams recalled, "We halted and took a little of that liquid which is not unnecessary to exhilarate the animal spirits upon such occasions."

Greene then formed his men up for the battle. He planned to attack in three lines. Going back to Daniel Morgan's plan at Cowpens, militia, troops from North and South Carolina, Marion's men, and Lee's Legion made up the front line, while the Marylanders, Virginian Continentals, and North Carolina troops made up the second. Meanwhile, the forces led by William Washington and Robert Kirkwood remained in reserve. The assault began around nine in the morning, with the militia engaging the enemy. "The militia advancing with alacrity, the battle became warm," Greene recalled. "The fire ran from flank to flank; our line still advancing, and the enemy adhering to his position."

The North Carolinians pushed the British back, but began sustaining heavy casualties. The militia carried muskets, but none of them had bayonets. Withering under the heavy British fire, the militia line began to bow. Sensing victory, the British charged. At this moment, Greene ordered the two Maryland regiments into action along with the Virginia Continentals. The Marylanders consisted of two battalions of roughly 250 men each, commanded by Williams. John Eager Howard led one battalion, while Major Henry Hardman led the other. Hardman had been one of Williams's officers since before Fort Washington, and he was also captured and later released in a prisoner exchange around the same time as Williams. The Continentals surged forward "through a heavy cannonade and a shower of musket balls. Nothing could exceed the gallantry and firmness of both officers and soldiers upon this occasion—they preserved their order and pushed on with such unshaken resolution, that they bore down all before them." At this critical moment in the battle, Greene issued the order: "Let Williams advance and sweep the fields with his bayonet." As the British fell back in response, Williams ordered his men to charge. A number of soldiers from both sides "fell transfixed by each other's bayonets."

Unable to halt the disciplined advance, the British began a hasty retreat, leaving behind two of their six-pound guns.

Amid the fighting Doctor Richard Pindell was dressing the wounds of injured soldiers. "I pushed on to join the troops just as the Grand Charge was ordered," he recalled. "Discovering some of our troops formed on the left of the road under the command of the brave and intrepid Ewing six [men] had the disposition to hang back and were getting in disorder unobserved by this Hero who was dauntlessly advancing in their front, I rode to him under Heavy fire of both cannon and musketry and aided him in forming his men at the risk of my life and a few minutes after they took two pieces of British artillery, killing and dispersing all the troops designated to guard them."

Victory was within Greene's grasp when disaster struck. As the men surged forward, they passed the British bivouac area, scores of tents on either side of the road that bisected the plantation. The tent poles and rigging became an obstruction and a hindrance to troops moving toward the brick Roche plantation house, which itself was a natural fortress. Riflemen from inside began picking off the Americans, who attempted to hide in the tents, their only source of cover. Ewing was wounded seven times, and "nearly all his men were killed or wounded," recalled Pindell.

One version of events states that because they felt confident that the enemy was on the run, the Marylanders, Virginians, and militiamen ceased fighting and instead began looting the British camp. As always, the troops were hungry. They fell on the stores they found, eating their fill and getting drunk on the stockpiled liquor. The officers attempted to get them to focus on the battle—which was not yet truly won—but to no avail. This version seems to conflict with the reports that Stewart had sent out foraging parties, indicating the British camp was lacking in food. No matter the reason, the Patriots' advance stalled, giving their enemy crucial time to regroup.

Stewart had given orders to his men to retreat into the plantation mansion in case of an American breakthrough. A footrace ensued between the forces, both of which realized the importance of the house's stout walls. Much like the Chew House in this battle of Germantown, the Roche house played a decisive role in this battle. Major Henry Sheridan and his force of Loyalists from New York got to the house first. The Patriot group closest to the house was that led by Lieutenant Edward Manning of Lee's Legion. Manning charged halfway through the door before Sheridan's men forced him out and barred the door just in time. To avoid the withering fire from inside the house, Manning and his men used British soldiers as human shields while they made their way back to the American lines.

Around the same time, another British group, led by Major John Majoribanks, moved closer to the house to support Sheridan. They occupied a thicket and creek bank, which provided some cover. Their position proved crucial as the battle played out.

The Patriots continued to approach the brick mansion, drawing close to several British six-pound cannon, which were located nearby. As the Maryland Line captured two of them, Lieutenant Edward Duvall, who fearlessly led the forlorn hope at Ninety Six, jumped on one of these cannons. He "took off his hat and gave three cheers. A bullet from a retreating British soldier knocked him off the artillery piece, mortally wounding him." Also assaulting the cannon was a young South Carolinian, Dick Johnson, who jumped from his horse as he approached one of the six-pounders, and "taking a nail from his pocket, stuck it in the touch hole and drove it home with his basket hilte-broadsword." Spiking the cannon in this way prevented it from firing—at least until the nail could be removed. Johnson's macabre appearance mirrored the gory nature of the clash. Facing the house, his white trousers and waistcoat in which he had ridden into the battle now "bloody as a butcher from head to foot" he bellowed, "You have plagued us all day, you shall plague us no more."

In an attempt to dislodge the enemy from the house, Greene called the artillery forward, both his own six-pounders and those captured from the British, intending to blast Sheridan out of his stronghold. But the artillerists made a crucial error, costing them many lives. They moved too close to the building, putting themselves within musket range of those inside. While the crews manned their guns as long as possible, they "drew all the fire from the windows" on themselves. Sheridan's musketeers "soon killed or disabled nearly the whole" of the American artillerists.

Sword in hand, Howard led his Marylanders in a charge on the residence. Like the artillerymen, the Marylanders ran into a "galling and destructive fire" from the brick building. Two of Howard's lieutenants were killed, and he himself was shot in the shoulder. Still, he continued directing the assault and "could not be prevailed on to leave the field . . . for many hours," recalled Doctor Pindell, who treated him during the melee.

Greene's army had not learned from the Americans' failure to bypass the British-held residence in the battle of Germantown; it would have been wise to abandon their plans to occupy the Roche house and instead continue to pursue the fleeing British troops. The attack on the residence was costly, depriving the Americans of momentum and thwarting their opportunity to win the battle decisively.

Greene made one last attempt to secure victory, ordering Lee, William Washington, and Kirkwood to charge both flanks of the battlefield.

Rushing into the woods where Majoribanks was holed up, Washington's horse was shot out from under him, and he went down, tangled with the animal and open to a bayonet attack. A British soldier came upon him and pinned Washington with his bayonet, but he was miraculously spared from certain death when a British officer intervened. The Redcoats captured the wounded commander, but shot and killed his second in command and two of his officers. In all, half of Washington's men were killed or wounded. Kirkwood and his "gallant band" of Delaware troops "rushed furiously" to the aid of Washington, making a bayonet charge that pushed the enemy back through a ravine and up the other side before their advance stalled. They also recaptured one of the British cannon and rolled it back to American lines. On the other side of the field, the British cavalry turned back the drive made by Lee's cavalry.

Majoribanks again counterattacked, turning the tide of the battle against the Patriots. Greene withdrew his troops, leaving Stewart to claim a pyrrhic victory. Mortally wounded in the fighting, Majoribanks was buried on the side of the road, where his marked grave remains to this day. The encounter with Stewart's army took a heavy toll on Greene: he lost 42 percent of his men in the bloody three-hour battle, one of the highest percentage losses of the entire war in a fixed battle in which neither side was completely victorious. His officers had been hit particularly hard. Three, including Washington and Howard, were wounded, and several were killed; only Williams and Lee were left unscathed by the melee. Williams summed up the feeling in the Patriot camp. "Victory is ours," he wrote, despite the fact that the Americans had been temporarily driven from the field. "A great many [Maryland officers] now sleep in the bed of honor while [the enemy are] leaving many wounded [on the battlefield]." Fearing a renewed assault, Stewart retreated to Moncks Corner without taking the time to bury the British dead. He left seventy wounded soldiers behind under a flag of truce.

Stewart did, however, pause long enough to set fire to the muskets and ammunition the Americans had left behind, setting off a round of explosions and firing. The eruption of fire caused a general panic in the British camp, and many, including those in charge of watching William

Washington, fled. Bound by his deeply embedded code of honor, Washington remained where he was until they returned and took him into custody again.

Despite Stewart's attempt to eliminate the stores they were leaving behind, Greene's army collected "not less than a 1000 stand of arms that were picked up on the field, and found broke and concealed in the Eutaw springs. They stove between 20 and 30 puncheons of rum, and destroyed a great variety of other stores which they had not carriages to carry off." The general also sent Lee and Marion to chase down Stewart and his men. In a panic because they believed Greene's army was engaging the rear guard, Stewart's wagoneers cut loose the horses and fled, allowing the Patriots to capture a trove of valuable wagons, baggage, and other supplies.

Though the battle, the bloodiest by far of the southern campaign, may have seemed a defeat for Greene as his army was the first to retire from the battlefield, it was a strategic victory. Except for intermittent, minor raids, the British retreated back to Charleston and never ventured into the interior of South Carolina again. Within the span of about ninety days, Greene's army, led by the Marylanders, had systematically eliminated nearly all the British outposts outside Charleston. The Marylanders and Kirkwood's Delaware Blues had kept the army together once again and had achieved Greene's strategic objectives. Bottled up in Charleston, the British in South Carolina would not be joining Cornwallis in Yorktown.

CHAPTER 41

"CONQUER OR DIE"—
YORKTOWN

A flag bearing the words "Conquer or Die" gently fluttered in the wind as General George Washington and his Life Guard, the unit responsible for his personal safety, rode toward Baltimore. It was September 8, 1781, and Baltimore's most distinguished residents and a company of Light Dragoons had ridden to the edge of town on horseback. They waited with anticipation for the arrival of the general, much as they had years before when he first visited the city. In the intervening years, the Marylanders had been fighting for Washington, saving his army on several occasions. Now they had come full circle, and once again they escorted him to the Fountain Inn.

As the general and his official escort approached Baltimore, the group included four officers, seven NCOs, 136 privates, one fifer, two drummers, and one surgeon. All were chosen for their "sobriety, honesty and good behavior," but they also had to be "five feet eight inches to five feet ten inches, handsomely and well made, . . . clean and spruce." Extremely accomplished at drill exercises, the group often served as an example when Baron Friedrich von Steuben was training other units. The élan of the Life Guard was manifested in its clothing: plumed hats and blue-and-buff coats as well as red waistcoats that set it apart from any other unit. On this occasion, the Guards' presence added extra pomp to the festivities.

Baltimoreans came out to greet Washington and his entourage as enthusiastically as if they had already won the war. As the visitors rode into town, an artillery company fired its cannon in salute. Lanterns blazed through the night, and the town fathers held a banquet in Washington's honor at a local coffeehouse. Samuel Smith, Mordecai Gist, William Smallwood, and Jack Steward attended, and several prominent citizens gave speeches. With the presence and countenance befitting a man who would become America's first president, Washington responded to the exaltations with his own uplifting words: "I thank you most cordially for your prayers and good wishes for my prosperity. May the author of all blessings aid our united exertions in the cause of liberty and universal peace; and may the particular blessing of heaven rest on you and the worthy citizens of this flourishing town of Baltimore."

While he was greeted with less ceremony, another noteworthy individual arrived in Baltimore on the same day General Jean-Baptiste Donatien de Vimeur, comte de Rochambeau. After the celebration in Baltimore, he and Washington both traveled to Mount Vernon, where they plotted strategy for the upcoming offensive against Cornwallis.

For the past several months, a siege mentality had persisted in Baltimore. The town had been gripped by fear because of Cornwallis's presence in Yorktown, Virginia: Baltimoreans were worried that he would strike deeper in the Chesapeake. The Chesapeake Bay was a pathway vulnerable to British invasion that the Crown had never fully exploited, but it would attempt to do so later during the War of 1812.

Since the battle of Camden, Gist, Smith, and Smallwood had been actively recruiting men to join Nathanael Greene's army as well as organizing a defense force within Baltimore. Gist came up with a complicated plan to divide the population into socioeconomic classes, which would each supply men for the Maryland Line. A bill to realize the plan passed the Maryland legislature, but General Washington doubted that it would work. In fact, the recruiting plan was not very successful, and Greene soon complained about the need for more Marylanders to fill the army's ranks.

A month earlier, on August 14, Washington had received startling news: twenty-nine French ships of the line carrying thirty-two hundred troops had sailed from the Caribbean to the Chesapeake and would arrive there in the first week of September.

During the Revolution up to this point, the Royal Navy had maintained naval superiority on the entire East Coast. Any city along the coast was vulnerable to an amphibious landing. Conversely, British troops that got into trouble could be easily extracted by ship. Admiral François-Joseph-Paul de Grasse's arrival altered the naval balance of power. At the time, neither Cornwallis nor General Henry Clinton completely understood the danger both were in. The Admiralty assured them that they had at least parity with the French. With the arrival of de Grasse's fleet the calculus of the war had changed. True to their name, ships of the line would form a line of battle at sea and unleash a devastating broadside against an adversary. Each ship bristled with guns; de Grasse's flagship, the multilevel *Ville de Paris*, alone sported 104, ranging in size from thirty-six-pound to eight-pound long guns.

Additional numbers, even small numbers, of these vessels could give one side the advantage over the other; conversely, the loss of these ships could be devastating. One Royal Navy officer admitted, "The loss of two line-of-battle ships in effecting the relief of the army is of much more consequence than the loss of the army."

But any joint operation with the French had a short life; de Grasse would be able to remain in the Chesapeake only until mid-October before he would have to return to the warm waters of the Caribbean. Washington now finally saw the potential for everything to align in his favor with French naval power and a massed Franco-American army more than twice the size of Cornwallis's. Seeing an opportunity to trap Cornwallis in Virginia, Washington immediately conferred with Rochambeau, and the two battle captains agreed to move the bulk of the American army, plus several thousand French soldiers currently in Rhode Island, to Maryland, where they could board ships that would take them the rest of the way to Virginia.

They had only three weeks to move the French and American armies south. After a successful disinformation campaign, Washington set the plan in motion, marching the French and American armies south, first feinting toward New York and then veering to Philadelphia. The deception plan, complete with spies furnishing false information, worked so well that not until September 2 did Clinton realize that the Continental Army wasn't heading to New York. In Philadelphia the bulk of the army boarded ships while the rest marched south; they all converged near Williamsburg, Virginia.

When the French fleet arrived, Brigadier General Gist sent Washington a message that ensured his plans for an attack on Cornwallis. For the past year and a half, Gist (as a recent widower) had remained in Baltimore, recruiting and sending reinforcements south to Greene. He had been funding the operation out of his own pocket, depleting his fortune and finding himself, "largely indebted for the Support of my table." Gist notified the commander in chief immediately of "the safe arrival in the Chesapeake of Admiral de Grasse, with [twenty-four] ships of the line." The very same day that the message arrived, de Grasse won the most decisive naval battle of the Revolution, the Battle of the Capes. De Grasse's ships and British Admiral Thomas Graves's nineteen warships pummeled each other in the mouth of Chesapeake Bay for two hours; the result was a tactical draw in terms of ships damaged on both sides. However, Graves made a fatal error: he failed to seal Chesapeake Bay from the French and sailed off to New York, leaving the French in control of the Chesapeake and Cornwallis's fate.

Following in the generals' wake, elements of the French force passed through Baltimore on September 11. Several transports carrying artillery, grenadiers, and light infantry arrived in Annapolis the next day. The French spent several days in the area before continuing on toward Yorktown. Energized by the possibility of taking out Cornwallis, Gist mobilized the Marylanders and raised the two new regiments. Washington sent messages to both French and American officers urging them to hurry. "Every day we now lose is comparatively an age," he wrote. "As soon as it is in our power, with safety, we ought to take our position near the enemy. . . . Lord Cornwallis is improving every moment to the best advantage; and every day that is given him to make his preparations may cost us many lives to encounter them."

* * *

After the costly Battle of Guilford Courthouse, Cornwallis faced a dilemma. With his troops significantly weakened, he lacked the strength to pursue Greene into South Carolina. However, he feared that if he did nothing and remained in Wilmington, Greene would "hem me in among the great rivers and by cutting off our subsistence render our arms useless," necessitating a retreat by sea, which Cornwallis believed "would be as ruinous and disgraceful to Britain as most events could be." With no good option before him, Cornwallis decided on his own to march into Virginia despite having no orders to that effect from Clinton—a fateful decision that put his army and the entire war at risk.

He sent Banastre Tarleton's dragoons and a company of Royal Welch Fusiliers ahead of him to capture the Virginia legislature, which was then meeting in Charlottesville. The once impressively dressed cavalrymen were now "in distress for want of arms, clothing, boots, and indeed appointments of any kind." But that didn't stop them from mounting a raid on June 4. Warned of the danger the night before by an alert militiaman, most of the politicians, including Thomas Jefferson, fled in time to avoid capture. However, Tarleton's men did manage to find seven lawmakers, whom they took prisoner. They also rounded up some of the finest stallions in the colonies, which gave the Legion unmatched celerity.

The most significant American military force in Virginia at this time was a group of thirty-six hundred effectives led by the Marquis de Lafayette. At the Green Spring plantation on the banks of the James River, Cornwallis attempted to draw the French general into an ambush. He hid the bulk of his army in the woods north of the river while the rest of the force, around sixteen hundred men, acted as bait, approaching the river as if they intended to cross. Lafayette sent a small group of Pennsylvanians commanded by Mad Anthony Wayne to attack, but the general, suspicious of the situation, wisely held the rest of his men back. As Wayne approached, the bulk of the British Redcoats suddenly appeared. In a surprise move, Wayne responded with a bayonet charge that threw the British off balance and allowed the bulk of his men to successfully withdraw. Cornwallis won the battle but again refrained from pursuing the Americans.

In July 1781 Clinton had ordered Cornwallis to occupy Old Point Comfort in the present-day city of Hampton, Virginia, near the mouth of the Chesapeake Bay. However, Cornwallis disliked the defensive situation of the point and instead positioned his men farther up on the same peninsula, in Yorktown. With its steep bluff overlooking the York River, the site was much more defensible, and Cornwallis set about constructing fortifications. The very next month, Cornwallis received the unwelcome news of the French fleet that was transporting thirty-two hundred soldiers. In preparation for the anticipated siege, the British general redoubled his efforts to strengthen the defenses at Yorktown. He wrote to Clinton, "I am now working hard at the redoubts of the place. The army is not very sickly. Provisions for six weeks."

While Cornwallis was feverishly fortifying Yorktown, the Marylanders and other American and French troops had boarded ships that took them down Chesapeake Bay to Williamsburg, Virginia. While they were en route, the French fleet defeated the British ships in the region; this victory allowed the French to set up a blockade of the York River, which the troops passed as they sailed. After landing, the ground troops proceeded to Yorktown. One of the officers with the American army described the scene: "As soon as the troops had all concentrated, with General Washington at their head, we left Williamsburg and proceeded on our route for Yorktown, where the British troops had fortified themselves, under the command of Lord Cornwallis. The whole army arrived in the evening and took possession of the ground around the town, driving in their outpost, which we effected without much loss or inconvenience on our part; [we] accomplished the end we had in view, that was to form our camp so as to encircle their whole outworks."

Thanks to the French reinforcements, the Americans now heavily outnumbered the British. In all, Washington had twenty-two thousand men at his disposal—fourteen thousand American and about eight thousand French—compared with seven thousand of Cornwallis's troops. The earl withdrew his men from the outer defenses at Yorktown in order to better defend a smaller area. Desperate, the British general sent an urgent message to Clinton in New York: "This place is in no state of defense. If you cannot relieve me very soon, you must be prepared for the worst." Clinton promised to send a fleet that would leave from New York at the beginning of October, which was still more than two weeks away.

The British were now in a precarious position. The large French fleet presented a critical threat: without reinforcements or an escape route, Cornwallis could not hold out long. But the British commanders were unable to rise to the occasion. Cornwallis was acting as he saw fit, regardless of orders from Clinton, and Clinton remained in New York, spending most of his time defending his actions to his generals instead of acting decisively. Rather than rushing the all-important fleet down to Virginia to relieve Cornwallis, Clinton sent several messages informing him that the ships would be delayed from sailing, first until October 5, then until October 12, and then until October 19.

Cornwallis's fate was sealed before Clinton's fleet could sail. On October 6, Washington began the siege of Yorktown. The French, who were masters of siege warfare, provided invaluable strategic advice as the Patriots began the process of digging trenches and then hammering the fortifications with their artillery. The Marylanders would be firmly in the center of the action, fighting under Baron von Steuben, who commanded the 2nd, or center, Division. The 3rd and 4th Maryland Regiments and the Delaware Recruits formed the 1st Brigade of the division, which was led by Brigadier General Mordecai Gist. Wayne led the 2nd Brigade, which consisted of the 1st and 2nd Pennsylvania Battalions and the Virginia Battalion.

As usual, Washington remained calm during the battle, despite being closer to the action than his aides would have liked. At one point, Colonel David Cobb urged the commander to move farther back for safety's sake. Washington coolly replied, "Colonel Cobb, if you are afraid, you have liberty to step back." Just moments later, a musket ball hit a nearby cannon and rolled to a stop near Washington's feet. Frightened, a second officer grabbed Washington's arm and cried, "My dear General, we can't spare you yet." As unconcerned for his personal safety as ever, Washington responded, "It is a spent ball, and no harm is done."

Gist, accompanied by Steward, recognized the end was near as he fought in the trenches. "I feel great happiness augmented . . . by having the honor to become one of the Generals commanding in the Trenches for the three last days of the Siege and particularly so when I reflect that the Surrender of Cornwallis and his Army must establish our Independence and pave the way to an honorable peace," he wrote.

On October 14 the French and Americans assaulted two of the redoubts in the British line. An axe-wielding forlorn hope once again led the way, chopping through the wooden abatis. Although casualties were high, both assaults succeeded, making it all but inevitable that the fort, would fall. Marylander John Boudy claimed to have taken part in the assault party, saying, "General Washington ordered us to storm [the] breastworks of the enemy which were galling us very much—and [I] was in the division under Colonel Hamilton that stormed and took one of the redoubts." Recognizing the hopelessness of the situation, Cornwallis wrote to Clinton: "We dare not show a gun to their old batteries. . . . Experience has shown that our fresh earthen works do not resist their powerful artillery, so that we shall soon be exposed to an assault in ruined works, in a bad position, and with weakened numbers. The safety of the place is, therefore, so precarious that I cannot recommend that the fleet and the army should run great risk in endeavouring to save us."

On October 16 Cornwallis launched a desperate counterattack: 350 British troops rushed out of their trenches and hit the American line, hoping to spike the American artillery. The raiders suffered heavy casualties and spiked only a few guns, which were quickly repaired and placed back in action. The assault didn't have any impact on the steady and methodical siege that was slowly pulverizing Cornwallis's army. Cornwallis also hoped to use the counterattack as a diversion while ferrying the bulk of his army to Gloucester Point, a small peninsula directly across the James River from Yorktown, in small boats. Cornwallis positioned Tarleton and additional British troops on the point to prevent the allies from placing artillery there and firing into the rear of the British fortifications. By linking up with Tarleton, he hoped to punch through the American and French lines and break out north to Maryland or New York. Weather dashed the bold gamble. A severe storm swamped many of the boats, and the British called off the operation. The siege went on; Washington and Rochambeau had Cornwallis in checkmate.

The crushing bombardment continued. Sergeant Roger Lamb, the intrepid veteran who escaped from captivity at Saratoga, recalled, "[The fortifications] were tumbling into ruin; not a gun could be fired from them, and only one eight inch, and a little more than one hundred cohorn [mortar shells] remained." Out of ammunition and with the numbers of dead and wounded piling up every day, Cornwallis dispatched a flag of truce on October 17, 1781, four years to the day after Burgoyne surrendered at Saratoga.

Disease, hunger, and battle had racked the British forces at Yorktown, yet all who were able put on their finest uniforms for the day of surrender. Led by Brigadier General Charles O'Hara, they slowly marched out along the Hampton Road. According to legend, although most historians now question it, the band played "The World Turned Upside Down" as they went. French and American forces silently lined the road as they passed. Harry Lee recalled, "On one side the commander in chief, surrounded by his suite and the American staff, took his station; on the other side, opposite to him, was the Count de Rochambeau, in like manner attended."

The British force earned the scorn of onlookers for two perceived slights: they left their fortifications later than they were supposed to, and General Cornwallis did not accompany his men. The Americans at the time thought he was feigning illness because he was too embarrassed to appear. One army surgeon wrote in his journal, "We are not to be surprised that the pride of the British officer is humbled on this occasion, as they have always entertained an exalted opinion of their own military prowess and affected to view the Americans as a contemptible, undisciplined rabble." He continued, "When it is considered that Lord

Cornwallis has frequently appeared in splendid triumph at the head of his army, by which he is almost always adored, we conceive it incumbent on him cheerfully to participate in their misfortunes and degradations, however humiliating; but it is said he gives himself up entirely to vexation and despair."

Similarly, Cornwallis's officers seemed to the onlookers to be behaving poorly and perhaps even to be drunk. One newspaper reported, "The British officers in general behaved like boys who had been whipped at school; some bit their lips, some pouted, others cried; their round, broad-brimmed hats were well adapted to the occasion, hiding those faces they were ashamed to show. The [Hessian] regiments made a much more military appearance, and the conduct of their officers was far more becoming men of fortitude."

Lieutenant Colonel John Laurens, who had drawn up the articles of surrender and was the son of Henry Laurens, a former president of Congress, took Cornwallis into custody. Gist also had a chance to meet the man who caused the death or capture of so many Marylanders at Brooklyn and throughout the war. For Gist and the Marylanders, the war had come full circle. So many of their compatriots had died at Cornwallis's hands while they fought at the old stone house in Brooklyn, but now Cornwallis was surrendering to the Americans. Surprisingly, given the length of the fight that pitted Cornwallis against the Marylanders, Gist laconically remarked, "His defense of the post was not so obstinate as might be expected from an experienced & determined Officer."

Reaching the end of the American and French lines, the Redcoats and Hessians made a sharp right turn onto the field of surrender. Twenty-eight British officers marched forward in formation to hand over their flags to the Americans. Proud to the end, the officers refused to give their colors to the sergeants the Americans had sent to receive them, finding it demeaning to surrender to noncommissioned officers. Eventually, the Americans solved the problem by telling a junior officer to take the flags from the British and hand them, one at a time, to the American sergeants.

As a further sign of surrender, O'Hara, who had fought so bravely against the Marylanders at Guilford Courthouse, handed over Cornwallis's sword. He first offered it to Rochambeau, either because he simply made a mistake or because he couldn't stand the thought of giving it to the Americans. A French officer soon corrected O'Hara, who then turned to Washington, on the opposite side of the road. Washington deferred the honor of accepting the sword to General Benjamin Lincoln, who had been humiliated and not afforded an honorable surrender of his forces at Charleston in 1780.

The Americans made prisoners of about eight thousand British troops (including around one thousand sailors) at Yorktown—a staggering one-quarter of all the British troops in America. They sent the captives to camps, where they stayed until their eventual release prior to the signing of the Treaty of Paris in September 1783. Minor skirmishes continued for two more years, but for all intents and purposes, the war was won. With Cornwallis's surrender to Washington, the world balance of power forever shifted, and an entirely new country was born.

1782–83

CHAPTER 42

THE LAST BATTLE

Not pausing to savor the decisive victory over Cornwallis, Gist and the Marylanders once again marched south. Departing Yorktown on November 4, 1781, the Immortals joined several regiments of Pennsylvanians commanded by Anthony Wayne and headed into the Carolinas to join Nathanael Greene. The general planned to eliminate one of the last British posts at Dorchester, a small town northwest of Charleston that housed an eight-hundred-man garrison.

Since Eutaw Springs, Greene had kept the British bottled up in Charleston and Dorchester. He hoped to strike another blow at the enemy while the bulk of the American army continued south toward Charleston under the command of Colonel Otho Holland Williams. Greene took a small detachment of Marylanders and Virginians into Dorchester to strike at the fort. According to Captain William Wilmot, a veteran officer of the 1776 Flying Camp who fought under Jack Steward in the doomed Staten Island raid and many other battles, "[The British] being apprised of his approach, reinforced that post and sallied out about two miles, when we fell in with them and drove them to the fort, leaving a small number of their killed and wounded on our hands." After the brief melee, the Redcoats and Loyalists unceremoniously burned their stores and fled to the safety of Charleston. Thwarted in his attempt to capture the garrison, Gist caught up with the rest of the army, and they continued to push south. After hundreds of miles of marching that burned through their shoe leather and left their uniforms, overalls, and hunting shirts in tatters, the men were in wretched condition, "naked and full of vermin."

As they trudged toward Charleston, the Marylanders protected Greene's right flank with orders to "strike at [the British] wherever you may find them." As usual, supplies were scarce and the countryside had been picked clean by both armies, prompting Gist to opine, "[The surrounding area was] so much ravaged" that it was "impracticable" to forage for food. With the end of the war in sight, the men began to worry about whether they would receive their back pay. Most had fought without payment for nearly two years.

The war had left many injured and in poor health, limiting their abilities to provide for themselves and their families. One of those injured officers was the indomitable John Eager Howard. Shortly after Eutaw Springs, rumors spread north that the Baltimore native had fallen in the battle, prompting his brother James to journey south. In reality, Howard had been seriously wounded in the left shoulder. Doctor Richard Pindell and later another physician treated the gaping wound. With the British spymaster John André out of the way, Howard courted Peggy Chew with a barrage of love letters sent during his convalescence. Eventually, she "surrendered unconditionally to the noble colonel, and the couple became engaged" and after many weeks of rest, James and John made the six-hundred-mile journey back home, where the Maryland hero, with Miss Chew by his side, recuperated until the war was over.

In late August, Greene positioned Gist, now in charge of the southern army's light infantry, near Johns Island, a sizable isle located due south of the city of Charleston. Starved for supplies, the British were dispatching foraging parties, and Greene ordered Gist's Marylanders and the Delaware Regiment along with Light Horse Harry Lee's cavalry to protect the area where the enemy had been sighted. Formed into a quick reaction force, the light infantry and cavalry mobilized to deal with British excursions. On August 27, Lieutenant Colonel John Laurens, one of George Washington's favorite aides, was leading an element of this task force to join Gist when the British, hiding in the tall grassy wetlands, ambushed the young officer's group, cutting down many of the Continentals. Gist quickly marched his men to help Laurens, but they were too late; the brilliant young officer died in the clash. After Gist arrived, the British made a hasty withdrawal, but not before the Marylanders captured a British galley that mounted two nine-pound cannon.

Since Greene didn't have enough troops to seize the heavily fortified port of Charleston, skirmishing continued around the islands surrounding the city, culminating in what some consider one of the last engagements of the Revolution. Captain William Wilmot, known for his "love of adventure" and inability to resist a fight, led several raiding parties across the river to James Island, also located outside Charleston. On November 14, 1782, just one month prior to the evacuation of Charleston by the British, Polish-born Thaddeus Kosciuszko, the engineer who had conducted the siege operations at Ninety Six, suggested the idea of ambushing a group of woodcutters on the neighboring island. Kosciuszko and Wilmot planned the raid with an African American who was later believed to be sent by the British to lead the Americans into a trap. Historians recorded, "The enemy was well prepared for the 'surprise' and poured into the little party so deadly a fusillade that Captain Wilmot was killed instantly.... Kosciuszko escaped injury, although 'his weapon was shattered in his hand and his coat pierced by four balls.'" Marylander John Boudy remembered that "our Colonel Laurens, who was far in advance, fell in the outset of the engagement. I remember seeing four men carry him into our rear, where it was said he died before we left the field." Boudy recalled the deaths of "Lieutenant James Bettis and some five or six privates."

According to Greene's biographer William Johnson, "This was the last bloodshed in the American War."

But Wilmot wasn't the last Maryland soldier to die during the Revolution. Tragically, an accident claimed one of Maryland's bravest officers. Word of Cornwallis's surrender had spread fast, and the recently liberated William Washington had married Jane Elliot, a wealthy Charlestonian who owned Sandy Hill Plantation on the outskirts of town. Jack Steward was riding to Sandy Hill for an "evening given in entertainment to the officers of the army" when his horse fell. "And the Colonel pitching on his head in a ditch, dislocated his neck.

He lived till Sunday morning about seven o'clock and then died." Maryland's indestructible man, who had survived Brooklyn, escaped a prison ship, led the forlorn hope at Stony Point, and fought at Cowpens and Yorktown, died in a freak accident. The officers of the Maryland Line, his friends, gathered to mourn. The next day they interred Steward with every military honor in the burying ground of the old church near Sandy Hill. "This gentlemen, whose untimely death is much to be limented, had served with great reputation during the war, and was much beloved by the army."

The Americans had won the war, but negotiating the peace dragged on for many months. Representatives from both countries met in France to hammer out the details of what became known as the Treaty of Paris. Benjamin Franklin, John Jay, Henry Laurens (father of the late John Laurens), and John Adams met with British representatives David Hartley and Richard Oswald. The group signed a preliminary agreement on November 30, 1782. The treaty between Britain and the United States did not include France; this was remarkable considering that the negotiations took place in France. That evening, Franklin rode to Versailles and broke the news to the French king. He had the confidence to ask for additional loans, which he secured along with French consent to the treaty.

Meanwhile, the Marylanders settled into routine garrison duty at Johns Island and James Island while waiting for the British to leave Charleston, which they did on December 14. Under the terms of a truce, the Americans could enter the city as long as they allowed the British to leave freely. Led by Wayne, Gist, and Greene, the triumphant Marylanders and other American troops entered the city. "The British moved out of town unusually slow, and repeatedly complained to our General that we pressed too close upon them," recalled Boudy. "Whereupon Wayne ordered us to march 'more slowly.'" When the Americans arrived near the statehouse, the officers gave them permission to visit the town. Boudy added, "Discipline now being almost suspended in the afternoon all the troops were liberally treated with the most choice spirits, and that much ceremony and parade was used—General Greene, Brigadier General Gist, the governor and others marched in procession into the City, followed by the whole of the light horse belonging to the Army. The doors I remember and windows were thronged with the people of Charleston, cheering the procession and giving it many a hearty welcome."

Up north, the bulk of the army waited another year for the British to evacuate New York City. On April 11, 1783, the fledgling American Congress issued a proclamation "declaring the cessation of arms, as by sea as by land, agreed upon between the United States of America and his Britannic Majesty." Congress approved the preliminary treaty articles on April 15, 1783, which many colonists considered to be the end of the war. However, the countries didn't officially sign the treaty until September 3, and Congress didn't ratify it until January 14, 1784. It encapsulated the dreams of the Americans who had fought so long and hard, declaring, "His Britannic Majesty acknowledges the said United States, viz. New Hampshire, Massachusetts Bay, Rhode Island and Providence Plantations, Connecticut, New York, New Jersey, Pennsylvania, Delaware, Maryland, Virginia, North Carolina, South Carolina and Georgia, to be free, sovereign and independent states: that he treats with them as such, and for himself, his heirs and successors, relinquishes all claims to the Government, propriety and territorial rights of the same, and every part thereof."

On April 21, 1783, Baltimore celebrated the end of the war. The residents set the city ablaze with lights and constructed a temporary building especially for the party. Thirteen times they toasted their victory, and thirteen cannon sounded in salute after each toast. Afterward, they held a ball and a dinner for local dignitaries, who, according to the *Maryland Gazette*, "with unfeigned satisfaction congratulated each other on the blessings of Peace—the rising glory of their country—the prospects of her commerce, her future grandeur and importance in the scale of nations."

Far removed from the glitz of Baltimore, what was left of the Immortals moldered away outside Charleston. Relief finally came that spring when the state furloughed the Marylanders. Without money, new clothing, transport, or food, the men began the six-hundred-mile journey home. Many, including John Boudy, were able to sail home on

Lady Washington, a ship provided by the Maryland government. Among those who had survived to the end were Private James Gooding, who was twice taken captive by the British and twice escaped to rejoin the Patriots; John Bantham, who had been severely wounded when serving on the forlorn hope at Ninety Six but recovered and fought through the battle on James Island; Thomas Carney, the African American who had fought in most of the Maryland engagements since Brandywine; and the surviving leadership of the Maryland Line, including Otho Holland Williams, Gassaway Watkins, Mordecai Gist, and William Smallwood. The Marylanders were finally going home.

CHAPTER 43

"OMNIA RELIQUIT SERVARE REMPUBLICAM"

On December 23, 1783, General George Washington solemnly entered the State House in Annapolis wearing his finest buff-and-blue uniform. His commanding presence attracted every eye in the chamber. In anticipation of the day's events, several prominent women had crowded into the upper gallery, and numerous dignitaries filled the room, including the entire Continental Congress, the consul general of France, and the leadership of the Maryland Line: William Smallwood, Otho Holland Williams, Samuel Smith, John Eager Howard, and Mordecai Gist. In November, the Continental Congress had moved from Princeton to Annapolis, where it was then in session. As Washington gracefully made his way to his reserved seat, the members of Congress remained seated with their hats on, but the numerous other men in attendance stood and removed their hats as a sign of respect.[35]

After Washington found his seat, the president of Congress stood and announced, "The United States in Congress assembled, are prepared to receive your communications."

His countenance etched with dignity, Washington rose and addressed the room. He clutched a prewritten speech in his right hand, which trembled until he used his other hand to steady it. Reading aloud in a voice that occasionally faltered with emotion, he congratulated Congress and announced that he was "retiring from the service of my country." He expressed his gratitude to God and his fellow Americans,

---

35. Artist John Trumbull immortalized the scene in a painting called *General George Washington Resigning His Commission* that proudly hangs in the Rotunda of the U.S. Capitol.

and committed the new country to "to the protection of Almighty God." He closed, "Having now finished the work assigned me, I retire from the great theatre of action, and bidding an affectionate farewell to this august body, under whose orders I have so long acted, I here offer my commission, and take my leave of all the employments of public life."

Washington then turned to the president of Congress and handed him his commission.

Those in attendance understood that Washington's resignation was a momentous event in the establishment of the young nation and in the history of the world. Rather than remain in control of the army, possibly setting himself up as a dictator, the general chose to keep the army under civilian control. This decision influenced the course of United States history from that day forward. Those present felt a wellspring of emotion, as the event marked the culmination of their cause, the realization of the liberty from Great Britain they had fought so long to attain. Many that day felt overcome by gratitude for Washington's leadership and for his humility in leaving his position when his task was accomplished. The editor of the *Maryland Gazette*, who attended the speech, wrote, "Few tragedies ever drew so many tears from so many beautiful eyes as the moving manner in which his Excellency took his final leave of Congress."

Afterward, Washington warmly greeted many Marylanders, including the officers who were present. He then left Maryland and quickly rode home to Mount Vernon, arriving in time for Christmas Eve. There he wrote, "I feel eased of a load of public care. I hope to spend the remainder of my days in cultivating the affections of good men, and in the practice of the domestic virtues."

It ended much as it had begun—in a tavern. On November 7, 1783, the officers of the Maryland Line assembled at Mann's Tavern in Annapolis. The men formed the Maryland Chapter of the Society of the Cincinnati, a fraternal organization composed of veterans of the American Revolution. The group took its name from Lucius Quinctius Cincinnatus, a farmer who temporarily ruled the Roman Republic during a time of war but who resigned and went back to his fields when the emergency was over. The society chose the motto *Omnia reliquit servare rempublicam*, which means "He relinquished everything to save the Republic." Its stated goals were "to preserve the rights so dearly won; to promote the continuing union of the states; and to assist members in need, their widows, and their orphans." Brigadier General Otho Holland Williams served as the temporary chairman, with Nathaniel Ramsay as treasurer.

Washington's Immortals were true citizen-soldiers—a group of men of family, fortune, and honor who followed the same path throughout the Revolution. When the war was over, they hung up their muskets and uniforms and began the hard work of building a nation. Many of the men were as successful after the war as they were during it.

John Eager Howard recovered from his wounds and married the love of his life, Peggy Chew, whose former home sat on the site of the Battle of Germantown. He built a magnificent mansion called Belvedere in the heart of Baltimore and owned a vast amount of real estate in the city. He was elected governor in 1788 and was later elected to the U.S. House of Representatives and then the Senate.

William Smallwood never married but returned to his plantation. He later became governor of Maryland after the adoption of the U.S. Constitution.

Otho Holland Williams remained active in the Society of the Cincinnati. He was appointed commissioner of the Port of Baltimore and was later elected to the House of Representatives. He suffered from repeated bouts of influenza and attempted to mitigate his ailments by traveling south to Barbados. He died in Virginia in 1794.

Mordecai Gist relocated to South Carolina and remained an ardent believer in individual freedom and states' rights. Reflecting his beliefs, he named his two sons Independent and States. He also remained active in the Freemasons, serving as Grand Master in South Carolina. He died on September 12, 1792, at the age of fifty and was laid to rest in Charleston.

Gist's friend Samuel Smith recovered from his wounds and after the war became a member of the Maryland House of Representatives. He later rose to the rank of major general in the Maryland militia and successfully commanded Baltimore's defenses during the siege of Fort McHenry and Battle of Baltimore in the War of 1812. After the war, Smith was elected to the U.S. House of Representatives and the Senate. His final position in public service before he died in 1839 was mayor of Baltimore.

The statuesque Gassaway Watkins lived to the age of eighty-eight. He settled in Howard County, Maryland; built a home called Walnut Grove; and raised a family.

Like many of the men of the Maryland Line, the intrepid Doctor Richard Pindell went west, settling in Kentucky. He applied for and received a pension. Later he was the personal physician for Speaker of the House Henry Clay.

Captain Bob Kirkwood continued to serve his country. After moving west into the Northwest Territory, he once again took up arms for the United States. He was killed in November 1791 by Native Americans led by Little Turtle and Blue Jacket in the Battle of the Wabash (also known as St. Clair's Defeat), one of the worst defeats ever suffered by an American army, a battle that left 623 Americans dead. One of the lucky survivors recorded Kirkwood's demise: "There resting beneath the tree, lay old Kirkwood, scalped, his head smoking like a chimney." It was Kirkwood's thirty-sixth battle fighting for his country.

General Cornwallis returned to Britain in 1782; having been released on parole after his surrender at Yorktown, then he sat out the rest of the Revolution. In 1785 he went to Prussia as an ambassador to the court of Frederick the Great, and 1786 he became the governor general and commander in chief of India, where he enacted many important reforms. He later served as master of the ordnance during the French Revolutionary Wars, as lord lieutenant and commander in chief of Ireland during the Irish Rebellion of 1798, and as pleni-potentiary minister to France during the negotiation of the Treaty of Amiens. He returned to his post as governor general of India in 1805 and died the same year.

Banastre Tarleton was elected to the House of Commons in 1790 and became an outspoken advocate for the slave trade, frequently mocking well-known abolitionists. He later recounted his activities in the Revolution (and criticized Cornwallis's decisions) in a book titled *A History of the Campaigns of 1780 and 1781 in the Southern Provinces of North America.* He died in 1833, leaving behind a wife but no children.

Like Tarleton, General Sir Henry Clinton served in Parliament and also published a book that blamed the loss of the war on Cornwallis. He died in October 1793.

Many of the Americans who fought for the Maryland Loyalist Regiment never saw their homes again. Many left the United States and relocated to other portions of the British Empire, such as Nova Scotia. James Chalmers didn't remain idle long after the war. He again went into action writing pamphlets on the Revolution and other political topics. He attempted to resecure some of the vast holdings that he lost in Maryland. Eventually, he became an inspector general of colonial troops in the West Indies. He died in London on October 4, 1806.

The war never left many of the men and officers. Some were haunted by the condition we now call post-traumatic stress disorder (PTSD). Peter Jaquett was "a cross, morose and quarrelsome man. It was a hard matter for anyone to keep on speaking terms." Many combat veterans experienced the night terrors that accompany PTSD. Ensign Bryan Philpot's son later recalled his father's nightmares, which involved seeing men drown in Gowanus Creek or watching a cannonball sheer off the head of a wounded soldier sitting next to him.

The lucky ones could apply for a pension. Initially, Congress granted pensions only in very special cases. If the veteran was impoverished, he or a surviving spouse could apply in 1818 for a pension of half his wages. In 1832 things became a little easier, but only a handful of veterans were still alive then. The veteran typically went to the local courthouse and swore under oath to his recollections of the war. These applications could be challenged for a variety of reasons. Even Peter Francisco's pension was initially challenged, likely because his exploits were so extraordinary. The giant resubmitted his application and provided affidavits from Ansolem Bailey and several officers, who confirmed that he was at Stony Point and other battles. His application was eventually accepted. Virginia and Massachussets even voted to name March 15 Peter Francisco Day.

Shoemaker George Dias wasn't so lucky. The African American who was severely wounded during the war and was "so poor and sickly that he cannot [could not] earn any thing." He was "so poor he has not had a Bed to sleep on for three years and his whole personal Property consisting of a few Instruments of his Proffesion, he carries about with him in a small Bag." Another African American, Thomas Carney, suffered a similar fate. He was afflicted with rheumatism and "unable to do much work." He had very few possessions: a pair of "cartwheels and shafts, two old straw beds, some furniture, one plow," and some farm animals. What he did have was a strong bond of friendship with his brothers-in-arms, including Captain Perry Benson, whose life he saved at Ninety Six.

In the eighteenth century and until 1833, the United States maintained debtors' prisons under federal law, and some states maintained them even longer. Those who didn't pay their personal debts could be sent to these facilities, a fate suffered by many veterans. Despite his brilliant success during the war, Light Horse Harry Lee found himself behind bars for failing to pay what he owed. The traumatic experience was something his famous son Robert E. Lee never forgot. When Harry Lee wasn't performing physical labor to work off his debts, he spent his remaining free time writing his memoirs.

Gist and Nathanael Greene, along with many other officers, incurred substantial debts in order to pay their men's expenses and keep the army in the field. Even after the state of Georgia awarded Greene a Loyalist plantation, debts that he had accrued during the war remained. He died nearly bankrupt, leaving his widow to battle with Congress to be made whole.

Afterword

The actual burial site of the 256 Immortals who fell in the Battle of Brooklyn remains unknown to this day. An archaeological study in 1957 by the National Park Service and another in 2008 were conducted on the supposed site, but the nature of the soil makes it difficult for ground-penetrating radar to identify objects buried in the area. The earliest known mention of a mass grave dates back to 1869, when Henry Field, who wrote an early history of the Battle of Brooklyn, identified the block of Third Avenue between Seventh and Eighth streets as the resting place of the Marylanders. The claim was based on testimony from Adrian Van Brunt, who bought the property soon after the Revolution and "was often heard to say that the ground was sacred . . . because it held the remains of the Maryland Regiment." In the early 1900s an apartment house was built on the site, and the landowner claimed that there were fifteen burial trenches, each one hundred feet long, on the lots. The son of the contractor who did the work later stated that his father had found "the bones of some thirty bodies, in regular or military order." However, these reports have never been substantiated with remains. The Marylanders' bodies may yet be under a city street, buried under an automobile repair shop, or in the general area of the Old Stone House. Every month the Defense POW/MIA Accounting Agency finds the lost remains of American service members in locations around the world, including remote islands in the Pacific. Surely its attention can be drawn to Brooklyn. In a country with a four-trillion-dollar budget and many of the world's billionaires, funds should be allocated to find these heroes and purchase this hallowed ground.

It is a national tragedy that the Immortals—whose collective sacrifices changed the course of the Revolution and, ultimately, this nation—have yet to receive the full honor they deserve.

ACKNOWLEDGMENTS

The writing of this book was an astonishing journey that spanned more than five years spent combing through the letters, diaries, pension files, and other words of this great generation. It involved not only finding the documents of the Revolution but also walking the grounds where the Marylanders fought and lived. I'd like to thank the many park rangers and other volunteers that I met along the way. I strongly encourage my fellow Americans to visit these hallowed sites, such as the Old Stone House, Green-Wood Cemetery, Hobkirk's Hill, Stony Point, Cowpens, Eutaw Springs, Guilford Courthouse, Camden, Valley Forge, and all the other major battlefields where the Marylanders fought. It is ironic that some of the most beautiful places in America are also the grounds where so many Americans gave their full measure of devotion.

This book would not have been possible without the help of many valuable repositories of historical information. I'd like to thank the staff at the Old Stone House in Brooklyn, including Executive Director Kimberly Maier. I'd also like to thank the staff at the National Archives Record Administration in Washington, D.C., the Maryland State Archives, the professional and extremely knowledgeable staff at the Maryland Historical Society, the New York Public Library, the Library of Congress, the Public Records Office in Kew, the Brooklyn Historical Society, the Long Island Historical Society, and other historical societies and libraries around the country that I visited many, many times. Thanks in particular to the New-York Historical Society, which opened its doors just for me during its renovation; specifically, I'd like to thank Dr. Louise Mirrer and Jean Ashton.

In addition, words can't express how grateful I am to historian, author, and editor of the Journal of the American Revolution, Don Hagist for going through the manuscript line-by-line and making improvements to the book. Don, also an expert on Britain's role in the Revolution, furnished several priceless sources from the British perspective.

Every author has many friends on whom he leans for advice and early reads, and I leaned on mine and am most grateful for their time and thoughtful comments. Thanks to Cyndy Harvey for all of her wisdom and editorial advice. Thanks to Justin Oldham for looking at many drafts and providing feedback. I'm extremely grateful to Glenn F. Williams, historian at the U.S. Army Center of Military History, who examined the book in detail and provided valuable comments. I'm also indebted to historian and editor of the *Journal of the American Revolution* Don Hagist, who spent several weekends going through the manuscript line by line. Also thank you, David Mitchell, Ben Ibach, Lieutenant Commander Gray Connelly, Rick McQualter, Dean Hall, James Noel Smith, and Theana Kastens. Special thanks also to historian and literary agent Roger S. Williams. I'm grateful to my family, including my beautiful daughter, Lily, for their support. I'm deeply in debt to my fiancée, the beautiful and brilliant Dr. Lori Snyder, who provided countless comments and suggestions to strengthen the book. In addition, I appreciate the hard work of my literary agent, Andrew Zack.

I'm most grateful for the brilliant comments and reshaping provided by my outstanding editor, Jamison Stoltz. And this book would never have become a reality without the vision and support of my publisher, the legendary Morgan Entrekin.

SOURCES

My journey with the Marylanders began more than five years ago when I found the "MARYLAND HEROES" sign in New York City. An extremely important aspect of my research for this book involved going to all the major battlefields where the Marylanders fought. I traveled from north to south, from Stony Point to Eutaw Springs.

In 2010 I had the pleasure of touring the Brooklyn battlefield with Colonel Willy Buhl, a seasoned military officer who helped plan the operation to clear Fallujah. Willy was the commanding officer of the Marines of 3/1, with whom I was embedded during that epic battle, and he later helped introduce me to many great stories that later became my books We Were One and Give Me Tomorrow. Running across the sign with one of the finest fighting Marine officers was just one of many full-circle and serendipitous moments I've had in career. Although many experts doubted there were enough sources to tell the untold story, his words convinced me to pursue the Marylanders' story: "If anyone could tell their story it's you, Pat."

To reconstruct the Marylanders' story, I utilized thousands of original sources housed in hundreds of libraries, repositories, and archives. The Maryland Historical Society, located in Baltimore, was an invaluable resource, and I am most grateful for the assistance the staff offered. The New-York Historical Society was also extremely helpful, as was the Library of Congress. Pension files were obtained through Fold3, which had taken the original paper and microfilm files from the National Archives and digitized them.

Many of the quotations in this book retain their original spelling and punctuation; however, some were edited slightly to allow for greater readability.

NOTES

PREFACE

xi "gentlemen of honour, family, and fortune." Gist Papers, Roll 1, Maryland Historical Society (MHS). The papers were microfilmed, and the author has complete copies of all the microfilm rolls and spent hundreds of hours reviewing them. To appeal to a large readership, the author decided to use the term "Patriots" versus "Whigs" for Americans who advocated independence. Although patriots existed on both sides, depending on your point of view, the book does closely examine the nature of the conflict as both a revolution and a civil war. Please see the "Sources" section of the book for a description of the first time the author encountered the sign regarding the Marylanders' mass grave and his motivtion for writing the book.

xii "Close up! Close up!" Henry Whittemore, *Heroes of the American Revolution and Their Descendants: Battle of Long Island* (Brooklyn, NY: Heroes of the Revolution Publishing Co., 1897), Preface.

xii "[continued] pouring the . . . of hail." Joseph Plumb Martin, *Private Yankee Doodle: Dangers and Sufferings of a Revolutionary Soldier* (Jamestown, VA: Eastern Acorn Press, 1962), 26.

xii "the flower of . . . to atoms." Walt Whitman, *Brooklyn Daily Eagle*, August 27, 1846.

xii "closed their ranks over . . . the foe." Thomas Field, *The Battle of Long Island* (New York: Long Island Historical Society, 1869), 201.

xii "Good God! What . . . day lose!" Maryland Gazette Collection, Maryland State Archives (MSA) SC 2731 January 9, 1772–September 10, 1779 M 1282

xiii The Immortals or the Maryland 400. The number of Marylanders killed and captured remains a mystery and in dispute. Some historians believe that more than 100 men were captured and 256 killed to come to the figure 400.

xiii "an hour, more . . . its history." John Thomas Scharf, *History of Maryland, 1765–1812* (Hatboro, PA: Tradition Press, 1879), 247.

CHAPTER 1: "GENTLEMEN OF HONOUR, FAMILY, AND FORTUNE"

3 "infinitely, the dirtiest place I was ever in." David Hackett Fischer, *Washington's Crossing* (Oxford: Oxford University Press, 2004), 143.

3 "the Damndest Hole in the World." Ibid.

3 Biographical detail on Mordecai Gist from "Mordecai Gist," Maryland State Archives (MSA SC 3520-15852).

3 "frank and genial manner." Ibid.

4 "a company composed . . . of humanity." Gist Papers, MHS.

4 "by all the Sacred . . . and Country." Articles of Incorporation, Gist Papers, MHS; *Maryland Historical Magazine*, 4 (1909): 372–74.

5 "We, the Baltimore . . . Continental Congress." Baltimore Independent Cadets, Articles of Incorporation, Maryland State Archives (MSA).

5 "contrary to the true . . . this Engagement." Ibid.

7 "The arrangement essentially . . . the Crown." M. Christopher New, *Maryland Loyalists in the American Revolution* (Centreville, MD: Tidewater, 1996), 4.

9 "a Uniform Suit . . . half Boote." Papers of Mordecai Gist, MHS, Roll 1 microfilm.

9 "for the defense of the state." The colonies didn't officially become states until July 4, 1776. However, for the purposes of this book, the terms state and colony are used interchangeably.

10 "You are to be drawn . . . four quarters." James R. Gaines, *For Liberty and Glory: Washington, Lafayette, and Their Revolutions* (New York: W. W. Norton, 2007), 44.

11 "About three hundred . . . Twenty thousand." Mordecai Gist Papers, MHS; Gist Letterbook, Meyers Collection, New York Public Library.

CHAPTER 2: SMALLWOOD'S BATTALION
AND THE BIRTH OF AN ARMY

12 Description of the Fountain Inn from Mary Ellen Hayward and Frank R. Shivers Jr., eds., *The Architecture of Baltimore: An Illustrated History* (Baltimore: Johns Hopkins University Press, 2004), 17.

12 "satisfaction in the appearance . . . and men." Scharf, *History of Maryland*, 72.

12 "May the town . . . an end." Ibid.

13 "a mixed multitude . . . every department." George Washington Papers, Library of Congress.

14 "He possessed the . . . great command." Ron Chernow, *Washington: A Life* (New York: Penguin Press, 2010), 185.

14 "at the expense of the Continent." John Adams to Elbridge Gerry, letter, June 18, 1775, in *Letters of Members of the Continental Congress*, Edmund Cody Burnett, ed. (Washington, DC: Carnegie Institution of Washington, 1921), 135.

14 The Maryland Convention. Maryland's Whig or patriot government, was first called the Annapolis Convention and included all the counties of Maryland. In 1775, the Annapolis Convention was renamed the Assembly of Freemen.

14 "in the pay and for the defense." "William Browne," MSA, 18:4.

14–15 "of a battalion . . . of firearms." Maryland Convention 1776, *Proceedings 1774–1776* (Baltimore, 1836), 94. The battalion also included a company of marines.

15 "encamp out among . . . or Tents." He complained, "We stand here exposed and remain in a most Defenceless state." R. Beall to Council, May 29, 1776, MSA, 11:452.

16 "Success alone is . . . Mordecai Gist." Gist to Robert Munford, October 24, 1775, Mordecai Gist Papers, MHS.

17–18 "There are a good . . . we have." "Journal and Correspondence of the Maryland Council of Safety, August 29, 1775 to July 6, 1776," Maryland State Archives (MSA), 11:212.

18 Biographical detail on Edward Veazey from Edward C. Papenfuse et al., *A Biographical Dictionary of the Maryland Legislature, 1635–1789*, 2 vols. (Baltimore: Johns Hopkins University Press, 1979–1985); MSA, 426:851.

18 Biographical detail on Bryan Philpot Jr. from "Muster Rolls and Other Records of Service of Troops in the American Revolution, 1775–1783," *Archives of Maryland* 18.

18 Biographical detail on William Sterrett from "William Sterrett," MSA 3520-16728.

18 Biographical detail on James Fernandis from "James Fernandis," MSA SC 3520-16770.

18 Biographical detail on John Bantham from pension application of John Bantham. Pension applications are located at NARA (Revolutionary War Pension and Bounty-Land Warrant Application Files), NARA M804, S 2806, 33, and accessed via microfilm or online at Fold3.com. We also consulted an excellent transcription at the Southern Campaigns Revolutionary War Pension Statements and Rosters transcribed and annotated by C. Leon Harris.

19 "have a very Respectable . . . this Town." Ewing to Smallwood, January 10, 1776, "Journal and Correspondence of the Maryland Council of Safety, August 29, 1775 to July 6, 1776," MSA, 11:95.

19 Age and height information from Muster Rolls from MSA.

19–20 Free African Americans also . . . remained enslaved. One document, "Return of Negros in the Army," provides a rough tally of African Americans serving in the American army. Smallwood's Battalion lists sixty men while Gist's 2nd Maryland lists thirty-five African Americans on the muster rolls.

20 Information about Daniel Brophy from Woolford to Council of Safety, March 25, 1776, MSA.

20 "man of magnificent . . . in battle." Whittemore, *Heroes of the American Revolution*, 62.

CHAPTER 3: GIRDING FOR WAR

22 "It was just . . . ineffective." Major General B. P. Hughes, *Firepower: Weapons and Effective Use on the Battlefield, 1630–1850* (New York: Charles Scribner's Sons, 1975), 26.

22 "Powder is not . . . four men." Maurice de Saxe, *Reveries on the Art of War*, trans. Gen. Thomas R. Phillips (London, 1757; reprint, Mineola, NY: Dover Publishing, 2007), 32.

22 "Mr. Keener . . . he comply'd." Ewing to Council of Safety, letter, February 12, 1776, MSA, 11:155.

22 "stamp'd all that prov'd good." Ibid.

22 "vile trash." R. Beall to Council of Safety, May 29, 1776, MSA, 11:452.

22 "of the guns which were in the hands of the minute Company." "Journal and Correspondence of the Maryland Council of Safety, August 29, 1775 to July 6, 1776," MSA, 11:212.

23 "very indifferent, indeed . . . worse one." Ibid., 11:221.

23 "very uneasy . . . with Cloaths." T. Smyth to Maryland Council of Safety, letter, April 9, 1776, MSA.

23 Biographical detail on Jack Steward from Francis R. Heitman, *Historical Register of Officers of the Continental Army during the War of Revolution* (Washington, DC: US Government Printing Office, 1914), 467.

23 "You only live once." Steward Papers, MHS.

23 Information about gunpowder from James M. Potts, *French Covert Action in the American Revolution* (New York: iUniverse Inc., 2005), 33.

23 "take the most . . . the province." John E. Selby and Edward M. Riley, *Dunmore* (Williamsburg: Virginia Independence Bicentennial Commission, 1977), 55.

24 These efforts were . . . and arrows. Helen Augur, *The Secret War of Independence* (New York: Duell, Sloan and Pearce, 1955), 65.

25–25 "Deserted. From the . . . forty shillings." *Maryland Journal and Baltimore Advertiser*, March 29, 1775.

CHAPTER 4: AMERICA'S FIRST CIVIL WAR

26 "it was better . . . they were." "Journal and Correspondence of the Maryland Council of Safety, August 29, 1775 to July 6, 1776," MSA, 11:309.

26 "My brave boys . . . be stretched." Ibid.

26 "was satisfied he was right." Ibid.

27 "I confess . . . myself carfully." Ibid., 11:310.

28 Information about colonial debts from Kevin Phillips, *1775: A Good Year for Revolution* (New York: Penguin Group, 2012), 108.

28 "was an ardent . . . a Tory." A. A. Gunby, *Colonel John Gunby of the Maryland Line* (Cincinnati: Robert Clark Company, 1902), 24–25.

28 "one of the most . . . Gen. Smallwood." *Salisbury* (Maryland) *Times*, September 7, 1959, Edward H. Nabb Research Center for Delmarva History and Culture at Salisbury University.

29 "I am determined . . . of England." Ibid.

29 "a name to . . . endure oppression." Gunby, *Colonel John Gunby*, 24–25.

29 "The worthy proprietor . . . fertile territory." New, *Maryland Loyalists in the American Revolution*, 20.

29–30 "shamefully misrepresents facts . . . SYNONYMOUS TERMS." James Chalmers (Candidus), *Plain Truth* (Philadelphia: R. Bell, 1776).

30 "repel force by force." Ibid.

CHAPTER 5: THE *OTTER*

33 "becoming, subsequently, on the most friendly terms." Samuel Smith Papers, Columbia University Library. The author painstakingly transcribed the handwritten papers, which were a biography written in the third person.

34 "We hear that . . . you can." "Journal and Correspondence of the Maryland Council of Safety, August 29, 1775 to July 6, 1776," MSA, 11:201.

34–35 "moved with astonishing . . . with Men." Ibid., 11:236.

35 "was done without . . . inconsiderate midshipman." Ibid.

35 "We cannot sufficiently . . . our power." Ibid., 11:226.

36 "It evidently appears . . . our Enemies." Ibid., 11:334.

CHAPTER 6: THE ARMADA

37 "a wood of pine trees trimmed." Daniel McCurtin, "Journal of the Times at the Siege of Boston," in *Papers Related to the Maryland Line during the Revolution*, Thomas Balch, ed. (Philadelphia: Printed for the Seventy-Six Society, 1857), 40.

37 "I declare, at . . . was afloat." Ibid.

37 Part of a small advance group. Two companies of Marylanders, including a main figure in this book, Otho Holland Williams, took part in the siege of Boston.

38   "The Congress have . . . of tyranny." John Hancock to the Convention of Maryland, letter, July 4, 1776, from *Letters of Members of the Continental Congress*, 525–26.

38   "I do therefore . . . defend ourselves." Ibid.

39   "silent as a rock." Chernow, *Washington: A Life*, 239.

39   "had no objection . . . enjoyed madam." David McCollough, *1776* (New York: Simon & Schuster, 2005), 75.

40   "a shy bitch." Andrew Jackson O'Shaughnessy, *The Men Who Lost America* (New Haven, CT: Yale University Press, 2013), 214.

40   Information on terms of enlistment from Fischer, *Washington's Crossing*, 33.

41   "the most arrogant army in the world." A. Graydon, *Memoirs of His Own Time*, J. S. Littell, ed. (Philadelphia: Lindsay and Blakiston, 1846), 208.

41   "Their army is . . . motley crew." Michael Stephenson, *Patriot Battles: How the War of Independence Was Fought* (New York: HarperCollins, 2007), 20.

41   Information on purchase of commissions and British troops' experience from Fischer, *Washington's Crossing*, 34; and Sylvia R. Frey, *The British Soldier in America* (Austin: University of Texas Press, 1981), 135.

42   "For men on . . . deeply believed." Fischer, *Washington's Crossing*, 50.

42   "leaping, running, climbing . . . remarkable rapidity." Bennet Cuthbertson, *Cuthbertson's System, for the Complete Interior Management and Œconomy of a Battalion of Infantry* (Briston: A. Gray, 1776), 191.

43   "two pistols, a short-barreled carbine, and a long cavalry sword." Fischer, *Washington's Crossing*, 36.

44   "any disgrace which . . . cruel misfortune." James Browne, *A History of the Highlands and of the Highland Clans* (London, Edinburgh, and Dublin: A. Fullarton, 1854), 133.

44   "the largest suppliers . . . most expensive." Fischer, *Washington's Crossing*, 52.

45   "Never in this . . . them rich." Johann Ewald, *Diary of the American War: A Hessian Journal*, Joseph P. Tustin, ed. (New Haven, CT: Yale University Press, 1979), 118.

46   "The time is . . . this Army." Chernow, *Washington: A Life*, 212.

46   "The whole army . . . take it." Henry Onderdone Jr., ed., *Revolutionary Incidents of Suffolk and Kings Counties with an Account of the Battle of Long Island, and the British Prisons and Prison-Ships at New-York* (New York: Leavitt & Company, 1849), 133–34.

46   Note on Marylanders in New York: An independent company of Marylanders took part in the siege of Boston and therefore arrived in Manhattan before Smallwood or the Flying Camp.

46   "They met, they talked, they parted." Ambrose Serle, *The American Journal of Ambrose Serle, 1776–1778*, Edward H. Tatum Jr., ed. (San Marino, CA: Huntington Library, 1940), 70.

CHAPTER 7: MARYLAND GOES TO WAR

47 "Never did a . . . hunting-shirts." "Account of Smallwood's Regiment in Philadelphia," in George Washington Park Custis, Mary Randolph Custis Lee, and Benson John Lossing, *Recollections and Private Memoirs of Washington* (New York: Derby and Jackson, 1860), 265.

47 "Colonel Smallwood's battalion . . . the Union." John Thomas Scharf, *The Chronicles of Baltimore* (Baltimore: Turnbull Brothers, 1874), 265.

47–48 "was obliged . . . the Service." Washington to Robert Morris, superintendent of finance, letter, January 29, 1783, in John C. Fitzpatrick, ed., *The Writings of George Washington from the Original Manuscript Sources 1745–1799*, Volume 26, *January 1, 1783–June 10, 1783* (Washington, DC: Library of Congress, 1939), 79.

48 "Having fondness for . . . the revolution." *Selected Papers of Charles Willson Peale and His Family*, Volume 5, Lillian Miller, ed. (New Haven, CT: Yale University Press, 2000), 119.

48 "She said she . . . to her." Ibid., 123.

48 "You can aid . . . seen before." Ibid., 124.

49 "We are advised . . . the Ospitals." Sands Collection, Williams Sands letter, August 14, 1776, MSA SC 2095.

49 Percentage of army listed as sick from Fischer, *Washington's Crossing*, 87.

49 "typically easing themselves in the ditches of the fortifications." Nathanael Greene, General Orders, July 28, 1776, in *Papers of Nathanael Greene, 1776*, Richard Showman, ed. (Chapel Hill: University of North Carolina Press, 1989), 1:278.

50 "The whores (by information) . . . one another." John J. Gallagher, *Battle of Brooklyn, 1776* (New York: Da Capo Press, 1995), 79.

50 Details on prostitute population from Fischer, *Washington's Crossing*, 86.

50 Details on whore's march from Christopher Ward, *The War of the Revolution* (New York: Macmillan, 1952). 123–25.

51 "We shall have . . . our all." Council to Maryland Deputies, August 16, 1776, MSA, 12:211–13.

51 "the amenity of . . . of friends." Thomas Wyatt, *Memoirs of the General, Commodores, and Other Commanders Who Distinguished Themselves in the American Army and Navy* (Philadelphia: Carey and Hart, 1848), 78.

51 "deserves a statue . . . Grecian heroes." *A Memoir of the Late Col. John Eager Howard, Reprinted from the* Baltimore Gazette, *October 15, 1827* (Baltimore: Kelly, Hedian & Piet, 1863), 4.

51 "was apptd. an Ensign . . . 3d July." Papers of Captain William Beatty, MHS.

52 "tall and brawny . . . genuine courage." Balch, *Papers Related to the Maryland Line*, 46–48.

CHAPTER 8: THE STORM BEGINS

53   "In a few ... every side." Henry P. Johnson, *The Campaign of 1776 around New York and Brooklyn* (Brooklyn, NY: Long Island Historial Society, 1878), 113.

53   "the tips of ... if roasted." McCullough, *1776*, 156.

53   "ships and vessels ... the rain." Serle, *American Journal*, 70.

53–54   "The peach and ... readily apparent." Bruce Burgoyne, trans. and ed., *An Anonymous Hessian Diary* (Bowie, MD: Heritage Books, 1980), 54–55.

54   "regaled themselves with ... trees together." Serle, *American Journal*, 71–73.

54   "The Enemy being ... [by the] lines." Mordecai Gist, letter, Camp New York, August 1776, New-York Historical Society (NYHS).

54   "over desire of being popular." George Washington to Congress, letter, June 17, 1776 in James Thomas Flexner, *George Washington* (New York: Little, Brown, 1965), 6:112.

54   "carts and horses ... in tumult." Philip Vickers Fithian, "August 25, 1776," in *Philip Vickers Fithian Journal, 1773–1776* (Princeton, NJ: Princeton University Press, 1934), 218.

55   "A few more ... in America." Henry Clinton, *The American Rebellion: Sir Henry Clinton's Narrative of His Campaigns, 1775–1782*, William B. Willcox, ed. (New Haven, CT: Yale University Press, 1954), 19.

55   "The distinction between ... the latter." George Washington to Israel Putnam, letter, August 25, 1776 in Flexner, *George Washington*, 6:126–27.

55   "a continuous barrier ... be sustained." Henry P. Johnston, *Memoirs of the Long Island Historical Society* (Brooklyn, NY: Long Island Historical Society, 1878), 3:143.

58   "at all hazards ... the wood." George Washington to Israel Putnam, letter, August 25, 1776.

CHAPTER 9: THE BATTLE OF BROOKLYN

59   Details on the devil's footprint from Whittemore, *Heroes of the American Revolution*, xiv.

60   "Now you are ... the enemy." Onderdone, *Revolutionary Incidents*, 138–39.

61   "overweight, rheumatic, vain, pompous, gluttonous inebriate." Paul David Nelson, *William Alexander, Lord Stirling* (Tuscaloosa: University of Alabama Press, 1987), 88.

61   "I fully expected ... our lines." Johnston, *Memoirs of the Long Island Historical Society*, 2:357.

61–62   "We began our ... the attack." "Extract of a letter from a gentleman from Maryland," New York, August 30, 1776, in *Peter Force's American*

Archives (Washington, DC, 1837–53), 5th series, 1:1231–32; Papers of Mordecai Gist, MHS.

62 "with a Red and angry Glare." "Extract of a letter"; Papers of Mordecai Gist, New-York Historical Society.

62 "immediately advanced and . . . the front." "Extract of a letter"; Papers of Mordecai Gist, NYHS.

62 "immediately drew up . . . English taste." Unknown (Nathaniel Ramsay), "Extract of a Letter from New-York, Dated September 1, 1776," in *Journal of the Transactions of August 27, 1776, upon Long-Island, Peter Force's American Archives*, 5th series, 2:107–8.

62 "Our men stood . . . our number." Ibid.

62–63 "We gave them . . . touched any." Captain Enoch Anderson, *Personal Recollections* (Wilmington: Historical Society of Delaware, 1895), 121.

63 "[Grant] may have . . . mill pond." William Duer, *The Life of William Alexander, Earl of Stirling* (New York: Wiley & Putnam, 1847), 102.

63 "Our men behaved . . . side ceased." "Extract of a letter from a gentleman from Maryland," New York, August 30, 1776, *Peter Force's American Archives*, 5th series, 1:1231–32.

63 "We soon heard . . . our camp." Ibid.

64 "with colors flying . . . their bayonets." Christopher Longstreth Ward, *The Delaware Continentals, 1776–1783* (Literary Licensing, 2012), 37.

64 Details on bayoneting of stragglers from Henry R. Stiles, *A History of the City of Brooklyn* (Brooklyn, NY, 1867), 1:274.

64 "ten or fifteen grenadiers." Samuel Smith Papers, Columbia University Library.

64 "that the left . . . for stragglers." Ibid.

64 "When the regiment . . . in line." Ibid.

64–65 "We soon fell . . . in ambuscade." "Extract of a Letter from a Marylander, Dated New York, August 30, 1776," *Peter Force's American Archives*, 5th series, 1:1231–32.

65 "They entirely overshot . . . I made." "Extract of a Letter from a Marylander, Dated New York, August 28, 1776," *Peter Force's American Archives*, 5th series, 7:615.

65 "came to the marsh . . . brisk fire." Onderdone, *Revolutionary Incidents*, 146.

65 "During this interval . . . a marsh." "Extract of a Letter from a Marylander, Dated New York, August 30, 1776," *Peter Force's American Archives*, 5th series, 1:1231–32.

65 Details about bridge from Scharf, *History of Maryland*, 246.

65 "rather corpulent." O'Shaughnessy, *The Men Who Lost America*, 249.

66   "I found it . . . the creek." Lord Stirling to General Washington, letter, August 29, 1776, *Peter Force's American Archives*, 5th series, 1:1245.

66   "We were then . . . our battalion." "Extract of a Letter from a Marylander, Dated New York, August 28, 1776," *Peter Force's American Archives*, 5th series, 7:615.

67   "We continued the . . . several times." There's a conflict between Gist's and Stirling's accounts regarding the number of charges. Stirling, letter to George Washington, Stirling Papers, New-York Historical Society.

67   "our little line . . . second attack." "Extract of a Letter from a Marylander, Dated New York, August 30, 1776," *Peter Force's American Archives*, 5th series, 1:1231–32.

67   "Our men fought with more than Roman valor." Unknown (Nathaniel Ramsay), "Extract of a Letter from New-York, Dated September 1, 1776," in *Journal of the Transactions of August 27, 1776, upon Long-Island*, Peter Force's *American Archives*, 5th series, 2:107–8; Onderdone, *Revolutionary Incidents*, 147.

67   "encouraged and animated . . . invincible resolution," "Extract of a Letter from a Marylander, Dated New York, August 30, 1776," *Peter Force's American Archives*, 5th series, 1:1231–32.

67   "Surrounded on all . . . and confusion." Ibid.

67–68   "The Hessians and . . . their hands." Onderdone, *Revolutionary Incidents*, 138.

68   "We were greatly . . . was decided." Ibid.

68   "My captain was . . . was taken." Pension application of William McMillan, NARA.

69   "Major Gist [and his men] . . . them again." "Extract of a Letter from a Marylander, Dated New York, August 28, 1776," *Peter Force's American Archives*, 5th series, 7:615.

69   "Gen. Washington wrung . . . day lose!'" *Maryland Gazette*, January 9, 1772–September 10, 1779; "Mordecai Gist," Archives of Maryland (Biographical Series).

69   "out of the water . . . water-rats." Martin, *Private Yankee Doodle*, 16.

69   "Most of those . . . their lives." Smallwood Papers, MHS.

69   "He and a sergeant . . . not swim." Samuel Smith Papers, Columbia University Library.

69   "hold up his . . . his mouth." Charles Willson Peale, *The Autobiography of Charles Willson Peale*, in *The Selected Papers of Charles Willson Peale and His Family*, Lillian B. Miller and Sidney Hart, eds. (New Haven and London: Yale University Press, 2000), 5:123.

69–70   "[My father spoke] . . . his head." Pension application of Bryan Philpot, NARA.

70 Details about decapitation from pension applications of Patrick Sims and Bryan Philpot, NARA.

70 "A party retreated . . . safe in." "Extract of a Letter from a Marylander, Dated New York, August 30, 1776," *Peter Force's American Archives*, 5th series, 1:1231–32.

70 "The men were . . . they could." Samuel Smith Papers, Columbia University Library.

70 "Captain Veazey is . . . are missing." Unknown (Nathaniel Ramsay), "Extract of a Letter from New-York."

70 "torn with shot." Ward, *Delaware Continentals*, 41.

70–71 "soon found it . . . the Hessians." Stirling Papers, NYHS.

71 "General Stirling fought like a wolf." Cornwallis Papers, UK Public Record Office (PRO).

71 "an hour, more . . . its history." Thomas W. Field, *The Battle of Long Island* (Brooklyn, NY: Long Island Historical Society, 1869), 208.

CHAPTER 10: ESCAPE FROM LONG ISLAND

72 "The enemy came . . . has begun," "Maryland Soldier's Letter," *Peter Force's American Archives and Maryland Gazette*, September 5, 1776.

72 Details on killed and missing from Onderdone, *Revolutionary Incidents*, 146.

72 "It required repeated . . . the attempt." Howe's Memoirs in *Memoirs of the Long Island Historical Society* (Brooklyn, NY: Long Island Historical Society, 1869), 2:378; also found in George Trevelyan, *The American Revolution* (London: C. J. Fox, 1899), 1:311.

72–73 "We had no . . . every part." Whittemore, *Heroes of the American Revolution*, 24.

73 "When I looked . . . dearly bought." Trevelyan, *The American Revolution*, 1:311.

73 "There fell a . . . our ammunition." Martin, *Private Yankee Doodle*, 17.

74 "that at the Battle . . . taken prisoner." Pension application of John Hughes, NARA.

74 "Troops fired off . . . own lines." Philip Vickers Fithian, *Journal, 1775–1776*, Robert Greenhalgh Albion and Leonidas Dodson, eds. (Princeton, NJ: Princeton University Press, 1934), 220–21.

74 "so much that . . . with water." W. H. W. Sabine, ed., *The New York Diary of Lieutenant Jabez Fitch* (New York: New York Times and Arno Press, 1971), 61–62.

75 "had but one . . . enemy's approaches." Smallwood to Maryland Convention, letter, October 12, 1776, http://lincoln.lib.niu.edu/cgi-bin/philologic/getobject.pl?p.24520:2.amarch.

75 "remarkably still, the water smooth as glass." Whittemore, *Heroes of the American Revolution*, 32.

76 "The effect was at once alarming and sublime." Alexander Gratin, *Memoirs* (New York: New York Times and Arno Press, 1969), 167.

76 "Good God! General . . . the line!" George F. Scheer and Hugh F. Rankin, eds., *Rebels and Redcoats: The American Revolution through the Eyes of Those Who Fought and Lived It* (New York: Da Capo Press, 1957), 170–71.

76 "sink it to hell." Stiles, *History of the City of Brooklyn*, 1:387.

76–77 "Those of us . . . yards' distance." Benjamin Tallmadge, *Memoir of Colonel Benjamin Tallmadge* (New York: TK, 1858), 10–11.

77 "One of the corporals . . . to [us]." Samuel Smith Papers, Columbia University Library.

77 Details on losses from Onderdone, *Revolutionary Incidents*, 136. The British tallied, and likely understated, their own losses as follows: "5 officers and 56 non-commissioned officers, and rank and file killed; 12 officers, and 245 non-commissioned officers and rank and file wounded; one officer and 20 grenadiers of the marines taken, by mistaking the enemy for the Hessians. The Hessians had two privates killed, three officers and 23 rank and file wounded."

CHAPTER 11: MANHATTAN

78 "All of a sudden . . . go first." Martin, *Private Yankee Doodle*, 34.

78–79 "I have often . . . Connecticut troops." "Journal and Correspondence of the Maryland Council of Safety, July 7–December 31, 1776," MSA.

79 "Wretches, who, however . . . one Shot." Smallwood Papers, MHS.

79 "a New England . . . for Cowardice." Papers of Captain William Beatty, MHS.

79 "to restore to . . . be hanged." *Papers of George Washington*, Library of Congress; 6:171–77.

79 "so vexed at . . . than life." Flexner, *George Washington*, 2:123.

80 "Washington expressly sent . . . upon us." "Journal and Correspondence of the Maryland Council of Safety, July 7: December 31, 1776," MSA, 342.

81 "Come on, boys!" Henry Phelps Johnson, *Battle of Harlem Heights* (New York, 1897), 55; also Bruce Blizen, *The Battle for Manhattan* (New York: Holt, 1955), 85–87.

81 Expending most of their ammunition. Knowlton's men unleashed about eight rounds per man. See Johnson, *Battle of Harlem Heights*, 155.

81 "The enemy appeared . . . our disgrace." *Peter Force's American Archives*, 5th series, 2:443–45.

82 "Never did troops . . . on them." September 17, 1776, *Peter Force's American Archives*, 5th series, 2:370.

82 "The Marylanders, were . . . gave way." Ibid.

82 "The action was . . . not broke." Papers of Captain William Beatty, MHS.

82 "[From] the appearance . . . and wounded." General Washington to Governour Cooke, letter, September 17, 1776, *Peter Force's American Archives*, 5th series, 2:367.

83 "striking Sergeant [William] . . . Colonel Silliman." "Proceedings of a General Court-Martial of the Line, held on the Heights of Harlem, by order of General Washington, for the trial of all prisoners to be brought before them," *Peter Force's American Archives*, 5th series, 2:467.

83 "I'll go to . . . damn you." Ibid.

83 "I drew near . . . a battle." Anderson, *Personal Recollections*, 23.

84 "A pardon, a pardon! . . with pleasure." Ibid., 24.

84 "I would burn . . . to theirs." Greene to Washington, September 5, 1776, *Papers of Nathanael Greene*, 1:295.

84 "but was absolutely forbid." John Hancock to George Washington, September 3, 1776, *Papers of George Washington*, Revolutionary War Series, 6:207.

84 "The sick, the aged . . . ever beheld." Frederick Mackenzie, *The Diary of Frederick Mackenzie* (Cambridge, MA: Harvard University Press, 1930), 58–60.

84 "I must break . . . fight them." William Smallwood to the Maryland Convention, letter, October 12, 1776, in Scharf, *Chronicles of Baltimore*, 152.

CHAPTER 12: WHEN TWENTY-FIVE MEN HELD OFF AN ARMY

87 Comment about potential mental illness from Phillip Papas, *Renegade Revolutionary: The Life of General Charles Lee* (New York: New York University Press, 2014).

88 "the British officer . . . no control." Samuel Smith Papers, Columbia University Library.

88 "near two hundred . . . the Doctor." "Minutes of Council of Safety, October 26, 1776," MSA, 12:404.

88 "could not from . . . they pleased." Clinton, *The American Rebellion*, 45–55.

89 "and asked how . . . British out." Pension application of John Hughes, NARA.

89 "[I] with Twelve . . . this accident." Ibid.

89   "The sun shone . . . more advantage." William Heath, *The Revolutionary War Memoirs of Major General William Heath*, Sean M. Heuvel, ed. (Jefferson, NC: McFarland, 2014), 54.

89   "A cannon commenced. . . . our artillery." Samuel Smith Papers, Columbia University Library.

89   "construct a rough . . . across them." Pension applications of John Hughes and Samuel Smith, NARA.

89   "more than halfway . . . into disorder." Ward, *The War of the Revolution*, 264.

90   "The enemy advanced . . . great fury." "Extract of a letter from White Plains," *Maryland Gazette*, October 28, 1776, MSA.

90   "It was a gallant . . . the slope." Samuel Smith Papers, Columbia University Library.

90   "first took the . . . a heap." Edward G. Lengel, *General George Washington: A Military Life* (New York: Random House, 2005), 163; "Extract of a letter from White Plains."

90   "in this Battle . . . the hospital." Pension application of William Brooks, NARA.

90   "A ball struck . . . Sergeant Westlay." Samuel Smith Papers, Columbia University Library.

90   "[We marched] down . . . militia aforeward." "Extract of a letter from White Plains."

90   "fled in confusion . . . scattering fire." John Haslet to Caesar Rodney, letter, Delaware Historical Society.

91   "very heavy fire . . . an hour." Ibid.

91   "a soldier of . . . and expired." Anderson, *Personal Recollections*, 25.

91   "The Americans overpowered . . . was found." Samuel Smith Papers, Columbia University Library.

91   "about a hundred stragglers, and marched them within the lines." Smallwood Papers, MHS.

91   "A young . . . satisfied ourselves." Samuel Smith Papers, Columbia University Library.

91   Details on losses from Gist to Council, November 2, 1776, Archives of Maryland, 12:418.

92   "The rebels had . . . extraordinary tenacity." Bruce E. Burgoyne, trans., *The Diary of Lieutenant Von Bardeleben and Other Von Donop Regiment Documents* (Bowie, MD: Heritage Books, 1998), 90.

92   "Since the skirmish . . . much haste." "Journal and Correspondence of the Maryland Council of Safety, July–December 1776," MSA, 12:418.

92   "I being very . . . two weeks." Papers of Captain William Beatty, MHS.

CHAPTER 13: FORT WASHINGTON

93   Note on Williams: He was an officer in the Maryland and Virginia Rifle Regiment, also known as Rawling's Regiment, a unit of light infantry and riflemen. As the name suggests, both states contributed troops to the unit. They acted as scouts, skirmishers, and forward outposts in front of the main army.

94   "great hopes the enemy was entirely repulsed." "General Washington to the President of Congress," November 16, 1776, *Peter Force's American Archives*, 5th series, 3:706.

94   "All that are my grenadiers, march forwards!" Johannes Reuber, Journal, December 25 [26], 1776, in McCullough, *1776*, 242.

95   "Commission was stain'd . . . the action." Otho Holland Williams Papers, MHS. The author has microfilm copies of all of the Williams papers.

95   "Of the Maryland . . . of them." Samuel Chase to Maryland Council of Safety, letter, November 22, 1776, *Peter Force's American Archives*, 5th series, 3:809.

95   "escaped in a . . . the porch." After the escape, Everhart quit the infantry and joined the Light Dragoons, mounted infantry led by Washington's nephew, the indomitable William Washington. Pension application of Lawrence Everhart, NARA.

95   "Their odd figures . . . our soldiers." Frederick Mackenzie, *Diary of Frederick Mackenzie* (Cambridge, MA: Harvard University Press, 1930), 111–12.

95   "lowered the colours . . . his breeches." One of the lucky prisoners, Atkinson escaped confinement in New York City. He was placed "in a sugar house, and then in a vessel of war, that he was soon after taken sick & removed to the hospital, on his recovery he was compelled to attend on the sick in the hospital and subsequently permitted to go in and out when he pleased, that at length he effected his escape about the month of June (1777)." Pension application of Richard Thomas Atkinson, NARA.

96   Details on captured prisoners from Edwin G. Burrows, *Forgotten Patriots: The Untold Story of American Prisoners during the Revolutionary War* (New York: Basic Books, 2008), xi.

96   "Among the prisoners . . . for officers." E. J. Lowell, *The Hessians and Other German Auxiliaries of Great Britain in the Revolutionary War* (New York: Harper and Brothers, 1884), 64–66.

96–97   "he replied, that . . . his offence." Osmond Tiffany, *A Sketch of the Life and Services of Gen. Otho Holland Williams* (Baltimore, MD: John Murphy, 1851), 8.

97   "about sixteen feet . . . loathsome filth." Otho Holland Williams Papers, MHS.

97   "Their health was . . . his imprisonment." Ibid.

97 "Sunday 17th. Such . . . Deaths multiply." Henry Steele Commager and Richard Brandon Morris, eds., *The Spirit of 'Seventy-Six: The Story of the American Revolution as Told by Participants* (New York: Harper and Row, 1967), 856–57.

98 "said I should . . . threaten us." William Sterrett to James McHenry, letter, April 2, 1778, MHS.

98 "much to the . . . to myself." Burrows, *Forgotten Patriots*, 108.

98–99 "Ten of us . . . but death." Pension application of William McMillan, NARA, via Fold3.

99 "with little port-hole . . . external air." William Dunlap, *History of the New Netherlands, Province of New York, and State of New York, to the Adoption of the Federal Constitution*, 2 vols. (New York: Carter and Thorp, 1840), 1:136, 141–42.

99 "from Exposure, bad treatment, Cold & Hunger." Pension application of Elijah Wright, NARA.

99 "that she had . . . always happened." Pension application of William McMillan, NARA.

99 "murdered a great . . . year 1776." Elias Boudinot, *Journal of the Events in the Revolution* (original edition, 1894; reprint, New York: New York Times and Arno Press, 1968), 35–36.

CHAPTER 14: THE CRISIS

100 "A thick cloud . . . every countenance," Archives of Delaware, 3:1358; Ward, *Delaware Continentals*, 104.

100 "Our army began . . . the Enemy." Papers of Captain William Beatty, MHS.

101 "dark, cold, and . . . their blankets." Fischer, *Washington's Crossing*, 125.

101 "No nation ever . . . of tatterdemalions." Ibid.

101 "Was taken sick . . . of April." Gassaway Watkins, "An Interesting Personal Record," *The Spirit of '76*, 1 (December 1894):69.

102 "This march being . . . very hard." Papers of Captain William Beatty, MHS, PAM 10699.

102 "informed him that . . . guard duty." Papers of Samuel Smith, Columbia University Library.

102 "I can assign . . . and damper." Ibid.

102 "Even the bones . . . of one." Maryland Archives Online, 2:1166–67.

103 "[We] are badly . . . their baggage." "Journal and Correspondence of the Maryland Council of Safety, July 7–December 31, 1776," MSA.

103 "[I] am much . . . get none." Captain Hindman to Maryland Council of Safety, letter, October 12, 1776, *Peter Force's American Archives*, 5th series, 2:1006.

103 "Let them go . . . ten rebels." Ewald, *Diary of the American War*, 30–35.

103 "ending the war . . . needless way." Ibid.

104 "Two or three . . . to Philadelphia." William Beatty, Journal, MHS.

105 "[Our] numbers by . . . a few officers." Samuel Stelle Smith, *The Battle of Princeton* (Monmouth Beach, NJ: Westholme, 1967; reprint, 2009), 28–30, 34–36.

106 "Colonel Haslet came . . . no shoes." Anderson, *Personal Recollections*, 25.

106 "comfortable lodgings in the college." Fischer, *Washington's Crossing*, 131.

107 "We continued on . . . his pioneers." Anderson, *Personal Recollections*, 28.

107 "the most hellish . . . brother James." Peale, *Autobiography*, 50.

107 Note on size of battalion: The regiment was now down to 5 officers, 19 NCOs, and 139 enlisted men. Charles H. Lesser, *The Sinews of Independence: Monthly Strength Reports of the Continental Army* (Chicago: University of Chicago Press, 1976), 40, 43.

107–8 "Entre nous, a certain . . . are lost." Lee to Gates, December 13, 1776, American Archives, Northern Illinois University Libraries Digital Collections and Collaborative Projects.

108 "I ordered my . . . they could." McCullough, *1776*, 265.

108 "he trusted he . . . a gentleman." Ibid., 275.

109 "the greatest coolness . . . not killed." Friedrich von Münchhausen, *At General Howe's Side, 1776–1778: The Diary of General William Howe's Aide-de-Camp, Captain Friedrich von Muenchhausen*, Ernest Kipping, trans. (Monmouth Beach, NJ: Philip Freneau, 1974), 6.

109 "It became clearly . . . and peacefully." Ewald, *Diary of the American War*, 17–25.

109 "General Howe appeared . . . his escape." Charles Stedman, *The History of the Origin, Progress, and Termination of the American War*, 2 vols. (London: J. Murray et al., 1794).

109 "scattered through the . . . ragged condition." Horace Wells Sellers, "Charles Willson Peale, Artist-Soldier," *Pennsylvania Magazine of History and Biography* 38, no. 3 (1914):257–87.

109 "All the plantations . . . declared booty." Ewald, *Diary of the American War*, 30–35.

110 "These are the . . . and women." Thomas Paine, "The American Crisis," December 23, 1776.

110 "flew like wildfire . . . the counties." George Otto Trevelyan, *The American Revolution*, pt. 2 (New York and London: Longmans, Green, 1898–1926), 2:81.

110   "people began to . . . it quickly," Fischer, *Washington's Crossing*, 142

111   "I think the game is pretty near up." Chernow, *Washington: A Life*, no
      page number.

CHAPTER 15: VICTORY OR DEATH—
THE GAMBLE AT TRENTON

112   "not to suffer . . . attempts either." George Washington, General Orders,
      December 25, 1776, *Papers of George Washington*, Revolutionary War Series,
      7:436.

112   "I was struck . . . 'or Death.'" Benjamin Rush, *The Autobiography of Benja-
      min Rush: His 'Travels through Life' Together with His Commonplace Book for
      1789–1813*, George W. Corner, ed. (Princeton, NJ: American Philosophical
      Society, 1948), 124.

112   Details on Hessians from Fischer, *Washington's Crossing*, 396.

113   "I have not . . . the bayonet." "The Affair at Trenton, Finding of Hessian
      Court Martial, Colonel's Report," Lidgerwood Transcripts, Morristown
      National Historical Park Library; and Fischer, *Washington's Crossing*, 196.

113   "not to be troubled . . . manage it." Fischer, *Washington's Crossing*, 203.

113–14 "our General halted . . . our beloved." Pension application of Henry
      Wells (Wales), NARA.

114   "but thinly clad . . . extremely cold." Pension application of John Boudy
      (Bondy, Bodray), NARA.

114   "greatest fatigue"; "breaking a passage." George Washington to T. Cad-
      walader, December 26, 1776, *Papers of George Washington*, Revolutionary
      War Series, 7:450.

115   "Many of our . . . broken shoes." Ward, *Delaware Continentals*, 121.

115   "Our Army was destitute of shoes and clothing — . . . It was snowing at
      this time and the night was unusually stormy. Several of our men froze
      to death." Pension application of John Boudy (Bondy, Bodray), NARA.

115   "Soldiers, keep by . . . your officers!" Scheer and Rankin, *Rebels and Red-
      coats*, 212.

115   "Tell General Sullivan . . . take Trenton." Ward, *Delaware Continentals*, 122.

115   "Press on! Press on, boys!" Ibid.

115   "*Der Feind! Heraus! Heraus!*" Fischer, *Washington's Crossing*, 240.

116   "These are the times that try men's souls!" Thomas Paine, "The American
      Crisis," December 23, 1776.

116   "All who are my grenadiers forward!" Johannes Reuber, Journal, Decem-
      ber 25–26, 1776, in Fischer, *Washington's Crossing*, 246.

116   "Here succeeded a . . . saw before." Henry Knox to Lucy Flucker Knox, December 28, 1776, quoted in William S. Stryker, *The Battles of Trenton and Princeton* (Boston, 1898), 371; and in Fischer, *Washington's Crossing*, 248.

116   "My blood chill'd . . . to bear." Joseph White, *A Narrative of Events, as They Occurred from Time to Time, in the Revolutionary War, with an Account of the Battles of Trenton, Trenton-Bridge, and Princeton* (Charlestown, MA: 1833), 77, quoted in Fischer, *Washington's Crossing*, 248.

117   "reeled in the saddle." Fischer, *Washington's Crossing*, 246–48.

117   "March on, my brave fellows, after me!" *The Revolutionary Services of John Greenwood of Boston and New York, 1775–1783* (New York: De Vinne Press, 1922), 83.

117   "Sir, they have . . . and German." William M. Dwyer, *The Day Is Ours! An Inside View of the Battles of Trenton and Princeton, November 1776–January 1777* (New York: Viking, 1983), 259.

117   "[Prisoners] should have . . . unfortunate brethen." Chernow, *Washington: A Life*, 282.

117   "policy of humanity." Charles Francis Adams, ed., *Familiar Letters of John Adams and His Wife Abigail Adams* (New York: Hurd and Houghton and Cambridge: Riverside Press, 1876), 247.

117   Note on treatment of prisoners: Fighting in the South or Southern Department was more violent and involved many clashes between Loyalist and Whig partisan units that did not view quarter in a uniform manor. But Continentals treated prisoners properly in both the North and the South.

117–18   "With [Hessian] brass . . . or Defense." Joseph Reed, "General Joseph Reed's Narrative of the Movements of the American Army in the Neighborhood of Trenton in the Winter of 1776–77," *Pennsylviania Magazine of History and Biography*, December 1, 1884, 391–92.

118   "as many muskets . . . and swords." George Washington to John Hancock, December 27, 1776 Founders online: NARA.

118   "very trifling indeed . . . privates wounded." Dwyer, *The Day Is Ours!* 271.

118–19   "My brave fellows . . . other circumstances." Sergeant R—, "The Battle of Princeton," *Wellsborough* (Pennsylvania), *Phoenix*, March 24, 1832, quoted in Fischer, *Washington's Crossing*, 272–73.

119   "most affectionate manner." Ibid.

119   "Defend the bridge . . . man, excellency." Custis, Lee, and Lossing, *Recollections and Private Memoirs of Washington*, 413.

119–20   "This was the . . . and them." Robert Beale, "Revolutionary Experiences of Major Robert Beale," *Northern Neck of Virginia Historical Magazine* 6 (1956): 500–6.

120   "If there ever . . . valorous sons." James Wilkinson, *Memoirs of My Own Times* (Philadelphia: Abraham Small, 1816; reprint, 1923), 1:138.

120   "On one hour . . . conquered rebels!" Edwin Martin Stone, *The Life and Recollections of John Howland* (Providence, RI: George H. Whitney, 1857), 74.

120   "Well, boys, you . . . leg them." Harry M. Ward, *Charles Scott and the Spirit of '76* (Charlottesville: University Press of Virginia, 1988), 27.

121   "The noble horse . . . and station." Stone, *Life and Recollections*, 74.

121   "The enemy came . . . soon defeated." Ward, *Delaware Continentals*, 142.

122   "They continued to . . . and fled." Dwyer, *The Day Is Ours!* 323.

122   "Officers reformed the . . . the bridge." Ibid.

122   "It was then . . . one man." Ibid.

122   "They came on . . . cannot conceive." Ibid.

122   "The bridge looked . . . red coats." White, *Narrative*, 74–79.

122   "Their dead bodies . . . just passed." Pension application of William Hutchinson, NARA.

122   "We've got the . . . the morning." Benton Rain Patterson, *Washington and Cornwallis* (Lanham, MD: Taylor Trade Publishing, 2004), 95.

CHAPTER 16: PRINCETON

126   "Orders were given . . . lightly planted." Trevelyan, *The American Revolution*, pt. 2, 2:144.

126   "The morning was . . . every object." Wilkinson, *Memoirs of My Own Times*, 141.

126–27   "We drew up . . . Brigade lay." H. C. Wylly, ed., *1913 Regimental Annual, The Sherwood Foresters* (London, 1913), 18, quoted in Fischer, *Washington's Crossing*, 329.

127   Mawhood's troop numbers from Fischer, *Washington's Crossing*, 330.

127   "remaining fragment." Samuel Stelle Smith, *The Battle of Trenton/The Battle of Princeton: Two Studies* (Monmouth Beach, NJ: Westholme Publishing, 2009), 20.

127   "rushed without reconnoitering . . . of cannon." Ibid.

127   "too far off." Ibid., 24.

127   "so that every . . . fire incessantly." Ibid.

127   "threw the whole in confusion." Ibid.

128   "expostulated to no purpose." Ibid.

128   "Parade with us . . . them directly." Douglas Southall Freeman, *George Washington: A Biography*, 7 vols. (New York: Scribner, 1948–1957).

128   "O my Susan! . . . of myself." James Read, letter, 1777, in *The Pennsylvania Magazine of History and Biography* 16:465–66.

128   "They fly, the day is our own." "An Account of the Battle of Princeton. From the *Pennsylvania Evening Post,* Jan. 16, 1777, Extract of a letter from an Officer of Distinction in General Washington's Army, Jan. 5, 1777," in *Pennsylvania Magazine of History* 8, no. 3 (October 1884):310–12.

128   "It is a fine fox chase, my boys!" Wilkinson, *Memoirs of My Own Times,* 1:145.

129   "all the blood . . . the surface." Smith, *The Battle of Trenton/The Battle of Princeton,* 27.

129   "Gen'l Washington . . . and people." Pension application of Jesse Ford, NARA.

129   "The achievements of . . . military achievements." North Callahan, *Henry Knox: General Washington's General* (New York: Rinehart, 1958), 98.

130   "Thus had times . . . our defense." Ewald, *Diary of the American War,* 44–45 for entry of December 30–31, 1776.

130   "a church, a tavern, . . . better sort." Ward, *The War of the Revolution,* 319.

130–31   "The Tories in . . . the Whiggs." In Maryland Archives Online.

131   "an armed force, . . . their country." Theodore Corbett, *Revolutionary Chestertown: Loyalists and Rebels on Maryland's Eastern Shore* (Charleston, SC: History Press, 2014), 113.

131   "their ravaging and . . . of Gold." New, *Maryland Loyalists in the American Revolution,* 40.

132   "but, undismayed, [she] . . . the rebel." Ibid., 50.

132   "a suit of clothes yearly." "Instructions to Recruiting Officers," October 23, 1776," *Peter Force's American Archives,* 5th series, 2:1204.

132   Information on difficulty in recruiting troops from Charles H. Lesser, ed., *Sinews of Independence: Monthly Strength Reports of the Continenetal Army* (Chicago: University of Chicago Press, 1976), 54.

133   "the whole Army, . . . the smallpox." Pension application of John Boudy (Bondy, Bodray), NARA.

133   "fired by the love of liberty." Richard Pindell, "A Militant Surgeon of the Revolution: Some Letters of Richard Pindell, M.D.," *Maryland Historical Magazine Vols. 17–18* (MHS: Baltimore, 1922), 309–23

133   "repeatedly rejected the . . . for life." Ibid.

134   Information on Revolutionary-era medicine from Elizabeth Rorke, "Surgeons and Butchers," Brandywine Battlefield Historic Site, http://www. ushistory.org/brandywine/special/art06.htm.

134   "Our hospital, or . . . wretched clothing." Anthony Wayne to Gates, December 1, 1776, *Peter Force's American Archives,* 5th series, 3:1032.

135   Information on troop strength from Ward, *Delaware Continentals,* 162.

136 "The whole of . . . then retreated." Joseph Nourse, February 29, 1777, *Peter Force's American Archives*, 5th series, 3:1031.

136 Information on troop strength from Fischer, *Washington's Crossing*, 359.

137 "whose head was . . . of him." Papers of Captain William Beatty, MHS.

137 "mostly Barefoot though . . . us Daily." John Sullivan to George Washington, letter, August 7, 1777, Sullivan Papers, Rhode Island Historical Society, 1:423–27.

137 "The court passed . . . the road." William Beatty, Journal, MHS.

138 "only those who . . . a march." From Ward, *Delaware Continentals*, 179, citing Sullivan Papers, 1:437.

138 "My line of . . . then run." Anderson, *Personal Recollections*.

138–39 "Our people [were] . . . were ineffectual." Ward, *Delaware Continentals*, 179.

139 "lawful plunder." Anderson, *Personal Recollections*.

139 "Run, run, . . . safe over." AIbid.

139–40 "They came down . . . the Barn." Spelling errors have been corrected from the original. Normally, the author attempts to preserve the original language, including the spelling errors, but in this case, there were so many errors that the text became difficult to read. Francis B. Culver, "General Sullivan's Descent upon the British on Staten Island—The Escape of William Wilmot," *Maryland Historical Magazine* 6, no. 2 (June 1911).

CHAPTER 17: BRANDYWINE

141 "[No] dancing along . . . the case." George Washington, General Orders, August 23, 1777, *Papers of George Washington*, Revolutionary War Series, 9:127.

141 "with a lively smart step." Chernow, *Washington: A Life*.

141–42 "We have such . . . the enemy." Ibid.

142 "I confess the . . . our comprehension." Ibid.

142 "must mean to . . . strange one." Ibid.

142 "they are utterly . . . strenuous exertions." Ibid.

144 "As the Approach . . . respective camps." William Beatty, Journal, MHS.

144 "*Marsch, schräg nach rechts! . . . Angriff!* (Charge!)" McGuire, *The Philadelphia Campaign: Brandywine and the Fall of Philadelphia* (Mechaniecsburg, PA: Stockpole Books, 2006), 216.

145 "The balls [were] . . . the grapeshot." Robert Middlekauff, *The Glorious Cause: The American Revolution, 1763–1789*, rev. ed. (Oxford and New York: Oxford University Press, 2005), 394.

145　"Colonel [Nathaniel] Ramsay . . . the Yagars." Samuel Smith Papers, Columbia University Library.

145　"much stained with blood." Sheer and Rankin, *Rebels and Redcoats*, 270.

146　"The general was . . . fallen in." Joseph Townsend, "Some Account of the Adventures of One Day—The Memorable September 11th, 1777," Historical Society of Pennsylvania.

146　"I neither knew . . . with them." Stephenson, *Patriot Battles*, 274.

146　"rode up to Consult the other General officers." Ibid.

147　"By the time . . . of battle." John Stone to William Paca, letter, September 23, 1777, in Scharf, *Chronicles of Baltimore*, 166–68.

148　"Lord Cornwallis's men . . . good order." McGuire, *The Philadelphia Campaign: Brandywine and the Fall of Philadelphia*, 222.

148　"received a wound . . . Winter following." Pension application of John Boudy (Bondy, Bodray), NARA.

148　"The firing, while . . . war began." Joseph Clark, Diary, New Jersey Historical Society, 256.

148　"During the fight . . . our discomfiture." Pension application of Henry Wells (Wales), NARA.

148　"The American fire . . . wings collapsed." McGuire, *The Philadelphia Campaign: Brandywine and the Fall of Philadelphia*, 223.

148　"I rallied a . . . Bristled Bayonetts." Pindell, "Militant Surgeon," 308–20.

148–49　"We began to . . . their batteries." Francis Downman, *The Services of Lieut.-Colonel Francis Downman, R.A. in France, North America, and the West Indies between the Years 1758 and 1784*, Colonel F. A. Whinyates, ed. (Woolwich, UK: Royal Artillery Institution, 1898), 33.

149　"We renew our . . .all quarters." Ibid.

149　"Never was a . . . and wounded." Scharf, *Chronicles of Baltimore*, 167.

149　"well over six . . . great strength." William L. Calderhead, "Thomas Carney: Unsung Soldier of the American Revolution," *Maryland Historical Magazine* 84, no. 4 (Winter 1989):321.

149　"when said frigate . . . at Brandywine." Pension application of Michael Ellis, NARA.

149　"wounded in the hand and in the face." Pension application of Jacob Allen, NARA.

149–50　"We were led . . . this day." Pension application of Henry Wells (Wales), NARA.

150　"We retreated about . . . great execution." Scharf, *History of Maryland*, 321.

150　"discovered a flanking . . . near sunset." Samuel Smith Papers, Columbia University Library.

150 "assured him he . . . forced me!" J. Smith Futhey and Gilbert Cope, *History of Chester County, Pennsylvania* (Philadelphia: Louis H. Everts, 1881), 80.

CHAPTER 18: WAYNE'S AFFAIR

151 "Oh my Daddy's killed, my dear Daddy's killed!" Persifor Frazer, *General Persifor Frazer: A Memoir Compiled Principally from His Own Papers by His Great-Grandson* (Philadelphia, 1907), 155–56.

151 "I fought with . . . to me." Ward, *Delaware Continentals*, 537.

152 "Every one Rejoiced . . . few hours." Journal and Order Book of Captain Robert Kirkwood of the Delaware Regiment of the Continental Line, Delaware Historical Society, 167–70.

152 "The order of . . . immediately arranged." Futhey and Cope, *History of Chester County*, 83.

152 "An extraordinary thunderstorm . . . the world." Ewald, *Diary of the American War*, 89.

153 "The inferiority of . . . this occasion." Howard to Bentalou, March 1826, Bayard Papers, MHS.

153 "Hard rain that . . . the arms." Papers of Captain William Beatty, MHS.

153 "cutting off the . . . of Ambuscades." Washington to Brigadier Gneral Anthony Wayne, September 18, 1777, Washington Papers, Library of Congress; Fitzpatrick, *The Writings of George Washington*: 235–36.

153 "I believe a . . . human gore!" Chernow, *Washington: A Life*, 361.

153 "surprise these gentlemen . . . a frolic." Nahum Parker Journal, September 20, 1777, Parker Family Papers, NARA.

154 "Turn out my . . . the Smoak." Martin Hunter, *The Journal of Gen. Sir Martin Hunter*, James Hunter, Anne Hunter, and Elizabeth Bell eds. (Edinburgh: Edinburg Press, 1894), 29–30.

154 "Dash, Light Infantry!" "HUZZAH!" Ibid.

154 "One of our . . . of since." Smallwood to Johnson, September 23, 1777, MHS, MSS 1875.

154 "The Rear taking . . . their friends." Ibid.

154 "My Horse received . . . their Hands." Mordecai Gist to John Smith, September 23, 1777, Emmet Collection, Manuscripts and Archives Division, New York Public Library, Astor, Lenox and Tilden Foundation, no. 6610.

155 "The fire of . . . from foe." Hamilton B. Tompkins, "Contemporary Account of the Battle of Germantown," *Pennsylvania Magazine of History and Biography* 11, no. 3 (October 1887):330–31.

156–57 "encampment of the British . . . and retreated." "Col. John Eager Howard's Account of the Battle of Germantown," *Maryland Historical Magazine* 4, no. 4 (December 1909):314.

157 "survived the hottest . . . little red." Papers of Captain William Beatty, MHS.

157 "engaged from behind . . . the field." "Col. John Eager Howard's Account of the Battle of Germantown," 315.

158 "the rebels pressed . . . the door." "Battle of German Town from a British Account," *Pennsylvania Magazine of History and Biography* 11, no. 1 (April 1887):113.

158 "was wounded at . . . back bone." Pension application of James Keelan (Keland), NARA.

158 "Hurrah to the King! Hurrah to the English." McGuire, *The Philadelphia Campaign: Germantown and the Roads to Valley Forge* (Mechanicsburg, PA: Stokpole Books, 2007).

158-59 "The Bravest [Americans] . . . great Slaughter." Jeremiah Green-man, *Diary of a Common Soldier in the American Revolution*, Robert C. Bray and Paul E. Bushnell, eds. (DeKalb: Northen Illinois University Press, 1978), 82.

159 "Seventy-five dead Americans . . . spattered around." Chernow, *Washington: A Life*.

159 Numbers of Loyalist troops provided by author and historian Don N. Hagist.

159 "We drove the . . . proper place." Asher Holmes to Sallie, letter, October 6, 1777, in George Crawford Beekman, *Early Dutch Settlers of Momnouth County, New Jersey* (Freehold, NJ: Moreau Bros., 1901), 118.

159–60 "A thick foggy . . . their line." Mordecai Gist Papers, MHS.

160 "A few Minutes . . . several redoubts." Ibid.

160 "found that the . . . to Maryland." Ibid.

160 "We are still . . . our advantage." James Cox to Mary Cox, letter, October 3, 1777, James Cox Papers, MHS.

160 "Your loving husband. . . hour afterwards." George Welsh to Mary Cox, letter, October 7, 1777, in Scharf, *Chronicles of Baltimore*, 165–66.

160 "brave and valuable officer." Ibid., 166.

161 "The Weakness of . . . the Ground." Mordecai Gist Papers, MHS.

161 "Upon our troops . . . the pursuit," "Battle of German Town from a British Account," 114.

161 "The enemy sallied . . . checked them." "Col. John Eager Howard's Account of the Battle of Germantown," *Maryland Historical Magazine* 4, no. 4 (December 1909):314.

161   "When Cornwallis Coming . . . to retreat." William Beatty, Journal, MHS, 9.

161   "They appeared to . . . from us." Thomas Paine to Benjamin Franklin, letter, May 16, 1778, *The Writings of Thomas Paine* (New York and London: G. P. Putnam's Sons, 1906).

162   "The British Grenadiers . . . move off." Officer B [Wetherall], *British Journal, 1776–1778*, Feinstone Collection, in McGuire, *The Philadelphia Campaign: Germantown*, 48.

162   "It was a . . . for us." Chernow, *Washington: A Life*, 311.

162   "nothing struck him so much." Ibid.

CHAPTER 19: MUD ISLAND

164   "to defend [Fort Mifflin] to their last extremity." Martin, *Private Yankee Doodle*, 90–91.

164   "The keeping of . . . persevering defense." Washington to Smith, letter, September 23, 1777, *Papers of George Washington*, Revolutionary War Series, Volume 12; Samuel Smith Papers, Columbia University Library.

164   "nothing more than . . . hewn stone." Martin, *Private Yankee Doodle*, 49.

164   "The island, because . . . by assault." Lt. Col. Von Cochenhausen to Major General von Jungkenn, letter, November 28, 1777, in "The Philadelphia Campaign, 1777–1778, Letters and Reports from the von Jungkenn Papers," *Journal of the Johannes Schwalm Historical Association* 6, no. 2 (1998):18.

164   "He is a Young . . . public service." Samuel Smith, "The Papers of General Samuel Smith. The General's Autobiography," in The Historical Magazine Vol VII., No. 2 (February 1870): 87.

165   "sinister black painted." Fischer, *Washington's Crossing*, 134. Details on the navy and guns from the same source.

165   "A mosquito couldn't live there under my guns." Smith, *Autobiography*, 87.

165   "A shell would sink any of my galleys." Ibid.

165   "Yes, and falling . . . or paid." Ibid.

166   "fired two shot . . . of Artillery." Smith to Washington, letter, October 11, 1777, *Maryland Historical Magazine, 1910*, 5:214; Washington Papers, Library of Congress; Smith Papers, MHS.

166   "conveyed it to a Major Stuart." Samuel Smith Papers, Columbia University Library.

166   "Yesterday a red . . . more damage." Smith to Washington, letter, October 20, 1777. NARA.

166   "The rebels opened . . . our guns." Downman, *The Services of Lieut.-Colonel Francis Downman*, 42.

166   "they fired a . . . so accurately." Münchhausen, *Diary*, 43.

167   "Our men were . . . be broiled." Martin, *Private Yankee Doodle*, 49. The wounded included Marylander Neal Peacock.

167–168   "What are you . . . to lose!" Smith to Washington, letter, October 11, 1777, *Maryland Historical Magazine, 1910*, Volume 5; Washington Papers, Library of Congress; Smith Papers, MHS.

168   "[De Fleury] was . . . stroke at." Martin, *Private Yankee Doodle*, 50.

168   "We would watch . . . us out." Ibid.

168   "The enemy are . . . next week." Greene to Washington, letter, November 14, 1777, *Maryland Historical Magazine, 1910*, 5:214; Washington Papers, Library of Congress; Smith Papers, MHS.

168   "I wish we . . . cursed fort." Münchhausen, *Diary*, 43–44.

168   "I imprudently went . . . the Chimney." Smith to Washington, letter, November 12, 1777, *Maryland Historical Magazine, 1910* 5:214; Washington Papers, Library of Congress; Smith Papers, MHS.

168   "rolled over and . . . front door." Smith, *Autobiography*, 89–90.

169   "some of our . . . for duty." De Fleury to Washington, letter, November 12, 1777, NARA.

169   "The flag was . . . this evening." Greene to Washington, letter, November 14, 1777, NARA.

169   "very severe . . . firing range." Ibid.

170   "amusing himself in . . . the cellar." Martin Luther Brown, *Baroness von Riedesel and the American Revolution* (Chapel Hill: University of North Carolina Press, 1965), 55–59.

172   "I believe no . . . heartfelt joy." Washington to Continental Congress, Washington Papers, Library of Congress.

172   "This morning . . . Main Channel." Greenman, *Diary*, 85.

172   "Mud Island was . . . lay about." Loos to Junkenn, "In Camp near Philadelphia 30 October 1777," cited by McGuire, *The Philadelphia Campaign: Germantown*.

173   "Up with the . . . was here." Martin, *Private Yankee Doodle*, 52.

173   "We left our . . . the island." Ibid.

173   "hid himself in . . . our lines." Münchhausen, *Diary*, 43.

173   "having taken too . . . British uniform." Martin, *Private Yankee Doodle*, 54.

173   "Colonel Osborn took . . . and bloodstains." Cochenhausen to Jungkenn, letter, November 28, 1777, cited by McGuire, *The Philadelphia Campaign: Germantown*.

174   "The house of . . . been there." Bruce Burgoyne, *Enemy Views: The American Revolutionary War as Recorded by the Hessian Participants* (Berwyn Heights, MD: Heritage Books, 2009), 236.

174 "hauled down the . . . English Jack." McGuire, *The Philadelphia Campaign: Germantown.*

174 "trifling snow." *The Montresor Journals*, G. D. Scull, ed. (Ann Arbor: University of Michigan Library, 1882), 477.

CHAPTER 20: VALLEY FORGE AND WILMINGTON

175 "The only alternative . . . frozen ground." Martin, *Private Yankee Doodle*, 58.

175 "not only starved . . . especially blankets." Ibid.

176 "Poor food—hard . . . and discouraged." Diary of Surgeon Albigence Waldo, of the Connecticut Line, Valley Forge, 1777–1778, Historical Society of Pennsylvania.

176 "three or four . . . our destruction." Washington to Continental Congress, letter, December 23, 1777, *Papers of George Washington*, LOC.

177 "Naked and starving . . . the soldiery." Washington to Governor George Clinton, letter, February 16, 1778. Washington Papers, LOC.

177 "Our army suffered . . .collect provisions." Pension application of John Boudy (Bondy, Bodray), NARA.

177 "a smart widower . . . brave officer." Sally Wister, *Journal* (Philadelphia, PA: Ferris & Leach Publishers, 1902).

177 "I have been . . . my design." Mordecai Gist Papers, MHS..

177 "I have the . . . his subjects." Ibid.

178 "The enchanting pleasures . . . his Country." Gist to Steward, June 13, 1777, New York Public Library Collection. The author has complete copies of the Gist letterbook and letters in the Emmett and Meyers Collections at the New York Public Library and has spent hundreds of hours interpreting General Gist's penmanship.

178 "1st with wounding . . . and Discipline." George Washington, General Orders, December 3, 1777, *Papers of George Washington*.

178 "however Justifiable the . . . a riot." Ibid.

178 "Scandalous and Infamous . . . disorderly manner." "The Journal of Lieut. William Feltman, 1781–1782," Collections of the Historical Society of Pennsylvania, 319.

179 "Maryland officers in . . . other corps." Peale, *Autobiography*, 5:125.

179 "fared very . . . Prize of cloathing." William Beatty, Journal, MHS.

179 "very unpopular, owing . . . of Motion." *Papers of Nathanael Greene* (Chapel Hill: University of North Carolina Press, 1980), 2:366–67.

179 "A pretty Condition . . . the morning," George Luck to Nathanael Greene, letter, *Papers of Nathanael Greene*, 2:367.

179 "[Chaplin] and sixteen . . . leave America." *London Morning Post*, June 2, 1778.

179–180 "Lieutenant General in the King of Prussia's service." Benjamin Franklin, *The Complete Works of Benjamin Franklin* (New York and London: G. P. Putnam's Sons, 1888), 6:105.

180 "Over here! Swear at him for me!" Austin Washington, *The Education of George Washington* (Washington, DC: Regnery History, 2014), 244.

CHAPTER 21: "A DAMNED POLTROON"

184 "to face about . . . the Rebels." O'Shaughnessy, *The Men Who Lost America*, 221.

184 "I desire to . . . and confusion." Lee P. Anderson, *Forgotten Patriot: The Life and Times of Major-General Nathanael Greene* (Columbia: University of South Carolina Press, 2012), 162.

184 "a damned poltroon." Ibid.

184 "a terrific eloquence of unprintable scorn." Ibid.

185 "It was at . . . from heaven." Ibid.

185 "General Washington was . . . the troops." Harlow Giles Unger, *Lafayette* (Hoboken, NJ: John Wiley, 2002), 79.

185 "If you can . . . my army!" *Col. N. Ramsay—A Monograph Published by the MHS*, Fund Publication no. 24.

185 "I will stop them or fall." Ibid.

186 "rather noted . . . the line." Scharf, *History of Maryland*, 333.

186 "making it equal . . . whole army." Ibid.

186 "Our Great good . . . the Artillery." Otho Holland Williams to Philip Thomas, letter, June 29, 1778, Otho Holland Williams Papers, MHS.

187 "prisoners" and "endeavoured . . . situation permitted." Peale, *Autobiography*, 5:126.

187 "the very flower . . . the army." Stryker, *Battles of Trenton and Princeton*, 212.

188 "While in the . . . her occupation." Martin, *Private Yankee Doodle*. 75.

188 "The Whole of . . . all night." William Beatty, Journal, MHS.

188 "The Enemy took . . . had taken." Ibid., 12.

189 "Three sergeants, fifty-six rank and file died with fatigue." Henry Beebee Carrington, *Battles of the American Revolution* (London, 1904; reprint, Forgotten Books, 2013), 444.

190 "I have never . . . cross belts." Charles Albert Moré, Chevalier de Pontgibaud, *A French Volunteer of the War of Independence*, Robert B. Douglas, ed. and trans. (New York: D. Appleton, 1898), 93.

190 "It is a maxim . . . its interest." George Washington to Henry Laurens, letter, *Papers of George Washington.*

190 "his hand under . . . of water." John Adams, *The Works of John Adams, Second President of the United States* (Boston: Little, Brown and Company, 1853), 8:4.

CHAPTER 22: LIGHT INFANTRY

191 "[I am] old and would die here!" J. G. Simcoe, *Simcoe's Military Journal* (New York: Bartlett and Welford, 1844), 86.

192 "a Corps of . . . Partizan Officers." George Washington, General Orders, August 8, 1778, *Papers of George Washington.*

192 "alertness, daring, and military efficiency." Ward, *Delaware Continentals*, 296.

193 "Our light infantry . . . superior party." Benjamin Ford to Governor Johnson, September 1778 (Camp White Plains), MSA.

193 "It won't be . . . this occasion." Ibid.

194 Details of British troops from O'Shaughnessy, *The Men Who Lost America*, 224.

194 "With the present . . . of arms." Ibid., 163.

194 "If fifty thousand . . . far extended." Ibid.

CHAPTER 23: DESPOTS

199 "charged with disobedience . . . in chief." Otho Williams to Elie Williams, letter, July 6, 1778, in *Calendar of the General Otho Holland Williams Papers in the MHS* (Baltimore: Maryland Historical Records Survey Project, 1940), 5.

199 "most important [trial] that has occurred so far." Ibid.

199 "Captain [Edward] Norwood . . . of honour." *Maryland Gazette*, January 5, 1779.

200 "for only saying . . . precarious tenure." Ibid.

200 "Your scurrilous observations . . . of camp." Maryland Officers to William Smallwood, March 1, 1780, in Scharf, *Chronicles of Baltimore*, 183–85.

200 "not furnishing the . . . military manner." George Washington, General Orders, March 22, 1780, *Papers of George Washington.*

200 "Was present when . . .were frozen." Gassaway Watkins, Journal, MHS.

200 "in general the . . . and unmilitary." Washington, General Orders, March 22, 1780.

201 "painful as it . . . of orders." Ibid.; George Washington to Arthur St. Clair, February 24, 1780, *Papers of George Washington.*

201 "It is with . . . Excellency's orders." Mordecai Gist to George Washington,

February 18, 1779, Gist Letterbook, Meyers Collection, New York Public Library.

201   "like those from a favorite son." Otho Holland Williams Papers, November 22, 1779, MHS.

201   Among them was Lieutenant James Peale, who resumed his life as an artist. Pension application of James Peale, NARA.

202   Details on substitutes from William Richardson to Governor, June 14, 1778, Maryland State Archives, MSA.

203   Inflation figures from O'Shaughnessy, *The Men Who Lost America*, 147.

203   "a bad supper . . . thousand dollars!" Freidrich Kapp, *The Life of John Kalb, Major-General in the Revolutionary Army* (Bedford, MA: Applewood Books, 1884), 184.

204   "We have the . . . exorbitant prices." Michael S. Adelberg, *The American Revolution in Monmouth County: The Theatre of Spoil and Destruction* (Charleston, SC: History Press, 2010), 65.

204   "Col. Gist has . . . at Middletown." Ibid., 66.

205   "continued very peaceable . . . was 22." William Beatty, Journal, MHS, 17.

CHAPTER 24: THE GIBRALTAR OF AMERICA— THE MIDNIGHT STORMING OF STONY POINT

207   "Should there be . . . to death." General Anthony Wayne, Order of Battle, July 15, 1779, in Henry Dawson, *The Assault on Stony Point* (New York: New-York Historical Society, 1863), 38.

207   "The column was . . . the body." Hull Manuscript, *Magazine of American History* 28 (1892):182–83.

207   "You performed a . . . Be satisfied." Ibid.

207   "desperadoes led by officers of distinguished merit." Ward, *Delaware Continentals*, 305.

209   "like a parcel of devils." Woodhull to Malcolm, letter, 7 June 1779, in Henry Phelps Johnston, *The Storming of Stony Point on the Hudson* (New York: James T. White, 1900), 154.

209   "Pillars of Hercules . . . of America." Washington Irving, *A History of New York*, (Philadelphia: Inskeep & Bradford, 1809).

210   "The importance of . . . the fortifications." George Washington to Anthony Wayne, letter, July 1, 1779, in *The Life of General Washington, First President of the United States*, Charles Wentworth Upham, ed. (London: Office of the National Illustrated Library, 1851), 349.

211   "I have now . . . of them." Washington to Major Henry Lee Jr., letter, June 28, 1779, ibid., 348–49.

212 "What do you . . . Washington out?" McLane Manuscript, New-York Historical Society, NYHS.

212 "I know nothing . . . attempt impossibilities." Ibid.

212 "only obstructed by a slight abatis." George Washington to Anthony Wayne, letter, July 9, 1779, *The Writings of George Washington*, Worthington Chauncey Ford, ed. (New York and London: G.P. Putnam's Sons and Knickerbocker Press, 1890), 486–87.

212–13 "My ideas for . . . from them." George Washington to Anthony Wayne, letter, July 10, 1779, ibid.

213 "Conceal the intended . . . your hopes." Ibid.

213 Some information about Steward and Gassaway Watkins comes from the pension application of Michael Ellis, NARA: "He joined the Maryland troops at Wilmington on the Brandywine, then continued with them as a Volunteer till after the battle of Monmouth (not then enlisting) having escaped from on board a British man of War and landed at Chester on the Delaware and he was captured by said man of War (the Daphne a twenty gun sloop commanded by Capt. McKendrick) on a voyage from Charleston to Hispaniola and after the Battle of Monmouth he is listed in the 2nd Maryland Regiment Capt. Longs company, Long resigned shortly after he joined the Company and John Gassaway took the command of s'd company and I continued in said company about three years, that his company was at West Point when Wayne stormed Stony and some of the men of his company volunteered on that expedition. Woolford was the Colonel and John Stewart the Major of the Regiment to which this Company belonged that Stewart went with Wayne to storm Stony Point and was called by the British Lucy Jack as he understood."

213 "spoke very clever." Pension application of Vincent Vass, NARA.

214 Information about Elias Pollock from pension application of Elias Pollock, NARA.

214 "fresh shaved and well powdered." Ward, *Delaware Continentals*, 297.

214–15 "I must acknowledge . . . other Virtue." Anthony Wayne to George Washington, letter, July 4, 1779, in Paul David Nelson, *Anthony Wayne, Soldier of the Early Republic* (Bloomington: Indiana University Press, 1985), 3.

215 "We were to . . . our canteens," Pension application of Vincent Vass, NARA.

215 "much of the . . . the distance." Dawson, *Assault on Stony Point*, 41–42.

215 "Off we went . . . every difficulty." Pension application of Vincent Vass, NARA.

215 "I am called . . . Other World." Dawson, *Assault on Stony Point*, 46–47.

215 "we had white . . . our hats." Pension application of Vincent Vass, NARA.

215 "Guards were placed . . . person passing." Pension application of Robert Devin, NARA.

216 "I heard the . . . TOWARD us." Court-martial of Lt. Col. Henry Johnson, Public Records Office (PRO), Kew.

216 "often courted Danger beyond his tour of Duty." Pension application of Richard Waters, NARA.

216 "Lotts were drawn . . . upon me." John Gibbon to Capt. Allan McLane, letter, November 27, 1871, McLane Papers, New-York Historical Society.

217 "[We] fired five or six rounds a man." Court-martial of Lt. Col. Henry Johnson, PRO.

217 "A large body . . . to defend." Ibid.

217 "passing the abatis . . . know it." Pension application of Noel Battles, NARA.

217 "[My commanding officer] . . . his firelock." Testimony of Lt. John Ross, court-martial of Lt. Col. Henry Johnson, PRO.

217–18 "[*One of my men*] . . . damned Scoundrel!" Ibid.

218 "The Cannon was . . . this time." Pension application of Thomas Pope, NARA.

218 "Seventeen out of . . . the three-pounder." Testimony of Lt. William Hornden, Royal Artillery, court-martial of Lt. Col. Henry Johnson, Public Records Office (PRO). The author accessed the originals, located in the Public Records Office in Kew. Most of the original language was retained, although some spelling was modernized and pronouns were occasionally changed from third to first person. Another fine book—Don Loprieno, *The Enterprise in Contemplation: The Midnight Assault of Stony Point* (Westminster, MD: Heritage Books, 2009)—also contains a copy of Johnson's court-martial.

218 "The rebels are . . . [him] insensible." Court-martial of Lt. Col. Henry Johnson, PRO.

218 "Face the damn rascals!" Ibid.

219 "Damn ye, who are you!" Ibid.

219 "narrowly escaped from that party." Ibid.

219 "muddy to the . . . to rags." Ward, *Delaware Continentals*, 299.

219 "John O'Hara received . . . through life." Pension application of John O'Hara, NARA.

219 "Father Joseph Coffman . . . Stony Point." Pension application of Joseph Coffman, NARA.

219 "[I] escaped receiving . . . literally riddled." Pension application of Isaac Jackson, Virginia, NARA.

220 "in the hottest . . . the Slaughter." Pension application of Peter Francisco, NARA.

220 "spear in hand," Dawson, *The Assault on Stony Point*, 50.

220 "Forward, my brave fellows, forward!" Ibid.

220 "For God's sake . . . the water?" John Roberts, deposition, court-martial of Lt. Col. Henry Johnson, PRO.

221 "The Enemy were . . . the Barrier." Ibid.

221 "told us we . . . upper works." Deposition of Simon Davies, ibid.

221 "He ordered two . . . in front." Ibid.

221 "offered if we . . . the shipping." Ibid.

221 "Throw down your . . . our rear." Ibid.

221–22 "[I] forded a . . . I swam." Testimony of Lt. John Roberts of the Royal Artillery, ibid.

222 "The fort's our own!" Johnston, *The Storming of Stony Point*, 191.

222 "blares of Cannon . . . my thigh." Pension application of Vincent Vass, NARA, Fold3.

222 "My messmate Samuel . . . took place." Ibid.

222 "endured all the . . . was wounded." Pension application of Peter H. Triplett, NARA.

222 "Colonel Flury [de Fleury] struck the colors with his hands." Pension application of Vincent Vass, NARA.

222 Detail about de Fleury not accepting the bounty is from pension application of Thomas Craig, NARA.

222 Detail on bounty recipients from Ward, *Delaware Continentals*, 300.

223 "Quarters, quarters brave . . . quarter, quarter!" Pension application of Vincent Vass, NARA.

223 "I was far . . . ten yards." Julia Isabel Jarvis, *Three Centuries of Robinsons: The Story of a Family* (Toronto: J. Jarvis, 1967), 78–79.

223 Thirty-three minutes. A British soldier recalled that an American officer looked at his watch just before the assault. Court-martial of Lt. Col. Henry Johnson, PRO.

223 Additional detail on losses: The light infantry lost 15 men killed and 84 wounded, while the British lost 20 killed, 74 wounded, and 472 captured.

223 "Dear General,—The . . . be free." General Anthony Wayne's First Dispatch to General George Washington, in Henry B. Dawson, *Battles of the United States* (New York: Johnson, Fry, 1858), 524.

224 "were tried, Deserting . . . suffer Death." Edward Boynton, *The History of West Point* (Bedford, MA: Applewod Books, 1864), 83.

224 "At daylight the . . . the dead." Pension application of George Hood, April 23, 1829, NARA.

224 "It was a great . . . the Carolinas." Ward, *Delaware Continentals*, 537; Alexander Garden, *Anecdotes of the American Revolution* (Charleston, SC: A. E. Miller, 1828), 2:382.

CHAPTER 25: INTERLUDE

226 "The situation of . . . a fortnight." George Washington to Caesar Rodney, in H. Niles, *Principles and Acts of the Revolution* (Baltimore, MD: 1822), 332.

226 "almost perishing." Ward, *Delaware Continentals*, 316

226–27 "They have borne . . . necessary subsistence." George Washington to John Trumbull, January 1780, in Fitzpatrick, *The Writings of George Washington*, 366.

227 "The winter of . . . regiments mutinied." Pension application of John Boudy (Bondy, Bodray), NARA.

227 "the handkerchiefs covering . . . and brains." Gaines, *For Liberty and Glory*, 150.

228 Information on Henry Carbery from William Thompson, *Report of the Adjutant General of the State of Maryland* (New York: New York Public Library, 1912), 285–86.

228 "northern army was . . . military name." Otho Holland Williams to Forrest, letter, April 28, 1784, Otho Holland Williams Papers, MHS.

228 "A liberal dose . . . the trick." Stephenson, *Patriot Battles*, 99.

229 Information about Freemason members from William R. Denslow, *10,000 Famous Freemasons* (Richmond, VA: Macoy Publishing & Masonic Supply Co., 1957) and Freemasons Grand Lodge of Maryland, *Proceedings of the Grand Lodge of Maryland* (Baltimore: Griffin, Curley, 1887), 8.

229 "What we have . . . is immortal." Quote comes from noted Freemason Albert Pike, who was the only Confederate officer honored with an outdoor statue in Washington, DC

229–30 "Unhappily, the distinctions . . . in America." *National Freemason* 9, no. 9 (August 31, 1867):130.

230 "save us from . . . other Lodges." Ibid.

230 "When we contemplate . . . ancient fraternity." Ibid.

230 Details about Freemasons from Freemasons Grand Lodge of Maryland, *Proceedings of the Grand Lodge of Maryland*, 8.

CHAPTER 26: THE MARCH SOUTH

235 Mileage marched from Kirkwood, Journal and Order Book, Delaware Historical Society. Three hundred fifty miles were deducted from the total for when the men sailed from Head of Elk to Petersburg, VA.

238 "a perfect Ariovistus, more than six feet tall." Ward, *Delaware Continentals*, 289.

238 "temperance, sobriety, and . . . in lodging." Ibid., 289–90.

238 "inquire into the intentions of the inhabitants." Kapp. *The Life of John Kalb*, 47.

239 "as a provision in case of my being taken prisoner." John Eager Howard to Sheldenmire Estate, May 26, 1809, Bayard Papers, MHS.

241 "The officers, however . . . them example." Otho Holland Williams, "A Narrative of the Campaign of 1780" (hereafter cited as Williams, "Narrative"), in William Johnson, *Sketches of the Life and Correspondence of Nathanael Greene* (Charleston, SC: A. E. Miller, 1822; reprint, New York: Da Capo Press, 1973), 488–99. (Hereafter cited as Johnson, *Sketches*.)

241 "The tick, a . . . these stings." Kapp, *The Life of John Kalb*, 200, 201.

242 "a vast number . . . the enemy." William Seymour, *A Journal of the Southern Expedition, 1780–1783* (Wilmington: Historical Society of Delaware, 1896).

242 "rum and rations." Williams, "Narrative," 486.

243 "As for this . . . catch him." George F. Scheer, *The Elusive Swamp Fox* (New York: American Heritage, 1958).

243–44 "Fearless and inexorable . . . British regulars." Robert D. Bass, *Gamecock: The Life and Campaigns of General Thomas Sumter* (Orangeburg, SC: Sandlapper, 1961; reprinted 2000).

CHAPTER 27: A "JALAP" AND A NIGHT MARCH

245 "Instead of rum . . . to evacuate." Seymour, *Journal of the Southern Expedition*.

245 "I will breakfast . . . my table." This quotation was passed down by legend, but may have been false. It was quoted in William Gilmore Simms, *The Life of Nathanael Greene, Major General in the Army of the Revolution* (New York: Houghton Mifflin Company, 1884).

246 "fit for duty." Ward, *Delaware Continentals*, 352.

246 "Sir, it will be enough for our purpose." Johnson, *Sketches*, 485–500.

246 "overheard Gates and . . . battle plan." Pension application of Michael Awald, North Carolina Militia, 1832, NARA.

246 "Others could not . . . the enemy." Williams, "Narrative," in Johnson, *Sketches*, 493.

246–47 "Now, my brave . . . turn out." John Robert Shaw, *A Narrative of the Life and Travels of John Robert Shaw, the Well-Digger, Now Resident in Lexington, Kentucky* (Lexington, KY: Daniel Bradford, 1807).

247 "except a few . . . military stores." Ibid.

247 "executed their orders gallantly." Otho Holland Williams to his sister, letter, November 24, 1780, MHS.

247 "The enemy, no . . . of hostilities." Ibid.

247   "astonishment could not be concealed." Ibid.

248   "Well, And has . . . the Army?" Ibid.

248   "the unwelcome news" Ibid.

248   "Gentlemen, what is best to be done?" Ibid.

248   "remained mute for a few moments." Ibid.

248   "Gentlemen, is it . . . but fight?" Ibid.

CHAPTER 28: CAMDEN

249   "Don't shoot until . . . their eyes." Pension application of Vincent Vass, NARA.

249   "We see them . . . as ours." Ibid.

249   "seemed disposed to . . . as possible!" Otho Holland Williams to his sister, letter, November 24, 1780, MHS.

250   "[We] formed the . . . of Day." Journal of Captain Robert Kirkwood, August 16, 1780, Delaware Historical Society.

250   "I believe my . . . killing me." Pension application of William Gipson, NARA.

250   "almost instantly collapsed . . . utmost consternation." Lt. Col. H. L. Landers, F.A., *The Battle of Camden South Carolina August 16, 1780* (Washington, DC: United States Government Printing Office, 1929), 46.

250   "like electricity, it . . . it touches." Simms, *The Life of Nathaniel Greene*, 373.

250   "the action became . . . half an hour," Kirkwood, Journal.

251   "General Gist preserved . . . left division." Banastre Tarleton, *A History of the Campaigns of 1780 and 1781 in the Southern Provinces of North America* (London: T. Cadell, 1787).

251   "the ugliest officer" in the British Army. John S. Pancake, *This Destructive War: The British Campaign in the Carolinas, 1780–1782* (Tuscaloosa: University of Alabama Press, 1985), 193.

251   "The enemy threw . . . was [in] doubt." Matthew H. Spring, *With Zeal and with Bayonets Only: The British Army on the Campaign in North America, 1775–1783* (Norman: University of Oklahoma Press, 2010), 113–14.

251   "who had the . . . little emotion." Johnson, *Sketches*, 485–95.

251   "A dead calm . . . both sides." Tarleton, *A History of the Campaigns*, 128.

251   "with great coolness . . . soldier remembers." Spring, *With Zeal*, 114.

252   "Volunteers of Ireland, you are fine fellows! Charge the rascals—By heaven, you behave nobly!" Ibid., 114; *The London Chronicle* 48, no. 3729 (October 26, 1780):398; extract from letter by officer in the Volunteers of Ireland to his friend in Glasgow, 25 August 1780.

252 "[De Kalb] fell into . . . and hands." Jim Piecuch, *The Battle of Camden: A Documentary History* (Charleston, SC: History Press, 2006), 45–46.

252 "[I] called upon . . . with bayonets." Williams, "Narrative," 496.

252 "who, however, was not to be found." Johnson, *Sketches*, 496.

252–53 "The men, to . . . with them." Major Charles Magil to his father, letter, in Piecuch, *Battle of Camden*, 44.

253 "Rout and slaughter ensued in every quarter." Tarleton, *A History of the Campaigns*.

253 "Brigadier General Gist . . . of battle." Ibid.

254 "I am sorry . . . of man." Rufus Wilmot Griswold, William Gilmore Simms, and Edward Duncan Ingraham, *Washington and the Generals of the American Revolution* (Philadelphia: J. B. Lippincott, 1856), 271.

254 "I saw in . . . British troops." John J. Jacob, *A Biographical Sketch in the Life of the Late Captain Michael Cresap* (Cincinnati: J. F. Uhlhorn, 1866), 54. On John Eager Howard, see 42.

254 "who bore his part under Howard." William Calderhead, "Thomas Carney: Unsung Soldier of the American Revolution," *Maryland Historical Magazine* (1989): 119–26.

254 "I retreated with . . . a stand." Johnson, *Sketches*, 496–503.

254 "The cries of . . . [fled the battlefield]." Ibid.

255 Two hundred wagons and account of American plundering. Ibid.

255 "The road for . . . the Americans." Ibid.

255 "every day picking . . . of value." Seymour, *Journal of the Southern Expedition*, 7.

256 "capturing some, plundering . . . they met." Johnson, *Sketches*, 496–503.

256 "[I] was wounded . . . three months." Pension application of James Gooding, NARA.

256 "Our Regiment was . . . bad company." Ward, *Delaware Continentals*, 538.

256 "a great number . . . mortifying picture." Williams, "Narrative," in Johnson, *Sketches*, 1:501.

257 "was pursued by . . . the woods." Pension application of Gassaway Watkins, NARA; J. D. Warfield, *The Founders of Anne Arundel and Howard Counties, Maryland: A Genealogical and Biographical Review from Wills, Deeds, and Church Records* (Baltimore: Kohn and Pollock, 1905), 413–15.

257 "I can give . . . the 21st." Kirkwood, Journal and Order Book.

257 "The fugitives from . . . and blankets." David Schenck, *North Carolina 1780–1781: Being a History of the Invasion of the Carolinas* (Raleigh, NC: Edwards and Broughton, 1889), 100.

257 "Attacked a Guard . . . Maryland line." Ward, *Delaware Continentals*, 591.

258 "His army is . . . before him." Spring, *With Zeal*, 73.

CHAPTER 29: "LAY THEIR COUNTRY WASTE WITH FIRE AND SWORD"

259 "very much shattered . . . blood vessel." Anthony Allaire, "Diary of Lieut. Anthony Allaire," in Lyman Copeland Draper, *King's Mountain and Its Heroes* (Cincinnati: Peter G. Thomson, 1881), 506. Lyman Draper interviewed scores of veterans from the battle of King's Mountain and wrote the indispensable account of that battle.

259 Troop numbers from John Ferling, *Almost a Miracle: The American Victory in the War of Independence* (New York: Oxford University Press, 2007), 416.

260 "whole country . . . of rebellion." Charles, Earl Cornwallis to Henry Clinton, letter, August 6, 1780, in Charles Ross, ed., *Correspondence of Charles, First Marquis Cornwallis* (London: J. Murray, 1859), 54.

261 "Major Ferguson joined . . . the militia." Allaire, "Diary," 505.

261 "If they do . . . and sword." Draper, *King's Mountain*, 169.

261–62 "Gentlemen: unless you . . . protect them." *Virginia Gazette*, November 11, 1780.

262 "dangerous example." Mark Mayo Boatner, *Encyclopedia of the American Revolution* (Harrisburg, PA: Stackpole Books, 1973), 523.

262 "[They] appeared . . . the Carolinas." Draper, *King's Mountain*, 313.

262 "We were formidable. . . . to find." "Vance's Narrative of the Battle of King's Mountain," in David Schenck, ed., *Narrative of the Battle of Cowan's Ford . . . and Narrative of the Battle of King's Mountain* (Greensboro, NC: Reece and Elam, 1891), 28; John Buchanan, *The Road to Guilford Courthouse: The American Revolution in the Carolinas* (New York: John Wiley, 1997), 232.

263 Information about rifles from http://www.customflintlock.com/dickert_history.php.

263 "I will not . . . Cornwallis's lines." Draper, *King's Mountain*, 229.

263 "How many are there of you?" Ibid., 230.

263 "Enough to whip . . . that mountain." Ibid., 230.

264 "Dismount and tie . . . your saddles." Ibid., 235.

264 "We got swords . . . the blacksmiths." Pension application of James P. Collins, NARA.

264 "We were paraded . . . escape suffering." Ibid.

264 "could not well . . . of 'coward.'" James P. Collins, *Autobiography of a Revolutionary Soldier* (Clinton, LA: Feliciana Democrat, 1859). Reprinted as *A*

Revolutionary Soldier, John M. Roberts, ed. (New York: Arno Press, 1979), 259.

264　"Fresh prime your . . . he dies." Ibid.

264　"The orders were . . . "reload quick." Ibid., 260–61.

265　"Their great elevation . . . desired effect." Ibid.

265　"The fight seemed . . . his men." Ibid.

265　"Hurrah, my brave fellows! Advance!" Ibid.

265　"Give them Buford's play!" Ibid.

265　"[We] continued to . . . bad example." Scheer and Rankin, *Rebels and Redcoats*, 419.

265　"Don't shoot! It . . . cease firing!" Draper, *King's Mountain*, 283.

265　"The poor Tories . . . every direction." Collins, *Autobiography*, 22.

266　"It appeared that . . . to pieces." Ibid., 261.

266　"The next morning . . . or dying." Ibid.

266　"The hogs in . . . every direction." Ibid.

266　"Several of the . . . the mire." Allaire, "Diary," 518.

267　"State legislatures, especially . . . Continental Regiments." Lawrence E. Babits, *Long, Obstinate, and Bloody: The Battle of Guilford Courthouse* (Chapel Hill: University of North Carolina Press, 2013), 8.

267　"Just as such . . . hated Monster." General Gist to Colonel Mumford, October 24, 1780, *Maryland Historical Magazine* 4 (1909): 369–70.

267　"[King's Mountain] unhappily . . . of America." Clinton, *The American Rebellion*, 226.

CHAPTER 30: WASHINGTON'S BEST GENERAL

268　"intimated the . . . Gates's army." Johnson, *Sketches*, 1:502.

269　"six feet in . . . and corpulent." Buchanan, *Road to Guilford Courthouse*, 298.

269　"military exploits announce . . . of preparation." Henry Lee, *The Revolutionary War Memoirs of General Henry Lee*, Robert E. Lee, ed. (New York: 1869; reprint, Da Capo Press, 1998), 588.

269　"War was his . . . at it." Daniel Morgan to William Snickers, letter, January 26, 1781, New-York Historical Society (NYHS).

269–70　"in March 1778 . . . your Country." George Washington to Nathanael Greene, letter, August 15, 1780, *Papers of Nathanael Greene*, 6:217.

270　"I'm well satisfied . . . of conduct." Buchanan, *Road to Guilford Courthouse*, 219.

CHAPTER 31: THE RAGTAG ARMY

273   "The officers have . . . military complexion." Nathanael Greene to Alexander Hamilton, letter, 10 January, 1781, *The Papers of Alexander Hamilton*, Harold C. Syrett and Jacob Cooke, ed. (New York: Columbia University Press, 1961–79), 2:532.

273   "new lords, new laws." William Gordon, *The History of the Rise, Progress, and Establishment of the United States* (London, 1788), 4:28.

273   "camp of repose." Nathanael Greene to Thomas Jefferson, letter, December 6, 1780, *Papers of Nathanael Greene*, 6:530–31.

274   Troop numbers. Ibid.

276   "either offensively or . . . possible precaution." Ward, *Delaware Continentals*, 369.

276   Information about Cornwallis's intelligence from Roderick MacKenzie, *Strictures on Lt.-Col. Tarleton's History* (London, 1787).

276   Information about Tarleton's strike from Tarleton, *A History of the Campaigns*, 220–23.

277   "Dear Tarleton, If . . . be lost." Robert D. Bass, *The Green Dragoon: The Lives of Banastre Tarleton and Mary Robinson* (New York: Holt, 1957), 142–43.

277   "My Lord . . . King's Mountain." Ibid.

277   "Dear Tarleton . . . intentions perfectly." Ibid.

277   "Here we cannot . . . the Enemy." Daniel Morgan to Nathanael Greene, letter, January 4, 1781, *Papers of Nathanael Greene*.

277   "harass their rear . . . this way." Greene to Morgan, letter, January 8, 1781, in James Graham, *The Life of General Daniel Morgan of the Virginia Line of the Army of the United States* (New York: Derby & Jackson, 1856), 273.

278   "Col. Tarleton is . . . proper dismission [*sic*]." Greene to Morgan, letter, January 13, 1781, ibid., 275.

CHAPTER 32: HUNTING THE HUNTER

279   Information about Morgan's sword from pension application of William Neal, NARA.

279   "of which only . . . one lash." Lee, *Revolutionary War Memoirs*, 393–94; Henry Lee, *The American Revolution in the South*, Robert E. Lee, ed. (New York: Arno Press, 1969), 580.

280   "Here is Morgan's grave or victory." Pension application of Dennis Tramell, December, 10 1833, NARA, Fold3.

280   "As to retreat . . . lives dearly." Johnson, *Sketches*, 1:576; Lee, *Revolutionary War Memoirs*, 226.

281 "The [militia] were . . . his progress." Lee, *Revolutionary War Memoirs*, 226 and 222.

281 "Two of my Cosins . . . shattered Constitution." Pension application of Henry Wells, January 29, 1834, NARA, Fold3.

281 "I knew my . . . downright fighting." Don Higginbotham, *Daniel Morgan: Revolutionary Rifleman* (Chapel Hill: University of North Carolina Press, 1979), 245.

282 "No burning, no . . . the country." Johnson, *Sketches*, 382.

282–83 "I shall never . . . gallant conduct." Thomas Young, "Memoirs of Major Thomas Young," *Orion* 3 (October and November 1843):85.

283 "sle[ep] a wink that night." Ibid.

283 "Boys, get up, Benny's Coming!" Joseph McJunkin, "Memoirs of Major Joseph McJunkin, Revolutionary Patriot," James Hoge Saye, ed. *Richmond Watchman and Observer* (1847): 38.

CHAPTER 33: COWPENS

284 "The enemy . . . of time." Collins, *Autobiography*.

284 Additional detail about the battle from Young, "Memoirs," 100.

284 "Aim for the men with the epaulets." Ward, *Delaware Continentals*, 374.

285 "fleetest race horses . . . the men." Pension application of Lawrence Everhart, NARA.

285 "information of the approach of the Enemy." Ibid.

285 "Do you expect . . . Tarleton, sir." Ibid.

285 "*They are* . . . by God!" Young, "Memoirs," 100.

287 "[Morgan] galloped along . . . their eyes." Ibid.

287 "with great firmness." Ibid.

287 "The British line . . . ever saw." Ibid.

287 "When they came . . . let fly." Lawrence E. Babits, *A Devil of a Whipping: The Battle of Cowpens* (Chapel Hill: University of North Carolina Press, 1998), 90. This outstanding book is highly recommended for additional reading on the battle.

287 "[He] fixed his . . . officer fall." McJunkin, "Memoirs," 33.

287 "POP! POP! POP!" Young, "Memoirs," 100.

287 "the effect of . . . a recoil." Lee *Revolutionary War Memoirs*, 257.

287 "Two-thirds of . . . of privates." MacKenzie, *Strictures on Lt. Col. Tarleton's History*, 98.

287 "rent the air . . . their advance." Ibid., 97–98.

287 "The British approached . . . much slaughter." Daniel Morgan to Nathanael Greene, letter, January 19, 1781, *Papers of Nathanael Greene*, 7:152–55.

288 "seven wounds on . . . brains." Incapacitated for nearly thirty days, Whelchel would survive the war. Pension application of James Kelly, NARA; pension application of John Whelchel, NARA; pension application of Joshua Palmer, NARA.

288 "Prime and load! . . . "Fire!" Babits, *A Devil of a Whipping*, 104.

288 Casualty information from Delaware muster rolls as calculated by Babits.

288 "with great bravery . . . and bloody." Seymour, *Journal of the Southern Expedition*, 15; Stedman, *The History of the Origin, Progress, and Termination of the American War*, 321–22; MacKenzie, *Strictures on Lt. Col. Tarleton's History*, 98.

289 "[I] saw [Morgan] . . . of Cowpens." Pension application of Andrew Rock, NARA.

289 "thought the advance . . . this maneuver." Tarleton, *A History of the Southern Campaign*, 217.

289 "I had about . . . my flank." John Eager Howard to John Marshall, letter, 1804, Bayard Papers, MHS; Wyatt, *Memoirs*.

289 "soon removed [Morgan's] . . . that order." "John Eager Howard," in *The National Portrait Gallery of Distinguished Americans with Biographical Sketches by Celebrated Authors* (Philadelphia: Rice, Rutter & Co., 1865).

289 "Thinking that We . . . no order." Anderson, *Personal Recollections*, 209.

289 "Battalion! Halt! To the Right About,—Face!" Babits, *A Devil of a Whipping*, 116; Friedrich Wilhelm Ludolf Gerhard Augustin Baron von Steuben, *Regulations for the Order and Discipline of the Troops of the United States* (Albany, NY: Daniel & Samuel Whiting, 1803), 46.

289 "perfectly formed." John Eager Howard to John Marshall, 1804, Bayard Papers, MHS; Wyatt, *Memoirs*.

289–90 "The enemy pressed . . . deadly fire." *Papers of General Nathanael Greene*, 7:159.

290 "They are coming . . . charge them." Johnson, *Sketches*, 1:381.

290 "Form, form, my . . . never beaten." Collins, *Autobiography*, 57; Johnson, *Sketches*, 1:380.

290 "powerful and trumpet-like . . . every arm." Pension application of Henry Wells, January 29, 1834, NARA.

290 "We then advanced . . . right flank." Collins, *Autobiography*, 57.

290 "close and murderous." Anderson, *Personal Recollections*, 209.

290 "Nearly half of the Redcoats." Lee, *Revolutionary War Memoirs*, 257; Hugh McCall, *The History of Georgia*, 2 vols. (Savannah: Seymour and Williams, 1811), 507–8.

290 "threw down their . . . their faces." John R. Shaw, *A Narrative of the Life and Travels of John Robert Shaw* (Lexington, KY: Daniel Bradford, 1807), 54–55.

290 "The order was obeyed with great alacrity." Anderson, *Personal Recollections*, 209.

290 "in amongst them . . . infantry prisoners." Ibid.

290 "Officers and men . . . or fear." Seymour, *Journal of the Southern Expedition*, 15.

290 "received three severe . . . by bayonet." Pension application of John Bantham, April 2, 1818, NARA, M804.

290 "in the thigh . . . through it." Pension application of Cudbeth Stone, NARA.

291 "seeing the fortune . . . had changed." Gordon, *History*, 4:34–35; Stedman, *History*, 322–23.

291 "in a panic . . . rout ensued." Tarleton, *A History of the Campaigns*, 217.

291 "about to put . . . the gun." Anonymous, "The Account of Richard Anderson," *Niles Weekly Register*, 32 (May 19, 1827):200.

291 "I saw some . . . his match." Wyatt, *Memoirs*, 74

291 "[Till all] were either killed or wounded." Tarleton, *A History of the Campaigns*, 217.

291 "received a severe . . . left arm." Pension application of Andrew Rock, NARA.

291–92 "with his Sword . . . my Sholder." Pension application of Henry Wells, NARA.

292 "Tarleton's quarters." Young, "Memoirs," 101.

292 "Surrender! Lay down your arms!" Wyatt, *Memoirs*, 74; John Eager Howard to John Marshall, letter, 1804, Bayard Papers, MHS.

292 "Upon getting on . . . was about." Wyatt, *Memoirs*, 74.

292 "they had orders . . . him ill." Ibid.

292 "[They] broke, and . . . of running." Young, "Memoirs," 101.

292 "forsake their leader and left the field of battle." Tarleton, *A History of the Campaigns*, 217–18.

292 "Buford's Play!" Quoting Lawrence Everhart, who was then Tarleton's prisoner, pension application of Lawrence Everhart, NARA.

293 "Some officers went . . . the flight." George Hanger, *An Address to the Army* (London: James Ridgway, 1789), 109–10.

293   "Fourteen officers and . . . brave men." Tarleton, *A History of the Campaigns*, 218.

293   "perhaps 30 yards." John Eager Howard to John Marshall, letter, 1804, Bayard Papers, MHS; Wyatt, *Memoirs*.

293   "saw the American . . . at him." Wyatt, *Memoirs*.

293   "Tarleton made a . . . he parried." Ibid.

293   "The officer of . . . disabled him." Ibid.; Johnson, *Sketches*, 382–83.

293   "The noble animal . . . its rider." Wyatt, *Memoirs*.

293–94   "[Everhart] pointed out . . . the Surgeons." Pension application of Lawrence Everhart, NARA.

294   "should have escaped . . . unfortunate carcass." Murtie June Clark, *Loyalists in the Southern Campaign of the Revolutionary War* (Baltimore: Genealogical Publishing, 1981), 245; Ward, *Delaware Continentals*, 536–38.

294   "My love for . . . love Dougherty." Ward, *Delaware Continentals*, 538.

294   "[I] resolved upon . . . contained gold." Young, "Memoirs," 101.

294–95   "[I] put spurs . . . horse's neck." Ibid., 101–2.

295   "[We were] instrumental . . . day's Work." Seymour, *Journal of the Southern Expedition*, 15; Anderson, *Personal Recollections*, 209.

295   "You have done . . . shooting me." Cary Howard, "John Eager Howard," *Maryland Historical Magazine* 62 (September 1967):303.

295   "Our poor fellows . . . of clothes." Samuel Shaw, "Revolutionary War Letters to Captain Winthrop Sargent," *Pennsylvania Magazine* (1946):321.

295   Information on Amercian casualties from John Eager Howard to John Marshall, letter, 1804, Bayard Papers, MHS; and Wyatt, *Memoirs*. The American losses may have not included the militia and therefore were likely higher.

295   Information on British casualties from Daniel Morgan to Nathanael Greene, January 19, 1781, *Papers of Nathanael Greene*, 7:152; Seymour, *Journal of the Southern Expedition*, also gives similar figures.

296   "I was left . . . two waiters." Pindell, "Militant Surgeon."

CHAPTER 34: "TO FOLLOW GREENE'S ARMY
TO THE END OF THE WORLD"

297   Scene between Tarleton and Cornwallis from Tarleton, *A History of the Campaigns*, 220; Franklin and Mary Wickwire, *Cornwallis* (Boston: Houghton Mifflin, 1970), 268–69.

298   "You have forfeited . . . the 17th." Tarleton, *A History of the Campaigns*, 222.

299   "teeth as white . . . past age." Buchanan, *Road to Guilford Courthouse*, 336.

299 "Lord Cornwallis sett . . . a murmur." Charles O'Hara, "Letters of Charles O'Hara to the Duke of Grafton," George C. Rogers Jr., ed., *South Carolina Historical Magazine* 65, no. 3 (July 1964):174.

299 "Without Baggage, necessaries . . . the world." Ibid.

299 "one pair of spare soles." Cornwallis to Germaine, letter, March 17, 1781, Cornwallis Papers, UK Public Record Office (PRO); and *The Cornwallis Papers: The Campaigns of 1780 and 1781 in the Southern Theatre of the American Revolutionary War* (South Carolina Naval & Military Press, 2010).

300 "The sources of the most infamous plundering." A. R. Newsome, "British Orderly Book," *North Carolina Historical Review* 9 (1932):291–92 and 378.

300 "I am not . . . the Country." Nathanael Greene to Isaac Huger, letter, January 29, 1781, *Papers of Nathanael Greene*, 7:220–22.

300 "Cornwallis will push on." Daniel Morgan to Nathanael Greene, ibid., 7:178, 200–201.

300 "filling up all . . . obstruction imaginable." Ibid.

301 "a very Heavy . . . for Desertion." Papers of Captain William Beatty, MHS.

301 "drunk all your . . . than ever." Otho Holland Williams to Daniel Morgan, letter, January 25, 1781, in James Graham, *Life of General Daniel Morgan* (New York: Darby and Jackson, 1856), 323.

301 "Feu de Joy." Beatty describes the men firing their muskets in a line of succession to celebrate the victory at Cowpens.

CHAPTER 35: "SAW 'EM HOLLERIN' AND A SNORTIN' AND A DROWNIN'"

302 "that tho' Genl. . . . on it." Archibald D. Murphey, *The Papers of Archibald D. Murphey*, William Henry Hoyt, ed. (Raleigh, NC: E. M. Uzzell & Co., 1914)2:257.

303 "We went up . . . more whisky." Robert Henry, *Narrative of the Battle of Cowan's Ford, February 1st, 1781* (Reece & Elam, 1891).

303 "The British! The British!" Ibid.

303 "Lord Cornwallis, according . . . after them." Roger Lamb, *British Soldier's Story: Roger Lamb's Narrative of the American Revolution*, Don N. Hagist, ed. (Baraboo, WI: Ballindalloch Press, 2004).

303 "Fire away, boys! Help is at hand!" Ibid.

303 "[I] fired and . . . return fire." Henry, *Narrative*.

304 "rolled with him . . . forty yards." Lamb, *British Soldier's Story*.

304 "There wasn't many . . . off bank." Henry, *Narrative*.

304 "It's time to run, Bob!" Ibid.

304 "not less than . . . his home." Ibid.

304–5 "In February, the . . . and Morgan." Watkins, "An Interesting Personal Record."

305 "We marched all . . . come up." Seymour, *Journal of the Southern Expedition*, 396.

305 "[We were] in . . . them barefoot." Ibid.

305 "every step being . . . the way." Thomas Anderson, *Journal of Lieutenant Anderson of the Delaware Regiment, 1780–1782* (Morrisiana, NY: Henry B. Dawson, 1867), 209.

305–6 "More than one-half . . . their waists." Nathanael Greene to Abner Nash, letter, January 7, 1781, and Greene to Thomas Sumter, January 15, 1781, Greene Letterbook, New York Public Library, 37–46 and 74–75.

306 "rheumatic from head to toe." Higginbotham, *Daniel Morgan*, 152.

306 "violently attacked with the piles [hemorrhoids]." *Papers of Nathanael Greene*, 7.

307 "His pen never . . . immediately resumed." John S. Pancake, *This Destructive War: The British Campaign in the Carolinas, 1780–1782* (Tuscaloosa: University of Alabama Press, 1985), 165.

307 "from Cornwallises pushing . . . capital misfortune." Nathanael Greene to Isaac Huger, letter, February 5, 1781, *Papers of Nathanael Greene*, 7:251.

CHAPTER 36: THE RACE TO THE DAN

308 "If I should . . . must fall." Nathanael Greene to Thomas Sumter, February 9, 1781, *Papers of Nathanael Greene*, 7: 152–89.

308 "avoid a general action at all Events." *Papers of Nathanael Greene*, 13:297.

308 "Great god what . . . more men?" Daniel Morgan to Thomas Jefferson, letter, February 1, 1781, Julian P. Boyd, ed., *The Papers of Thomas Jefferson*, 41 vols. (Princeton, NJ: Princeton University Press, 1950), 4:495–96.

309 "Great generals are . . . be found." Nathanael Greene to Daniel Morgan, August 26, 1781, in Graham, *Life of General Daniel Morgan*, 395.

309 Details on reinforcements from Orderly Book, Otho Holland Williams Papers, MHS.

310 Distance traveled from Charles Royster, *A Revolutionary People at War: the Continental Army and the American Character, 1775–1783* (Chapel Hill: University of North Carolina Press, 1996), 241.

310 "We marched from . . . light troops." Seymour, *Journal of the Southern Expedition*, 297.

310 "Accident informed me . . . a Bridge." Otho Williams to Nathanael Greene, letter, February 11, 1781, *Papers of Nathanael Greene*, 7:283.

310 "The enemy was . . . to escape." Lee, *Revolutionary War Memoirs*, 241.

311 "note on paper . . . his friends." Ibid., 242.

311 "had not slept four hours." George W. Greene, *Life of Nathanael Greene, Major-General in the Army of the Revolution* (Boston: Charles C. Little and James Brown, 1845), 151.

311 "North Carolina militia . . . more critical." *Papers of Nathanael Greene*, 7:285.

311 "My Dr General . . . of that?" Ibid.

311–12 "More than once . . . Irwin's Ferry." Lee, *Revolutionary War Memoirs*, 243–44.

312 "deep and broken . . . with alacrity." Ibid., 248.

312 "The greater part . . . is clear." *Papers of Nathanael Greene*, 7:287

312 "became renovated in . . . the body." Lee, *Revolutionary War Memoirs*, 249.

312 "Every measure of . . . vigorously executed." Tarleton, *A History of the Campaigns*, 229.

312 "Notwithstanding the Enemies . . . of [territory]." Papers of Captain William Beatty, MHS PAM 10,699.

CHAPTER 37: GUILFORD COURTHOUSE—
"A COMPLICATED SCENE OF HORROR AND DISTRESS"

313 "in a great rage for battle." Pension application for David Williams, August 23, 1832, NARA.

313 "My brave boys . . . before night." Ibid.

313 "scarlet uniforms, burnished . . . the breeze." Eli W. Caruthers, *Revolutionary Incidents and Sketches in Character Chiefly in the Old North State*, Ruth F. Thompson, ed. (Greensboro, NC: Guilford County Geological Society, 1994), 134.

313–14 "You hear damnation . . . two fires." Ibid.

314 "We marched yesterday . . . strong enough." Buchanan, *Road to Guilford Courthouse*, 369.

314 "If [the militia] . . . our hopes." Daniel Morgan to Nathanael Greene, letter, February 20, 1781, *Papers of General Nathanael Greene*, 7:324.

314 "Put the rifleman . . . who runs." Ibid.

316–17 "killed by the . . . the body." Caruthers, *Revolutionary Incidents*, 142.

317 "[We were] in . . . nicest precision." Roger Lamb, *An Original and Authentic Journal of Occurrences during the Late American War* (Dublin: Wilkinson and Courtney, 1809), 361.

317 "armor which was . . . momentary disorder." Caruthers, *Revolutionary Incidents*, 142.

317 "most galling and . . . the spot." Schenck, *North Carolina*, 349–52.

317 "After they delivered . . . his cradle." Caruthers, *Revolutionary Incidents*, 134.

317 "At this awful . . . anxious suspense." Lamb, *Original and Authentic Journal*, 361.

317 "Come on, my brave Fuzileers[!]" Ibid.

318 "[The men] broke . . . by dogs." St. George Tucker to Francis Bland Tucker, letter, March 18, 1781, in *Magazine of American History* 7 (1881):39.

318 "Some made such . . . like heroes." Samuel Houston, Journal, in William Henry Foote, *Sketches of Virginia, Historical and Biographical*, 2nd series (Philadelphia: J.B. Lippincott & Co., 1855), 146–47.

318 "Riflemen and musketry . . . the enemy." Seymour, *Journal of the Southern Expedition*, 378–79.

318 "fired away fifteen . . . per man." St. George Tucker to Francis Tucker, letter, March 17, 1781, in *Magazine of American History* 7 (1881):39.

318 "[They] continued their . . . ever heard." Otho Williams to E. Williams, letter, March 16, 1781, Williams Papers, MHS.

319 "All [the] officers were wounded." Tarleton, *A History of the Campaigns*, 275.

319 "I saw Lord . . . the woods." Lamb, *Original and Authentic Journal*, 362.

319 "The first [Maryland] . . . 1st regt." John Eager Howard to John Marshall, letter, 1804, Bayard Papers, MHS.

320 "flattering himself with . . . finishing blow." Scheer and Ranken, *Rebels and Redcoats*, 449.

320 "Ford ordered a . . . some distance." Pension application of William Davie, NARA.

320 "The Second has . . . was ordered." Williams Papers, MHS.

321 "Col. Morris calling . . . to retire." Nathanael Greene to Samuel Huntington, letter, March 16, 1781, and Greene to Catherine Greene, letter, March 18, 1781, *Papers of General Nathanael Greene*, 7:433–34 and 446.

321 "Capt. Gibson, Deputy . . . take them." Gunby, *Colonel John Gunby*, 51; John Eager Howard to John Marshall, letter, 1804, Bayard Papers, MHS.

321 "Face about." Ibid.

321 "[We] immediately engaged ... continued firing." John Eager Howard to John Marshall, 1804, Bayard Papers, MHS.

321 "They fired at ... to meet." Thomas Baker, *Another Such Victory* (New York: Eastern Acorn Press, 1981), 65; pension application of Daniel Spence, July 3, 1845, NARA.

321 "were thrown into confusion by a heavy fire." Charles, Earl Cornwallis to George Germain, March 17, 1781, Cornwallis Papers, UK Public Record Office (PRO).

322 "The swords of ... lay dead." Pension application of Philemon Holcombe, April 14, 1834, NARA.

322 "[I] was wounded ... to others." Pension application of Peter Francisco, NARA.

322 "bore a conspicuous part as a soldier ... when the Maryland troops came to the charge, he bayonetted seven of the enemy." *National Intelligencer* 13 (February 1837).

322 "They bayoneted and ... British Guards." Otho Holland Williams to Josias Hall, letter, March 1781, Otho Williams Papers, MHS.

322 "an accidental ... [at Elizabethtown, New Jersey]." Pension application of James Nowell, February 21, 1811, NARA.

323 "Smith and ... only stunned him." Samuel Mathis to William R. Davie, June 26, 1819, in *Revolutionary Sketches of William R. Davie*, Blackwell P. Robinson, ed. (Raleigh, NC: Archives and History, 1976).

323 "a cannon's being ... much injured since." Pension application of James Gooding, June 18, 1821, NARA.

324 "The Maryland brigade ... great slaughter." Henry B. Carrington, *Battles of the American Revolution* (New York: A. S. Barnes, 1904), 561.

324 "I observed Washington's ... the guards." Wyatt, *Memoirs*, 75–76.

324 "*The whole were in our power.*" Ibid.; John Eager Howard, Bayard Papers, MHS.

324 "At this period ... each army." Tarleton, *A History of the Campaigns*, 281.

324 "Columns of the ... we retired." Howard, Bayard Papers, MHS; Wyatt, *Memoirs*, 75–76.

324 "with greatest alacrity." John Hairr, *Guilford Courthouse* (Cambridge, MA: Da Capo Press, 2002), 129.

325 "The artillery horses ... and regularity." Otho Holland Williams Papers, MHS.

325–26 "There were two ... the village." Caruthers, *Revolutionary Incidents*, 164–65.

326 Casualty information from Cornwallis Papers, PRO 30/11/65 and PRO 30/11/103.

326 "a violent and constant rain." "Letters of Charles O'Hara," 177–78.

326 "40 hours." Ibid.

326–27 "I never did . . . the Wounded." Ibid.

327 "The night was . . . military life." Stedman, *The History of the Origin, Progress, and Termination of the American War*, Volume 2.

328 "rogues and idiots." Richard M. Ketchum, *Victory at Yorktown: The Campaign That Won the Revolution* (New York: Holt, 2004), 141.

CHAPTER 38: HOBKIRK'S HILL

329 Details about Oldham from Francis Bernard Heitman, *Historical Register of Officers of the Continental Army during the War of the Revolution, April, 1775, to December, 1783* (Washington, DC: F. B. Heitman, 1893), 312.

329–30 "To the name . . . of fame." Lee, *Revolutionary War Memoirs*, 362.

331 "scattering fire was kept up all night." Kirkwood, Journal.

331 "[We] had a smart . . . the Army." Ibid.

332 "Burnt a House . . . Enemy's Redoubts." Ibid.

332 "The ugliest officer in the British Army." Pancake, *This Destructive War*, 193.

332 "By arming our . . . sick soldiers." Lord Francis Rawdon's Report on the Battle of Hobkirk's Hill, http://www.hobkirkhill.org/hobkirk/primary .aspx.

333 "filing close to the swamps." Ibid.

333 "were still washing . . . joined us." John Eager Howard to John Gunby, letter, March 22, 1782, Bayard Papers, MHS.

334 "heavy showers of Grape." Rawdon to Cornwallis, April 26, 1781, in *The Remembrancer, or Impartial Repository of Public Events for the Year 1783*, pt.1 (London: J. Debrett, 1783), 1.

334 "[It] put the . . . of them." Seymour, *Journal of the Southern Expedition*, 25.

334 "universal blaze of . . . his soul." Pension application of Guilford Dudley, October 12, 1832, NARA.

334 "The Enemy were staggered . . . left retiring." Nathanael Greene to Samuel Huntington, April 27, 1781, *Papers of General Nathanael Greene*, 8:158.

334 "to charge bayonets without firing." Otho Holland Williams to his brother Elie Williams, letter, April 27, 1781, http://southerncampaign.org/hobkirk/ ps.html.

334 "an ornament to his profession." Nathanael Greene to Samuel Huntington, April 27, 1781, *Papers of General Nathanael Greene*, 8:157.

334 "the promising young . . . amiable girl." Otho Holland Williams to his brother Elie Williams, letter, April 27, 1781.

334 "confusion and [the men] dropped out of line." Gunby, *Colonel John Gunby*, 73.

335 "exerting himself." John Eager Howard to John Gunby, March 22, 1782, Bayard Papers, MHS.

335 "I aided the . . . personal exertions." Pindell, "Militant Surgeon," 318.

335 "ordered him to . . . the cannon." Samuel Mathis, letter, 1819, in Thomas J. Kirkland and Robert MacMillan Kennedy, *Historic Camden*, Volume 1 (reprint, Nabu Press, 2012).

336 "fought like bulldogs . . . of action." Ibid.

336 "hung around his neck in his bosom." Ibid.

336–37 "A number . . . as Deserters." Rawdon to Cornwallis, April 26, 1781, in *The Remembrancer*, 2.

337 "The dye is . . . became swelled." Pindell, "Militant Surgeon," 309–10.

337 "Ford died a . . . still left." Otho Holland Williams to his brother Elie Williams, letter, April 27, 1781.

337 "If white men . . . to him." Otho Holland Williams Papers, MHS.

337 "that Capt. Smith . . . for mercy." Samuel Mathis, letter, 1819.

338 "Nothing can be . . . the army." Babits, *Long, Obstinate, and Bloody*, 183.

338 "all the most obnoxious loyalists." Lee, *Revolutionary War Memoirs*, 345.

338 "commandant of the . . . and wounded." Pension application of Guilford Dudley, NARA.

338 "a smile of complacency." Ibid.

338 "We fight, get beat, rise and fight again." Nathanael Greene to George Washington, May 1, 1781, in *Correspondence of the American Revolution*, Jared Sparks, ed. (Boston: Little, Brown, and Company, 1853), 3:299.

338 "feel the Effects of British tiriny," Williams Papers, MS908, MHS.

338 "stripped him, bound . . . bare back." Johnson, *Sketches*, 2:97.

CHAPTER 39: NINETY SIX

339 "[Ninety Six] must be . . . upon it." Cornwallis Papers, PRO.

340 carried to 96 . . . that place." Pension application of Major Joseph McJunkin, NARA.

343 "amid the thunder . . . every side." Scharf, *History of Maryland*, 422.

343 "carried . . . on his shoulder . . . was stationed." *National Intelligencer* (February 1837):247.

344 "in an attempt . . . Breast works." Pension application of Ransom Day, NARA.

344 "a [musket] ball . . . his shoulder." Alexander Garden, *Anecdotes of the Revolutionary War in America* (1822; reprint, London: Forgotten Books, 2013), 408–9.

344 "To this end . . . be quick.'" Ibid.

344 "got his skull bone broke." Pension application of John Bantham, NARA, S44344, transcribed and annotated by C. Leon Harris.

344 "had a furlough . . . his wound." Pension application of Briant Munrow, NARA, S34444, transcribed and annotated by C. Leon Harris.

345 "Gloom and silence . . . the troops." Lee, *Revolutionary War Memoirs*, 130.

346 "Army in good . . . constantly saddled." Otho Holland Williams Papers, MHS.

346 "Never did we . . . our epicures." Lee, *Revolutionary War Memoirs*, 145.

347 "We fought the . . . of America." Johnson, *Sketches*, 2:220.

347 "Hundreds of my . . . their guns." Ibid.

347 "rendered it impossible [to scout], by waylaying the bye-paths and passes through the different swamps." Bruce Lancaster, *The American Revolution* (New York: American Heritage, 1971), 307.

CHAPTER 40: EUTAW SPRINGS

348 "Most of [them] . . . or captured." Seymour, *Journal of the Southern Expedition*, 31.

349 "determined to fight . . . dangerous consequences." Alexander Stewart to Charles, Earl Cornwallis, letter, September 9, 1781, in K. G. Davies, ed., *Documents of the American Revolution*, 21 vols. (Dublin: Irish University Press, 1972–1981), 20:227.

349 "We halted and . . . such occasions." Otho Holland Williams Papers, MHS.

349 "The militia advancing . . . his position." Lee, *Revolutionary War Memoirs*, 284.

350 "through a heavy . . . before them." Ibid., 465.

350 "Let Williams advance . . . his bayonet." Scharf, *History of Maryland*, 334.

350 "fell transfixed by each other's bayonets." Lee, *Revolutionary War Memoirs*, 283.

350 "I pushed on . . . guard them." Pindell, "Militant Surgeon," 319.

351 "nearly all his . . . or wounded." Ibid.

351 Details about incident at the Roche house from Patrick O'Kelley, *Nothing But Blood and Slaughter: Military Operations and Order of Battle of the Revolutionary War in the Carolinas* (booklocker.com, 2005), 3:352.

351–52 "took off his . . . wounding him." Ibid., 3:351.

352 "taking a nail . . . no more." Draper, *King's Mountain*, 354.

352 "drew all the fire from the windows." Otho Holland Williams Papers, MHS.

352 "soon killed or disabled nearly the whole." Ibid.

352 "galling and destructive fire." Ibid.

352 "could not be. . . many hours." Pindell, *Militant Surgeon*, 319.

353 "gallant band . . . rushed furiously." Ibid.

353 "Victory is ours . . . the battlefield]." Otho Holland Williams Papers, MHS.

354 "not less than . . . carry off." Nathanael Greene, Report of Eutaw Springs, September 11, 1781, Papers of the Continental Congress, NARA.

CHAPTER 41: "CONQUER OR DIE"—YORKTOWN

355 Details about the makeup of the Life Guard from Fred Anderson Berg, comp., *Encyclopedia of Continental Army Units, Battalion, Regiments, and Independent Corps* (Harrisburg, PA: Stackpole Books, 1972), 135.

355 "sobriety, honesty and . . . and spruce." Fitzpatrick, *Writings of George Washington*, 388.

356 "I thank you . . . of Baltimore." Scharf, *Chronicles of Baltimore*, 191.

357 "The loss of . . . the army." Don Cook, *The Long Fuse: How England Lost the American Colonies, 1760–1785* (New York: Atlantic Monthly Press, 1995), 347.

357 The estimates about the number of French troops have varied over time. Initially estimates were lower, but a more scholarly analysis has revealed the number to be closer to seven thousand. The numbers of American troops are also debatable. The author used Jerome Greene's *Guns of Independence* for a source. John Furling's *Almost a Miracle* was also referenced. Cornwallis's numbers came from his official papers and included sailors although his actual effective force strength was much lower during the battle.

358 "largely indebted for . . . my table." Mordecai Gist to Sim Lee, letter, August 7, 1781, in William Hand Browne, *Archives of Maryland* (Baltimore: Maryland Historical Society, 1930), 47:398.

358 "the safe arrival . . . the line." Scharf, *History of Maryland*, 467.

358 "Every day we . . . encounter them." Ibid., 460.

359 "hem me in . . . could be." Charles Cornwallis, *Correspondence*, Charles Ross, ed. (London: John Murray, 1859), 1:95.

359 "in distress for . . . any kind." Sir Henry Clinton, *The Campaign in Virginia 1781* (London: Benjamin Franklin Stevens, 1888), 1:477.

360 "I am now . . . six weeks." Stephenson, *Patriot Battles*, 349.

360 "As soon as . . . whole outworks." Ward, *Delaware Continentals*, 472.

361 "This place is . . . the worst." Stephenson, *Patriot Battles*, 349.

361 Source for the units at Yorktown: National Park Service Yorktown Order or Battle. "Colonel Cobb, if . . . step back." Washington Irving, *The Life and Times of Washington* (New York: G. P. Putnam and Sons, 1876), 618.

361–62 "My dear General, . . . you yet." Ibid.

362 "It is a spent . . . is done." Ibid.

362 "I feel great . . . honorable peace." Mordecai Gist Papers, MSA.

362 "General Washington ordered . . . the redoubts." Pension application of John Boudy (Bondy, Bodray), NARA. The author has not been able to verify Boudy's account, and it is unknown whether other Marylanders participated in the attack.

362 "We dare not . . . save us." Charles Edward Cornwallis to Sir Henry Clinton, letter, October 15, 1781, in Cornwallis, *Correspondence*, 1:124.

363 "[The fortifications] were . . . remained." Lamb, *Original and Authentic Journal*, 378–79.

363 "On one side . . . manner attended." Henry Phelps Johnston, *The Yorktown Campaign and the Surrender of Cornwallis, 1781* (New York: Harper and Brothers, 1881), 167, quoted in Jerome Green, *The Guns of Independence: The Siege of Yorktown, 1781* (El Dorado Hills, CA: Savas Beatie, 2009), 295.

363–64 "We are not . . . and despair." Ibid., 294–95.

364 "The British officers . . . of fortitude." Ibid., 299.

364 "His defense of . . . determined Officer." Mordecai Gist to John Sterrett, October 12, 1781, Mordecai Gist Papers, MHS.

CHAPTER 42: THE LAST BATTLE

369 "[The British] being . . . our hands." W. Wilmot, "A Letter from the South," *Maryland Historical Magazine* 5, no. 4 (December 1910):330–40.

369 "naked and full of vermin." Ward, *Delaware Continentals*, 474.

370 "strike at [the British] . . . find them." William Pierce Jr. to Mordecai Gist, letter, August 23, 1782, Mordecai Gist Papers, MHS.

370 "[The surrounding area was] . . . impracticable." Mordecai Gist to John Sterrett, letter, April 12, 1782, Mordecai Gist Papers, MHS.

370 "surrendered unconditionally to . . . became engaged." Margaret Oswald Chew Howard, MSA.

371 "love of adventure." Scharf, *History of Maryland*, 489.

371 "The enemy was ... 'four balls.'" Francis B. Culver, "The Last Blood-shed of the Revolution," *Maryland Historical Magazine* 5, no. 4 (December 1910):330–40.

371 "our Colonel Laurens ... six privates." Pension application of John Boudy, NARA.

371 "This was the last ... American War." Johnson, *Sketches*, 345.

371 "evening given in ... then died." *Charlestown* (South Carolina) *Gazette*, March 25, [1783].

372 "This gentlemen, whose ... the army." Ibid.

372–73 "The British moved ... hearty welcome." Pension application of John Boudy, NARA.

373 "declaring the cessation ... Britannic Majesty." "A Century of Law-making for a New Nation: U.S. Congressional Documents and Debates, 1774–1785," *Journals of the Continental Congress, 1774–1785*, 34 vols. (Washington, DC: Government Printing Office, 1904–1937), 24:24.

373 "His Britannic majesty ... part thereof." Ibid., 26:238.

373 "with unfeigned satisfaction ... her commerce, her future grandeur and importance in the scale of nations." Scharf, *History of Maryland*, 491.

CHAPTER 43: "*OMNIA RELIQUIT SERVARE REMPUBLICAM*"

375 "The United States ... your communications." Scharf, *History of Mary-land*, 499.

375–76 "retiring from the ... public life." Ibid., 499–500.

376 "Few tragedies ever ... of Congress." Ibid., 500.

376 "I feel eased ... domestic virtues." Ibid., 501.

376 Information about the Society of the Cincinnati. Ibid., 502.

377 "to preserve the ... their orphans." Ibid.

379 "a cross, morose ... speaking terms." Williams Whiteley, "Revolutionary Soldiers of Delaware," read before the two houses of the Delaware legislature, February 15, 1875, 47–48.

379 Information about Philpot's nightmares from pension application of Bryan Philpot, NARA.

380 "so poor and ... small Bag." Pension application of George Dias, NARA.

380 "unable to do ... one plow." Pension application of Thomas Carney, NARA.

381 "was often heard ... Maryland Regiment." Field, *The Battle of Long Island*.

381 "the bones of ... military order." U.S. National Park Service Historical Orientation Report for Archaeological Investigation, Marylanders' Burial Site, Brooklyn, NY, Appendix.

INDEX